CONSCIOUSNESS, CREATIVITY, AND SELF AT THE DAWN OF SETTLED LIFE

Over recent years a number of scholars have argued that the human mind underwent a cognitive revolution in the Neolithic. This volume seeks to test these claims at the Neolithic site of Çatalhöyük in Turkey and in other Neolithic contexts in the Middle East. It brings together cognitive scientists who have developed theoretical frameworks for the study of cognitive change, archaeologists who have conducted research into cognitive change in the Neolithic of the Middle East, and the excavators of the Neolithic site of Çatalhöyük who have over recent years been exploring changes in consciousness, creativity, and self in the context of the rich data from the site. Collectively, the authors argue that when detailed data are examined, the theoretical evolutionary expectations are not found for these three characteristics. The Neolithic was a time of long, slow, and diverse change in which there is little evidence for an internal cognitive revolution.

Ian Hodder is Dunlevie Family Professor at Stanford University and Director of the Stanford Archaeology Center. He is the author and editor of many books, most recently *Religion and the Emergence of Civilization, Entangled: An Archaeology of the Relationships between Humans and Things*, and *Religion at Work in a Neolithic Society*.

CONSCIOUSNESS, CREATIVITY, AND SELF AT THE DAWN OF SETTLED LIFE

Edited by

IAN HODDER

Stanford University

CAMBRIDGE
UNIVERSITY PRESS

CAMBRIDGE
UNIVERSITY PRESS

University Printing House, Cambridge CB2 8BS, United Kingdom

One Liberty Plaza, 20th Floor, New York, NY 10006, USA

477 Williamstown Road, Port Melbourne, VIC 3207, Australia

314–321, 3rd Floor, Plot 3, Splendor Forum, Jasola District Centre, New Delhi – 110025, India

79 Anson Road, #06–04/06, Singapore 079906

Cambridge University Press is part of the University of Cambridge.

It furthers the University's mission by disseminating knowledge in the pursuit of
education, learning, and research at the highest international levels of excellence.

www.cambridge.org
Information on this title: www.cambridge.org/9781108484923
DOI: 10.1017/9781108753616

First published 2020

Printed in the United Kingdom by TJ International, Padstow Cornwall

A catalogue record for this publication is available from the British Library.

Library of Congress Cataloging-in-Publication Data
NAMES: Hodder, Ian, editor.
TITLE: Consciousness, creativity, and self at the dawn of settled life / Edited by Ian Hodder, Stanford University, California.
DESCRIPTION: Cambridge, United Kingdom ; New York, NY : University Printing House, 2019.
IDENTIFIERS: LCCN 2019013845 | ISBN 9781108484923 (hardback) | ISBN 9781108718875 (paperback)
SUBJECTS: LCSH: Neolithic period–Turkey. | Neolithic period–Middle East. | Excavations (Archaeology)–Turkey. |
Excavations (Archaeology)–Middle East. | Consciousness–Research. | Cognition and culture.
CLASSIFICATION: LCC GN776.32.T9 C66 2019 | DDC 939/.21–dc23
LC record available at https://lccn.loc.gov/2019013845

ISBN 978-1-108-48492-3 Hardback

CONTENTS

List of Contributors	*page* vii	
Acknowledgments	ix	

I INTRODUCTION TO THE THEMES, SITE, AND REGION — I

1 INTRODUCTION TO THE THEMES OF THE VOLUME: COGNITION
AND ÇATALHÖYÜK — 3
Ian Hodder

2 HUNTER-GATHERER HOME-MAKING? BUILDING LANDSCAPE
AND COMMUNITY IN THE EPIPALEOLITHIC — 31
Lisa Maher

II HIGHER LEVELS OF CONSCIOUSNESS — 63

3 WHEN TIME BEGINS TO MATTER — 65
Marion Benz

4 COGNITIVE CHANGE AND MATERIAL CULTURE: A DISTRIBUTED
PERSPECTIVE — 90
Michael Wheeler

5 CONSCIOUS TOKENS? — 107
Lucy Ebony Bennison-Chapman

6 BRICK SIZES AND ARCHITECTURAL REGULARITIES AT NEOLITHIC
ÇATALHÖYÜK — 133
Marek Z. Barański

CONTENTS

III GREATER INNOVATION AND CREATIVITY 151

7 THE MERONOMIC MODEL OF COGNITIVE CHANGE
AND ITS APPLICATION TO NEOLITHIC ÇATALHÖYÜK 153
Chris Thornton

8 CONTAINERS AND CREATIVITY IN THE LATE NEOLITHIC UPPER
MESOPOTAMIAN 168
Olivier Nieuwenhuyse

9 CREATIVITY AND INNOVATION IN THE GEOMETRIC WALL PAINTINGS
AT ÇATALHÖYÜK 190
Ian Hodder and Nazlı Gürlek

IV GREATER AWARENESS OF AN INTEGRATED PERSONAL SELF 207

10 PERSONAL MEMORY, THE SCAFFOLDED MIND, AND COGNITIVE
CHANGE IN THE NEOLITHIC 209
John Sutton

11 ADORNING THE SELF 230
Milena Vasić

12 FROM PARTS TO A WHOLE? EXPLORING CHANGES IN FUNERARY
PRACTICES AT ÇATALHÖYÜK 250
*Scott D. Haddow, Eline M. J. Schotsmans, Marco Milella, Marin A. Pilloud,
Belinda Tibbetts, and Christopher J. Knüsel*

13 NEW BODIES: FROM HOUSES TO HUMANS AT ÇATALHÖYÜK 273
Anna Fagan

Notes 289
Index 291

CONTRIBUTORS

Marek Z. Barański
Academy of Fine Arts, Gdańsk, Poland

Lucy Ebony Bennison-Chapman
The Netherlands Institute for the Near East,
Leiden University, Netherlands

Marion Benz
University of Freiburg, Germany, Institute of
Near Eastern Archaeology

Anna Fagan
Department of Archaeology, University of
Melbourne, Australia

Nazlı Gürlek
Cihangir Caddesi, Istanbul, Turkey

Scott D. Haddow
Department of Cross-Cultural and Regional
Studies, Copenhagen University

Ian Hodder
Department of Anthropology, Stanford
University, USA

Christopher Knüsel
University of Bordeaux, France

Lisa Maher
Department of Anthropology, University of
California, Berkeley, USA

Marco Milella
Department of Anthropology
Institute of Forensic Medicine University
of Bern

Olivier Nieuwenhuyse
Free University, Berlin, Germany

Marin A. Pilloud
Forensic Anthropology, University of
Nevada, Reno, USA

Eline M. J. Schotsmans
School of Archaeological and
Forensic Sciences, Bradford University, UK

John Sutton
Macquarie University, Australia

Belinda Tibbetts
Department of Archaeology, Exeter
University, UK

Chris Thornton
Centre for Research in Cognitive Science,
University of Sussex, UK

Milena Vasić
Free University, Berlin, Germany

Michael Wheeler
Department of Philosophy, University of
Stirling, UK

ACKNOWLEDGMENTS

This volume results from research conducted by the Çatalhöyük Research Project between 2015 and 2017 and funded by a grant (Number 52003) from the John Templeton Foundation as well as by the British Institute at Ankara and commercial sponsors (Yapı Kredi, Boeing, Koçtaş, and Shell). The project involved research at Çatalhöyük and culminated in a conference held at the McDonald Institute of Archaeological Research in Cambridge on July 27–30, 2017. Some of the speakers and participants at the conference then came together to produce this volume.

Apart from those already listed, I am very grateful to the British Institute at Ankara, the Turkish Ministry of Culture and Tourism in Ankara, and Konya Museums, as well as to the many hundreds of archaeologists who have worked at Çatalhöyük between 1993 and 2018. I am also very grateful to the McDonald Institute in Cambridge for help in housing and organizing the conference. The organization of the conference was handled very efficiently by Bilge Küçükdoğan.

PART I

INTRODUCTION TO THE THEMES, SITE, AND REGION

INTRODUCTION TO THE THEMES OF THE VOLUME

Cognition and Çatalhöyük

Ian Hodder

OVER RECENT YEARS, A NUMBER OF scholars have argued that the human mind underwent a cognitive revolution in the Neolithic. This book seeks to test these claims at the Neolithic site of Çatalhöyük in Turkey and in other Neolithic contexts in the Middle East. The volume brings together cognitive scientists who have developed theoretical frameworks for the study of cognitive change, archaeologists who have conducted research into cognitive change in the Neolithic of the Middle East, and the excavators of the Neolithic site of Çatalhöyük, who have over recent years been exploring changes in consciousness, creativity, and self in the context of the rich data from the site.

Cognitive archaeology has focused on ways in which different material worlds afford different potentials of mind. Thus external symbols allow more information to be stored. Or systems of weights allow new notions of value and worth. Or writing and numbering allow more complex quantification. This may all be true, but what is "cognitive" about it? External symbols (including material culture but also later number systems and writing) might

mean that a society has more information available to it, but does that mean that a human mind can store more information? Or might it mean the opposite, that the human mind becomes less complex, less able to remember large amounts of complex data? After all, there are accounts of small-scale societies like the Polynesian Tikopia that have prodigious abilities to navigate vast oceans without measuring devices (Firth 1959). Systems of weights and measures might underpin more complex social and economic systems, but might that not mean that a human mind has become less attuned to quantifying weights and making measurements? One might call this the "smart phones, dumb people" syndrome!

Perhaps more important, if we were to make such arguments and in fact suggest that human dependence on material symbols, number systems, and writing (and libraries and computers) actually made the mind less complex, less able to construct abstract thoughts, less able to remember large numbers of social contacts, how would one test these alternative hypotheses as an archaeologist? It is striking that cognitive archaeology set itself up as a more rigorous, scientifically testable domain (Renfrew 1982), and yet it is not at all clear that there are methods available to test these alternative hypotheses. Certainly it is possible for archaeology to attest to the emergence of abstract symbol systems, and this will be part of the task in this volume. But it is not at all clear that such evidence is telling us anything at all about "the cognitive." Rather, the evidence is telling us about how societies are able to store information, construct abstractions, and develop social memories. It may not be telling us about mind.

Of course, mind is responsive to and constitutive of context, and so presumably in all contexts humans think differently and have different cognitive potential. The notion of the extended mind suggests that the mind is responsive to material context at both the habituated, embodied level of practice (Malafouris 2013) and at more abstract levels. How the mind cognizes the world is a product of the context. But because as archaeologists we cannot access mind or test theories about it directly (rather than through proxies), it is not clear what a cognitive archaeology can contribute except insofar as it is confined to social cognition – that is, to the concepts, abstractions, memories, thoughts of a society. It cannot then be right for archaeologists to separate the cognitive from social meanings and representations.

Something would be added by a cognitive archaeology, of course, if it were argued that the wiring in the physical brain had an impact on how humans cognized the world. And such arguments are made in evolutionary accounts of shifts from modular to generalized minds (e.g., Mithen 2004), or when links are made between tool-making and language (closely connected parts of the brain are involved). It remains unclear that any such limitations provided by brain architecture have influenced the development and history of the mind of *Homo sapiens*. Rather, there is much evidence of brain structure and organization being responsive to contextual changes.

Something too would be added if it was argued that learned patterns of mental action became habituated such that they limited cognitive capacities. Such arguments are the domain of psychology or have long been key to critiques of ideology. In such contexts, most starkly, it would be difficult to distill out a cognitive domain. The mind is thoroughly embedded in psyche and ideology.

The danger in cognitive archaeology is thus that it often asserts something to do with mind, even writing of "the archaeology of mind" (Renfrew 1982), when in fact all it can do is test hypotheses about how societies function in terms of information, values, concepts, memories. These might indeed all be termed aspects of the "social mind," but they do not give insight into the mind itself if by that is meant the workings of individual minds. Cognitive archaeologists often claim to discuss aspects of "the human mind" when in fact all they can explore scientifically is specific social minds embedded within sociomaterial contexts.

Of course, it might be countered that the notion of a distributed mind makes a nonsense of any attempt to make a distinction between universal characteristics of the human mind and social minds. According to this view, all minds are dependent on and continuous with the world around them. So there can be no universal human mind separated from context. As discussed by Wheeler in Chapter 4 of this volume, there are two main versions of this distributed connectionist argument. The first, embedded hypothesis is close to the argument presented earlier and states that the introduction of new symbol systems such as language or material symbol systems allows more complex cognitive performance without necessarily causing changes in biological brain capacity. This is because, according to this embedded view, the biological capacities of the human brain are highly dependent on body and world in order to function, but they have generalized capabilities that are not necessarily changed by that functioning. Within such a view, it is difficult or impossible for archaeologists to move beyond the embedded social mind to ascertain biological human minds in the past, except by making assumptions about universal characteristics of the human mind.

Wheeler argues that an alternative extended hypothesis rejects the embedded notion that external elements such as language and material symbols act as noncognitive factors that support and augment the wholly internal cognitive states and processes. Rather, the extended view takes the more radical position that external symbols are themselves part of the cognitive process. From such a standpoint, any change in material symbols involves cognitive change. There are two difficulties here. The first is that because all material culture has symbolic dimensions, the statement that changes in material culture involve cognitive change becomes trivial and self-fulfilling (see Wheeler, Chapter 4 in this volume, for a

discussion of this issue). The second is that archaeology itself cannot resolve the argument between the embedded and extended views, for the reasons stated earlier. Archaeologists can explore hypotheses about ancient symbol systems, but they have little purchase on the relationships between those (social) systems and mind.

In this volume we attempt to avoid the confusions of cognitive archaeology by focusing on specific and well-defined aspects of "social minds." We show that specific questions concerned with levels of consciousness, degrees of creativity, and notions of self can be explored by understanding mind as social action, situated in context, and thus as dependent on interpretation as any other form. In this volume the archaeological case studies focus on cognitive change as change in social minds that is distributed within a material–social milieu.

Over recent years a number of scholars have argued that "the human mind" underwent a cognitive revolution in the Neolithic. In my view, this argument results from a confusion between an evolutionary account of the universal nature of a separate cognitive domain (the human mind) on the one hand and a recognition of the context-dependent nature of mind on the other. When tested against detailed data from the Neolithic of the Middle East and Anatolia, and in particular against the large amounts of high-quality data obtained from Çatalhöyük, the confusions are made clear, and an alternative account emerges.

THEORIES OF NEOLITHIC COGNITIVE CHANGE

There has long been an assumption that the modern mind somehow differed cognitively from the "primitive" or "savage" mind – and here we seem to be talking about universal aspects of individual minds. In *La Pensée Sauvage* Lévi-Strauss (1962) argued that the "savage mind" was in many ways similar to the "civilized mind," and that both had the ability to be "scientific." But he also noted a difference between premodern (including Neolithic) science, which was limited to putting together bits of sensory practical knowledge (in a process he called bricolage) and the more open questioning of modern science. For Lévi-Strauss, the Neolithic mind was not dissimilar from the Paleolithic mind; both were embedded in concrete and sensible things rather than being distanced from them. Over recent years, a number of authors have drawn continuities across the period of the adoption of farming. For example, David Lewis-Williams has interpreted sites like Çatalhöyük in terms of ethnographic parallels with hunter-gatherers and argued that altered states of consciousness are relevant to Neolithic as much as to Paleolithic art (Lewis-Williams 2004; Lewis-Williams and Pearce 2005). Finlayson and Warren (2010) have warned against the assumption that the Neolithic mind suddenly became more like the modern mind, pointing to the undoubted complexity of Upper Paleolithic thought processes in Europe, as indicated in cave paintings and complex tool technologies.

On the other hand, work in cognitive evolution, especially that by Merlin Donald (1991), has encouraged the notion that cognitive changes have occurred in human history, whether genetically linked or not. At the same time, work on the plasticity and distributed nature of cognitive processes argues strongly that mind is embedded in context.

For example, for Fuchs and Schlimme (2009), consciousness does not develop in an isolated brain, but only in a living organism enmeshed in its environment. Clark (1997) argues that recent work on cognitive models, neuroscience, and robotics indicates that our thinking comes about as an interaction between brain and world.

Given this notion of a contextually distributed and plastic mind, it might be expected that the Neolithic, with its panoply of new techniques and ways of life, would be associated with cognitive change. For Gordon Childe (1936), the emergence of pottery technology in the Neolithic had great significance for human thought and the emergence of science in that it involved the transformation of substance. Perhaps the clearest early statement on the cognitive changes that may have accompanied the adoption of farming and a settled way of life is by the Jesuit priest Teilhard de Chardin, who argued that the Neolithic was a key moment in the gradual process by which human consciousness, an awareness of personal self, and the horizons of human possibility (innovation and creativity) all increased. In his 1955 *The Phenomenon of Man*, de Chardin wrote a chapter on "The Neolithic Metamorphosis" in which the Neolithic was seen as a "critical age and one of solemn importance among all the epochs of the past" (p. 68). The greater exchange and interaction between people meant that "from Neolithic times onwards the influence of psychical factors begins to outweigh – and by far – the variations of ever-dwindling somatic factors" (p. 68). More specifically, de Chardin argued that the increased spreading out of ideas in the Neolithic meant that people created more complex thoughts as they converged and integrated. Trade, exchange, movement, and interaction led to what he termed "complexification" – an evolutionary process of increased organizational complexity. The same processes also led to an intensification of mental subjective activity – "the evolution of progressively more conscious mind" – the raising of mental potential.

In a series of important articles, Renfrew (e.g., 1998, 2012) builds on the work of Merlin Donald (1991) and proposes a phase in cognitive development between the phase of linguistic or mythic culture associated with *Homo sapiens* and the phase of theoretic culture associated with urban societies with writing. In this intermediate period associated with the Neolithic, Renfrew describes a phase of symbolic material culture in which information is stored externally, not in texts, but in the complexities of material symbols. The substantive engagement with greater amounts of material culture associated with sedentism (pottery, polished axes, and domesticated plants and animals) led to a nexus of weights, values, commodities, and exchanges that involved cognitive change (more accurate measurement of relative value and the objectification of things as commodities). The substantive engagement with more material culture brought forth symbol and concept. Material symbol preceded concept in that it was the experience and comparison of heavy/light things that led to abstract ideas about weight and metrication/measurement. The large body of work by Schmandt-Besserat (e.g., 2007) argued for a gradual development from the use of tokens into early writing in the Middle East from 7,500 to 3,000 BC, a process described by her in

terms of the human acquisition of complex cognitive processes such as abstraction (for a critique of this argument, see Chapter 5, this volume).

Watkins (2010) follows Renfrew in suggesting that the Neolithic saw the emergence of the cognitive and cultural abilities to create symbolic vocabularies and formulate symbolic constructions using material culture (as distinct from spoken or written language), but he follows Wilson (1991) in arguing that in particular the built environment of houses and ritual structures was the driver of rapid cultural development in the first village communities. The steep upward turn in the graph of cognitive and symbolic abilities was associated with the construction of built environments that allowed humans to manage the complex social relations that emerged in the Neolithic. In fact, there are two separate hypotheses within Watkins's account. First, starting in the increasingly sedentary societies of the Late Epipaleolithic in the Middle East, architecture and the built environment provided a stage on which complex ideas and relations could be mapped, expressed, and stored. Second, there is the rather different point that dense settlements required complex organizational skills to manage the processes of living together permanently.

For Mithen (2004), too, it is the dense settlements of the Neolithic that made the biggest difference in terms of cognitive evolution, along with increases in trade and exchange. During the Neolithic, such developments as (a) closer relations with plants and animals and their cycles of reproduction, (b) larger houses necessitating more complex architectural and construction techniques, (c) use of lime plaster involving burning limestone to temperatures between 750 and 850°C, and (d) the production of textiles, all engendered new modes of thought. In addition there were increases in basketry, brewing, and pottery – all this involved new bodies of knowledge and the evolved propensities of the mind. As a result, a more "scientific" mode of thought emerged in which humans made accurate observations and tested hypotheses about causality, even if scientific cognition at that time was tied up with religious thought (a claim not dissimilar to Lévi-Strauss's account of premodern science and its relation to myth).

While the preceding authors associate cognitive change with sedentism, agriculture, trade, and exchange and the new technologies of the Neolithic, Cauvin (2000) takes the view that cognitive, symbolic, and psychological change must have preceded other aspects of the Neolithic package. Increased intervention in the environment associated with agriculture implies the predevelopment of a human agency obtained from envisaging the power of personal divinities. The birth of agriculture is linked to and preceded by the birth of human-like divinities. Such divinities allowed humans to see themselves as separate from external reality (p. 209) and then to act upon it so as to transform and domesticate. The initial change was "a purely mental development" (p. 32) involving a greater sense of agency and an alienated sense of self (p. 209). However, toward the end of his book, Cauvin takes a more dialectical stance: The symbolic and the economic "are simply two faces, interior and exterior, of a single revolution" (p. 220).

While all the authors in this book describe in broad-brush terms the evidence for cognitive change in the Neolithic of the Middle East and the causes for those changes, there has been little specific testing of the claims made. Scholars have assumed that the cognitive changes they describe are loosely linked to sedentism, changes in technology, trade, and exchange, increases in amounts of material culture in the Neolithic as a whole, without exploring or testing any specific correlations. The dating of sites and events in the Neolithic of the Middle East remains imprecise, and many of the processes involved took place over millennia (e.g., sedentism, cultivation, and domestication) and varied in nature and speed in different parts of the Middle East: The process of Neolithicization has come to be understood as a complex polycentric process (Gebel 2004; Özbaşaran and Buitenhuis 2002; Özdoğan 2010). It has proved much easier to talk about cognitive change in broad-brush terms than to test specific hypotheses against the data from the Middle East as a whole.

All the earlier discussions of Neolithic cognitive change make broad claims about overall evolutionary transformations, although it is not always clear whether changes in universal aspects of human minds or changes in social minds are being proposed. The chapters in this volume seek to test claims for cognitive change in social minds and the causes of the changes by taking a five-part strategy. First, a single excavated site, Çatalhöyük, with large amounts of data that cover part of the Neolithic sequence, will be used as an important laboratory for testing hypotheses about the causes of cognitive change. Second, specific measures of cognitive change will be proposed, building on the work of Renfrew and others (Renfrew 1982; Renfrew and

Bahn 2004; Renfrew and Zubrow 1994; Renfrew et al. 1985), but will be critically evaluated. Third, both at Çatalhöyük and at other sites in the Middle East, careful consideration will be given to the interpretation of the social and economic context within which cognitive change may have occurred rather than assuming an overall "Neolithic" transformation. Fourth, cognitive change will be understood as change in the capacity of social minds, that is, in the ability of a society and its technology to manage information, produce abstractions, innovate, and develop notions of self. Fifth, claims for overall evolutionary transformations will be critically scrutinized.

ÇATALHÖYÜK

The focus of this volume, Çatalhöyük East (7,100–6,000 BC) in central Turkey, is one of the best-known Neolithic sites in Anatolia and the Middle East, roughly contemporary with latest Pre-Pottery and the following Pottery Neolithic in the Levant. It became well known because of its large size (32 acres and 3,500–8,000 people), with numerous levels inhabited over 1,100 years, and dense concentration of "art" in the form of wall paintings, wall reliefs, sculptures, and installations. Within Anatolia, and particularly within central Anatolia, recent research has shown that there are local sequences that lead up to and prefigure Çatalhöyük (Gérard and Thissen 2002; Özdoğan 2002), especially as a result of recent work at Boncuklu (Baird et al. 2018). In southeast Turkey, the earlier villages of Çayönü (Özdoğan and Özdoğan 1998) and Göbekli Tepe (Schmidt 2001, 2006) already show substantial agglomeration and elaborate symbolism. In central Anatolia, Aşıklı Höyük (Esin and Harmankaya 1999) has dense packed housing through the millennium prior to Çatalhöyük. There are many other sites either contemporary or partly contemporary with Çatalhöyük that are known in central Anatolia and the adjacent Burdur-Lakes region (Duru 1999; Gérard and Thissen 2002). Yet Çatalhöyük retains a special significance because of the complex narrative nature of its art, and many syntheses (e.g., by Cauvin 1994 or Mithen 2003) give it a special place.

Much of the symbolism of the earlier Neolithic and later (into historic times) periods of the Middle East can be "read" in terms of the evidence from Çatalhöyük, and the rich evidence from the site enables interpretation of the evidence from other sites.

The site was first excavated by James Mellaart (see 1967) in the 1960s. After 1965, it was abandoned until a new project under my direction began in 1993 (Hodder 1996, 2000, 2005a, 2005b, 2005c, 2006, 2007a, 2010, 2013a, 2013b, 2014a, 2014b, 2014c). Through both Mellaart's and my projects, only 5 percent of the mound has been excavated, but the whole mound has been sampled using surface survey, surface pickup, geophysical prospection, and surface scraping (see reports in Hodder 1996). The main architectural components of the site are densely clustered houses, with areas of refuse or midden between them. The art and symbolism and burial all occur within houses. There is evidence of productive activities in all houses and on roofs of houses. None of the sampling has found evidence of large public buildings, ceremonial centers, specialized areas of production, or cemeteries. The population of the settlement at any one time has been conservatively estimated (Cessford 2005a) using a variety of techniques and making a variety of assumptions about how many houses were inhabited at any one time.

All of the extensive excavation in the 1960s took place without screening, and with limited recording and no scientific analysis (except radiocarbon dating). The current project (since 1993) has used a range of modern scientific techniques. In the earliest phase of the current project (1993–1995), we concentrated on regional survey and on planning and studying the surface of the mound, conducting surface pickup, drawing eroded profiles of the earlier excavation trenches, and using geophysical prospection. We also undertook a reevaluation of the material in museums that had been excavated by Mellaart. This work has been published (Hodder 1996).

In the second phase of fieldwork and publication (1996–1999), the research aim focused on individual buildings. We excavated in two main areas on the mound (Figure 1.1). In the North area we concentrated on excavating two buildings in great detail in order to discern depositional processes and to understand how individual houses functioned. In the South area we continued the trenches that had been started by Mellaart in order to understand the overall sequence of the site and to see how individual houses were rebuilt and reused over time. At the same time paleoenvironmental work was conducted (Roberts et al. 1999), regional survey continued (Baird 2002), and excavations were undertaken on the later Chalcolithic mound at Çatalhöyük West. Publication of the monographs for this second phase of

work has been completed (Hodder 2005a, 2005b, 2005c, 2007a). The methods used by the project were published in an earlier volume (Hodder 2000). Articles have also been published in journals and in the project's own archive reports and newsletters available on the web at www.catal hoyuk.com.

The research aims for the third phase of the project (2000–2008) turned from individual houses to the social geography of the settlement and to the changes in social organization through time. The work from this cycle and postexcavation analysis between 2009 and 2012 led to four volumes describing the results of the excavations and two further interpretive volumes (Hodder 2010, 2013a, 2013b, 2014a, 2014b, 2014c).

The fourth phase of excavation and research at Çatalhöyük (2009–2017) focused on the hypothesis that social organization at the site was based around "history houses" made up of groups of houses centered on a central house in which the dead were preferentially buried and ritual and symbolic markers were amassed (human heads, animal heads, horns, tusks, claws, etc.). The hypothesis argued that religion and history were closely tied in the production of these special houses, and that these houses acted to produce the long-term social relations and structures that are the hallmark of settled agricultural societies. It was hypothesized that we can chart the development of the history house system in the growth and development of the site, and indeed that the whole town of Çatalhöyük and the surrounding landscape were organized so that historical relations and connections could be charted.

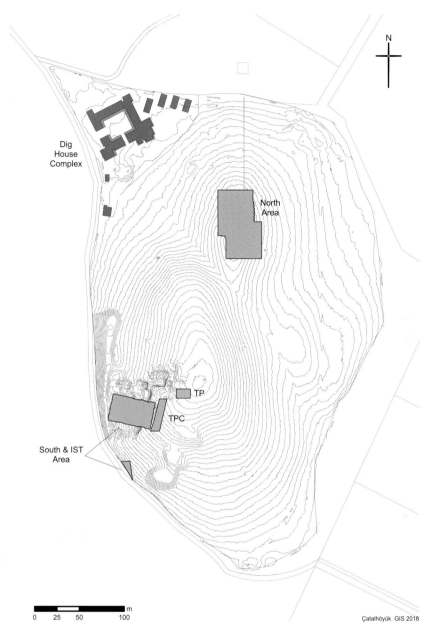

FIGURE 1.1 Map of the Neolithic East Mound at Çatalhöyük, with the main excavation areas identified.

NEOLITHIC SOCIETIES OF THE MIDDLE EAST AND ANATOLIA

It is now widely accepted that the processes of sedentism and domestication of plants and animals in the Middle East lasted many millennia: There was a long slow process of gradual change in many arenas of life. It is important to note these changes as they underpinned or were related to the cognitive changes that have been claimed for this time period. In particular, cognitive change has been related to sedentism, technological change, domestication of plants and animals, and trade and exchange. Cognitive change has also been related to shifts in ritual and religious practice and social change.

The Levantine sequence involves Epipaleolithic groups such as the Kebaran and Natufian (the latter from approximately 12,500 BC to 10,000 BC) with increasingly intensive hunting, gathering, and cultivation of wild plants, followed by the Pre-Pottery Neolithic A (PPNA) from 10,000 to 8,700 BC, and then the Pre-Pottery Neolithic B (PPNB) from 8,700 to 6,800, in which a wide range of domesticated plants and animals emerged associated with large, dense, and sedentary communities (Zeder 2011). The PPNB is followed by the PPNC and Pottery Neolithic (PN). Because of the polycentric character of the processes of sedentism and domestication (Gebel 2004) throughout the Middle Eastern and Anatolian region, it is incorrect to use these terms and sequences outside the Levant, and others have been proposed for Anatolia (e.g., Özbaşaran and Buitenhuis 2002). However, the Levantine sequence is best understood and documented and provides a benchmark for the sequences elsewhere.

In the southern Levant we can see the size of settlements gradually increase over time (Kuijt 2008). The largest Late Natufian settlements are about 0.2 ha each. The largest PPNA settlements average over 1 ha. The largest MPPNB sites are 4.5–5.0 ha. It is not until the LPPNB that settlements such as Basta and 'Ain Ghazal reach 10–14 ha, more in line with Çatalhöyük East. Also of note is that through these time periods the density of occupation in sites increases. Kuijt (2008) has estimated that the ratio of the area with

buildings to open space in settlements increases from the Late Natufian through to the LPPNB; in addition, houses were often double-story by the LPPNB. There is also some evidence that through time hearths, that in the Natufian are usually found inside structures, are through time increasingly found in external midden deposits (Goring-Morris and Belfer-Cohen 2012), perhaps indicating an expansion of domestic activity and production. It is the megasites such as Basta and 'Ain Ghazal that are most relevant in size and date to Çatalhöyük, even though the deposits in these sites in Jordan are usually not as thick and deep (Verhoeven 2006). Only small portions of these sites have been excavated, but so far there is no evidence of social segmentation or hierarchical divisions of power and authority. Mortuary practices and residential architecture show little evidence of social differentiation (Verhoeven 2006). Many large sites collapse toward the end of the PPN, though 'Ain Ghazal and Abu Hureyra to the north continued to be occupied up to the mid-Chalcolithic. Sites generally become smaller and more dispersed toward the beginning of the sixth millennium in the early Pottery Neolithic. However, one PN Yarmoukian site, Sha'ar Hagolan, was very large (c. 20 ha), although the houses were not densely packed.

It has often been argued that through time in the southern Levant there is a shift from nuclear family households to extended households that own independent property (Flannery 2002; Goring-Morris and Belfer-Cohen 2008; Kuijt 2008; Kuijt et al. 2011). Through time, houses shift from round to rectangular (PPNA to PPNB), become larger, internally divided, and double-story (by LPPNB). They have more evidence of in-house storage. It is also possible that as the processing of plant and animal products became more intensive, these were most effectively achieved in domestic space (intensive processing of plants, bones, meat, and milk) that was also more controlled and private. Perhaps the most significant process was a change from neighborhood clusters and collective labor to more autonomous house units (Byrd 1994; Düring and Marciniak 2006; Marciniak 2008). Through time these autonomous units gradually expanded. For example, Goring-Morris and Belfer-Cohen (2012) note that in the PN in the southern Levant, Sha'ar Hagolan has courtyards with external enclosure walls, and there are rectangular domestic structures together with ancillary storage and cooking facilities. This increasing focus on appropriating the space around houses in order to support productive activities is also a feature of Çatalhöyük. The increasing autonomy can be seen most clearly in storage. There is very limited evidence of storage in Natufian settlements, but at the PPNA site of Dhra' near the Dead Sea in Jordan there is evidence for large-scale storage structures (Kuijt and Finlayson 2009). These granaries were placed in extramural locations and were presumed to have been collective. Going through time in the Levant, from 9,500 BC onward in the PPNA there are large silos like Dhra' but also small bins. Kenyon (1981) also identified possible collective storage structures at PPNA Jericho near the tower. By 8,500 BC storage bins occur in houses in MPPNB, and by 7,500 BC there are dedicated storage rooms in houses in LPPNB Neolithic villages (Kuijt et al. 2011).

In the Levant it is generally assumed that the Middle and Late PPNB sites in which there is much symbolism and ritual reflect communal practices (Kuijt 2000). Kenyon (1957) identified PPNB structures as shrines or temples at Jericho. Bar-Yosef (1986) suggested that the PPNA tower at Jericho had a primarily ritual function. At Beidha in the PPNB, nondomestic buildings were identified as serving some communal purpose (Byrd 1994). At 'Ain Ghazal, Rollefson (pers. comm.) has argued for kinship groups or sectors in the layout of the settlement, but also for the presence of specialized shamans or priests rather than an egalitarian society. At the Middle/Late PPNB funerary site of Kfar HaHoresh, Goring-Morris (2005) argues for perhaps some incipient social differentiation, based on the burial data. Claims for social differentiation and ranking (e.g., Davis 1998) have not withstood more critical analysis, and even in MPPNB any social differentiation that cross-cuts age and sex is best described as emergent or incipient (Price and Bar-Yosef 2010). Verhoeven (pers. comm.) suggests the presence of sorcerers and shamans in the PPNB who had social authority but within an overall focus on communality.

Moving to the northern Levant and southeast Turkey, Rosenberg and Redding (2000, 48–9) have tentatively suggested that two of the very few circular huts excavated at Hallan Çemi may have been public structures, with perhaps an aurochs skull hung on one interior wall. In Syria in the PPNA site of Tell Qaramel, monumental towers and a "shrine/common house" have been identified (Mazurowski 2004). It is still early to be sure of the spatial geography of the monumental stone circles at Göbekli Tepe (dated to

9,100–8,500 cal BC – that is from the PPNA to the Middle/Late PPNB). For the excavator Klaus Schmidt (2006), they indicate a sanctuary that served a region. On the other hand, Banning (2011) argues that the circular structures at Göbekli may not be temples but symbolically elaborate houses. Whether there was a contemporary settlement around the main circles remains unclear, but the circles seem to represent collective endeavor: There is no associated evidence of elites or elite residences.

The situation is clearer at Jerf al-Ahmar in the PPNA, where throughout the sequence there are distinct cult buildings, which are described by Stordeur (2000) as communal, perhaps including shared storage. Through time the sunken ritual buildings become larger and more elaborate. Large, more elaborate structures in contrast to residential structures are found at Tell 'Abr 3, upstream of Jerf al-Ahmar (Yartah 2005). The evidence from PPNB Nevali Çori consists of houses but also a cult building (Hauptmann 2007) with T-shaped pillars (as at Göbekli). The cult building with terrazzo floors had been built into earlier buildings in a repeated series.

The sequence at Çayönü is important as the occupation continues on into the period contemporary with Çatalhöyük. Mehmet Özdoğan (2002) argues (for example, in the Cell subphase) that there is an eastern area of the site with temple or cult buildings associated with domestic buildings bigger and better built than houses found in the western area (see also Davis 1998). There is more evidence of lithic production in the western area, but special and high-quality materials predominate in the eastern area. The evidence may indicate social differentiation, but it remains possible that the eastern area contains public buildings for collective use rather than elites.

In central Anatolia, by the second half of the ninth millennium, there are both small settlements as at Boncuklu and Pınarbaşı (Baird 2007b) and the large highly agglomerated village at Aşıklı Höyük (8,400–7,400 BC) (Esin and Harmankaya 1999; Özbaşaran 2011). At the latter site there is very little evidence of storage facilities. As a result of large-scale area excavation, a clear social geography has been identified, with public ritual buildings (frequently renewed) separated from other dwellings by a monumental street. The dwellings are organized into sectors by narrow spaces or narrow streets, and there are collective common middens. The area with public ritual buildings is distinctive in having larger numbers of pressure-retouched projectiles and higher percentages of cattle bones. There is evidence of butchering and sharing of meat. Overall, the evidence is interpreted in terms of the collective and communal rather than in terms of centralized elites.

On the Konya Plain itself, Boncuklu in the period 8,500–7,500 BCE has painting, bucrania and subfloor burials all very reminiscent of Çatalhöyük, presaging its ritual complexity, but in a small wetland site with dispersed oval houses (Baird 2007a). There is an overall increase in house size in the area, as seen in the Levant, but the changing density of settlements shows a rather more complex picture. Regional survey by Baird (2002, 2005) shows increasing population densities, but also concentration through time into the one large site of Çatalhöyük, followed by dispersal into multiple tells in the Chalcolithic.

Central Anatolia is located at a cusp between East and West in terms of the spread of farming (Özdoğan 2010). In many aspects the cultural assemblage from Çatalhöyük has similarities with the Marmara and Balkan regions (bone spoons, stamp seals, bone hooks) rather than with the southeast of Turkey. This difference also includes the social organization of settlements and ritual. As Özdoğan has argued, to the east special buildings are more commonly found, and there is a general focus on ancestors and history making. But to the west of Çatalhöyük special buildings do not dominate, and there are extramural cemeteries (for example, in the Fikirtepe culture sites with rectangular architecture in the Marmara region) (Özdoğan 2011). In the Neolithic of Greece, starting around 7,000/6,700 BC, there is again less obvious ritual and an overall focus on communality, especially in the flat extended settlements. It may be possible to observe a dialectic tension between communality and a focus on power, history, and memory in the tell sites in Greece. Sesklo is comprised of a tell (acropolis) and a surrounding settlement (polis). The percentage of painted pottery is higher on the tell, suggesting some form of social division expressed within the social geography of the site.

Overall, then, Çatalhöyük has to be set within larger-scale temporal and spatial trends. The site is part of a local sequence characterized by dense agglomerate settlement (as at Aşıklı Höyük and Can Hasan III). Yet there are differences between Konya and Cappodocia. There is little ritual elaboration at Aşıklı Höyük, but at Boncuklu, close to and prior to Çatalhöyük, there is already evidence for painted floors, bucrania, head

removal, and subfloor burial and divisions between "dirty" and "clean" parts of houses. Thus Çatalhöyük is part of a distinct local tradition on the Konya plain, certainly linked culturally and by the exchange of obsidian with Cappodocia but with its own distinctive focus on symbolic elaboration. It is now widely recognized that local traditions occurred throughout Turkey and the Middle East. But there were also contacts and spreads of technologies and ideas (e.g., Hodder and Meskell 2011), and Çatalhöyük participated in these wider economic, social, and demographic trends.

This broad account of the changes leading up to Çatalhöyük and the broader Pottery Neolithic are important in any attempt to argue that cognitive change occurred "in the Neolithic." The processes described earlier took place over millennia, and it is often not easy to see overall evolutionary developments. The central Anatolian plateau is one of many areas with distinct sequences, and the differences between, for example, Cappadocia and the Konya Plain are striking. There is much evidence for variation across space and time in ritual practices and in forms of social organization. Given this variation, we might immediately be suspect of any suggestion of an overall cognitive shift. But it might be countered that whatever the variation, Neolithic societies throughout the region all went through similar processes of larger and longer-term settlement associated with symbolic and ritual elaboration. The archaeological evidence needs to be examined to see if overall cognitive shifts can be observed.

Two introductory chapters to this volume explore the wider and longer-term context of

Neolithic change and demonstrate the complex and diverse ways in which cognitive change may have been involved. In Chapter 2 Lisa Maher uses the careful and detailed excavations at the Epipaleolithic (23,000–11,500 cal BP) site of Kharaneh IV in eastern Jordan to demonstrate that even at this early time period, many of the components of complex dwellings so characteristic of "The Neolithic" were already present. Place-making, innovation and creativity, and greater interaction between individuals and groups were already found. The evidence suggests that there is little indication of an overall cognitive Neolithic "break." Instead she focuses on the continuous nature of the changes. Rather than the Neolithic marking the beginning of the so-called modern mind, the Kharaneh IV data suggest a continuity with hunter-gatherer behavior involving place-making, home-making, dwelling, and the creation of communities.

In Chapter 3, Marion Benz makes a similar point regarding concepts of time. She defines episodic, cyclical, and linear concepts of time and suggests that in the Neolithic of the Middle East there was no linear evolution from episodic, to cyclical and then on to linear concepts of time. It seems that increasing circular and linear concepts of time were related to concepts of increasingly well-defined social identities in sedentary agricultural communities. Anticipating and assessing environmental conditions and long-term planning became crucial cognitive capacities within farming communities. Episodic concepts of time were thus marginalized because of a specific social and economic context. Benz goes on to argue in the light of these data that the hypothesis that early Neolithic

communities were more innovative or more creative than Paleolithic hunter- gatherers seems highly questionable. The substantial surge in new things during the Neolithic is thus not to be considered a result of a higher level of creativity, but as a consequence of social differentiation and social identities, which became more and more based on and expressed by material things and prescribed familial relationships.

In both these cases we can talk of cognitive changes, at times nondiscursive and embodied, but these seem situational and specific, and there is little evidence of an overall evolutionary development in universal aspects of "the human mind." Rather, specific aspects of "social minds" such as memory making, place making, and notions of time emerge within social institutions (such as forms of community, family, and economy).

MEASURING NEOLITHIC COGNITIVE CHANGE

Turning to the Neolithic of the Middle East itself, in this volume there is consideration of three of the claims about cognitive change that have been made in the literature described earlier.

1. *Higher levels of consciousness.* The claim that higher levels of consciousness became necessary in the Neolithic is found in a number of guises in the literature, including increases in abstract thought and distanced thought. The claim is most specifically made by Teilhard de Chardin (1955) as discussed earlier. In addition, a number of authors (e.g., Schmandt-Besserat 2007) have linked abstract thought to metrication and the appearance of tokens. Recent definitions of

consciousness have argued that it involves the dual processes of abstraction and objectification (Bekaert 1998). Much human knowledge is practical (know-how, savoir faire) and tied to motor habits, while more abstract levels of conscious and discursive thought involve representations, metaphors, and codic oppositions (Bekaert 1998; Pelegrin 1990; Wynn 1993). The abstractions thus depend on objectifications in the form of symbols or tokens. Archaeologically, the dual processes of abstraction and objectification can be identified in material symbols and tokens (objectifications) that are generalized and recombinable (abstractions). As noted earlier, however, it does not follow that the existence of material symbols and tokens necessarily implies that individual minds became more capable of abstract thought. Rather, they allowed societies to develop more elaborate representations, a more complex social consciousness – regardless of whatever was happening at the level of individual internal cognition. At Çatalhöyük, much of the early art and symbolism is iconic, fixed, and tied to parts of buildings and houses. In the upper levels, however, moveable tokens appear that have a limited range of nonrepresentational shapes (disks, cones, cubes, balls, etc.), appear to show continuities with later writing systems (as demonstrated by Schmandt-Besserat), and are found in a range of combinations in different contexts at Çatalhöyük (Bennison-Chapman 2013). Stamp seals too appear in the upper levels, with a limited range of designs (Türkcan 2005, 2013). While we do not know with any certainty what they were used for, the most likely explanation is for stamping designs on animal and human skin (Türkcan 2005). Whatever their specific

use, they are generalized and recombinable symbols (Kamerman 2014). In Chapter 5, Bennison-Chapman shows that tokens at Çatalhöyük do not in fact suggest social institutions devoted to complex accounting (for a further discussion of the Bennison-Chapman work, see Chapter 4, this volume).

Initial work by the Çatalhöyük Research Project (Love 2013) has explored variation in the sizes of bricks through time (following on from the work by Mellaart 1967). But there has been no attempt to use the extremely large dataset of recorded brick dimensions to identify whether standardized units of measurement were used in brick manufacture and house construction. Early work on the existence of a "megalithic yard" (Thom 1955, 1962) in Neolithic and Bronze Age Britain has been subjected to statistical evaluation (Broadbent 1955; Kendall 1974). In Chapter 6, Barański uses similar statistical techniques to evaluate whether the corpus of sizes of bricks in buildings at Çatalhöyük shows evidence of statistically significant units of measurement. Such units of measurement might indicate abstract metric systems, although clearly in the public domain. Indeed, Barański finds that patterning in brick size at Çatalhöyük is not related to the development of mental abstraction but to the practicalities of making walls that stand up in different conditions. Some standardization and formalization of brick sizes is identified over time, but these features are best seen as the result of changes in building techniques, which themselves are embedded in practical and social processes.

It seems then that careful analyses of "tokens" and brick sizes at Çatalhöyük do not show a step change in the complexity of measuring devices, and this result accords with our current understanding of the social and economic organization of the community at the site. There is limited evidence of specialization of production, at least in most levels. Most production seems small-scale and house-based but also involving considerable sharing and interdependence. There are strong sodalities and little evidence of social differentiation beyond age groupings and beyond the coalescing of individual houses around ritually elaborate ancestral or "history" houses. In such a context it is perhaps not surprising that there is so little evidence of codified metrical systems. As a result, it is difficult to make a larger claim for increased abstraction and objectification. The gradual processes identified by Maher and Benz in Chapters 2 and 3 seem to continue through the Neolithic.

By defining "higher levels of consciousness" very precisely in terms of abstraction/objectification and by further defining abstraction/objectification in terms of the existence of generalizable and recombinable symbols (such as tokens and metrical systems), it has been possible to test the argument that "higher levels of consciousness," as measured by these proxies, increased during the Late Neolithic at Çatalhöyük. Careful examination of the evidence from the site does not support such a claim. Of course, it remains possible that the string of proxies that has been used is flawed. For example, it might be possible to have a metrical system based on body parts such as arm length without having an abstract system of measures – as discussed by Barański in Chapter 6. It is also possible that "higher levels of consciousness" became prevalent in other domains, such as in the

religious or social spheres. However, to pursue such an investigation would demand equally careful attention to definitions and chains of proxies, which at present do not seem substantiated. We can turn instead to another set of cognitive changes that has been claimed.

2. *Greater innovation/creativity.* Early village societies in the Middle East show a remarkable degree of continuity and are characterized by slow rates of change. This is particularly true of central Anatolia and Cappadocia, where Aşıklı Höyük has streets, houses, and hearth locations that remain stable over hundreds of years (Özbaşaran 2011). Çatalhöyük is often described in similar terms, and indeed the continuity of houses and of the use of space is remarkable throughout the sequence (Düring 2006; Hodder and Cessford 2004). However, detailed dating has shown that the rate of change in the rebuilding of houses speeds up in the upper levels (Düring 2006; Hodder 2014a). While in the lower levels of occupation at the site the length of house occupation is 70–100 years, in the upper levels it is 40–80 years (Cessford 2005b).

More generally there is much evidence for variation in innovation rates throughout the Neolithic of Anatolia and the Middle East, and it is often argued that rates of change increased in the Neolithic in comparison to earlier periods. As noted earlier, Renfrew has argued that increased amounts of material "stuff" allowed greater external symbolic storage, and it might be argued that an increasing load of material culture forced humans into creative ways of managing and organizing this material. Certainly in Chapter 8 Nieuwenhuyse argues that increasing material entanglements with containers of all sorts provided an impetus to, and a need for, new and expressive forms of creativity.

Another argument, discussed by Mithen (2004) and Watkins (2010), is that increased rates of innovation/creativity occurred in the Neolithic in tandem with increases in the size and density of settlement (see earlier). The Çatalhöyük Research Project has gradually amassed a large amount of data concerning change through time in settlement size and density. Surface pickup has taken place in combination with surface scraping, systematic shovel testing, and extensive use of Ground Penetrating Radar and other geophysical techniques, coupled with deep excavation in the South Area, as well as stratigraphic excavation in the North and IST Areas (Hodder 2014a). The extent and density of occupation at different moments in time can in this way be judged, if only approximately. More reliable estimates of settlement density can be obtained from the size and packing of houses at different levels in the excavated parts of the mound (the South and North Areas). Analyses of these data have shown clear evidence for a rise in settlement density (fewer open spaces between buildings) in the Middle phase of occupation, with decline and dispersal in the Late and Final levels (for a summary of these data, see Hodder 2014a). It is also of interest that the increased density of houses in the Middle levels corresponds with the maximum concentration of burials in houses (Düring 2006) and with the period of highest human fertility (Hillson 2013).

A good case can be made for heightened creativity and innovation in the Middle levels. It is undoubtedly the case that this is the period of "classic" Çatalhöyük with the most elaborate wall installations such as bucrania, reliefs, and complex internal divisions of space. Many types of data show peaks in this period. This is also a period in which there seems to be much competition between houses, with some amassing large numbers of burials and symbolic elaboration in contrast to others. So it is not clear if it is population density or social jockeying that is most closely linked to higher rates of innovation. In addition this is also the period of most evidence for increased workload and various types of generative disease (Hodder 2014a), suggesting that hardship may also have been a contributing factor to innovation rates.

Another hypothesis might be that increased rates of innovation/creativity occurred during the occupation of Çatalhöyük in tandem with increases in trade and exchange (as argued by de Chardin 1955, see earlier). The Çatalhöyük Research Project has collected large amounts of quantified evidence for the trade and exchange of a wide range of materials and has studied the sourcing of many of these, including obsidian (the main material used for stone tools at the site – Carter et al. 2006), chert (Nazaroff et al. 2013), ceramics (Doherty and Tarkan 2013), shell (Bar-Yosef Mayer 2013), groundstone (Wright 2013), and speleothems (Erdoğu et al. 2013). There is much evidence from these different types of data of increases in the amount and scale of local and regional exchange in the upper levels, from South P onward.

And indeed one can take other variables and argue that it was in the Late levels that innovation reached its peak. After all, it is in this period that the wonderful narrative paintings are found showing the teasing, baiting, and hunting of wild animals; this is when the highly creative designs on stamp seals are found, and pottery starts to be more decorated. Taking this evidence, one might argue that greater innovation was associated with increased rates of exchange in the upper levels (Late and Final), rather than in the Middle levels.

The underlying problem is that evaluation of rates of innovation is extremely difficult, as shown in Chapter 9. When set aside the exuberant narrative scenes of hunting, teasing, and baiting wild animals in the Late levels, the geometric paintings found in the Middle levels and indeed throughout the occupation of the site seem remarkably straightforward. However, Hodder and Gürlek show in Chapter 9 that the apparently simple designs can often be seen to be enormously complex and multileveled. To focus on these geometric designs is to open up another world of creativity. The underlying difficulty is that evaluation of innovation rates depends on the definition of entities and categories. By studying decoration or "art" at different degrees of detail, one sees different rates of change.

If it is difficult to define innovation and creativity in the archaeological record, it is also difficult to link rates of material change with cognition. In Chapter 8, Nieuwenhuyse demurs from linking archaeological evidence for innovation with internal cognitive change. He notes that it is important for archaeologists to identify the specific social settings that stimulated individuals to establish conceptual connections and crossovers between components. Nieuwenhuyse emphasizes the particular historical contexts in which creativity was heightened, rather than describing overarching processes in the Neolithic as a whole. He shows how the early development of the innovation of pottery follows a meronomic process in that pottery "hitchhiked" onto already existing container traditions. It is an important part of Nieuwenhuyse's argument that innovation in pottery production and use did not emerge suddenly with the first pottery containers, but emerged as the affordances of pottery were gradually realized. This process suggests less an internal shift in cognitive universals than an emerging awareness of potentials as pottery was allied with new needs and functions.

Thornton in Chapter 7 provides a general framework for discussing the processes of innovation described by Nieuwenhuyse. At the same time he sidesteps the difficulties of determining internal cognitive change in the past by focusing on conceptual innovation, where concept is defined as a mental representation of a category. This approach makes no assumptions about mind other than that it involves identification of categories. Otherwise the meronomic process of building categories from combinations of existing categories is a generative and combinatorial process in the social world. Thornton shows that an analysis of meronomic processes can allow archaeologists to explore degrees of and potentials for innovation, but he is also at pains to note that understandings of innovation processes depend very much on how the relationships between categories are constructed by the archaeologist. There can, then, be no easy quantification of innovation rates.

3. *Greater awareness of an integrated personal self.* There has been much discussion in archaeology, anthropology, and related

disciplines of the notion of a distributed self (Bird-David 1999; DeMarais et al. 2005; Fowler 2004). Over recent years arguments have been made for changing notions of self and personhood in the Neolithic, prompted by anthropological accounts of differences between distributed, fragmented selves ("dividuals") and more holistic, integrated selves ("individuals") (Fowler 2004; Strathern 1988). Notions of self may have changed throughout the Paleolithic and Epipaleolithic as humans invested more in burial and bodily decoration. But it is possible to argue that in the early Neolithic of the Middle East, there remained an important focus on the collective and on sharing (e.g., Kuijt 2000), and treatment of the human corpse has been argued to indicate a partible sense of self; certainly after death the body could be divided up, skulls and other body parts separated, kept, exchanged, and redeposited (Goring-Morris and Belfer-Cohen 2014; Kuijt 2008,). Through much of the sequence at Çatalhöyük, skulls and body parts were treated in this same partible, distributed way. And the claim has been made (Hodder 2011; van Huysteen 2014) that through time a shift occurred from more to less distributed selves.

There are several forms of evidence that might be used to indicate changing notions of self at Çatalhöyük. The first concerns burial. The evidence for head removal and secondary burial of body parts might indicate a more partible self as has often been claimed. Evidence for adornment of the human body (beads, belt hooks, bone pins) in burial contexts may indicate changes through time. Many of the human figurines show evidence again of partible bodies in that clay figurine heads and dowels were found separated from clay human torsos, suggesting that heads were interchangeable on bodies. In the upper levels of the site there is more evidence of human figurines (as opposed to animal and other figurines), so that the frequencies of those with and without separatable parts can be quantified (Hodder 2011; Meskell 2007,). Other evidence of notions of self is provided by analysis of wear on bone objects of personal ornament or dress. Russell (2005) describes the occurrence of whole bone pendants in burials. She shows that they were at least sometimes worn around the neck. Together with their variability of form, this suggests that the pendants were a part of personal identities. Russell also notes the striking frequency of repair of these items in contrast to other bone artifacts. There is evidence of use after repair, and in some cases pendants that had lost their perforation and could no longer be worn were kept, perhaps as amulets. All this suggests that the pendants were linked to individual and shorter-term memories.

The earlier phases of occupation at Çatalhöyük have an agglomerated neighborhood pattern of occupation (Düring and Marciniak 2006); houses are tightly packed together, and open space seems shared, with movement occurring across house roofs. In the upper levels there is increased evidence of separation of productive tasks; adjacent midden space is taken over for yards, and outside activities associated with individual houses and doors appear linking houses to yards (see Hodder 2014a, 2014b). Human and animal isotopes suggest differences in diets and grazing patterns between buildings in the upper levels (Pearson 2013). There is more evidence of house-based production of groundstone artifacts (Wright 2013), bone tools, and chipped stone tools (Carter and Milic 2013; Russell and Griffitts 2013). As houses became more separate and self-sufficient economically, so perhaps there is increased evidence for a separate and integrated self.

Cattle through most of the sequence at Çatalhöyük were wild, but domestic forms appear in the uppermost levels (Twiss et al. 2013). According to Cauvin (2000), the use of increasingly domesticated cattle involves a changed relationship between humans and the natural world, involving a greater sense of domination and agency. It might then be expected that the increasing use of domesticated cattle at Çatalhöyük in the upper levels would be associated with increasing evidence of a separate and integrated self.

However, all these approaches assume that different forms of "self" (such as dividual and individual) can be separated and that these various material measures are valid proxies of "selfness." Sutton in Chapter 10 takes a more cautious approach, saying that "historical facts about, say, beads, bricks, or bones may be clear enough without settling anything about which cognitive processes they indicate or what kind of 'self' they implicate." He suggests that a more helpful way may be to think in terms of memory, in particular personal or autobiographical memory. The basic capacities for memory were in place well before the Neolithic, but through time they were deployed in different ways. How and what we remember, and for how long, depend on specific sets of biosociomaterial entanglements. He uses the term "sociocognitive tuning" to describe the ways in which specific memory capabilities were built historically upon basic memory mechanisms,

and he describes in detail the factors that may have led to increased autobiographical or personal memory construction in the Neolithic.

Sutton critiques the anthropological model that has been widely adopted in archaeology of a distinction between partible "dividual" and integrated "individual" selves, and Vasic in Chapter 11 confirms these concerns in the detailed evidence for personal ornament from Çatalhöyük. She shows that there is no evidence for a shift from partible to integrated self. Rather, there was a strong notion of both integrated and partible selves throughout the occupation of the settlement. In particular, the evidence for the moving and sharing of beads in necklaces and in burials demonstrates a great level of sociality and sociocentric decoration. But individuality and elements of personal preferences are witnessed in the variability in the body treatment of the dead. Vasic concludes by arguing that the self at Çatalhöyük must have been highly dynamic and changing according to the social context.

We have seen that it has often been argued in archaeology that the secondary distribution and burial of parts of human bodies in the Neolithic have been used to indicate a more partible and distributed self. In the case of Çatalhöyük, the expectation was that secondary burial as an indicator of partible selves should decrease over time. But the human remains evidence discussed by Haddow et al. in Chapter 12 show exactly the opposite: increased secondary burial over time. Haddow et al. note that this shift may have been tied into practical concerns: Greater mobility occurs in the upper levels, so individuals who died away from site might not have been available for immediate burial. Their evidence for delayed burial throughout the occupation of the site may indicate that the disarticulated bones found in secondary and perhaps tertiary contexts may represent the final deposition of a fragmented and skeletally incomplete individual, not the redistributed parts of a "dividual." They thus throw doubt on evidence for an increased emphasis on the "individual" in the upper levels and demonstrate the possibility of much nuanced diversity of practice.

In Chapter 13, too, Fagan argues against the hypothesis that throughout the occupation of Çatalhöyük, there was a growing awareness of a separate and integrated personal self. She situates this critique within a broader reevaluation of the Western dichotomies that she suggests undergird cognitive archaeology more generally. She identifies an overall shift at the site between the earlier levels focusing on the house (and the renewal of its vitality) and the later levels focusing on the body and social difference. She places changing notions of body and human–human relationships within transformations of ontology rather than within cognitive change.

Once again cognition proves difficult to separate from meaning. Changing notions of self seem, in this reading, far from the cognitive.

CONCLUSIONS

The main result of the studies and analyses included in the chapters in this volume is to comprehensively undermine the evidence for cognitive change associated with the Neolithic, at least at Late Neolithic Çatalhöyük but also more broadly. When scrutinized closely, many of the theoretical assumptions are found wanting. And when examined in contextual detail, the archaeological evidence simply does not support causal relationships between greater population density, trade, new technologies, and greater hierarchy and higher levels of consciousness, creativity and a more integrated notion of self.

Certainly there was much variation across space and time in the ways in which social minds functioned. There is much evidence for diversity in the ways in which farming and sedentism were adopted, and these variations were undoubtedly related to different ways of conceptualizing the world. But there is little evidence for an overall long-term shift, an evolutionary "moment." Any cognitive variation in social minds seems highly dependent on context, and social minds were effective at adapting to changing circumstances and to the challenges of harder work, settled life, and denser agglomerations. But there seems little evidence for basic changes in internal components of the universal human mind. It is difficult, if not impossible, for archaeologists to move beyond demonstrating the complex performance of social minds to show changes in biological brain capacity, and certainly no such changes have been identified in this volume.

Even when considering social minds, this volume demonstrates the difficulty of making assumptions about proxies that can be used to measure higher levels of consciousness, creativity, and notions of self. In all cases it seems that multiple lines of evidence need to be collected in order to demonstrate changes in these attributes. In some cases at Çatalhöyük it has been possible to demonstrate that both bricks and tokens, or both burial and personal adornment, point in the same direction as regards changes in social mind. But the claim that these are primarily cognitive changes is dogged by the issue raised by Fagan in Chapter 13. She notes that how we understand the world is primarily an ontological question. Epistemology (how we know the world) is dependent on ontology (how we understand and experience the world). In such a context it is very difficult to separate the cognitive from "being-in-the-world." There may well have been ontological shifts as humans in the Middle East settled down into agricultural villages; they came to experience the world differently. Changes in treatment of the dead, personal adornment, and so on may have cognitive dimensions (in the sense of changes in social minds) but embedded within ontological schemes.

The chapters in this volume take a hard look at claims for cognitive changes in the Neolithic in the Middle East. Many archaeologists now argue that the development of the Neolithic was slow and diverse (see Chapter 2, this volume and also Hodder 2018). The authors in this volume demonstrate that a similar claim can be made for change in social minds, at least with reference to the use of measuring devices, creativity, and notions of self. They also argue that any understanding of mind needs to be situated within current cognitive theories (as seen in Chapters 4, 7, and 10, this volume) and needs to be careful about proxies that are used to

TABLE 1.1 The groupings of levels at Çatalhöyük

Temporal groupings of levels	South	North	Cal BC
Final	TP.O-R and TPC Trenches I and 2 (B109 and 115)		6,300–5,950 BC
Late	GDN South.T.TP.N. TPC B110 and Bl50 South.S. TP.M. TPC BlSO and B122 South.R South.Q South.P	North.H, I, J, and IST	6,500–6,300 DC
Middle	South.O South.N South.M	North.F, G	6,700–6,500 DC
Early	South.L South.K South.J South.I South.H South.G		7,100–6,700 DC

measure mind. Discussion of Neolithic cognitive change has been dogged by broad-brush accounts and a lack of careful attention to arguments and methods. We hope in this volume to have demonstrated the need for a change in approach.

REFERENCES

Baird, D. 2002. Early Holocene settlement in Central Anatolia: problems and prospects as seen from the Konya Plain. In Gérard, F. and Thissen, L. (eds.) *The Neolithic of Central Anatolia. Internal developments and external relations during the 9th–6th millennia cal BC, Proceedings of the International CANeW Round Table, Istanbul, 23–24 November 2001.* Istanbul: Ege Yayınları. Pp. 139–52.

Baird, D. 2005. The history of settlement and social landscapes in the Early Holocene in the Çatalhöyük area. In Hodder, I. (ed.) *Çatalhöyük perspectives: themes from the 1995–1999 seasons.* Cambridge, UK: McDonald Institute for Archaeological Research/British Institute of Archaeology at Ankara Monograph. Pp. 55–74.

Baird, D. 2007a. The Boncuklu Project: the origins of sedentism, cultivation and herding in Central Anatolia. *Anatolian Archaeology* 13, 14–18.

Baird, D. 2007b. Pınarbaşı: from Epipalaeolithic camp site to sedentarising village in central Anatolia. In Özdoğan, M. and Başgelen, N. (eds.) *The Neolithic in Turkey: new excavations and new discoveries.* Istanbul: Arkeoloji ve Snatat Yayinlari. Pp. 285–311.

Baird, D., Fairbairn, A., Jenkins, E., Martin, L., Middleton, C., Pearson, J., Asouti, E., Edwards, Y., Kabukcu, C. 2018. Agricultural origins on the Anatolian Plateau. *PNAS* 115(14), E3077–E3086.

Banning, E. B. 2011. So fair a house: Göbekli Tepe and the identification of temples in the Pre-Pottery Neolithic of the Near East. *Current Anthropology* 52(5), 619–60.

Bar-Yosef, M. D. 2013. Mollusc exploitation at Çatalhöyük. In Hodder, I. (ed.) *Humans and landscapes of Çatalhöyük: reports from the 2000–2008 seasons.* *Çatalhöyük Research Project Series Volume 8.* British Institute at Ankara Monograph No. 47 / Monumenta Archaeologica 30. Los Angeles: Cotsen Institute of Archaeology Press. Pp. 323–32.

Bar-Yosef, O., 1986. The Walls of Jericho. An alternative interpretation. *Current Anthropology* 27, 157–62.

Bekaert, S. 1998. Multiple levels of meaning and the tension of consciousness. *Archaeological Dialogues* 5 (1), 6–29.

Bennison-Chapman, L. 2013. Geometric clay objects. In Hodder I. (ed.) *Substantive technologies at Çatalhöyük: reports from the 2000–2008 seasons.* Çatalhöyük Research Project Series Volume 9. British Institute at Ankara Monograph No. 48 / Monumenta Archaeologica 31. Los Angeles: Cotsen Institute of Archaeology Press. Pp. 253–76.

Bird-David, N. 1999. "Animism" revisited. Personhood, environment, and relational epistemology. *Current Anthropology* 40 Supplement, 67–90.

Broadbent, S. R. 1955. Quantum hypotheses. *Biometrika* 42, 45–57.

Byrd, B. 1994 Public and private, domestic and corporate: the emergence of the Southwest Asian Village. *American Antiquity* 59, 639–66.

Carter, T. and Milic, M. 2013. The chipped stone. In Hodder, I. (ed.) *Substantive technologies at Çatalhöyük: reports from the 2000–2008 seasons.* Çatalhöyük Research Project Series Volume 9. British Institute at Ankara Monograph No. 48 / Monumenta Archaeologica 31. Los Angeles: Cotsen Institute of Archaeology Press. Pp. 417–78.

Carter, T., Poupeau, G., Bressy, C. and Pearce, N. J. 2006. A new programme of obsidian characterization at Çatalhöyük, Turkey. *Journal of Archaeological Science* 33(7), 893–909.

Cauvin, J. 1994. *Naissance des divinités, Naissance de l'agriculture.* Paris: CNRS.

Cauvin, J. 2000. *The birth of the gods and the origins of agriculture.* Cambridge: Cambridge University Press.

Cessford, C. 2005a. Estimating the Neolithic population of Çatalhöyük. In Hodder, I. (ed.) *Inhabiting Çatalhöyük: reports from the 1995–1999 seasons.* Cambridge: McDonald Institute for Archaeological

Research/British Institute of Archaeology at Ankara Monograph.

Cessford, C. 2005b. Absolute dating at Çatalhöyük. In Hodder, I. (ed.) *Changing materialities at Çatalhöyük: Reports from the 1995–1999 seasons.* Cambridge, UK: McDonald Institute for Archaeological Research/British Institute of Archaeology at Ankara Monograph. Pp. 65–100.

Clark, A. 1997. *Being there. Putting brain, body, and world together again.* Cambridge, MA: MIT Press.

Davis, M. K. 1998. Social differentiation at the Early Village of Çayönü, Turkey. In Çambel, H., Arsebük, G. and Schirmer, W. (eds.) *Light on the top of the Black Hill studies presented to Halet Çambel.* Istanbul: Ege Yayınları.

De Chardin, P. T. 1955. *The phenomenon of man.* New York: Harper and Row.

DeMarais, E., Gosden, C. and Renfrew, C. (eds.) 2005. *Rethinking materiality: the engagement of mind with the material world.* Cambridge, UK: McDonald Institute for Archaeological Research/British Institute of Archaeology at Ankara Monograph.

Doherty, C. and Tarkan, D. 2013. Pottery production at Çatalhöyük: a petrographic perspective. In Hodder I. (ed.) *Substantive technologies at Çatalhöyük: reports from the 2000–2008 seasons.* Çatalhöyük Research Project Series Volume 9. British Institute at Ankara Monograph No. 48 / Monumenta Archaeologica 31. Los Angeles: Cotsen Institute of Archaeology Press. Pp. 183–92.

Donald, M. 1991. *Origins of the modern mind.* Cambridge, MA: Harvard University Press.

Duru, R. 1999. The Neolithic of the Lake District. In Özdoğan, M. and Başgelen, N. (eds.) *Neolithic in Turkey: the cradle of civilization. New discoveries.* Istanbul: Arkeoloji ve Sanat Yayınları. Pp. 165–91.

Düring, B. 2006. *Constructing communities: clustered neighbourhood settlements of the Central Anatolian Neolithic, ca. 8500–5500 Cal. BC.* Leiden: Ned. Inst. voor het Nabije Oosten.

Düring, B. S. and Marciniak, A. 2006. Households and communities in the central Anatolian Neolithic. *Archaeological Dialogues* 12, 165–87.

Erdoğu, B., Uysal, I. T., Özbek, O. and Ulusoy, Ü. 2013. Speleothems of Çatalhöyük Turkey. *Mediterranean Archaeology & Archaeometry, 13*(1), 23–37.

Esin, U. and Harmanakaya, S. 1999. Aşıklı in the frame of Central Anatolian Neolithic. In Özdoğan, M. and Başgelen, N. (eds.) *Neolithic in Turkey: the cradle of civilization. New discoveries.* Istanbul: Arkeoloji ve Sanat Yayınları. Pp. 115–32.

Finlayson, B. and Warren, G. 2010. *Changing natures: hunter-gatherers, first farmers and the modern world.* London: Duckworth.

Firth, R. 1959. *Social change in Tikopia.* London: Allen Unwin.

Flannery, K. V., 2002. The origins of the village revisited: from nuclear to extended households. *American Antiquity* 67, 417–33.

Fowler, C. 2004. *The archaeology of personhood: an anthropological approach.* London: Routledge.

Fuchs, T. and Schlimme, J. E. 2009. Embodiment and psychopathology: a phenomenological perspective. *Current Opinion in Psychiatry* 22(6), 570–75.

Gebel, H. G. K. 2004. There was no center: the polycentric evolution of the Near Eastern Neolithic. *Neo-Lithics* 1/04, 28–32.

Gérard, F. and Thissen, L. 2002. *The Neolithic of Central Anatolia. Internal developments and external relations during the 9th–6th millennia CAL BC, Proceedings of the International CANeW Round Table, Istanbul, 23–24 November 2001.* Istanbul: Ege Yayınları.

Gordon Childe, V. 1936. *Man makes himself.* Nottingham: Spokesman.

Goring-Morris, A. N. 2005. Life, death and the emergence of differential status in the Near Eastern Neolithic: evidence from Kfar HaHoresh, Lower Galilee, Israel. In Clarke, J. (ed.) *Archaeological perspectives on the transmission and transformation of culture in the Eastern Mediterranean.* Oxford: Oxbow. Pp. 89–105.

Goring-Morris, A. N. and Belfer-Cohen, A. 2008. A roof over one's head: developments in Near Eastern residential architecture across the Epipalaeolithic-Neolithic transition. In Bocquet-Appel, J.-P. and Bar-Yosef, O. (eds.) *The Neolithic demographic transition and its consequences.* Heidelberg: Springer. Pp. 239–86.

Goring-Morris, A. N. and Belfer-Cohen, A. 2012. The Near eastern perspective. In Hofmann, D.

and Smyth, J. (eds.) *Tracking the Neolithic house in Europe – sedentism, architecture and practice*. London: Springer.

Goring-Morris, A. N. and Belfer-Cohen, A. 2014. Different strokes for different folks: Near Eastern Neolithic mortuary practices in perspective. In Hodder I. (ed.) *Religion at work in a Neolithic society: vital matters*. Cambridge, UK: Cambridge University Press. Pp. 35–57.

Hauptmann, H. 2007. Nevalı Çori. In *Die ältesten Monumente der Menschheit*. Karlsruhe: Badisches Landesmuseum. Pp. 86–93.

Hillson, S. 2013. The human remains I: interpreting community structure, health and diet in Neolithic Çatalhöyük. In Hodder, I. (ed.) *Humans and landscapes of Çatalhöyük: reports from the 2000–2008 seasons*. Çatalhöyük Research Project Series Volume 8. British Institute at Ankara Monograph No. 47 / Monumenta Archaeologica 30. Los Angeles: Cotsen Institute of Archaeology Press. Pp. 333–88.

Hodder, I. (ed.) 1996. *On the surface. Çatalhöyük 1993–95*. Cambridge, UK: McDonald Institute for Archaeological Research/British Institute of Archaeology at Ankara Monograph.

Hodder, I. (ed.) 2000. *Towards reflexive method in archaeology: the example at Çatalhöyük*. Cambridge, UK: McDonald Institute for Archaeological Research/British Institute of Archaeology at Ankara Monograph.

Hodder, I. (ed.) 2005a. *Inhabiting Çatalhöyük: reports from the 1995–1999 seasons*. Cambridge, UK: McDonald Institute for Archaeological Research/British Institute of Archaeology at Ankara Monograph.

Hodder, I. (ed.) 2005b. *Changing materialities at Çatalhöyük: reports from the 1995–1999 seasons*. Cambridge, UK: McDonald Institute for Archaeological Research/British Institute of Archaeology at Ankara Monograph.

Hodder, I. (ed.) 2005c. *Çatalhöyük perspectives: themes from the 1995–1999 seasons*. Cambridge, UK: McDonald Institute for Archaeological Research/British Institute of Archaeology at Ankara Monograph.

Hodder, I. 2006. *The leopard's tale: revealing the mysteries of Çatalhöyük*. London: Thames and Hudson.

Hodder, I. (ed.) 2007a. *Excavating Çatalhöyük: reports from the 1995–1999 seasons*. Cambridge, UK: McDonald Institute for Archaeological Research/British Institute of Archaeology at Ankara Monograph.

Hodder, I. 2007b. Çatalhöyük in the context of the Middle Eastern Neolithic. *Annual Review of Anthropology* 36, 105–20.

Hodder, I. (ed.) 2010. *Religion in the emergence of civilization. Çatalhöyük as a case study*. Cambridge, UK: Cambridge University Press.

Hodder, I. 2011. An archaeology of the self: the prehistory of personhood. In van Huyssteen, J. W. and Wiebe, E. P. (eds.) *In search of self*. Grand Rapids, MI: Eerdmans. Pp. 50–69.

Hodder, I. (ed.) 2013a. *Humans and landscapes of Çatalhöyük: reports from the 2000–2008 seasons*. Çatalhöyük Research Project Series Volume 8. British Institute at Ankara Monograph No. 47 / Monumenta Archaeologica 30. Los Angeles: Cotsen Institute of Archaeology Press.

Hodder, I. (ed.) 2013b. *Substantive technologies at Çatalhöyük: reports from the 2000–2008 seasons*. Çatalhöyük Research Project Series Volume 9. British Institute at Ankara Monograph No. 48 / Monumenta Archaeologica 31. Los Angeles: Cotsen Institute of Archaeology Press.

Hodder, I. (ed.) 2014a. *Çatalhöyük excavations: the 2000–2008 seasons*. Çatalhöyük Research Project Series Volume 7. British Institute at Ankara Monograph No. 46 / Monumenta Archaeologica 29. Los Angeles: Cotsen Institute of Archaeology Press.

Hodder, I. (ed.) 2014b. *Integrating Çatalhöyük: themes from the 2000–2008 seasons*. Çatalhöyük Research Project Series Volume 10. British Institute at Ankara Monograph No. 49 / Monumenta Archaeologica 32. Los Angeles: Cotsen Institute of Archaeology Press.

Hodder, I. (ed.) 2014c. *Religion at work in a Neolithic society: vital matters*. Cambridge, UK: Cambridge University Press.

Hodder, I. 2018. Things and the slow Neolithic: the Middle Eastern transformation. *Journal of Archaeological Method and Theory* 25(1), 155–77.

Hodder, I, and Cessford C. 2004. Daily practice and social memory at Çatalhöyük. *American Antiquity* 69, 17–40.

IAN HODDER

Hodder, I. and Meskell, L. 2011. A "curious and sometimes a trifle macabre artistry": some aspects of symbolism in Neolithic Turkey. *Current Anthropology* 52(2), 1–29.

Kamerman, A. 2014. The use of spatial order in Çatalhöyük material culture. In Hodder I. (ed.) *Religion at work in a Neolithic society: vital matters.* Cambridge, UK: Cambridge University Press. Pp. 304–33.

Kendall, D. G. 1974. Hunting quanta. *Philosophical Transactions of the Royal Society of London A*, 276, 231–66.

Kenyon, K. M. 1957. *Digging up Jericho.* London: Benn.

Kenyon, K. M. 1981. *Excavations at Jericho. Vol. 3: The Architecture and Stratigraphy of the Tell.* London: The British School of Archaeology in Jerusalem.

Kuijt, I. 2000. (ed.) *Life in Neolithic farming communities: social organization, identity, and differentiation.* New York: Kluwer Academic/Plenum Publishers.

Kuijt, I. 2008. The regeneration of life. Neolithic structures of symbolic remembering and forgetting. *Current Anthropology* 49(2), 171–97.

Kuijt, I. and Finlayson, B. 2009. Evidence for food storage and predomestication granaries 11,000 years ago in the Jordan Valley. *Proceedings of the National Academy of Science* 106 (27), 10966–70.

Kuijt, I., Guerrero, E., Molist, M. and Anfruns, J. 2011. The changing Neolithic household: household autonomy and social segmentation, Tell Halula, Syria. *Journal of Anthropological Archaeology* 30 (4), 502–522. doi:10.1016/j.jaa.2011.07.001.

Lévi-Strauss, C. 1962. *La pensée sauvage.* Paris: Pion.

Lewis-Williams, D. 2004. Constructing a cosmos architecture, power and domestication at Çatalhöyük. *Journal of Social Archaeology*, 4(1), 28–59.

Lewis-Williams, J. D. and Pearce, D. G. 2005. *Inside the Neolithic mind: consciousness, cosmos and the realm of the gods.* London: Thames & Hudson.

Love, S. 2013. An archaeology of mudbrick houses from Çatalhöyük. In Hodder, I. (ed.) *Substantive technologies at Çatalhöyük: reports from the 2000–2008 seasons.* Çatalhöyük Research Project Series Volume 9. British Institute at Ankara Monograph No. 48 / Monumenta Archaeologica 31. Los Angeles: Cotsen Institute of Archaeology Press. Pp. 81–96.

Malafouris, L. 2013. *How things shape the mind.* Cambridge MA: MIT Press.

Marciniak, A. 2008. Communities, households and animals. Convergent developments in central Anatolian and central European Neolithic. *Documenta Praehistorica* 35, 93–109.

Mazurowski, R. F. 2004. Tell Qaramel excavations 2003. *Polish Archaeology in the Mediterranean* 15, 355–70.

Mellaart, J. 1967. *Çatal Hüyük: a Neolithic town in Anatolia.* London: Thames and Hudson.

Meskell, L. 2007. Refiguring the corpus at Çatalhöyük. In Renfrew, C. and Morley, I. (eds.) *Material beginnings: a global prehistory of figurative representation.* Cambridge, UK: McDonald Institute for Archaeological Research/British Institute of Archaeology at Ankara Monograph.

Mithen, S. 2003. *After the ice. A global human history, 20,000–5000 BC.* London: Weidenfeld and Nicolson.

Mithen, S. J. 2004 Human evolution and the cognitive basis of science. In Carruthers, P, Stich, S. and Siegal, M. (eds.) *The cognitive basis of science.* Cambridge, UK: Cambridge University Press. Pp. 23–40.

Nazaroff, A. J., Baysal, A. and Çiftçi, Y. 2013. The importance of chert in Central Anatolia: lessons from the Neolithic assemblage at Çatalhöyük, Turkey. *Geoarchaeology* 28(4), 340–62.

Özbaşaran, M. 2011. The Neolithic on the plateau. In Steadman, S. R. and McMahon, G. (eds.) *The Oxford handbook of ancient Anatolia.* Oxford, UK: Oxford University Press. Pp. 99–124.

Özbaşaran, M. and Buitenhuis, H. 2002. Proposal for a regional terminology for Central Anatolia. In Gérard, F. and Thissen, L. (eds.) *The Neolithic of Central Anatolia. Internal developments and external relations during the 9th–6th millennia cal BC, Proceedings of the International CANeW Round Table, Istanbul, 23–24 November 2001.* Istanbul: Ege Yayınları. Pp. 67–77.

Özdoğan, M., 2002. Defining the Neolithic of Central Anatolia. In Gérard, F. and Thissen, L. (eds.) *The Neolithic of Central Anatolia, internal developments and external relations during the 9th–6th millennia cal BC, Proceedings of the International CANeW Round Table, Istanbul, 23–24 November 2001.* Istanbul: Ege Yayınları, Pp. 253–61.

Özdoğan, M. 2010. Westward expansion of the Neolithic way of life: sorting the Neolithic package into distinct packages. In Matthiae, P., Pinnock, F., Nigro, L. and Marchetti, N. (eds.) *Proceedings of the 6th International Congress on the Archaeology of the Ancient Near East.* Wiesbaden: Harrassowitz Verlag.

Özdoğan, M. 2011. Eastern Thrace: the contact zone between Anatolia and the Balkans. In Steadman, S. R. and McMahon, G. (eds.) *The Oxford handbook of ancient Anatolia.* Oxford, UK: Oxford University Press. Pp. 657–82.

Özdoğan, M. and Özdoğan, A. 1998. Buildings of cult and the cult of buildings. In Arsebük, G., Mellink, M. and Schirmer W. (eds.) *Light on top of the Black Hill. Studies presented to Halet Cambel.* Istanbul: Ege Yayinlari. Pp. 581–93.

Pearson, J. 2013. Human and animal diets as evidenced by stable carbon and nitrogen isotope analysis. In Hodder, I. (ed.) *Humans and landscapes of Çatalhöyük: reports from the 2000–2008 seasons.* Çatalhöyük Research Project Series Volume 8. British Institute at Ankara Monograph No. 47 / Monumenta Archaeologica 30. Los Angeles: Cotsen Institute of Archaeology Press. Pp. 265–92.

Pelegrin, J. 1990. Prehistoric lithic technology: some aspects of research. *Archaeological Review from Cambridge* 9, 116–25.

Price, T. D., and Bar-Yosef, O. 2010. Traces of inequality at the origins of agriculture in the ancient Near East. In Price, T. D. and Feinman, G. M. (eds.) *Pathways to power.* New York: Springer New York, Pp. 147–68.

Renfrew, C. 1982. *Towards an archaeology of mind: an inaugural lecture delivered before the University of Cambridge on 30 November 1982.* Cambridge, UK: Cambridge University Press.

Renfrew, C. 1998. Mind and matter: cognitive archaeology and external symbolic storage. In Renfrew, C. and Scarre, C. (eds.) *Cognition and material culture: the archaeology of symbolic storage.* Cambridge, UK: McDonald Institute for Archaeological Research/British Institute of Archaeology at Ankara Monograph.

Renfrew, C. 2012. Towards a cognitive archaeology: material engagement and the early development of society. In Hodder, I. (ed.) *Archaeological theory today.* Cambridge, UK: Polity Press. Pp. 124–45.

Renfrew, C. and Bahn, P. 2004. *Archaeology: theories, methods and practice.* London: Thames and Hudson.

Renfrew, C., Mountjoy, P. A. and Macfarlane, C. 1985. *The archaeology of cult: the sanctuary at Phylakopi.* London: British School of Archaeology at Athens.

Renfrew, C. and Zubrow, E. B. (eds.) 1994. *The ancient mind: elements of cognitive archaeology.* Cambridge, UK: Cambridge University Press.

Roberts, N., Black, S., Boyer, P., Eastwood, W. J., Griffiths, H. I., Lamb, H. F., Leng, M. J., Parish, R., Reed, M. J., Twigg, D. and Yiğitbaşioğlu, H. 1999. Chronology and stratigraphy of Late Quaternary sediments in the Konya Basin, Turkey: results from the KOPAL Project. *Quaternary Science Reviews* 18, 611–30.

Rosenberg, M. and Redding, R. W. 2000. Hallan Çemi and early village organization in eastern Anatolia. In Kuijt, I. (ed.) *Life in Neolithic farming communities: social organization, identity, and differentiation.* New York: Kluwer Academic/Plenum. Pp. 39–61.

Russell, N. 2005. Çatalhöyük worked bone. In Hodder, I. (ed.) *Changing materialities at Çatalhöyük: reports from the 1995–99 seasons.* Cambridge, UK: McDonald Institute for Archaeological Research/British Institute of Archaeology at Ankara Monograph. Pp. 339–68.

Russell, N. and Griffitts, J. L. 2013. Çatalhöyük worked bone: South and 4040 areas. In Hodder I. (ed.) *Substantive technologies at Çatalhöyük: reports from the 2000–2008 seasons.* Çatalhöyük Research Project Series Volume 9. British Institute at Ankara Monograph No. 48 / Monumenta Archaeologica 31. Los Angeles: Cotsen Institute of Archaeology Press. Pp. 277–306.

Schmandt-Besserat, D. 2007. From tokens to writing: the pursuit of abstraction. *Bulletin of the Georgian National Academy of Sciences* 175(3), 162–67.

Schmidt, K. 2001. Göbekli Tepe, Southeastern Turkey: a preliminary report on the 1995–1999 excavations. *Paléorient* 26 (1), 45–54.

Schmidt, K. 2006. *Sie bauten den ersten Tempel. Das rätselhafte Heiligtum der Steinzeitjäger.* Munich: C. H. Beck.

Stordeur, D. 2000. New discoveries in architecture and symbolism at Jerf el Ahmar (Syria), 1997–1999. *Neo-Lithics* 1/00:1–4.

Strathern, M. 1988. *The gender of the gift: problems with women and problems with society in Melanesia.* Berkeley: University of California Press.

Thom, A. 1955. A statistical examination of the megalithic sites in Britain. *Journal of the Royal Statistical Society. Series A (General)* 118(3), 275–95.

Thom, A. 1962. The megalithic unit of length. *Journal of the Royal Statistical Society* 125 (2), 243–51.

Türkcan, A. 2005. Some remarks on Çatalhöyük stamp seals. In Hodder, I. (ed.) *Changing materialities at Çatalhöyük: reports from the 1995–99 seasons.* Cambridge: McDonald Institute for Archaeological Research/London: British Institute for Archaeology at Ankara. Pp. 175–85.

Türkcan, A. 2013. Çatalhöyük stamp seals from 2000 to 2008. In Hodder, I. (ed.) *Substantive technologies at Çatalhöyük: reports from the 2000–2008 seasons.* Çatalhöyük Research Project Series Volume 9. British Institute at Ankara Monograph No. 48 / Monumenta Archaeologica 31. Los Angeles: Cotsen Institute of Archaeology Press. Pp. 235–46.

Twiss, K., Russell, N., Orton, D. and Demirergi, A. 2013. More on the Çatalhöyük mammal remains. In Hodder, I. (ed.) *Humans and landscapes of Çatalhöyük: reports from the 2000–2008 seasons.* Çatalhöyük Research Project Series Volume 8. British Institute at Ankara Monograph No. 47 /

Monumenta Archaeologica 30. Los Angeles: Cotsen Institute of Archaeology Press. Pp. 203–52.

Van Huyssteen, W. 2014. The historical self: memory and religion at Çatalhöyük. In Hodder, I. (ed.) *Religion at work in a Neolithic society: vital matters.* Cambridge, UK: Cambridge University Press. Pp. 109–33.

Verhoeven, M. 2006. Megasites in the Jordanian Pre-Pottery Neolithic B. Evidence for "Proto-Urbanism"? *Neo-Lithics* 1(6), 75–9.

Watkins, T. 2010. Changing people, changing environments: how hunter-gatherers became communities that changed the world. In Finlayson B. and Warren, G. (eds.) *Landscapes in transition.* Oxford, UK: Oxbow Books. Pp. 106–14.

Wilson, P. J. 1991. *The domestication of the human species.* New Haven, CT: Yale University Press.

Woodburn, J. 1980. Hunters and gatherers today and reconstruction of the past. In Gellner, E. (ed.) *Soviet and Western anthropology.* London: Duckworth. Pp. 95–117.

Wright, K. 2013. The ground stone technologies of Çatalhöyük. In Hodder I. (ed.) *Substantive technologies at Çatalhöyük: reports from the 2000–2008 seasons.* Çatalhöyük Research Project Series Volume 9. British Institute at Ankara Monograph No. 48 / Monumenta Archaeologica 31. Los Angeles: Cotsen Institute of Archaeology Press. Pp. 365–416.

Wynn, T. 1993. Layers of thinking in tool behavior. In Gibson, K. R. and Ingold, T. (eds.) *Tools, language and cognition in human evolution.* Cambridge, UK: Cambridge University Press. Pp. 389–406.

Yartah, T. 2005. Les bâtiments communautaires de Tell 'Abr 3 (PPNA, Syrie). *Neo-Lithics* 1/05, 3–9.

Zeder, M. A. 2011.The origins of agriculture in the Near East. *Current Anthropology* 52(54), 221–35.

HUNTER-GATHERER HOME-MAKING? BUILDING LANDSCAPE AND COMMUNITY IN THE EPIPALEOLITHIC

Lisa Maher

INTRODUCTION

This chapter stems from a paper given at the "Consciousness and Creativity at the Dawn of Settled Life: The Test-Case of Çatalhöyük" workshop held in Cambridge, UK, in July 2017. This workshop focused on several key debates related to possible changes in human cognition at the onset of the Neolithic period. To address these workshop themes, I explore whether the Neolithic represents a cognitive "break" from cultural practices of preceding hunter-gatherers, specifically asking whether the Neolithic is a key "moment" marked by critical changes in (1) ways of perceiving and using space (e.g., place-making, built environment, sedentism), (2) innovation and creativity (e.g., new technologies and symbolic expressions, including burials), or (3) greater interaction between individuals and groups (e.g., aggregation, new social organizations, long-distance exchange networks, social interactions networks). As a case study of place-making and the creation of community in the Epipaleolithic (EP;

23,000–11,500 cal BP), the site of Kharaneh IV provides a rich dataset to explore the nature of pre-Neolithic dwelling, including how so-called ephemeral structures can be considered as economically, socially, and symbolically charged spaces (even "homes") and how the spaces between sites – "the landscape" – is full of "places" where the concept of dwelling can also apply. The former is accomplished through examination of the construction, use, and destruction of hut structures from the Early EP occupations, while the latter is accomplished through examination of the connections between Kharaneh IV and the surrounding landscape, including other EP sites, documented through material culture and resource use. I suggest here similarities between the highly socialized and built environments of farmers and hunter-gatherers – in this sense, hunter-gatherers also created a built environment. Rather than revisit the continued debates around the nature of the transition to agriculture and post-Pleistocene lifeways, adeptly summarized elsewhere (Asouti and Fuller, 2013; Belfer-Cohen and Goring-Morris, 2011; Finlayson, 2013; Finlayson and Makarewicz, 2013; Goring-Morris and Belfer-Cohen, 2011; Price and Bar-Yosef, 2011; Watkins, 2013; Zeder, 2011), instead I focus here on the treatment of entirely hunter-gatherer places occupied by peoples without intent to "become" Neolithic, thereby, addressing the idea of a Neolithic "break" and favoring the continuous nature of these changes. Following the suggestion by Finlayson and Warren (2010), I caution against a dichotomous view of EP hunter-gatherers and Neolithic farmers in Southwest Asia, with the latter presumptively marking the beginning of the so-called modern mind, and I do so by exhibiting the complexity of EP behaviors related to place-making, home-making, dwelling, and the creation of communities within the framework of entirely *hunter-gatherer* worldviews.

BEING HUNTER-GATHERER OR BECOMING NEOLITHIC?

The transition from mobile hunter-gather to sedentary food-producing societies in Southwest Asia was a pivotal shift in human prehistory, and its impacts on landscape and resource sustainability, long-distance interaction networks, technological innovation, and social issues, such as overcrowding and migration, continue to resonate today. The Neolithic remains a highly debated and high-profile period, yet, despite decades of research, comparatively less focus is placed on hunter-gatherer populations that represent the first 10,000 years of this transition. Indeed, much hunter-gatherer research here focuses

on Late EP (Natufian) trajectories toward Neolithic agricultural lifeways, tracing the appearance of settled villages, elaborated symbolic behaviors, the creation of a built environment, long-distance social networks, and other features as markers of increased cognitive and social complexity. We now recognize that this transition was protracted, was nonlinear, and entailed multiple entangled social, technological, ideological, and economic facets and, crucially, that this process began millennia earlier in the EP. Here, I trace some of these Neolithic (and Natufian) lifeways back into the earlier EP, focusing in particular on the creation of socialized landscapes, or place-making. I highlight that hunter-gatherers throughout the EP imbued the landscape with symbolic meaning, creating places within "storied landscapes" (Langley, 2013; Maher and Conkey, 2019; McBryde, 2000). As with Neolithic sites, these places are visible in the structured use of space within sites and can be extended to include certain landscape features. In this light, the EP hunter-gather landscape was every bit as experiential and constructed or built as that of a Neolithic farmer. Here I draw on concepts of dwelling, microscale examination of the organization of space, reconstructions of daily practice and place life histories, social networks, and landscape-level datasets in an attempt to explore hunter-gatherer place-making and the role these activities might play in the creation of "consciousness and creativity at the dawn of settled life."

Prehistoric hunter-gatherer research in Southwest Asia has traditionally focused on the complex and multifaceted transitions toward settled village farming life (e.g.,

Belfer-Cohen and Bar-Yosef, 2000). Archaeologists have focused on finding the origins of agriculture – the earliest domestic plants or animals – or identifying the emergence of sedentism – uncovering the earliest architecture or burial or village – that will prove revolutionary for our reconstructions of dramatic cultural change (see Gamble, 2007 for a discussion of our focus on "origins and revolutions"). Even the term "Epipaleolithic" itself suggests that these hunter-gatherers lived in some "in-between" or liminal world, experiencing persistence in some hunter-gatherer lifeways, while simultaneously not yet and not quite Neolithic (for a less-explicit but nonetheless similar critique, see Goring-Morris and Belfer-Cohen, 2010; Richter and Maher, 2013; Watkins, 2010, 2011, 2013). Alternate approaches to "becoming Neolithic" are providing an increasingly nuanced picture of Neolithic economic and social transformations, including approaches that emphasize cultural niche construction (Kuijt and Prentiss, 2009; Rowley-Conwy and Layton, 2011; Smith, 2015; Sterelny and Watkins, 2015; Zeder, 2009) and changes in cognition (Hodder, 2012; Watkins, 2015). Yet, with some recent exceptions (Finlayson, 2013; Finlayson and Warren, 2010, 2017), emphasis remains firmly placed on establishing differences between hunter-gatherer and farming worldviews and consequent "ways of being" (Belfer-Cohen and Goring-Morris, 2011; Boyd, 2002; Goring-Morris and Belfer-Cohen, 2011).

By shifting some of this focus away from the process of "Neolithization" to how hunter-gatherer groups created, modified, and "lived in" their landscapes, creating meaning in places (including homes) and the social landscapes between places, we can attempt to reconstruct EP hunter-gatherers as themselves complex and multifaceted groups (e.g., Finlayson, 2013; Maher and Conkey, 2019; Olszewski and al-Nahar, 2016). To do this we can explore the rich examples of this approach from hunter-gatherer research elsewhere where past hunter-gatherers engaged and contemporary hunter-gatherers continue to engage in long-term landscape modification, such as the Jomon of Japan (Habu, 2004), Australian Aborigines (McNiven, 2004; Veth et al., 2017), and groups from the West Coast of North America (Grier, 2017). These groups, some even referred to as "socially complex hunter-gatherers" (Arnold, 1996; Sassaman, 2004), are afforded degrees of social hierarchy, "incipient" agricultural practices such as arboriculture (Matsui and Kanehara, 2006), fire management (Bird et al., 2008; Lightfoot and Cuthrell, 2015), clam bed cultivation (Lepofsky et al., 2015), and a built environment. While some Southwest Asian prehistorians have labeled Natufians as socially complex hunter-gatherers (Bar-Yosef, 2002), with direct comparisons to such groups of the Northwest Coast, preceding EP phases remain largely overlooked as the "evidence" is not as clear or extensive. Indeed, looking comparatively at records elsewhere forces us to reconsider the nature of prehistoric hunter-gatherer economies, technologies, social lives, and cosmologies in Southwest Asia, just as was done for the Mesolithic of Europe, where new research is showing not wholesale replacement, but long-term and complicated interactions between foragers and farmers (Bailey and Spikins, 2008; Rowley-Conwy, 2011). Perhaps we should expect this kind of "gray area" – arguably impossible to pin down in the archaeological record – to characterize this process or transition in Southwest Asia (see Finlayson and Warren, 2010 for a comparison between these two regions). And, of course, taking the point made by Veth et al. (2008) that hunter-gatherers have long had complicated relationships with plants and animals without ever becoming farmers, we should remember that there may have been many generations where so-called EP and Neolithic people practiced some combination of foraging, hunting, collecting, fishing, gardening, farming, or pastoralism, hinting at the problems associated with assumptions behind linking the EP with hunting and gathering and the Neolithic with farming. We should thus be focusing on hunter-gatherers with no "intention" of becoming farmers. Perhaps this approach in Southwest Asia lags behind that elsewhere because the adoption of agriculture here is often used as a turning point in human prehistory – a cognitive "break" or the point at which we became "modern." I attempt here to address this by exploring two interrelated concepts I believe are key to reshaping how we understand these prehistoric groups: hunter-gatherer place-making and the construction of community (albeit in a somewhat different way than Canuto and Yaeger, 2000; Cohen, 1985).

DWELLING, SPACE, AND PLACE IN HUNTER-GATHERER ARCHAEOLOGY

Dwelling is a term with multiple interrelated meanings in contemporary usage, including home, house, residence, abode, and habitation, to name just a few. Heidegger explores

the concept of dwelling in relation to architecture, asking specifically, "What is it to dwell?" and "How does building belong to dwelling?" (Heidegger, 1971). Deconstructing the term *dwelling* through its use in several languages, Heidegger argues that dwelling is "the very essence of human life on earth; it is the thing that we do, as humans; we are, by nature, dwellers of locations and spaces, independent of what we build" (1971: 141). Similarly, Ingold addresses dwelling, both directly as integral to human livelihood and indirectly through movement as a means of becoming knowledgeable in our everyday practices of negotiating the world (Ingold, 1995, 2000, 2010). Archaeological literature often uses the term *dwelling*, but with a great deal of ambiguity and vagueness, perhaps intentionally, given the difficulties of identifying it in the distant prehistoric past (Barrett, 1999; Goring-Morris and Belfer-Cohen, 2003; Hirsch and O'Hanlon, 1995; Hutson, 2009; Ingold, 1993, 1995, 2000; Knapp and Ashmore, 1999; Lévi-Strauss, 1966; Nadel, 2003; Roberts, 1996; Thomas, 2008; Wilson, 1991). Kolen defines dwelling as "the ordering and differentiation of space by a recognition of places, including a home, and the use of those places according to specific temporal rhythms and schemes" (Kolen, 1999: 139). For both Kolen and Ingold, a key aspect of dwelling is organized space with social and symbolic meanings, thus, something that prehistorians could detect and reconstruct at the intrasite scale. Although more challenging to detect, dwelling could also be read as occurring at the intersite scale, such as *dwelling* in a landscape (Fano et al., 2015; Garcia-Moreno, 2013).

The concepts of space and place have been extensively discussed within the realm of landscape archaeology, in particular, as distinct, although not mutually exclusive, concepts (Ashmore, 2002; Ashmore and Knapp, 1999; Bradley, 2000; Chapman, 1988, 2000; Crumley and Marquardt, 1990; David and Thomas, 2008; Hillier and Hanson, 1984; Hirsch and O'Hanlon, 1995; Ingold, 1993, 2006; Wagstaff, 1987; Whatmore, 2002; Whitelaw, 1991; Whitridge, 2004). Here, space often refers to a well-defined geographical entity with clear boundaries. As a physical location, archaeological spaces are generally the things we identify and sample as indicative of features, sites, bounded territories, or regions of study. They are tangible locations, often defined on the basis of changes in their biological, geological, or geographical structure. Importantly, they are universal and measureable (Whitridge, 2004). Place, on the other hand, is a locale or spot that is both real and representational; it is created through a combination of experience and practice; it is mutable and dynamic, sometimes even having a life of its own. Place-making is the locally contingent investment of a location with meaning and involves ways of inhabiting and dwelling in the world and, thus, is a ubiquitous human experience (Whitridge, 2004: 214). In many ways this distinction is reflected in the archaeological terminology, where place is the human social realm we are interested in reconstructing and space is the physical manifestation we study in order to decipher or interpret it.

Yet, space and place are not mutually exclusive; either can be a locale for human activity: a campfire, a structure, a collection of structures, or simply a rock, stream, or forest (Bradley, 2000). Examinations of the use-of-space in prehistoric and ethnographic hunter-gatherer societies demonstrate the inextricable nature of space and place (e.g., Gaudzinski-Windheuser, 2015; Kent, 1987, 1990). Indeed, in many societies, past and present, objective space and meaningful place are inseparable (e.g., Bradley, 2000; David et al., 2006; Whatmore, 2002; Whitridge, 2004). Taking an approach that reframes these terms to question whether hunter-gatherer societies view these as distinctly different concepts, Whitridge (2004: 213) argues that place-making is inherent to human experience in the way we view ourselves and others, plants, animals, things, architecture, and landscapes. Through archaeological and ethnographic examples, he argues that Inuit groups of the Canadian High Arctic create social geographies or "spatial imaginaries," where traditional, socially embedded places are enmeshed with technologies and techniques more commonly understood as ways to observe and measure space, namely, mapping and navigational technologies, travel, and physically marking the landscape, thereby transforming it (Whitridge, 2004) as a type of built environment. Archaeological reconstructions of past people's interactions with the world should reflect an encompassing concept of place-making because "[h]uman spatialities are everywhere complex and heterogeneous, at each historical moment articulating embodied actors with a simultaneously symbolic, social, and biophysical world ... The investment of particular locations with meaning (place-making) is a ubiquitous social and cognitive process" (Whitridge, 2004: 214).

Given the deep time frame for hunter-gatherer groups of Southwest Asia discussed later and the dramatic changes in local environments over the last 20,000 years, correlating or linking places and spaces is a challenging endeavor. In a period overwhelmingly concerned with identifying the earliest agriculture and emergence of new "Neolithic" societies, our ability to assess causal relationships between social change and landscape change, for example, are currently hindered by the differing scales and resolutions of archaeological and paleoenvironmental datasets (Maher, Banning, et al., 2011). In this respect, spatial constructs relate more to "objectively measurable" aspects of the landscape and its features using macro- and microscale analyses within and immediately around a site and regional settlement patterns/territories reconstructed on the basis of shared material culture. While we recognize that prehistoric peoples did not experience the landscape in these segmented terms, our archaeological reconstructions of past human behavior appear (in practice and imagination) "confined" to these constructs (Whitridge, 2004) – these are *our* archaeological spatial imaginaries. Evidence for place-making is narrowed to particularly well-defined locales with visible traces of human activity, where people have transformed the "natural" and made it obviously "cultural," intentionally or unintentionally reinforcing a nature/culture divide (Descola, 2013; Whatmore, 2002). Given the problems of recognizing place-making in the (distant) past, it is not surprising that theoretical paradigms that eschew humans as apart from nature, such as historical ecology (Crumley, 1994) and human eco-dynamics (McGlade, 1995) are not readily apparent approaches in Southwest Asian prehistory. Sites clearly have

definable characteristics and obvious signs of human "intervention." But, what about the less obvious "places" or spaces in between sites?; the traces of movement, inhabitation, and dwelling (Gamble, 1998) that do not leave signs obvious to us 20,000 years later, such as piles of stones, diversion or damming of streams, or changes in forest composition (Bradley, 2000)? Paleoenvironmental reconstructions are invaluable for framing the character and constraints of a landscape; however, recent work on reconstructing EP paleolandscapes in Jordan (e.g., Jones, Maher, Richter, et al., 2016; Maher, 2017; Munro et al., 2016; Olszewski and al-Nahar, 2016) highlights the locally contingent nature of these datasets where data from specific locales around sites reinforces a dynamic landscape of microhabitats that often contradict regional climatic models. This makes our task of identifying places between sites even more challenging.

A HUNTER–GATHERER BUILT ENVIRONMENT? HUNTER–GATHERER PLACE-MAKING AND THE LIFE HISTORY OF PLACE IN SOUTHWEST ASIA

Yet, complementing these locally contingent paleolandscape models, I suggest there are ways to use (or develop) these spatial constructs to get at past place-making, such as pairing microscale analyses of the use-of-space within sites and exploration of social networks and movements across a socialized landscape (e.g., Gamble, 1998; Ingold and Vergunst, 2008; Langley, 2013; Maher, 2016; McBryde, 2000; McDonald and Veth, 2012; Snead et al., 2011). Dwelling in the world occurs on multiple scales, only some of which are readily detectable to us archaeologically (at least with our current techniques). As a way to explore the places in between sites, we can extend well-proven ethnoarchaeological approaches to the use-of-space (e.g., David and Kramer, 2001; Kent, 1987, 1990, 1995) beyond the site. Applying micromorphological and geochemical techniques to ethnoarchaeology – geo-ethnoarchaeology (Brochier et al., 1992; Friesem, 2016) – provides high-resolution data on the traces of human action and activity preserved in archaeological deposits as "artifacts" of behavior that can be interpreted within a practice theory framework, where repeated practices (*habitus*), in particular, leave distinctive, tangible residues (Maher, 2018). For example, geo-ethnoarchaeological, especially micromorphological, techniques can be employed to identify and examine pathways as high-traffic zones of movement within and (albeit more challengingly) between sites. I emphasize here that this approach that sees archaeological landscapes as encompassing locales of place-making that are highly social, mutable, and experiential and filled with both individual and collective meaning – in other words, storied landscapes (Langley, 2013) – is a realistic way to conceive of hunter-gatherer experiences, past and present, and a meaningful way to attempt to reconstruct hunter-gatherer landscapes in Southwest Asia.

Here, I ask whether many of the tangible things (e.g., houses) and intangible things (e.g., mind-sets to "settle" and create places) we associate with the so-called Neolithic package are found strictly within Neolithic? In order to address this question, I draw on certain tenets of practice theory (Bourdieu, 1977) that prompts us to recognize explicitly the active agency of hunter-gatherers in their daily

practices, practices that engender the creation, maintenance, and transformations of space, technologies, and social relations within sites examined through use-of-space and site organization, as well as across landscapes by tracing movements and interactions between groups (see also Maher and Conkey, 2019). In particular, repeated daily activities, or what we may call *habitus*, as well as individual actions, provide valuable clues to past lifeways and the life histories of places (Ashmore, 2002) as they leave diagnostic traces of these activities in the material culture and archaeological sediments or residues they leave behind (Friesem, 2016; Maher, 2018; Shahack-Gross, 2017). It is largely through daily practices that places are created and reified, within a site and across a landscape (Boivin, 2000; Matthews, 2012b; Whitridge, 2004). A life history of place approach reminds that all space is actively inhabited (Ashmore, 2002); it is useful here as "places were formed through repeated human action, especially as marked tangibly in artifacts or construction. A space full of such places is key to understanding society" (p. 1176). According to Ashmore, the social meaning of places is inscribed through repeated action and performance. As places are culturally and socially contingent, a life history approach allows us to explore these variable place biographies.

Although rare, there are several examples of hunter-gatherer aggregation sites in Southwest Asia whose incredible size and density evidence long-term, repeated use and larger-than-usual numbers of people (Garrard and Byrd, 2013). Some sites, while smaller in scale, show persistent use over generations (Olszewski and al-Nahar, 2016). These sites also exhibit clear organization of space, with individual hut or tent structures, floors, caches, and other features. Interpretation of these structures, some of which are quite small, is challenging and depends heavily on fine-grained, microscale excavation and analyses, as well as ethnoarchaeological comparisons. While it is tempting to view these as ephemeral shelters, akin to tents providing refuge from the elements, Yellen (1977) and Kent (1995) both remind us that these features may have had many different "functions," from sleeping to materials processing to storage; all of which represent an intentional construction and use within clear, discrete, and bounded space and that provided a means of differentiating and, often, privatizing space through differential access and visibility (Banning, 1996). They were visible markers of space and reminders that certain things are done "inside" and others "outside." For a full discussion of the "meaning" of huts embodied in the very terminology we use to describe them in comparison to the homes of later farming communities see Maher and Conkey (2019). Here, we note that in Southwest Asia, mobile hunter-gatherers build and occupy huts or tents that, if found in multiples, form campsites, while sedentary farmers (and foragers) build houses and homes that form communities. Indeed, the appearance of stone structures, as with the Natufian, is one (of many) criteria for hunter-gatherer complexity and is used to mark part of the process of "becoming Neolithic" (see also Boyd, 2006). This language has the, perhaps implicit, effect of excluding hunter-gatherers from constructing homes and communities with literature focused on the symbolism of the Neolithic house, especially as tied to a farming way of life (although see Banning and Chazan, 2006).

The alternative presented here of EP place-making, home-making, community construction, and a built environment relates directly to several issues raised in other chapters in this volume and provides an excellent comparative framework for the rich datasets from Çatal-höyük. Similarities and differences in the nature of the archaeological record and in the reconstructions of EP and Neolithic lifeways allow a number of pertinent questions. For example, what, specifically, marks the onset of the Neolithic? What do we mean when we use the term *Neolithization*, or what does it mean to "become Neolithic"? How do we identify this process in the archaeological record? Is there such a thing, or are we retrospectively assigning intentionality to peoples of the past? Specifically, I address these as related to changes in consciousness emerging through (1) increased rates of trade and exchange with other communities or, in other words, examine the role of social connectedness between sites through material culture and technological knowledge interactions and exchange; (2) evidence for increased rates of innovation/creativity as related to increased size and density of settlements and changes in the organization of and use-of-space within, exploring the shift from bounded and discrete spaces in the Early EP to communal spaces in the Middle EP; and (3) exploring the meanings of associations between structures and human burials as a mortuary practice that becomes a notable feature of the Neolithic.

IDENTIFYING EPIPALEOLITHIC PLACES;
TRACING EPIPALEOLITHIC INTERACTIONS

In Southwest Asia, it seems that house and home are inextricable (Watkins, 1990). We focus on the more visible stone architecture of the Natufian assumed to be permanent and reflecting a shift to sedentary mind-sets and lifeways (for a critique of this, see Boyd, 2006). Brush hut structures represent the remains of temporary camps for mobile hunter-gatherers who accomplished tasks such as flintknapping or grinding or hide-processing within them, downplaying them as part of a built environment or as venues for the creation of complex social relationships. While there are undoubtedly significant differences in architectural features spanning the EP and Neolithic, I caution against seeing this as in any way a reflection of the so-called mobile mind-set or consciousness of a hunter-gatherer. Rather, hut structures in clearly organized spaces, especially when reused and maintained, should be considered evidence of place-making (and home-making) in just the same socially meaningful ways that stone houses do; they represent locales for the creation, maintenance, and transformation of social relationships between people, material things, and places. Taken even further, "sedentism and permanent architecture are not the defining features of dwelling; dwelling in a landscape (or any parts of one) is just as much home-making" (Maher and Conkey, 2019: 95). It is through daily practices that homes are created, but as these daily activities frequently include off-site places, homes can also be found within landscapes that extend beyond the site, or the places between sites are also imbued with meaning and "made manifest" (Crumley, 1994) through an array of human actions that can include movement along paths, tracks, and trails (Gamble, 1998). These practices, performed outside easily recognizable sites,

are preserved in these landscapes, sometimes in less obtrusive, but still visible and detectable ways. Reconstructing daily practices through understanding the organization of space and thus the creation of a built environment within sites can be extended to the regular movements (and creation of places) by people in a larger landscape – indeed this broad scope for "being-in-the-world" is exactly what creates and shapes a landscape as a number of highly socialized places. Yet, in Southwest Asia the landscape is rarely seen as a series of interconnected places related to group or social identity (Bar-Yosef, 1991; Maher and Conkey, 2019).

I am concerned with the archaeologically visible practices of place-making through examination of the everyday and repeated practices attainable by microscale excavation and analyses of the spaces within and between structures, paired with multiscale exploration of site organization and broader local landscapes. The effectiveness of these methods has been well illustrated at Çatalhöyük (Matthews, 2005, 2010, 2012a, 2012b; Shillito, 2011; Shillito, Bull, et al., 2011; Shillito et al., 2008; Shillito, Matthews, et al., 2011; Shillito and Ryan, 2013), demonstrating how microscale techniques can detect fine-grained events such as repeated floor replastering, oven repairs, or successive hearth or midden use, that allow archaeologists to reconstruct the detailed life history of a building and, thus, part of the lives of its occupants. Paired with ethnoarchaeological studies, one can link specific archaeological contexts or traces to specific behaviors and practices (Boivin, 2000; Friesem, 2016; Matthews et al., 2000). Archaeologists generally recognize the building of a house or a home as a cultural phenomenon (at Çatalhöyük, for example, see Love, 2012, 2013; Matthews, 2012b), something that involves technological, social, economic, and ideological/symbolic activities and interactions, and, thus it has meaning in all these realms. We can examine and explore these roles through microscale analyses of daily activities, and their rhythm, that relate to the entangled quotidian and symbolic lives of those who build, rebuild, maintain, use, and abandon or destroy these structures. These are ways of creating the life history of places, and they help us to investigate the less tangible aspects of dwelling and memory. A microscale examination of the domestic, symbolic, ideological, and technological evidence for activities associated with lived-in spaces in Southwest Asia suggests that a hunter-gatherer hut is little different than a Neolithic house (Maher and Conkey, 2019). Hunter-gatherers also create "homes" as both physical spaces through people-place-thing relationships and social places embodied with a certain permanence, through repeated visits and shared memories.

This approach is becoming increasingly common in hunter-gatherer archaeology, challenging established assumptions about hunter-gatherer mobility, the so-called permanence of farming settlements, and the transformative role of hunter-gatherers in shaping a landscape. Indeed, the agentive role of hunter-gatherers in the creation, maintenance, management, and modification of the landscape is widely recognized in numerous contexts, including the Canadian Arctic (Brody, 2000; Whitridge, 2004), coastal California (Grier, 2017; Lightfoot and Cuthrell, 2015), and, especially, Australia (McBryde, 2000; McNiven et al., 2006; Veth et al.,

2008; Veth et al., 2017). These examples serve to remind us that, while we cannot assume that prehistoric hunter-gatherers viewed their world in *the same way*, we can and should imagine that they viewed their world with similar degrees of investment in place and social connectivity. In this sense, use of the terms "home" in relation to hunter-gatherer structures and "communities" to describe hunter-gatherer aggregation sites in Southwest Asian prehistory (Maher and Conkey, 2019) does not seem inappropriate and allows us to explore the complexities of EP worldviews and lifeways without establishing them as cognitively or cosmologically different from the modern mind. Taking the latter term even further, a hunter-gatherer community can extend from the taskscape (Ingold, 1993), linked together by movements through the landscape (Ingold and Vergunst, 2008), to include other sites and the places in between sites as entangled together in an interconnected hunter-gatherer socialized landscape (Langley, 2013). Indeed, I argue that, despite an avoidance of the use of this term (especially considering its prevalence in Neolithic contexts), a sense of community across a landscape is inherent in the very way we describe hunter-gatherer lifeways and mobility. For example, by definition, an aggregation site implies the existence of other socially connected locations (e.g., indirect or imagined communities? [Anderson, 2006]) from which people came, and later disperse to, as well as direct, face-to-face connections as people gather at the aggregation locale.

As archaeologists, we attempt to reconstruct social group identity and belonging through similarities and differences in material culture as traces of human action, agency, and behavior and map these across space. We can explore the nuance of these similarities and differences as semiotics (e.g., Preucel, 2008), and having social connotations relating to ethnicity, identity, or a sense of belonging at the group and individual level – material culture is imbued with social information, including biographies of their makers, users, and discarders (Appadurai, 1988; Hoskins, 1998). Tracking the movements of these objects, knowledges, and traditions is a first step to tracking social interactions and connections. This provides a rich platform from which to explore the ties of individuals to particular structures and hunter-gatherer groups to specific places (or sites) and landscapes, allowing us to tack back-and-forth to explore traces of home from a structure to site to landscape. This approach to place-making also incorporates aspects of historical ecology (Crumley, 1994) and human eco-dynamics (McGlade, 1995) that view humans as integral aspects of landscape creation, maintenance, and transformation. Here, humans have a transformative role in shaping a landscape and have done so throughout prehistory (Kidder, 2002). We cannot live in a landscape without seeing it through a cultural lens, thus all landscapes are cultural. Humans are a part of the natural world, not set apart from it. As sites are connected to each other across a highly socialized landscape, and these connections are maintained across space and time, communities in direct and indirect relationships populate this landscape (Maher, 2018; Maher and Conkey, 2019).

PLACE-MAKING AT KHARANEH IV

The EP site of Kharaneh IV is located in the Azraq Basin of eastern Jordan (Figure 2.1). It sits less than 1 km southwest of Qasr Kharaneh as a low mound on the otherwise flat alluvial terraces of Wadi Kharaneh, built up about 2 m from these terraces by the accumulation of thick cultural deposits. Indeed, the flint pavement that covers the site today, all EP stone tool production debris, represents a deflated palimpsest of the latest EP occupations of the site. However, this pavement has protected the underlying cultural deposits from subsequent erosion, where intact, stratified EP deposits document numerous "continuous" (see later) phases of occupation and provide an unparalleled, high-resolution sequence of repeated and prolonged occupation of this site. While site-formation processes have concentrated archaeological remains in the surface deposits to create a pavement of artifacts, excavations throughout the site indicate similar high densities of in situ archaeological material preserved at depth. In addition to the staggering density of material culture, the site of Kharaneh IV also extends over 21,000 m^2, making it the largest pre-Natufian EP site known to-date. Again, soundings throughout this area, as well as a 9 m geological trench cutting through one side of the site, demonstrate that this 1.5–2 m depth of deposits extends across much of the extent of the site, petering out only at the edges.

The site was first mentioned by Harding in the 1950s (Harding, 1959), who noted the prehistoric mound in passing while musing about where a wild dog in the vicinity might be getting water (highlighting the current inhospitable conditions at the site). It was described in more detail as part of a survey of eastern Jordan by Stanley-Price and Garrard in 1975 (Garrard and Stanley-Price, 1975). In the

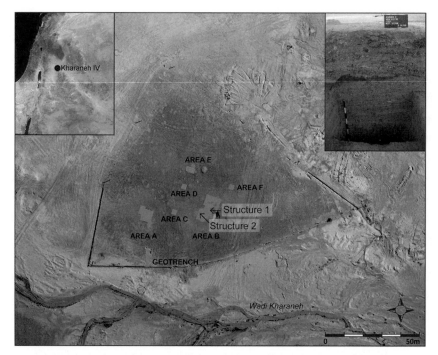

FIGURE 2.1 Aerial drone photomosaic of Kharaneh IV (courtesy of A. Evans, Fragmented Heritage Project, 2015) showing the locations of main excavation areas (Areas A and B) and smaller soundings across the low mound. Inset left: Map of the southern Levant showing the location of Kharaneh IV in eastern Jordan. Inset right: photograph of a section in Area B, showing the well-preserved stratigraphy of these artifact-rich deposits. A similar density of artifacts is found subsurface to depths of 1.5–2 m.

early 1980s the site was partially excavated by M. Muheisen of the Department of Antiquities of Jordan as part of his doctoral research at Bordeaux (Muheisen, 1983, 1988), where he reported traces of floors, hearths, postholes, and two human burials. He did not get the opportunity to continue his work at the site or fully publish his excavations; however, he did convince the Department of Antiquities to assume ownership of the site, protecting it from future destruction (most recently from the construction of a large water reservoir only a few hundred meters east of the site in 2011). In 2008, the Epipaleolithic Foragers in Azraq Project resumed work at the site, with excavations in 2008–2010, 2013, 2015, 2016, and 2018, interspersed with study seasons.

Radiocarbon dates from the depth of occupational deposits excavated so far suggest occupation of the site from 19,800 to 18,600 cal BP, spanning approximately 1,200 years (Richter et al., 2013). Current cultural-chronological frameworks for the EP subdivide the period into three main phases: Early, Middle and Late. Each of these phases is synonymous with several spatially (and temporally) bounded industries defined on the basis of nuanced differences in material culture, particularly stone tool technologies (Goring-Morris et al., 2009; Maher, Richter, and Stock, 2012, Figure 2). Despite some disagreement about the significance of variability between these industries (Olszewski, 2001), in general the Early EP includes the Kebaran and Nebekian, the Middle EP includes the Geometric Kebaran and Mushabian, and the Late EP includes the Natufian and Harifian. The boundaries between these phases (and industries) is also somewhat problematic, with overlap noted between individual dated sites of each phase (Maher, Banning, et al., 2011). With these caveats, the Kharaneh IV radiocarbon dates are stratified and consistent throughout the sequence of deposits, and with typological comparisons, indicate Early (~19,800–19,000 cal BP) and Middle (~19,000–18,600 cal BP) EP occupation of the site (see Macdonald et al., 2018 for a discussion of phases represented at the site). The Middle EP occupation is rather early compared to other Geometric Kebaran-type sites in the region, but see Maher, Banning, et al. (2011) and Richter et al. (2013) for an evaluation of Early and Middle EP cultural "boundaries." Notably, there is no evident hiatus in occupation of the site, with no obvious substantial interruptions in deposition, erosional episodes, or sterile deposits. However, this does not mean that the site was continuously occupied throughout this 1,200-year period, only that periods of abandonment were not substantial and may represent seasonal or yearly movements. A key component in the life history of Kharaneh IV as a place was regular reoccupation of the site.

Today, the landscape around the site is a stark desert, with less than 50 mm of precipitation per year and sparse vegetation. However, extensive geomorphological survey around the site and geoarchaeological analyses of on-site deposits provide a clear picture of landscape change from ~23,000 to the present day (Jones, Maher, Macdonald, et al., 2016; Jones, Maher, Richter, et al., 2016; Maher et al., 2016). The

site was first occupied during the last glacial maximum; yet, while cool and dry conditions predominated elsewhere, deposits in the area immediately around the site and in the basal deposits on-site indicate the presence of numerous freshwater sources. The earliest occupations were episodic and became more substantial as water levels receded slightly, with the site situated on a stable terrace. These wetlands, rivers, and seasonal lakes provided reliable water, supporting rich wetland and grassland vegetation (Ramsey et al., 2016) and drawing habitual and migratory game to the immediate vicinity. Indeed, faunal analyses from the site reflect a wide diversity of locally available species, many of which are water-dependent, even though the occupants of the site (during all phases) relied heavily on gazelle (Henton et al., 2017; Martin et al., 2010; Spyrou, 2015). Isotopic and tooth microwear data from gazelle indicates they were hunted throughout the year (Henton et al., 2017); analysis of changes in mortality profiles over time suggests shifts to more communal hunting, perhaps with drives, from the Early to Middle EP (Martin et al., 2010); and examination of the Middle EP faunal assemblage points to communal processing, drying, and storage of gazelle meat (Spyrou, 2015). Another key component in the life history of Kharaneh IV as a place was its prolonged, multiseasonal use as an aggregation locale within a rich wetland environment.

Detailed syntheses of the excavations are published elsewhere (Henton et al., 2017; Jones, 2012; Maher, 2016, 2017, 2018; Maher and Macdonald, 2013; Maher, Richter, Macdonald, et al., 2012, Maher, Richter, and Stock, 2012; Maher et al., 2014; Maher et al., 2016; Martin et al., 2010; Ramsey et al., 2018; Ramsey et al., 2016; Richter et al., 2011); here, I focus on the recent excavation of several hut structures in the Early EP occupational phases of Area B. To date, we have identified three structures here, and a further possible one in a test sounding to the north. Structure 1 has been fully excavated (Maher et al., in prep; Maher, Richter, Macdonald, et al., 2012), while Structure 2 excavation was started in 2016 and will be completed in 2018 (Figure 2.2). Interestingly, both structures show substantial similarities in construction, reuse and intentional destruction, but also some notable differences.

Structure 1 is an oblong shape, approximately 2 × 3 m in size, with its "foundation" or lowermost deposits partially dug into preexisting occupational deposits. Three well-defined, well-constructed, and well-maintained superimposed floors indicate substantial investment in the structure over time. Each floor is a compacted clay deposit, approximately 2–3 cm in thickness. While not entirely sterile, the clay floors contain very few artifacts, all less than 1 cm in size, which is a notable difference from artifact-rich deposits outside the structure. Large artifacts, such as large flint tools, bone points, large cobbles, shell, ocher, and articulated animal parts (i.e., fox paws), were placed on the floors, sometimes clustered as caches, after use of the floor and prior to the construction of a new floor on top. This suggests that each floor was cleaned, perhaps swept, and the macroscale artifacts on each floor were intentionally placed there as some kind of closing event. The last floor, and its collection of objects, were covered with a few cm of fill. Then, marking the end of the use of this structure, it appears that the brush superstructure was burned to the ground. Evidence for burning is confined to the area bounded by the hut floors, suggesting it was an intentional, controlled event. On top of the charcoal and ash produced by this burning event, near the center of the structure, were three distinct caches of marine shell, each cache containing hundreds of pierced and ocher-stained shells. Each cache also contained one large (5–10 cm diameter) chunk of red ocher. The caches were arranged around a large, flat anvil stone in the center of the structure. Several large, heavily burnt and fire-cracked nodules of local flint were also found in the remains of the burnt superstructure. These deposits were then entirely sealed in a near-sterile orange sand.

A detailed study of each of the floor assemblages and micromorphological examination of the Structure 1 deposits are ongoing (Macdonald and Maher, in press) (Figure 2.3); however, several notable features are emerging. For example, the fauna inside the structure are dominated by only five species (fox, gazelle, hare, tortoise, wild ass) and overwhelmingly represent partially articulated (often burnt) body parts, similar to that expected if carcasses were in containers or hanging from the supports of the structure (Allentuck, in prep). The placement of these objects on otherwise clean floors suggests a high level of maintenance and intentionality to the placement of objects. Typological and use-wear analysis of the lithic assemblage of the floors shows consistency between floors, with large tools like scrapers overrepresented and microliths virtually absent – a striking contrast to every other excavated Early EP context so far. Further, analyses of the

FIGURE 2.2 Structures 1 and 2 from the Early EP area (Area B) at Kharaneh IV. (a) Overview of Structure 1 after exposure of the burnt superstructure layer, with Structure 2 partially visible in the background. (b) Overview of Structure 2 with the burnt superstructure layer visible, and the partially burnt human burial visible in the western margins of the structure directly below this burnt layer. The photographs along the right are objects found placed on the floors of Structure 1: (c) one of three caches of marine shell and red ocher beside a large cobble placed on the burnt superstructure after destruction of the structure; (d) articulated auroch vertebrae, worked bone, and a fragment of groundstone; (e) articulated fox paw; (f) a string of marine shell beads; (g) polished bone point; and (h) articulated tortoise carapace.

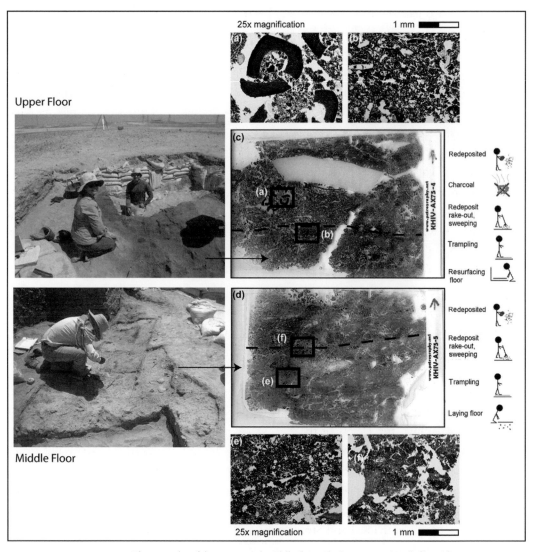

FIGURE 2.3 Photographs of the upper and middle floors during excavation (left), with scans of the micromorphological slides from these deposits, as well as the burnt superstructure (center) and interpretations of the sequence of events based on micro-stratigraphic and macroartifact analyses (right). The upper and lower center images are images from these slides at 25x magnification, showing burnt bone beads (upper left) and charcoal (upper right) and the compact, clayey, and "clean" floors (lower).

microwear traces on these large tools show use for predominantly butchery and fresh hide scraping. It seems that microlith products and retooling, the hallmark flintknapping activities of the EP, were not performed inside the structure. Or, if they were, the occupants were extremely diligent in cleaning up. Finally, phytolith analysis of the remains of the superstructure and on each of the floors indicates the superstructure was composed of predominantly wetland reeds and sedges, although grasses and reeds were both used for matting or bedding that may have covered the floors (Ramsey et al., 2018).

Structure 2 was partially excavated in 2016, uncovering the uppermost deposits of the structure to the level of the uppermost floor. Notably, a similar sequence of events was noted here, with a bright orange sand (of unknown origin) sealing the burnt remains of the hut superstructure. However, excavation beyond the burnt superstructure was slowed by the discovery of a human burial along the northern margins of the structure (Maher et al., in review). An adult female, approximately 50 years old, was found in a semiflexed position. She was of relatively small stature and exhibited advanced osteoarthritis and a healed radial fracture on her right wrist. Her skeletal remains were extensively charred, but not completely cremated, suggesting exposure to an intense, but short-lived fire as one might expect from the burning of dried grass and reeds from the hut superstructure. It is also likely that she was partially covered by clothing that served to dampen the effects of the fire. She was stratigraphically below the burnt layer of the structure, indicating that she was intentionally placed on the hut floor after death and then the structure set alight. It seems that the end of the life of this individual and Structure 2 are paralleled and, perhaps, connected. In addition, although the exact stratigraphic location of the two burials documented by Muheisen are unknown, they are reconstructed to be from the deposits immediately below Structure 1. Thus, it seems that the association of human remains and houses so prevalent for the Neolithic may have earlier roots.

Notably, no hearths were identified in either of these structures (reinforcing their intentional burning, rather than accidental). Instead, in the well-delineated space between these two structures, in stratigraphically equivalent deposits, we excavated one substantial stone-lined hearth, one large cache of burnt, disarticulated gazelle and ibex horn cores (Maher, Richter, Macdonald, et al., 2012), three burnt, articulated, upright gazelle horn core sets, and three caches of cored and bladelets from flintknapping events.

Hut structures and human burials have been documented at other Early EP sites, although not in such clear association. At Ohalo II, three hut structures are clustered together, with several hearths and middens, in one area of the site, with the burial of an adult male in a stone-marked grave near the peripheries of these living areas (Nadel, 1995b). At Ein Gev I, an adult female was found below a paved surface interpreted as the floor of a structure; however, whether she was placed there before or after the structure is unknown (Arensburg and Bar-Yosef, 1973). Now, at Kharaneh IV, we have clear evidence for a symbolic connection – both for the living and the dead – to these hut structures, regardless of their size, permanence, or "function." Although we do not yet know whether these structures are contemporaneous (and it is likely they are not), the complex sequence of events documented at Structures 1 and 2, and similarities between them in construction, use, and destruction – two examples among several more similar structures not yet excavated – suggest the enormous potential of Kharaneh IV for yielding insights into domestic and nondomestic spatial organization within hunter-gatherer sites and the important connections these groups made to particular places. The daily practices marked inside and outside these structures, including repeated themes of reuse, caching, domestic tasks, and funerary performances, integrated quotidian and symbolic behaviors. With the structures, these practices culminated in the destruction of these "places," probably homes. Given the entangled social "practices occurring in and around these structures, repeatedly, and ones notably different to other on-site areas, it seems that EP groups did invest in these structures as more than simple shelters" (Maher and Conkey, 2019: 103). Another key component in the life history of Kharaneh IV as a place was the highly structured use of space with the construction, reuse, and destruction of hut structures; delineation of activities inside and outside; and associated entanglement of domestic and symbolic activities. Notably, these notions of space also changed during occupation of the site from circumscribed and defined activities to communal activities.

Building on this evidence, I suggest that these hunter-gatherer structures were imbued with a variety of meanings, illustrated through their construction, reuse, maintenance, and intentional destruction associated with abandonment and death. There are interconnecting domestic and symbolic activities. There are preserved material and sedimentological traces of food preparation and hide-processing, caching, and traces of use by the living and the dead. Repeatedly occupied structures and repeatedly occupied sites, such as Kharaneh IV, Ohalo II (Nadel, 2006), Jilat 6 (Garrard and Byrd, 2013), and elsewhere (Olszewski and al-Nahar, 2016), provide evidence for hunter-gatherer place-making and communities. With groups congregating at and dispersing from Kharaneh IV, it is but one of many places connected to others across a landscape of hunter-gatherer communities.

Pre-Natufian sites are not always transitory, ephemeral, or unobtrusive occupations.

The Middle EP occupations of the site stand in contrast to those described earlier for the Early EP. In Area A, Early EP phases are noted stratigraphically below the Middle EP deposits in one deep sounding. However, work in Area A has focused on contiguous exposure of the Middle EP deposits to document a series of horizontally extensive and poorly bounded features, including several partially superimposed surfaces, each associated with several hearths (sometimes overlapping) and postholes. Here, at least three surfaces are identifiable on the basis of their compact, clayey texture, flat-lying artifacts, high density of lithic debris, and partially articulated animal remains. Each surface contains at least one hearth, and in some cases, hearths show clear indication of reuse with multiple, partly overlapping layers of ash and charcoal. All of these hearths are surrounded by several small posthole features; they are small in diameter, approximately 5–10 cm, and often filled with burnt sediment, bone, and lithics. Reconstructions of their position, angles, and locations suggest they are the remains of ephemeral structures around or beside fireplaces, perhaps as cooking, meat-drying, or smoking racks (Spyrou, 2015). Adjacent to each of the floors are extensive midden deposits, overwhelmingly dominated by gazelle remains, including large numbers of partially articulated carcasses with little evidence of extensive processing; all body parts are represented. Syprou (2015) suggests these are open, communal spaces of intensive gazelle processing for meat that was cooked/dried and either stored or, given the high density of gazelle, potentially eaten in mass consumption events. Mortality profiles of the gazelle here reinforce the possibility of communal hunting, with whole herd culling that could have been accomplished by the use of hunting blinds or drives. Martin et al. (2010) and Henton et al. (2017) both suggest these communal hunting efforts would have been quite effective in winter months when goitered gazelle form large, mixed herds. Isotopic, cementum, and dental microwear analyses of the gazelle remains clearly document year-round hunting. Thus, occasional multiseason occupation of the site and aggregations during the winter months are probable.

Over time, there is a shift from well-defined, delineated space, highly structured for different activities, including caching, working, cooking, and burial of the dead, to more public, communal living supported by the faunal record and the nature of features in the excavated Middle EP areas. Throughout occupation of the site, as an aggregation site, Kharaneh IV was a significant *place* in a social landscape where hunter-gatherer groups from the Azraq Basin and beyond came together repeatedly and for prolonged periods of time for a variety of economic, social, and ideological reasons. The material and microstratigraphic record from the site provides excellent evidence for technological innovation, food surpluses (involving storage and feasting), and caching of utilitarian and symbolic objects by hunter-gatherer groups. The presence of hut structures and human burials provides a rare opportunity to investigate the intersection of domestic and symbolic activities and the organization of space in and around these structures. The establishment of Kharaneh IV as a "place," a persistent place, in the Early and Middle EP landscape demonstrates complex behaviors associated with dwelling and a mind-set toward a built environment millennia before the Neolithic.

KHARANEH IV AND THE LARGER EP SOCIAL LANDSCAPE

Place-making at Kharaneh IV should be seen as only part of a bigger picture. It is complemented, of course, by connections between the site and others in the broader EP landscape.

As an aggregation site, Kharaneh IV served as a social hub of interaction for hunter-gatherer populations from throughout the region and, as such, was a focal point for a larger, fluid community composed of many different social groups who participated in diverse activities on-site during periods of aggregation *and* maintained connections to each other through long-distance exchange networks during periods of dispersal (Maher and Conkey, 2019: 105), with a range of behaviors enacted in an intensively-used landscape.

With marine shell ubiquitous to all phases of occupation (albeit more numerous in the Middle EP) and numbering in the thousands, we know that the occupants of Kharaneh IV were interacting with hunter-gatherer groups located between the site and the Mediterranean and Red Seas (Richter et al., 2011), either making the trek to these coasts themselves or trading with several intermediaries in a complex network of exchange. In either case, groups from the Azraq Basin to the Negev and Sinai and Coastal Plain and, perhaps, beyond would have known of each other and experienced face-to-face interaction or indirect connections through the movement of nonlocal material culture. Most of the marine shell from Kharaneh IV is modified, usually pierced and strung, but also including sectioned dentalium and carved and denticulated mother-of-pearl (Allcock, 2009). These shells likely served a variety of functions, including as social currency, helping to establish social relationships, and facilitating a variety of social and economic transactions. One might imagine a shell fair, where shell objects were traded for kind, or other objects, or services, or to cement social ties between groups. They may have been prominently displayed and markers of individual or group identity.

In addition, the Middle EP chipped stone assemblage here shows both a high degree of diversity in microlithc tool forms (more so than other contemporary sites) and strong similarities in tool types to several sites within and outside the Azraq Basin. Maher and Macdonald (2013) have used the types, numbers, and widths of trapezes at Kharaneh IV to make the point that if, as we often assume, differences in geometric types and sizes are indicative of lithic traditions, then the presence of such a wide range of geometrics at Kharaneh IV substantiates the idea of aggregation and interaction of many groups. As an aggregation site, we should expect to see the material traces of many different groups (from near and far) congregating, interacting, sharing, and exchanging both material goods and knowledge. If marine shell transport and exchange were mobilized over large distances, it is not surprising that lithic production knowledge was also shared during aggregation and dispersal events. Indeed, the so-called geometric variants at Kharaneh IV don't represent new types or industries, but rather show striking similarities in form to other Middle EP sites in southern Jordan, the Negev, the coastal plain of Israel, the Jordan Valley, and southern Syria and Lebanon (detailed in Macdonald, 2013; Maher, 2016; Maher and Macdonald, 2013). Indeed, Kharaneh IV shows an incredible diversity of geometric tools, representing "types" from all these areas, and reinforcing the notion that the site was a node of aggregation for otherwise potentially disparate hunter-gatherer groups. The presence of only local raw materials used for tool production (Delage et al., in prep) is striking when one considers the parallels in tool form between Kharaneh IV and other distantly located sites, suggesting that variation results from the movement of people and their knowledge of lithic technology, rather than the movement of already-made tools. Through various materials, paths and networks can be constructed to understand wider social networks and how hunter-gatherers constructed landscapes through regional interaction spheres. This work is now leading to interesting questions about the nature of intergroup interaction on site and in the larger region. For example, did each aggregating group at Kharaneh IV live in its own "community," creating subtle differences in how material culture was made and used on-site? Can we compare differences in technological style with other contemporaneous regional sites to link the communities at Kharaneh IV with those across the Levant? If patterns in technological style can be found between the assemblage at Kharaneh IV and other contemporaneous sites, then it might be possible to trace long-distance and maintained connections between dispersed populations.

A DISCUSSION OF EP PLACE-MAKING

I suggest here that, prior to the advent of permanent stone houses aggregated into villages in the Neolithic, Early, and Middle EP hunter-gatherer structures, or huts, were imbued with a variety of meanings, including symbolic ones related to differential use of space, regardless of their permanence. At Kharaneh IV, the presence of several Early EP hut structures and the structured use of space inside and outside these structures, including a deliberate human burial on a hut floor prior to its burning, provide evidence for entangled domestic and symbolic activities within these structures. They elaborate on practices documented at hut structures from Ohalo II and elsewhere, where use and reuse and clear separation of activities inside and outside (Nadel, 1995a, 2002, 2006), as well as associations with the dead (Arensburg and Bar-Yosef, 1973; Richter et al., 2016), suggest continuity in practices throughout the EP and into the Neolithic (Goring-Morris and Belfer-Cohen, 2008). Further, exploration of the organization and differential use of space in the Early EP occupations at Kharaneh IV contrasts notably with that of the Middle EP occupations, perhaps documenting a shift from private to more public or communal (and community-based?) concepts of space (see later).

Within these highly social(-ized) places, huts or *homes* are part of larger hunter-gatherer *communities*. Kharaneh IV served as an aggregation site, where Early and Middle EP groups congregated, repeatedly, and sometimes for prolonged periods (Henton et al., 2017; Jones, 2012; Maher, 2016, 2017; Spyrou, 2015). It was a "place," made socially, economically, and, with the burial of the dead, cosmologically meaningful in Early and Middle EP landscapes through repeated occupation, even if the particulars of these occupations changed (as we should expect it did) over time. In the Middle EP horizons, site features, stone tool technologies, and an abundance of marine shells suggest groups were congregating at and dispersing from Kharaneh IV; it was but one of many places connected to others across eastern Jordan and beyond. Even in the Early EP occupations, the abundance of marine shells, including in caches of hundreds of pierced and ocher-stained shells, demonstrates that connections to distant landscapes (Mediterranean and Red Seas) were actively sought and maintained (Richter et al., 2011). The nature of these interactions may remain elusive and likely included some combination of direct travel and down-the-line exchange; however, the high density of shells in all occupation phases, spanning the ~1,200 years the site was occupied, none-the-less, indicate maintained, long-distance interaction between groups over these distances. Kharaneh IV is thus a useful case study for place-making and connection across a highly socialized landscape traced through similarities in practice and material culture (Maher, 2016).

CONCLUSIONS

Kharaneh IV allows us to explore connections between sites and the potential pathways between them. While the tracks, trails, paths, and "roads," however well-travelled, remain largely elusive by their very nature and accepting the largely site-based ways in which research is necessarily conducted in the region, we can start by examining connections between known sites, including other aggregation sites. Within the Azraq Basin, Jilat 6, for example, is another probable aggregation site with evidence for ocher-colored floors, abundant marine shell, and with typological similarities to the Early EP microliths from Kharaneh IV (Garrard and Byrd, 2013). Ayn Qasiyyah, located within the Azraq Oasis, was a likely campsite and a burial locale with two distinct Early EP assemblages, the Kebaran one similar to Kharaneh IV (Richter et al., 2010, 2014). Outside the Azraq Basin, Ohalo II and Ein Gev I contain evidence for structures and stone installations; one of Ohalo II's excavated huts shows repeated use and clearly structured use of space (Nadel et al., 2004; 2011), and the stone pavement and burial at Ein Gev I was noted earlier. A structure is documented at Ein Qashish, alongside caches and several incised plaquettes (Yaroshevich et al., 2016). The Middle EP sites of Neve David (Kaufman, 1987), Wadi Mataha (Stock et al., 2005), and Uyyun al-Hammam (Maher, Stock, et al., 2011) all have human burials; Uyyun al-Hammam as a repeatedly occupied campsite and Middle EP burial ground. Neve David also contains at least one stone-built feature (Yeshurun et al., 2015). They also all have notable similarities in microliths tool form to the geometrics from Kharaneh IV (and some differences) (Macdonald et al., 2016; Maher and Macdonald, 2013). The persistent use of places tied to marshlands in the Wadi al-Hasa also attests to repeated patterns of landscape use (Olszewski and al-Nahar, 2016). Thus, "similarities in material culture and site organization...show that the evidence for social interaction and place- and home-making from Kharaneh IV is [not unique but]

indicative of broader trends in hunter-gatherer behaviors and connects this aggregation site to other large and smaller sites across the landscape" (Maher and Conkey, 2019: 105–106). Aggregations of groups tied to specific places and interconnected through long-distance social networks and exchange in objects and knowledge was a part of a hunter-gatherer way of life several millennia before the Neolithic.

These connections, at least the ones that drew the occupants of Kharaneh IV to the site for over 1,000 years, changed by ~18,600 years ago. Geoarchaeological work around the site and in the surrounding Azraq Basin indicate that the extensive wetlands dried up as a result of local responses to regional climatic changes, namely, increased rates of transevaporation and changing hydrological patterns with increased temperatures at the end of the last glacial maximum (Al-Kharabsheh, 2000; Jones, 2013; Jones, Maher, Macdonald, et al., 2016; Jones, Mayer, Richter, et al., 2016; Jones and Richter, 2011; Maher, 2017). Flora and fauna dependent on these water resources also disappeared. Kharaneh IV was no longer situated in a lush landscape, and the site was abandoned. The nature of this place for contemporary EP peoples changed dramatically, and its use changed accordingly.

I am not arguing here that Kharaneh IV, or other Early or Middle EP sites, can be equivocated with later Neolithic villages (or even Natufian sites), or that there isn't some cognitive or cosmological difference between life as a hunter-gatherer or farmer. I am, however, arguing that these differences are likely only in degree and do not represent a "break" – a clear line in the sand – between hunter-gatherer and farmer; the boundaries are increasingly blurred as we realize the complexities of EP lifeways over this 10,000-year time-span. EP hunter-gatherers were actively engaged in place-making and, even, home-making (Maher and Conkey, 2019), within the site of Kharaneh IV (and others), as well as in the socialization of the larger EP landscape through movements and interactions between people, material objects, and places.

ACKNOWLEDGMENTS

The author first presented some of the "place-making" ideas discussed in this paper as a joint endeavor with Meg Conkey at the 2013 SAA Annual Meetings in Honolulu as a comparison between the concept(s) of home in EP Southwest Asia and Upper Paleolithic Europe, and from there it has taken off. I must thank Meg profusely for pushing me to think bigger than Southwest Asia and for her unending encouragement in these endeavors. I also thank my codirector Danielle Macdonald for sharing the not-so-small task of working at Kharaneh IV and our tireless field crews over the last decade. Expanding from this work, this chapter is the result of several discussions with many of our colleagues over the last few years, too many to name individually here, as well as valuable insights provided by audiences from lectures and conferences at Berkeley and beyond.

This material is based upon work supported by the National Science Foundation under Grant No. 1727368 and the National Endowment for the Humanities under Grant No. RZ-255635. Any views, findings, conclusions, or recommendations expressed in this article, do not necessarily represent those of the National Endowment for the Humanities or National Science Foundation.

REFERENCES

Al-Kharabsheh, A. 2000. Ground-water modelling and long-term management of the Azraq basin as an example of arid area conditions (Jordan). *Journal of Arid Environments*, 44, 143–153.

Allcock, S. 2009. *Beyond trade and subsistence: the use of shell ornaments to infer social interaction and increasing complexity during the Early and Middle Epipalaeolithic, Jordan*. Masters of Science, University College London.

Allentuck, A. in prep. Taphonomy, subsistence and deposition of faunal remains in the early Epipalaeolithic. *In:* Maher, L. & Richter, T. (eds.) *A prehistoric oasis in the Azraq basin, Jordan: the epipalaeolithic foragers in Azraq Project 2005–2015*. Los Angeles: Cotsen Institute of Archaeology Press.

Anderson, B. 2006. *Imagined communities: reflections on the origin and spread of nationalism*. London: Verso Books.

Appadurai, A. 1988. *The social life of things: commodities in cultural perspective*. Cambridge, UK: Cambridge University Press.

Arensburg, B. & Bar-Yosef, O. 1973. Human remains from Ein-Gev I, Jordan Valley, Israel. *Paléorient*, 1, 201–206.

Arnold, J. E. 1996. The archaeology of complex hunter-gatherers. *Journal of Archaeological Method and Theory*, 3, 77–126.

Ashmore, W. 2002. "Decisions and dispositions": socializing spatial archaeology. *American Anthropologist*, 104, 1172–1183.

Ashmore, W. & Knapp, A. B. 1999. *Archaeologies of landscape: contemporary perspectives*. Malden, MA: Blackwell Publishers.

Asouti, E. & Fuller, D. 2013. A contextual approach to the emergence of agriculture in Southwest Asia: reconstructing early Neolithic plant-food production. *Current Anthropology*, 54, 299–345.

Bailey, G. & Spikins, P. 2008. *Mesolithic Europe*. Cambridge, UK: Cambridge University Press.

Banning, E. B. 1996. Houses, compounds and mansions in the prehistoric Near East. *In:* Coupland, G. G. & Banning, E. B. (eds.) *People who lived in big houses: archaeological perspectives on large domestic structures*. Madison, WI: Prehistory Press, 165–185.

Banning, E. B. & Chazan, M. (eds.) 2006. *Domesticating space: construction, community, and cosmology in the late prehistoric Near East*. Berlin: ex oriente.

Bar-Yosef, O. 1991. Stone tools and social context in Levantine prehistory. *In:* Clark, G. A. (ed.) *Perspectives on the past: theoretical biases in Mediterranean hunter-gatherer research*. Philadelphia: University of Pennsylvania Press.

Bar-Yosef, O. 2002. Natufian. A complex society of foragers. *In:* Fitzhugh, B. & Habu, J. (eds.) *Beyond foraging and collecting. Evolutionary change in hunter-gatherer settlement systems*. New York: Kluwer Academic/Plenum.

Barrett, J. 1999. Chronologies of landscape. *In:* Layton, P. J. & Ucko, R. (eds.) *The archaeology and anthropology of landscape: shaping your landscape*. New York: Routledge.

Belfer-Cohen, A. & Bar-Yosef, O. 2000. Early sedentism in the Near East: a bumpy ride to village life. *In:* Kuijt, I. (ed.) *Life in Neolithic farming communities: social organization, identity, and differentiation*. New York: Kluwer Academic/Plenum Publishers.

Belfer-Cohen, A. & Goring-Morris, N. 2011. Becoming farmers: the inside story. *Current Anthropology*, 52, S209–S220.

Bird, R. B., Bird, D. W., Codding, B. F., Parker, C. H., & Jones, J. H. 2008. The "fire stick farming" hypothesis: Australian Aboriginal foraging strategies, biodiversity, and anthropogenic fire mosaics. *Proceedings of the National Academy of Sciences*, 105, 14796–14801.

Boivin, N. 2000. Life rhythms and floor sequences: excavating time in rural Rajasthan and Neolithic Çatalhöyük. *World Archaeology*, 31, 367–388.

Bourdieu, P. 1977. *Outline of a theory of practice*. Cambridge, UK: Cambridge University Press.

Boyd, B. 2002. Ways of eating/ways of being in the Later Epipalaeolithic (Natufian) Levant. *In:* Hamilakis, Y., Pluciennik, M., & Tarlow, S. (eds.) *Thinking through the body: archaeologies of corporeality*. New York: Kluwer Academic/Plenum Publishers.

Boyd, B. 2006. On sedentism in the Later Epipalaeolithic (Natufian) Levant. *World Prehistory*, 38, 164–178.

Bradley, R. 2000. *An archaeology of natural places*. London: Routledge.

Brochier, J. E., Villa, P., Giacomarra, M., & Tagliacozzo, A. 1992. Shepherds and sediments: geo-ethnoarchaeology of pastoral sites. *Journal of Anthropological Archaeology*, 11, 47–102.

Brody, H. 2000. *The other side of Eden: hunters, farmers, and the shaping of the world*. New York: North Point Press.

Canuto, M. A. & Yaeger, J. 2000. *The archaeology of communities: a new world perspective*. New York: Routledge.

Chapman, J. 1988. From "space" to "place": a model of dispersed settlement and Neolithic society. *In:* Burgess, C., Topping, P., & Mordant, D. (eds.) *Enclosures and defences in the Neolithic of Western Europe*. Oxford, UK: BAR International Series.

Chapman, J. 2000. *Fragmentation in archaeology: people, places and broken objects in the prehistory of south eastern Europe*. London: Routledge.

Cohen, A. P. 1985. *The symbolic construction of community*. London: Tavistock.

Crumley, C. L. 1994. *Historical ecology: cultural knowledge and changing landscapes*. Santa Fe, NM: School of American Research Press.

Crumley, C. L. & Marquardt, W. H. 1990. Landscape: a unifying concept in regional analysis. *In:* Allen, K. M. S. & Zubrow, E. (eds.) *Interpreting space: GIS and archaeology*. New York: Taylor & Francis.

David, B., Barker, B. & McNiven, I. J. 2006. *The social archaeology of Australian indigenous societies*. Canberra: Aboriginal Studies Press.

David, B. & Thomas, J. 2008. Landscape archaeology: introduction. *In:* Thomas, J. & David, B. (eds.) *Handbook of landscape archaeology*. Walnut Creek, CA: Left Coast Press.

David, N. & Kramer, C. 2001. *Ethnoarchaeology in action*. Cambridge, UK: Cambridge University Press.

Delage, C., Mangado Llach, X., & Torres, M. in prep. The lithic landscape around Kharaneh IV. *In:* Maher, L. & Richter, T. (eds.) *A prehistoric oasis in the Azraq Basin, Jordan: the Epipalaeolithic foragers in Azraq Project 2005–2015*. Los Angeles: Cotsen Institute of Archaeology Press.

Descola, P. 2013. *Beyond nature and culture*. Chicago: University of Chicago Press.

Fano, M. Á., García-Moreno, A., Chauvin, A., Clemente-Conte, I., Costamagno, S., Elorrieta-Baigorri, I., Pascual, N. E., & Tarriño, A. 2015. Contribution of landscape analysis to the characterisation of Palaeolithic sites: A case study from El Horno Cave (northern Spain). *Quaternary International* 412(15), 82–98.

Finlayson, B. 2013. Imposing the Neolithic on the past. *Levant*, 45, 133–148.

Finlayson, B. & Makarewicz, C. 2013. Neolithic stereotypes: has South-west Asian archaeology outlived the Neolithic? *Levant*, 45, 119.

Finlayson, B. & Warren, G. 2010. *Changing natures: hunter-gatherers, first farmers and the modern world*. Bristol: Bristol Classical Press.

Finlayson, B. & Warren, G. (eds.) 2017. *Diversity of hunter-gatherer pasts*. Oxford: Oxbow Books.

Friesem, D. E. 2016. Geo-Ethnoarchaeology in action. *Journal of Archaeological Science*, 70, 145–157.

Gamble, C. 1998. Palaeolithic society and the release from proximity: a network approach to intimate relations. *World Archaeology*, 29, 426–449.

Gamble, C. 2007. *Origins and revolutions: human identity in earliest prehistory*. Cambridge, UK: Cambridge University Press.

Garcia-Moreno, A. 2013. To see or be seen . . . Is that the question? An evaluation of Paleolithic sites' visual presence and their role in social organization. *Journal of Anthropological Archaeology*, 32, 647–658.

Garrard, A. & Byrd, B. 2013. *Beyond the Fertile Crescent: Late Palaeolithic and Neolithic communities of the Jordanian Steppe. Volume 1: Project background and the Late Palaeolithic – geological context and technology*. Oxford, UK: Oxbow Books.

Garrard, A. & Stanley-Price, N. 1975. A survey of prehistoric sites in the Azraq Basin, eastern Jordan. *Paléorient*, 3, 109–126.

Gaudzinski-Windheuser, S. 2015. The public and private use of space in Magdalenian societies: evidence from Oelknitz 3, LOP (Thuringia, Germany). *Journal of Anthropological Archaeology*, 40, 361–375.

Goring-Morris, A. N. & Belfer-Cohen, A. 2003. Structures and dwellings in the Upper and Epi-Palaeolithic (c. 42–10k BP) Levant: profane and symbolic uses. *In:* Vasil'ev, S. A., Soffer, O., & Kozlowski, J. (eds.) *Perceived landscapes and built environments: the cultural geography of Late Paleolithic Eurasia*. Oxford, UK: BAR International Series 1122.

Goring-Morris, A. N. & Belfer-Cohen, A. 2008. A roof over one's head: developments in near eastern residential architecture across the epipalaeolithic-Neolithic transition. *In:* Bocquet-Appel, J. P. & Bar-Yosef, O. (eds.) *The neolithic demographic transition and its consequences*. New York: Springer.

Goring-Morris, A. N. & Belfer-Cohen, A. 2010. Different ways of being, different ways of seeing . . . changing worldviews in the Near East. *In:* Finlayson, W. & Warren, G. (eds.) *Landscapes in transition: understanding hunter-gatherer and farming landscapes on the early Holocene of Europe and the Levant*. London: CBRL Monographs.

Goring-Morris, A. N. & Belfer-Cohen, A. 2011. Neolithization processes in the Levant: the outer envelope. *Current Anthropology*, 52, S195–S208.

Goring-Morris, A. N., Hovers, E. & Belfer-Cohen, A. 2009. The dynamics of Pleistocene and Early Holocene settlement patterns and human adaptations in the Levant: an overview. *In:* Shea, J. & Lieberman, D. (eds.) *Transitions in prehistory: essays in honor of Ofer Bar-Yosef*. Oxford, UK: Oxbow Books.

Grier, C. 2017. Expanding notions of hunter-gatherer diversity: identifying core organizational principles and practices in coast Salish societies of the northwest coast of North America. *In:* Warren, G. & Finlayson, B. (eds.) *The diversity of hunter-gatherer pasts*. Oxford, UK: Oxbow Press.

Habu, J. 2004. *Ancient Jomon of Japan*. Cambridge, UK: Cambridge University Press.

Harding, G. L. 1959. *The antiquities of Jordan*. New York: Praeger.

Heidegger, M. 1971. *Poetry, language, thought: translations and introduction by Albert Hofstadter*. New York: Harper & Row.

Henton, E., Martin, L., Garrard, A., Jourdan, A.-L., Thirlwall, M., & Boles, O. 2017. Gazelle seasonal mobility in the Jordanian steppe: the use of dental isotopes and microwear as environmental markers, applied to Epipalaeolithic Kharaneh IV. *Journal of Archaeological Science: Reports*, 11, 147–158.

Hillier, B. & Hanson, J. 1984. *The social logic of space.* Cambridge, UK: Cambridge University Press.

Hirsch, E. & O'Hanlon, M. (eds.) 1995. *The anthropology of landscape. Perspectives on place and space.* Oxford, UK: Clarendon Press.

Hodder, I. 2012. *Entangled: an archaeology of the relationships between humans and things.* Chichester, UK: John Wiley & Sons.

Hoskins, J. 1998. *Biographical objects: how things tell the stories of people's lives.* New York: Routledge.

Hutson, S. R. 2009. *Dwelling, identity, and the Maya: relational archaeology at Chunchucmil.* Lanham, MD: Rowman & Littlefield.

Ingold, T. 1993. The temporality of the landscape. *World Archaeology,* 25, 152–174.

Ingold, T. 1995. Building, dwelling, living: how animals and people make themselves at home in the world. *In:* Strathern, M. (ed.) *Shifting contexts. Transformations in anthropological knowledge.* New York: Routledge.

Ingold, T. 2000. *The perception of the environment: essays on livelihood, dwelling and skill.* New York: Routledge.

Ingold, T. 2006. For space. *Journal of Historical Geography,* 32, 891–893.

Ingold, T. 2010. Footprints through the weather-world: walking, breathing, knowing. *Journal of the Royal Anthropological Institute,* 16, S121–S139.

Ingold, T. & Vergunst, J. (eds.) 2008. *Ways of walking: ethnography and practice on foot.* New York: Routledge.

Jones, J. 2012. Using gazelle dental cementum studies to explore seasonality and mobility patterns of the Early-Middle Epipalaeolithic Azraq Basin, Jordan. *Quaternary International,* 252, 195–201.

Jones, M. D. 2013. What do we mean by wet? Geoarchaeology and the reconstruction of water availability. *Quaternary International,* 308, 76–79.

Jones, M. D., Maher, L. A., Macdonald, D. A., Ryan, C., Rambeau, C., Black, S., & Richter, T. 2016. The environmental setting of Epipalaeolithic aggregation site Kharaneh IV. *Quaternary International.* 396, 95–104.

Jones, M. D., Maher, L., Richter, T., Macdonald, D., & Martin, L. 2016. Human-environment interactions through the Epipalaeolithic of Eastern Jordan. *In:* Contreras, D. (ed.) *Correlation is not enough: building better arguments in the archaeology of human-environment interactions.* New York: Routledge.

Jones, M. D. & Richter, T. 2011. Palaeoclimatic and archaeological implications of Pleistocene and Holocene environments in Azraq, Jordan. *Quaternary Research,* 76, 363–372.

Kaufman, D. 1987. Excavations at the Geometric Kebaran site of Neve David, Israel. A preliminary report. *Quartär,* 37/38, 189–199.

Kent, S. 1987. Understanding the use of space: an ethnoarchaeological approach. In Kent, S. (ed.) *Method and theory for activity area research: an ethnoarchaeological approach.* New York: Columbia University Press, 1–60.

Kent, S. 1990. Activity areas and architecture: an interdisciplinary view of the relationship between use of space and domestic built environments. *In:* Kent, S. (ed.) *Domestic architecture and the use of space: an interdisciplinary cross-cultural study.* Cambridge, UK: Cambridge University Press.

Kent, S. 1995. Ethnoarchaeology and the concept of home: a cross-cultural analysis. *In:* Benjamin, D. N., Stea, D., & Aren, E. (eds.) *The home: words, interpretations, meanings, and environments.* Avebury, UK: Aldershot.

Kidder, T. 2002. The rat that ate Louisiana: aspects of historical ecology in the Mississippi River Delta. *In:* Balee, W. (ed.) *Advances in historical ecology.* New York: Columbia University Press.

Knapp, A. B. & Ashmore, W. 1999. Archaeological landscapes: constructed, conceptualised, ideational. Introduction. *In:* Ashmore, W. & Knapp, B. (eds.) *Archaeological landscapes: contemporary perspectives.* Oxford, UK: Blackwell.

Kolen, J. 1999. Hominids without homes: on the nature of Middle Palaeolithic settlement in Europe. *In:* Roebroeks, W. & Gamble, C. (eds.) *The Middle Palaeolithic occupation of Europe.* Leiden: University of Leiden Press.

Kuijt, I. & Prentiss, A. M. 2009. *Niche construction, macroevolution, and the Late Epipalaeolithic of the Near East. Macroevolution in human prehistory.* New York: Springer.

Langley, M. C. 2013. Storied landscapes makes us (modern) human: landscape socialisation in the Palaeolithic and consequences for the archaeological record. *Journal of Anthropological Archaeology*, 32, 614–629.

Lepofsky, D., Smith, N. F., Cardinal, N., Harper, J., Morris, M., Bouchard, R., Kennedy, D. I., Salomon, A. K., Puckett, M., & Rowell, K. 2015. Ancient shellfish mariculture on the northwest coast of North America. *American Antiquity*, 80, 236–259.

Lévi-Strauss, C. 1966. *The savage mind*. Chicago: University of Chicago Press.

Lightfoot, K. G. & Cuthrell, R. Q. 2015. Anthropogenic burning and the Anthropocene in late-Holocene California. *The Holocene*, 25, 1581–1587.

Love, S. 2012. The geoarchaeology of mudbricks in architecture: a methodological study from Çatalhöyük, Turkey. *Geoarchaeology – an International Journal*, 27, 140–156.

Love, S. 2013. The performance of building and technological choice made visible in mudbrick architecture. *Cambridge Archaeological Journal*, 23, 263–282.

Macdonald, D. 2013. *Interpreting variability through multiple methodologies: the interplay of form and function in Epipalaeolithic microliths*. PhD, University of Toronto.

Macdonald, D. A., Allentuck, A., & Maher, L. A. 2018. Technological Change and Economy in the Epipalaeolithic: Assessing the Shift from Early to Middle Epipalaeolithic at Kharaneh IV. *Journal of Field Archaeology*, 43, 437–456.

Macdonald, D. & Maher, L. in press. Domestic tasks at Kharaneh IV: understanding the Epipalaeolithic toolkit through microwear. *In:* Gibaja, J., Clemente, I., Mazzucco, N., & Marreiros, J. (eds.) *Hunter-gatherers tool kit: a functional perspective*. Newcastle, UK: Cambridge Scholars Press.

Macdonald, D. A., Chazan, M., & Janetski, J. C. 2016. The Geometric Kebaran occupation and lithic assemblage of Wadi Mataha, southern Jordan. *Quaternary International*, 396, 105–120.

Maher, L. A. 2016. A road well-travelled? Exploring terminal Pleistocene hunter-gatherer activities, networks and mobility in Eastern Jordan. *In:* Chazan, M. & Lillios, K. (eds.) *Fresh fields and pastures new: papers presented in honor of Andrew M. T. Moore*. Leiden: Sidestone Press.

Maher, L. A. 2017. Late Quaternary Refugia: aggregations and palaeoenvironments in the Azraq Basin. *In:* Bar Yosef, O. & Enzel, Y. (eds.) *Quaternary environments, climate change and humans in the Levant*. Cambridge, UK: Cambridge University Press.

Maher, L. A. 2018. Persistent Place-Making in Prehistory: The creation, maintenance and transformation of an Epipalaeolithic landscape. *Journal of Archaeological Method and Theory*, 25, 1–86.

Maher, L A., Banning, E. B., & Chazan, M. 2011. Oasis or mirage? Assessing the role of abrupt climate change in the prehistory of the Southern Levant. *Cambridge Archaeological Journal*, 21, 1–29.

Maher, L. A., & Conkey, M. 2019. Homes for Hunters? Exploring the Concept of Home at Hunter-Gatherer Sites in Upper Palaeolithic Europe and Epipalaeolithic Southwest Asia. *Current Anthropology*, 60, 91–137.

Maher, L. A. & Macdonald, D. 2013. Assessing typo-technological variability in Epipalaeolithic assemblages: preliminary results from two case studies from the Southern Levant. *In:* Borrell, F., Molist, M., & Ibanez, J. J. (eds.) *The state of stone: terminologies, continuities and contexts in Near Eastern Lithics. Studies in early Near Eastern production, subsistence and environment 14*. Berlin: ex oriente.

Maher, L. A., Macdonald, D. A., Allentuck, A., Martin, L., Spyrou, A., & Jones, M. D. 2016. Occupying wide open spaces? Late Pleistocene hunter-gatherer activities in the Eastern Levant. *Quaternary International*, 396, 79–94.

Maher, L. A., Macdonald, D., Allentuck, A., Ramsey, M., Bode, L., & Martin, L. in prep. The making of a home? Spatial analysis of Structure 1 at Kharaneh IV. *Antiquity*.

Maher, L. A., Macdonald, D., Stock, J. T., & Pomeroy, E. in review. Burning down the house: a 20,000-year-old burial from Eastern Jordan. *Antiquity*.

Maher, L. A., Richter, T., Macdonald, D., Jones, M., Martin, L., & Stock, J. T. 2012. Twenty thousand-year-old huts at a hunter-gatherer settlement in Eastern Jordan. *PLoS ONE*, 7, e31447.

Maher, L. A., Richter, T. & Stock, J. 2012. The pre-Natufian Epipalaeolithic: long-term behavioral trends in the Levant. *Evolutionary Anthropology*, 21, 69–81.

Maher, L. A., Richter, T., Stock, J. & Jones, M. 2014. Preliminary results from recent excavations at the Epipalaeolithic Site of Kharaneh IV. *In:* Jamhawi, M. (ed.) *Jordan's prehistory: past and future research*. Amman: Department of Antiquities of Jordan.

Maher, L. A., Stock, J. T., Finney, S., Heywood, J. J. N., Miracle, P., & Banning, E. B. 2011. A unique human-fox burial from a pre-Natufian cemetery in the Southern Levant (Jordan). *PLoS ONE*, 6, 1–10.

Martin, L., Edwards, Y., & Garrard, A. 2010. Hunting practices at an Eastern Jordanian Epipalaeolithic aggregation site: the case of Kharaneh IV. *Levant*, 52, 107–135.

Matsui, A. & Kanehara, M. 2006. The question of prehistoric plant husbandry during the Jomon period in Japan. *World Archaeology*, 38, 259–273.

Matthews, W. 2005. Micromorphological and microstratigaphic traces of uses and concepts of space. *In:* Hodder, I. (ed.) *Inhabiting Çatalhöyük: reports from the 1995–1999 seasons*. Cambridge, UK: McDonald Institute for Archaeological Research.

Matthews, W. 2010. Geoarchaeology and taphonomy of plant remains and microarchaeological residues in early urban environments in the Ancient Near East. *Quaternary International*, 214, 98–113.

Matthews, W. 2012a. Defining households: micro-contextual analysis of early Neolithic households in the Zagros, Iran. *In:* Parker, B. & Foster, C. (eds.) *Household archaeology: new perspectives from the Near East and beyond*. Winona Lake, IN: Eisenbrauns.

Matthews, W. 2012b. Household life-histories and boundaries. *In:* Tringham, R. & Stevanovic, M. (eds.) *House lives: building, inhabiting, excavating a house at Çatalhöyük, Turkey. Reports from the BACH area, Çatalhöyük, 1997–2003*. Los Angeles and Ankara: Cotsen Institute of Archaeology Press and British Institute at Ankara.

Matthews, W., Hastorf, C., & Ergenekon, B. 2000. Ethnoarchaeology: studies in local villages aimed at understanding aspects of the Neolithic site. *In:* Hodder, I. (ed.) *Towards reflexive method in archaeology: the example at Çatalhöyük*. Cambridge, UK: McDonald Institute for Archaeological Research.

McBryde, I. 2000. Travellers in storied landscapes: a case study in exchanges and heritage. *Aboriginal History*, 24, 152–174.

McDonald, J. & Veth, P. 2012. The social dynamics of aggregation and dispersal in the Western Desert. *In:* McDonald, J. & Veth, P. (eds.) *A companion to rock art*. Malden, MA: Blackwell.

McGlade, J. 1995. Archaeology and the ecodynamics of human-modified landscapes. *Antiquity*, 68, 113–132.

McNiven, I. 2004. Saltwater people: spiritscapes, maritime rituals and the archaeology of Australian indigenous seascapes. *World Archaeology*, 35, 329–349.

McNiven, I. J., David, B. & Barker, B. 2006. The social archaeology of indigenous Australia. *In:* David, B., Barker, B. & McNiven, I. J. (eds.) *The social archaeology of Australian indigenous societies*. Canberra: Aboriginal Studies Press.

Muheisen, M. 1983. *La Préhistoire en Jordanie. Recherches sur l'Epipaléolithique. L'Example du Gisement de Kharaneh IV*. PhD, l'Université de Bordeaux I.

Muheisen, M. 1988. *Le Paléolithique et l'Epipaléolithique en Jordanie*. PhD, l'Université de Bordeaux I.

Munro, N. D., Kennerty, M., Meier, J. S., Samei, S., al-Nahar, M. & Olszewski, D. I. 2016. Human hunting and site occupation intensity in the Early Epipaleolithic of the Jordanian western highlands. *Quaternary International*, 396, 31–39.

Nadel, D. 1995a. The organization of space in a fisher-hunter-gatherers camp at Ohalo II, Israel. *In:* Otte, M. (ed.) *Nature et Culture: Colloques de Liège*. Liège: Université de Liège.

Nadel, D. 1995b. The visibility of prehistoric burials in the Southern Levant: how rare are the Upper Palaeolithic/Early Epipalaeolithic graves? *In:* Campbell, S. & Green, A. (eds.) *The archaeology of death in the ancient Near East*. Oxford, UK: Oxbow.

Nadel, D. 2002. Indoor/outdoor flint knapping and minute debitage remains: the evidence from the Ohalo II submerged camp (19.5 KY, Jordan Valley). *Lithic Technology*, 26, 118–137.

Nadel, D. 2003. The Ohalo II brush huts and the dwelling structures of the Natufian and PPNA sites in the Jordan Valley. *Archaeology, Ethnology and Anthropology of Eurasia*, 13, 34–48.

Nadel, D. 2006. Residence ownership and continuity from the early Epipalaeolithic into the

Neolithic. *In:* Banning, E. B. & Chazan, M. (eds.) *Domesticating space: construction, community, and cosmology in the Late Prehistoric Near East.* Berlin: ex oriente.

Nadel, D., Weiss, E., Simchoni, O., Tsatskin, A., Danin, A., & Kislev, M. 2004. Stone Age hut in Israel yields world's oldest evidence of bedding. *Proceedings of the National Academy of Sciences of the United States of America,* 101, 6821–6826.

Nadel, D., Weiss, E. & Tschauner, H. 2011. Gender-specific division of indoor space during the Upper Palaeolithic?: a brush hut floor as a case study. *In:* Gaudzinski-Windheuser, S., Jöris, O., Sensburg, M., Street, M., & Turner, E. (eds.) *Site-internal spatial organization of hunter-gatherer societies: case studies from the European Palaeolithic and Mesolithic.* Mainz: Verlag des Römisch-Germanischen Zentralmuseums.

Olszewski, D. My "backed and truncated bladelet," your "point": terminology and interpretation in Levantine Epipalaeolithic assemblages. *In:* Caneva, I., Lemorini, C., Zampetti, D., & Biagi, P. (eds.) *Beyond tools: redefining the PPN lithic assemblages of the Levant. Third Workshop on PPN Chipped Lithic Industries, 2001 2001 Ca'Foscari University of Venice.* Berlin: ex oriente, 303–318.

Olszewski, D. I. & al-Nahar, M. 2016. Persistent and ephemeral places in the Early Epipaleolithic in the Wadi al-Hasa region of the western highlands of Jordan. *Quaternary International,* 396, 20–30.

Preucel, R. W. 2008. *Archaeological semiotics.* New York: John Wiley & Sons.

Price, T. D. & Bar-Yosef, O. 2011. The origins of agriculture: new data, new ideas an introduction to Supplement 4. *Current Anthropology,* 52, S163–S174.

Ramsey, M. N., Maher, L. A., Macdonald, D. A., Nadel, D., & Rosen, A. M. 2018. Sheltered by reeds and settled on sedges: construction and use of a twenty thousand-year-old hut according to phytolith analysis from Kharaneh IV, Jordan. *Journal of Anthropological Archaeology,* 50, 85–97.

Ramsey, M. N., Maher, L. A., Macdonald, D. A., & Rosen, A. 2016. Risk, reliability and resilience: phytolith evidence for alternative "neolithization" pathways at Kharaneh IV in the Azraq Basin, Jordan. *PLoS ONE,* 11, e0164081.

Richter, T., Arranz-Otaegui, A., Boaretto, E., Bocaege, E., Estrup, E., Martinez-Gallardo, C., Pantos, G. A., Pedersen, P., Sæhle, I., & Yeomans, L. 2016. Shubayqa 6: a new Late Natufian and pre-pottery Neolithic A settlement in north-east Jordan. *Antiquity,* 90.

Richter, T., Garrard, A., Allcock, S., & Maher, L. 2011. Interaction before agriculture: exchanging material and shared knowledge in the Final Pleistocene Levant. *Cambridge Archaeological Journal,* 21, 95–114.

Richter, T., Jones, M., Maher, L., & Stock, J. T. 2014. The Early and Middle Epipalaeolithic in the Azraq Oasis: excavations at Ain Qasiyya and AWS-48. *In:* Jamhawi, M. (ed.) *Jordan's prehistory: past and future research.* Amman: Department of Antiquities of Jordan.

Richter, T. & Maher, L. 2013. Terminology, process and change: reflections on the epipalaeolithic of Southwest Asia. *Levant,* 45, 121–132.

Richter, T., Maher, L. A., Garrard, A. N., Edinborough, K., Jones, M. D., & Stock, J. T. 2013. Epipalaeolithic settlement dynamics in southwest Asia: new radiocarbon evidence from the Azraq Basin. *Journal of Quaternary Science,* 28, 467–479.

Richter, T., Stock, J. T., Maher, L., & Hebron, C. 2010. An Early Epipalaeolithic sitting burial from the Azraq Oasis, Jordan. *Antiquity,* 84, 1–14.

Roberts, B. K. 1996. *Landscapes of settlement: past and present.* New York: Routledge.

Rowley-Conwy, P. 2011. Westward ho! The spread of agriculture from Central Europe to the Atlantic. *Current Anthropology,* 52, S431–S451.

Rowley-Conwy, P. & Layton, R. 2011. Foraging and farming as niche construction: stable and unstable adaptations. *Philosophical Transactions of the Royal Society B-Biological Sciences,* 366, 849–862.

Sassaman, K. E. 2004. Complex hunter-gatherers in evolution and history: a North American perspective. *Journal of Archaeological Research,* 12, 227–280.

Shahack-Gross, R. 2017. Archaeological formation theory and geoarchaeology: state-of-the-art in 2016. *Journal of Archaeological Science,* 79, 36–43.

Shillito, L.-M. 2011. Simultaneous thin section and phytolith observations of finely stratified deposits from Neolithic Çatalhöyük, Turkey: implications for paleoeconomy and Early Holocene paleoen-vironment. *Journal of Quaternary Science*, 26, 576–588.

Shillito, L.-M., Bull, I. D., Matthews, W., Almond, M. J., Williams, J. M., & Evershed, R. P. 2011a. Biomolecular and micromorphological analysis of suspected faecal deposits at Neolithic Çatalhöyük, Turkey. *Journal of Archaeological Science*, 38, 1869–1877.

Shillito, L.-M., Matthews, W., & Almond, M. 2008. Investigating midden formation processes and cultural activities at Neolithic Çatalhöyük, Turkey. *Antiquity*, 82.

Shillito, L.-M., Matthews, W., Almond, M. J., & Bull, I. D. 2011b. The microstratigraphy of middens: capturing daily routine in rubbish at Neolithic Çatalhöyük, Turkey. *Antiquity*, 85, 1024–1038.

Shillito, L.-M. & Ryan, P. 2013. Surfaces and streets: phytoliths, micromorphology and changing use of space at Neolithic Çatalhöyük (Turkey). *Antiquity*, 87, 684–700.

Smith, B. D. 2015. A comparison of niche construction theory and diet breadth models as explanatory frameworks for the initial domestication of plants and animals. *Journal of Archaeological Research*, 23, 215–262.

Snead, J. E., Erickson, C. L., & Darling, J. A. 2011. *Landscapes of movement: trails, paths, and roads in anthropological perspective*. Philadelphia: University of Pennsylvania Press.

Spyrou, A. 2015. *Animal procurement and processing during the pre-Natufian Epipalaeolithic of the Southern Levant: zooarchaeological and ethnographic implications of meat and nutrient storage and social organization*. PhD, University College London.

Sterelny, K. & Watkins, T. 2015. Neolithization in Southwest Asia in a context of niche construction theory. *Cambridge Archaeological Journal*, 25, 673–691.

Stock, J. T., Pfeiffer, S. K., Chazan, M., & Janetski, J. 2005. F-81 skeleton from Wadi Mataha, Jordan, and its bearing on human variability in the Epipalaeolithic of the Levant. *American Journal of Physical Anthropology*, 126, 453–465.

Thomas, J. 2008. Archaeology, landscape and dwelling. In David, B. & Thomas, J. (eds.) *Handbook of landscape archaeology*. New York: Routledge.

Veth, P., Myers, C., Heaney, P., & Ouzman, S. 2017. Plants before farming: the deep history of plant-use and representation in the rock art of Australia's Kimberley region. *Quaternary International*, 489, 26–45.

Veth, P., Smith, M., & Hiscock, P. 2008. *Desert peoples: archaeological perspectives*. Malden, MA: Blackwell.

Wagstaff, J. M. 1987. *Landscape and culture: geographical and archeological perspectives*. New York: Basil Blackwell.

Watkins, T. 1990. The origins of house and home? *World Archaeology*, 21, 336–347.

Watkins, T. 2010. Changing people, changing environments: how hunter-gatherers became communities that changed the world. *In:* Finlayson, B. & Warren, G. (eds.) *Landscapes in transition*. London: Oxbow.

Watkins, T. 2011. Opening the door, pointing the way. *Paleorient*, 37, 29–38.

Watkins, T. 2013. The Neolithic in transition – how to complete a paradigm shift. *Levant*, 45, 149–158.

Watkins, T. 2015. The cultural dimension of cognition. *Quaternary International*, 405, 91–97.

Whatmore, S. 2002. *Hybrid geographies: natures, cultures, spaces*. London: Sage.

Whitelaw, T. 1991. Some dimensions of variability in the social organization of community space among foragers. *In:* Gamble, C. S. & Boismier, W. A. (eds.) *Ethnoarchaeological approaches to mobile campsites*. Ann Arbor, MI: International Monographs in Prehistory.

Whitridge, P. 2004. Landscapes, houses, bodies, things: "place" and the archaeology of Inuit imaginaries. *Journal of Archaeological Method and Theory*, 11, 213–250.

Wilson, P. J. 1991. *The domestication of the human species*. New Haven, CT: Yale University Press.

Yaroshevich, A., Bar-Yosef, O., Boaretto, E., Caracuta, V., Greenbaum, N., Porat, N., & Roskin, J. 2016. A unique assemblage of engraved plaquettes from Ein Qashish South, Jezreel Valley, Israel:

figurative and non-figurative symbols of Late Pleistocene hunters-gatherers in the Levant. *PLoS ONE*, 11, e0160687.

Yellen, J. E. 1977. *Archaeological approaches to the present: models for reconstructing the past.* New York: Academic Press.

Yeshurun, R., Kaufman, D., Shtober-Zisu, N., Crater-Gershtein, E., Riemer, Y., Rosen, A. M., & Nadel, D. 2015. Renewed fieldwork at the Geometric Kebaran site of Neve David, Mount Carmel. *Journal of the Israel Prehistoric Society*, 45, 31–54.

Zeder, M. A. 2009. Evolutionary biology and the emergence of agriculture: the value of co-opted models of evolution in the study of culture change. *In:* Prentiss, A., Kuijt, I., & Chatters, J. C. (eds.) *Macroevolution in human prehistory: evolutionary theory and processual archaeology.* New York: Springer.

Zeder, M. A. 2011. The origins of agriculture in the Near East. *Current Anthropology*, 52, S221–S235.

PART II

HIGHER LEVELS OF CONSCIOUSNESS

WHEN TIME BEGINS TO MATTER

Marion Benz

ALTHOUGH IDEAS OF SPACE AND TIME strongly influence human consciousness, decisions and activities, investigations into time concepts have been almost neglected in prehistoric archaeology. In this chapter new results of social neurobiology, sociology and archaeology are combined to focus on how time concepts might have changed at the transition to sedentary farming communities. Sociological studies have shown that, in every society, at least three concepts of time exist: episodic, cyclical and linear. The archaeological evidence from the early Neolithic of the Near East suggests that there was no linear evolution from episodic, to cyclical and then on to linear concepts of time. It seems that increasing circular and linear concepts of time were related to concepts of confined personal and social identities in sedentary agricultural communities. Anticipating and assessing environmental conditions and long-term planning became crucial cognitive capacities within farming communities. Episodic concepts of time were marginalized.

In light of these socio-anthropological investigations, the hypothesis that early Neolithic communities were more innovative or more creative than Palaeolithic hunter-gatherers seems highly questionable. It will be concluded that increasing linear concepts of time fostered material and social interdependencies and led into path dependencies. The substantial surge in new things during the Neolithic is thus not to be considered a result of a higher level of creativity, but as a consequence of social differentiation and social identities, which became more and more based on and expressed by material things and prescribed familial relationships.

CONCEPTS OF TIME – AN ALMOST NEGLECTED SUBJECT IN NEOLITHIC RESEARCH

Since the 1990s archaeological research has increasingly focussed on cognitive changes as a prime mover for the transition to agriculture and herding (Cauvin 1997; Hodder 1990; Watkins 2004, 2010; cf. Price and Bar-Yosef 2017:161). The intensified display of symbols and architecture were considered to have been mirroring major changes in human cognitive capacities (Renfrew 2005; Watkins 2004, 2010). Although the influence of built space on people has been acknowledged since Bourdieu, studies on time concepts have been limited to cultures with written records (Assmann 2002, 2003, 2005; Wendorf 1985). This is all the more striking because architectural and social research has incessantly emphasised that concepts of space and time are closely related (e.g. Safranski 2017; Steets 2015; Weidenhaus 2015). The lack of research on concepts of time in prehistoric research can only be partly compensated for by research on the role of the past in the past (e.g. Bradley 2002; Hodder and Pels 2010; Holtorf 2005; Watkins 2012).

Taking Einstein's "Raumzeit" as a challenge, Gunter Weidenhaus (2015) found convincing evidence in human biographies that time and space concepts are mutually related to social structure. The structuring of space and social interactions can thus shed light on collective concepts of time. Moreover, processes of commodification and decommodification (*sensu* Gebel 2010) can provide important evidence on these concepts.

In the first part of this chapter, I will introduce the three time concepts, cyclical, linear and episodic, and their related social and spatial concepts. Second, socio-neurobiological aspects will be presented, which are relevant for the interpretation. In the third part, two case studies are investigated: the early Holocene cultures of Northern Mesopotamia and Middle to Late Pre-Pottery Neolithic B communities of the Levant with an outlook to Çatalhöyük. These examples underline that Neolithic states of consciousness depended in many aspects on

insular concepts of space and cyclical concepts of time, but there is also some evidence for episodic and for increasing linear concepts of time, which became dominant with social differentiation, industrialization and eschatological religions (Assmann 2002; Wendorf 1985). Due to the diversity of Neolithic cultures, it will not be possible to describe a general Neolithic concept of "Space-time". Instead we have to search for contexts of different concepts of time within one society, as proposed by Assmann (2002:68–70) and compare different Neolithic communities. I will argue that the seemingly highly creative and innovative Neolithic people were not more or less creative or innovative than mobile hunter-gatherer groups. It was rather their different concepts of time, space and social relations – namely the reduction of sharing (Benz 2010) – that fostered stronger corporate identities and new relationships to objects. Creating physical, social and mental boundaries (Benz 2017; Gebel 2010) made them dependent on the production of ever "new" objects. Increasing commodification embraced all spheres of life: from landscapes to objects and invisible cognitive domains (Gebel 2010, 2014, 2017). It seems that time itself became one of the most precious and manipulated commodities humans have ever agreed upon (Safranski 2017:106–130).

DIFFERENT APPROACHES TO TIME

Three approaches to time should be differentiated (Figure 3.1): (neuro-) biological, physical and cultural. All three perspectives are mutually dependent and influence behaviour and mind (Weidenhaus 2015:30–31). Whereas neurobiological research focuses on the

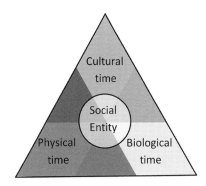

FIGURE 3.1 Mutually related domains of time.

perception of time (Helfrich 2011; Safranski 2017:121–124; Wittmann 2013), physical approaches to time study forms of measuring time. The focus of this chapter is on cultural time concepts and their influence on social communities, consciousness and creativity.

There is hardly any society that does not structure time. Two different forms of recording time exist: absolute and relative time accounts. Absolute chronologies are based on counting repetitions of cyclical events, such as astronomic, vegetative or meteorological processes, or respectively, dividing these cycles into ever smaller units. All calendars thus encompass cyclical and linear aspects. Whether cyclical or linear aspects are emphasized, is a matter of world view, personality and context (Assmann 2005; Helfrich 1996:108–109, 2011:1; Wittmann 2013).

Relative Chronologies

Relative chronologies combine cultural concepts of time and the measuring thereof. They refer to certain events in the past, but the time between these events is irrelevant. The relation between the remembered events and the present is decisive. Relative chronologies are thus social constructs; they might be related to

absolute chronologies, but do not have to be. What is remembered depends on its relevance for the present.

Relative chronologies embrace myths and genealogies, which often claim fictive ancestors at their beginnings. Even in historical settings, absolute chronologies are not of high relevance (Holtorf 2005:95). This statement may seem provocative, as it places myths, legends and history in the same trajectory, although it does not deny the difference between a sense of the past and history. However, it is an illusion to think that history is completely different from myth. Life is too complex to possibly remember everything, and a mere compilation of data remains meaningless. Reconstructions of the past are dependent on communication, discourse and sociopolitical contexts (Assmann 2002:34–48). Neurobiological research has confirmed this in many empirical studies (Hirst et al. 2018:440). Relative chronologies can occur in communities with cyclical concepts of time, but they gain importance with the dominance of linear time concepts.

The passing of time is experienced as irreversible. The universal experience of death can only be overcome by transcendental ideas. Even if a most detailed recording were to allow for a precise reproduction of the past, the context and the people who had witnessed these reconstructions would never be the same (*cf.* Safranski 2017:140). This shows that no society can experience time in a purely cyclical way. Overcoming death requires cultural efforts. The division of cold and hot societies as Claude Lévi-Strauss once suggested is thus only a gradual one and is never exclusive (Assmann 2005). Lévi-Strauss defined

TABLE 3.1 Domains that are influenced by different time concepts, translated modified and completed after Weidenhaus (2015:187, Table 2)

	Cyclical	Linear	Episodic
Relation to the past	Eternal present	Past and Future are of high relevance for the present	Sequence of unrelated events
Narrative structure	Cyclical, repetitive	Linear	Rather independent stories
Social relations	Few but close (almost familiar) relationships	Strong relationships with gradually decreasing intensity from the centre (ego) to the periphery	Networks of flexible relationships
Meaning of innovation	Innovation = restauration of the status quo	Innovation = Progress	Innovation = profiting of new opportunities
Space construction	Insular construction of space	Home with concentric circles of space	Network of equally relevant localities, highly mobile
Habitus/ planning	Importance of ritualized behaviour	Precise planning of the future	Open/future choice between opportunities

communities with cyclical concepts of time as cold in contrast to hot societies with linear concepts. Hunter-gatherers and traditional agricultural cultures were considered as cold. By cold he did not mean that there was no development. It is only within the paradigm of evolutionism that linear thinking was considered as progressive and the new as innovative per se (Safranski 2017:104). Jan Assmann (2002, 2005) has repeatedly emphasized that cyclical thinking is not less demanding or creative than linear concepts of time.

THE CULTURAL CONSTRUCTION OF TIME

With relative chronologies, the cultural dimension of time concepts has already been touched on. The question is if or how these concepts influenced or were influenced by the transition from mobile foraging communities to sedentary farmers. In modern societies, it seems that the global pacemaker is physically measured time. However, cultural concepts of time have at least as much influence on the behaviour of people as physically measured time. In his seminal thesis, "Soziale Raumzeit", Gunter Weidenhaus (2015) found good evidence for the close relationship of social structures with concepts of space and time. He differentiated three concepts of time: linear, cyclical and episodic (Table 3.1, Figure 3.2). Cyclical and linear concepts have been used for many years to differentiate between traditional societies and literate states (cf. Assmann 2003:25–29). Episodic concepts may seem a new type, emerging from the collapse of stable socioeconomic relations (Connerton 2009: 99–131), but as will be

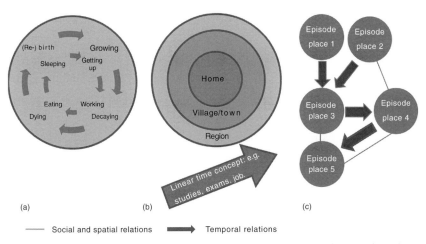

FIGURE 3.2 Graph of the correlation between concepts of time and space adopted from Weidenhaus 2015: (a) cyclical concept of time with insular bounded space concept; (b) linear concept of time with concentric space concept; and (c) episodic concept of time reflected by network-like spatial and social structures.

suggested later, episodic time concepts were probably the most dominant concepts for 99 per cent of the human past. All three concepts are inherent in all societies. However, their proportional relationship depends on spatial, economic, social, political or religious circumstances and paradigms.

Cyclical Concepts of Time

Societies with a cyclical concept of time aim at continuing life as it has always been (Assmann 2003:34, 2005:10–11; Müller 2005:34–37). Past, present and future merge into one eternal present mirroring the cosmic order of growth and decay. Rituals celebrate recurring natural events, but they also re-enact unique events continuously to keep the memory alive. Because natural and social conditions are changing constantly, the potential for creativeness and innovation in cyclical concepts of time is obvious.

Cyclical concepts of time are associated with the sacred, whereas linear concepts are considered profane (Assmann 2005:29). This division is not so clear-cut. Many people today conceive of their lives as cyclical or episodic whilst sequenced intersections are due to rare rituals. Cyclical and linear time concepts can thus be inherent in sacred and profane life. It is ritualization itself whether in a profane or sacred framing that strengthens a cyclical perspective. "[By] representing everlasting and fundamental patterns the ritual connects the past, present, and future and suspends history and time" (Meyerhoff 1984:152 cited in Kertzer 2013:370). However, not all rituals do so. Linear or cyclical aspects can exist in one and the same ritual. According to Victor Turner (Alexander 1991:27–44), the *rites de passage*, defined by van Gennep more than a hundred years ago, enact change and the progress of time: The performance of seclusion and of a liminal state dramatizes the potential for reflexivity by liberation from social norms. *Liminality* and *communitas* bear the germ of change. At the end of the ritual, participants are reintegrated into the social order. Although status and identities of participants have changed, the *rites de passage* naturalize this change and turn it into a constitutive part of the community for the sake of stability.[1]

Cyclical time concepts are paralleled by insular space concepts (Weidenhaus 2015:161–189). People with insular space concepts have stronger, often familial, but generally less social relations than people with episodic or linear time concepts. Insular space concepts imply that borders are emphasised. "Life with cyclical concepts of historicity happens beyond a world of accelerated processes of social change" (Weidenhaus 2015:101; translation MB). This parallels what Müller (2005:71) reports of rural communities who considered themselves as "living on wind still islands."

Linear Concepts of Time

In research, linear concepts of time have been associated with literate state societies. Linear concepts of time were considered means for consolidating hierarchical, large social systems. The past was used to legitimize status and create cohesion for unfamiliar people. In fact, one of myth and history's functions was to legitimize and naturalize territorial claims, social differentiation and hierarchies (Assmann 2005:11; Wendorf 1985). Furthermore, linear thinking was associated with recording, administration, scripture and an increase in trade volumes when debts and credits had to be archived. Assmann has turned the relationship of linear concepts and social hierarchies

upside down. He considers deprivation a strong incentive for change (Assmann 2002:72). Ironically, eschatological religions that postponed well-being in the present to life after death in order to avoid protest of the poor ultimately promoted linear concepts of time and thus change, even though religious rituals were a significant counterpart.

People with linear concepts of time construct their present as if it was a planned consequence of former achievements and conceive of their present as precondition for the future (Weidenhaus 2015:83–86, 107, 197–200). Past, present and future thus enter into a diachronic relationship with one period building on the other, but are clearly distinct from each other. Linear biographical concepts can only emerge where social and environmental conditions are stable, so that planning is realistic and that personal achievements can lead to a better performance. In rapidly changing conditions, people with linear concepts face major problems (Connerton 2009:75–77).

According to Weidenhaus (2015:81–85), linear concepts of time coalesce with concentric concepts of space and social relations. In the centre is ego, his family and a few close friends. Beyond this circle are local communities, followed by rather loose networks of anonymous relations within a region or nation. Although boundaries are not conceived of as strict as with the insular type, there is a clear segregation of the different levels. Spatial concepts mirror these social structures.

Linear concepts of time imply change. If linear concepts of time are combined with hierarchical structures and the objectification of identities, these communities are at risk to be caught in ever increasing spirals of production of the ever faster renewal of things (Connerton 2009). The contradiction *in adiecto* is obvious: although linear concepts of time need stability, they promote, create and need change. It can thus be hypothesized that Claude Lévi-Strauss's so-called hot societies are actually vulnerable social systems. In the long run, it may turn out that the dominance of linear thinking has only been a short interlude in human history.

Episodic Concepts of Time

Episodic concepts of time (see also discussion in Chapter II this volume) are characteristic of working "nomads" (Weidenhaus 2015:91–94). These people rarely have close familial ties because their flexible lifestyle is not compatible with stable social relations. Rapidly changing technologies and advances in science make acquired knowledge outdated within a short time. Past experiences thus have little relevance, but spatial, social and professional flexibility are of prime importance (Connerton 2009:99–131). This lifestyle has strong effects on how these people consider their past and future: they conceive of their life as a sequence of different opportunities, but past experiences are not considered as having an effect, neither on the present nor on the future. This might seem a fatalistic attitude, but the choices these people make are well reflected and often guided by higher aims. Yet, these aims are not oriented in pursuit of a linear career, but on the present.

People with episodic concepts live in spatially and socially loose networks. Parts of such networks can be homogenous with clearly represented social identities, but interacting in different networks makes the whole social structure multidimensional and multicultural.

The characteristic traits of episodic concepts of time resemble the worldview of recent mobile hunter-gatherer communities (Benz 2000:100–140; Guenther 2010; Widlok 2017). Their conception of the mythological past is characterized by the use of schematic templates to create relations between people and environments and by the use of moralizing social aspects. They rarely plan their future. The socioeconomic principle of sharing (Benz 2010; Widlok 2017) and the present-oriented time concept made cultivation an unfeasible option. At least in "immediate return systems" (Woodburn 1988) people focus on the present. This does not exclude that in other areas of life aspects of "delayed return" exist, e.g. objects for exchange-networks and aggregations of people are produced and planned in advance.

It is beyond the scope of this contribution to describe prehistoric hunter-gatherers, but it should be mentioned here that the archaeological record points to rather flexible structures of space, with a variety of settlement types from ephemeral huts to large, repeatedly visited aggregation sites (e.g. Bar-Yosef and Valla 2013; Benz et al. 2015; Maher et al. 2012; Weiss et al. 2004). Up to now, neither monumental stone built architecture like in the early Holocene (Mazurowski and Kanjou 2012; Schmidt 2011; Yartah 2013; Stordeur 2015), nor standardized symbolic repertoires (Benz and Bauer 2013; Hodder and Meskell 2011; Morenz 2014) have been discovered.[2] Groups of hunter-gatherer communities, like at Hayonim Cave and Mallaha seem to be genetically rather heterogeneous (Kranzbühler public comm. 2009)[3], but jewellery and technological traditions hint at emerging group identities within a wide social network (Belfer-Cohen and Goring-Morris 2017). Admittedly, reconstructions of familial relationships are only beginning, and many interpretations are still based either on analogy or on architecture (Kinzel 2013:14–15). Analyses of paleodiets have shown that the choice of resources was eclectic (e.g. Rössner et al. 2018; Savard et al. 2006; Weiss et al. 2004).[4] There is thus some evidence that not only hunter-gatherers of the recent past, but also of prehistoric periods had a rather flexible lifestyle.

To conclude this section we can surmise:

Hypothesis 1: *Time concepts are social constructs mutually related to space and socioeconomic structures.*

Hypothesis 2: *Episodic, cyclical and linear concepts of time exist in every society, but contexts and conditions determine the dominant concept.*

Hypothesis 3: *If the three concepts of time were mutually related to concepts of space and social structures, episodic thinking will have been the most influential concept for thousands of years as it is typical for socially and spatially flexible hunter-gatherer communities. Only with the beginning of agriculture and hierarchisation did linear and cyclical concepts start to dominate.*

NEUROBIOLOGICAL ASPECTS RELATED TO CULTURAL CONCEPTS OF TIME AND GROUP STRUCTURES

Before discussing the case studies, thee neurobiological aspects should be mentioned, as these are important for the understanding of early Neolithic cultures.

Memorizing

Neurobiological insights on memory help understand how *collective memories* are created.

More than 80 years ago Maurice Halbwachs emphasized that memory is a social construct (Assmann 2002:47). Neurobiology has provided evidence that memories can be influenced significantly (e.g. Edelson et al. 2011, with further references). In Western societies, the transmission of knowledge hardly withstands one generation. Common discourse influences the construction of the past so strongly that opinions about the past are formed according to templates despite more precise knowledge (Hirst et al. 2018:447). As Hirst et al. (2018:444) summarize: "Rather than memory being just a faculty to serve individual needs . . ., it turns out to be a social organ designed to promote the formation of collective memory".

Research on rituals has shown how synchronicity in sound and movement, best experienced in group dancing, enhances in-group bonding and the probability that such an action is remembered (Tarr et al. 2015; Winkelman 2002). Extraordinary structures and places, affecting or unexpected events can prime the mind strongly (Bauer 2013; Tambini et al. 2017; see also Whitehouse 2000).

These aspects on the workings of memory imply important consequences for the interpretation of material records and for the reconstruction of time concepts in prehistoric societies.

Assimilation

Humans depend on others for the formation of their body and brain (Over 2015). Their mind develops in dyadic processes. To attract attention, they have developed outstanding cognitive capacities. Besides various forms of communication and imitation (Dunbar 1992;

Rizzolatti and Sinigaglia 2008; Wulf 2005), humans tend to assimilate or even adopt the behaviour and opinions of peers. This tendency to *conform* is not restricted to children (e.g. Haun et al. 2013, 2014; Lakin et al. 2008; van Leeuwen et al. 2015).

Finding a balance of individualistic personal traits and assimilation is difficult (Brewer 1991; Hornsey et al. 2004). However, assimilation does not only cause tensions on the individual level, but also on a group level. The more homogenous groups tend to be, the more they segregate themselves from others. The larger the groups are, the more diacritical means they need to mark borders. The more unnatural these borders are, the more means are necessary to manifest them. To impress people, elites have to invent a lot of paraphernalia to make others believe in their "superiority". Elites are thus trapped in a vicious circle. If identities are based on the possession of things, possessing such things makes one appear like a member of the group. Imitation then leads to popularization, and elites will have to find new diacritical means.

Objectification

Both aspects, memory making and assimilation, are related to the cognitive capacity to attribute symbolic meaning to things. People do not only transmit knowledge to other people but they also fix knowledge, meaning and skills in things and landscapes, what was described as the "distributed mind" (Dunbar et al. 2010). Humans act according to the *meaning* things have for them (Blumler 2013:64; Thomas 1998:x). Objects and features in the landscape can thus become diacritical means or memory tokens. Groups that

grow too large need means to stabilize the commitment of their members and avoid fission (Dunbar 2013). External media, such as a common symbolic system, help to signal and to create trust and commitment (Cohen 1985). Rituals are considered one of the best means to strengthen loyalty and create lasting collective memories (Wulf 2005).

The more difficult it became to create social cohesion and the more status contradicted skills, the more important it became to reference the past.

CONCEPTS OF TIME IN EARLY NEOLITHIC CULTURES

In the last part of this chapter, two case studies, the early Holocene communities of Northern Mesopotamia between 10,000 and 8,800 BCE and the middle to late Pre-Pottery Neolithic cultures of the Levant, will be compared. For archaeological details, the reader is referred to more in-depth records and summaries (for Northern Mesopotamia e.g. Benz et al. 2015; Mazurowski and Kanjou 2012; Miyake et al. 2012; Özdoğan et al. 2011; Schmidt 2011; Stordeur 2015; Yartah 2013; for the Levant e.g. Bienert et al. 2004; Byrd 2005; Gebel 2010, 2017; Kuijt 2000; Kuijt and Goring-Morris 2002; Rollefson 2017).

CASE I: SEDENTARY HUNTER-GATHERERS OF NORTHERN MESOPOTAMIA

Since the discoveries of monumental architecture and permanent villages dating to the 10th millennium BCE[5] along the Middle Euphrates and the Upper Tigris, it has become obvious that early farming communities of Northern Mesopotamia developed from local Epipaleolithic cultures (Benz et al. 2015, 2016; Özkaya and Coşkun 2011). For the reconstruction of concepts of time, the most important observations are

(1) Permanence of settlements and of some buildings, but hardly for longer than one generation (Benz et al. 2015; Schreiber et al. 2014; Stordeur 2015);

(2) Segregation of standardized communal (monumental) buildings from domestic dwellings (Coqueugniot 2014; Mazur-owski and Kanjou 2012; Schmidt 2011; Stordeur 2015; Yartah 2013);

(3) Standardized, common figurative reper-toire represented on various media, from monumental pillars to miniature stone platelets discovered at almost every site (Benz and Bauer 2013; Morenz 2014);

(4) Deliberate destruction of buildings and objects (Benz et al. 2016; Özdoğan and Özdoğan 1998);

(5) No evidence for agriculture but the use of a broad spectrum of wild resources from vari-ous environments (Itahashi et al. 2017; Riehl et al. 2012; Rössner et al. 2018; Savard et al. 2006; Schmidt 2011:41–42; Willcox and Stordeur 2012). It might be possible that specialized hunting, incipient herd manage-ment (Arbuckle and Özkaya 2006; Peters publ. communication Sept. 2014; Rosen-berg et al. 1998) or cultivation (Rössner et al. 2018) were practiced.

Evidence for Episodic Concepts of Time

The eclectic use of various environments reflects a network of sites without strict terri-torial borders. Settlements were not marked by ditches, walls or clustered buildings, but resemble loose aggregations. Also in the internal structuring of the sites no boundaries are visible, neither in building style nor in the repartition of objects. Activity patterns or the distribution of objects has rarely been studied on these sites, but at least for Köritk Tepe it has been shown that there is no intra-site segregation of specific groups (Benz et al. 2016).

Figurative depictions show animals and humans in close relationship. Animals are not dominated by humans, except at Göbekli Tepe. This site is the most ancient place where representations of ("super-") humans in the form of monumental pillars appear in groups, but even these ("super-") humans are covered with animals (Figure 3.3). Göbekli is also the only site where hierarchies of human representations appear, with the pillars dom-inating other human figurines in size (Schmidt 2011). None of the human repre-sentations has individualistic traits (Dietrich et al. 2018). The heads of the stone-pillars have no faces (Schmidt 2011). Moreover, the animals depicted on the pillars are recom-bined in various numbers and versions on different pillars. So a pillar cannot be attrib-uted by its symbols to a specific person/god. It was thus not the individual but a general template that was depicted (Sütterlin 2013:88–95). Such schematic representations hardly fit with linear concepts of the past, but rather with episodic or cyclical thinking.

Evidence for Cyclical Concepts of Time

Northern Mesopotamia is characterized by strong seasonality. The snowmelt from the

FIGURE 3.3 Pillar 56 from Göbekli Tepe, Northern Mesopotamia: Although Göbekli Tepe is the earliest site where human representations dominate animals, some of the pillars were cluttered with depictions of various animals. None of the pillars can be identified by a specific symbol, and their faces remain anonymous. (Foto: N. Becker, DAI Berlin)

Taurus Mountains provides plenty of water during spring, compared to hot and dry summers. This was probably a strong incentive for a cyclical patterning of the year. The movement of wild gazelle may have intensified this. However, because there is no specialization on certain resources, these environmental conditions probably did not influence the prevalent concepts of time too much.

At Körtik Tepe valued objects were destroyed to cover some of the dead. The smashing of objects must have created affective and lasting memories. Although sedentism made the accumulation of objects possible, this deliberate destruction counteracted the accumulation. The lack of other evidence for social differentiation at Körtik Tepe, neither in architecture, nor in gender, diet or health status, underlines the egalitarian ethos (Benz et al. 2016; Koruyucu et al. 2018).

Even more instructive are the discoveries at Göbekli Tepe. The megalithic stone buildings are a gigantesque representation of the cycle, with a clear differentiation of inside and outside, of domestic and ritual. They show constant rebuilding and renovations with minor variations until the buildings were deliberately buried. Deliberate destruction has been evidenced for other communal buildings (Özdoğan and Özdoğan 1998; Stordeur 2015).

The deliberate destruction[6] of buildings and other objects may be interpreted as a conscious decision against the accumulation of wealth and concentration of power. These processes probably created strong collective memories. The place of the oldest backfilled monuments at Göbekli Tepe has never been built over (Schmidt 2011: Figure 2).

In sum, many observations seem to emphasize communal rituals with a focus on repetitive practices. The monumentality and the building material stone at Göbekli Tepe point to the aim of creating an eternal present. The past was the order that had to be maintained. New buildings do not seem to aim at change but copy the ancient standardized patterns (Schmidt 2011; Stordeur 2015). These patterns guide the movements of participants and dictate visual axes (John 2010). The monumentality and the style of the animal representations possibly primed the mind for certain emotions (Benz and Bauer 2015). As Maurice Bloch (2010:149) has proposed for Çatalhöyük, the stability of place implied "not only a static aspect to the perception of the passage of time, but … a concept of replacement of persons", i.e. not the individual but her role was constitutive for the community, mirrored by the anonymous faces. The participants of rituals at Göbekli Tepe thus probably perceived themselves not as individual actors but as part of a preconceived recurrent "drama" (Watkins 2004).

The same holds true for communal buildings at Jerf el Ahmar (Stordeur 2015) and Tell 'Abr 3 (Yartah 2013). Communal buildings still followed ancient ground plans (despite changes in interior layout) when domestic buildings were rectangular.

Domestic buildings at Körtik Tepe also indicate a rather strong building tradition. Multilayered floors were discovered in several buildings (Benz et al. 2015; Schreiber et al. 2014). They indicate constant renovations but possibly no longer than for one generation. No internal subdivision or structuring of internal space was observed (in contrast to later central Anatolian sites like Boncuklu [Baird et al. 2012] or Çatalhöyük [Hodder 2006]). The dead were buried beneath house floors, the burial pits covered with a floor. Graves were neither reopened for further burials, nor were they robbed. There is no evidence that the burials were marked, but the memory must have been transmitted because burials rarely overlap. It thus seems that after a burial the status quo had to be reestablished, and daily life continued above the dead.

The standardization of a symbolic repertoire over a large region created a communication network from northwestern Syria to the Upper Tigris Region (Benz and Bauer 2013; Morenz 2014). However, local traditions in the choice of some motifs, like the enigmatic larvae from Körtik Tepe or the fox at Göbekli Tepe, existed. Strikingly, complete vessels with elaborate "solar" symbols (Özkaya and Coşkun 2011: Figure 20) have never been found outside Körtik Tepe, although the motif itself was copied on various objects, and local copies of the vessels were made. Isolated sherds of this vessel type have been found at Tell Qaramel and Tell 'Abr 3. These sherds do not only provide information on spatial networks, but they also hint at emerging linear concepts of time (Benz et al. 2017a).

Evidence for Linear Concepts of Time

Because no complete vessel with the specific solar decoration has been found outside Körtik Tepe, it can be surmised that some sherds from the burial rituals were deliberately retained and brought to other places. Many of the restored vessels from Körtik Tepe lack a few sherds. Some of the sherds were reworked and very individualistically decorated. These small objects probably activated the memory of a specific communal event (Benz et al. 2017a).

Further evidence for emerging linearity might be installations for storage inside the older communal buildings at Jerf el Ahmar and near domestic dwellings at Körtik Tepe, but the archaeological evidence is poor (Stordeur 2015; Benz et al. 2017b: Figures 5, 9). In line with this observation is a deposit with thousands of beads at Körtik Tepe, which were probably not for personal use, but for exchange. The inhabitants of the early Holocene settlements were involved in a wide network of obsidian exchange (Carter et al. 2013). The uneven distribution of obsidian does not point to cyclical exchange networks. Moreover, the extraction of the raw material, transport and the production of tools required planning and was probably carried out by specialists.[7]

To summarize, there is good evidence for all three concepts of time. Ritual buildings were constantly renovated in the same style, even though innovations in domestic buildings and burials may announce new social structures (Benz et al. 2016; Stordeur 2015). The monumentality of stone buildings implied eternity and preconceived behaviour, obliterating the individual in awe-provoking inertia because any change would require strong efforts of erasing, burning or backfilling. The mediality of these buildings leaves hardly any possibility for reflexivity (Simon 2011). The circular concept of time reflected in the ritual sphere, matches with the segregation between ritual and domestic space and the inside-outside dichotomy.

The accumulation of things was actively hindered by deliberate destruction, reestablishing the status quo. Personal identities were not represented, but schematic templates prevailed (Sütterlin 2013:88–95).

In contrast, domestic settlements and daily subsistence activities were dominated by eclectic exploitation without clear-cut borders, indicating loose networks with episodic concepts of time. Souvenirs and commodities for exchange might point to some linear aspects. Concerning the spatial structure, a wide network of communication and exchange existed, but local communities were beginning to segregate on a symbolic level. As a tentative conclusion it can be suggested:

Hypothesis 4: *Daily practices of hunter-gatherers of Northern Mesopotamia were still deeply rooted in episodic time concepts with open access to various environments. This was mirrored by unbounded settlements and close relationships between animals and humans in figurative art. In contrast, the segregated monumental cult buildings and the standardized symbolic repertoire created repetitive cycles of an eternal present and bounded corporate identities characteristic of circular and linear concepts of time. Slight evidence for emerging linear concepts of time comes from obsidian exchange, possibly storage and the objects kept as souvenirs of specific communal rituals.*

CASE 2: THE MIDDLE TO LATE PRE-POTTERY NEOLITHIC COMMUNITIES OF THE LEVANT

The second case comprises the Middle to Late Pre-Pottery Neolithic cultures of the Central and Southern Levant of the ninth and eighth millenniums BCE (Bienert et al. 2004; Gebel 2010). Given the wide area and time frame, it is evident that not all sites comprise all characteristics. The most important features concerning our study are

(1) Inhabitants practised agriculture and herding with some hunting and collecting (Becker 2004; Neef 2004; Rollefson and Köhler-Rollefson 1989; von den Driesch et al. 2004);

(2) Settlements consisted of clusters of agglutinated buildings (Bienert et al. 2004; Byrd 2005; Gebel et al. 2006a; Kinzel 2013);

(3) Buildings seem to be in constant change (Purschwitz 2017:232–233; Purschwitz

and Kinzel 2007): Certain areas were abandoned, households buried in certain spaces, and other spaces were used as dumping area or burial grounds (Gebel et al. 2017);

(4) Production of specific objects en masse, with the emergence of coupons and commodities (Gebel 2010); hiding of objects (Gebel 2002);

(5) Burials were deposited inside the houses or in between houses in abandoned spaces;

(6) Increase of social differentiation and specialization (Purschwitz 2017:219), increasing importance of familial ties (Alt et al. 2013, 2015);

(7) Veneration of special individuals (Benz 2012; Stordeur and Khawam 2007).

Evidence for Episodic Concepts of Time

There is little evidence for episodic concepts of time. It might be that some hunting events, part-time mobility for herding, or occasional trips to procure raw materials were considered in such a loosely knit sequence of events. In contrast, raw material procurement by specialists (Purschwitz 2017:217–218), would rather hint at linear concepts of time.

Evidence for Cyclical Concepts of Time

Subsistence was dominated by agriculture with recurring cyclical activities. Farming depended on stable social entities to secure work forces. Commitment and trust were as important as planning in order to maintain herds and harvests. Sharing was partially replaced by balanced reciprocity (Benz 2010; Gebel 2010), increasing the need for recording past events (Müller 2005).

The architecture mirrors a closed system due to its agglutinated buildings. The late Pre-Pottery Neolithic B (PPNB) site of Ba'ja on a secluded intermontane plateau illustrates the insular character of such settlements well (Gebel et al. 2017).

One of the means to grant cohesion in these large groups was firm social relations. Epigenetic traits on teeth indicated very close familial ties for the inhabitants of Basta (Alt et al. 2013). Although there is no secure evidence for clan structures, strontium isotopes point to a local origin of these individuals. The architecture seems to underline the importance of familial clusters (Rollefson 2000:184).

Ties to late individuals were created by subfloor burials and special skull burials. Collective burial spaces required a constant reopening of graves and handling of bones (Gebel et al. 2006b). The heads of a few selected individuals were retrieved after death, plastered, exhibited and after some time reburied (Kuijt 1996, 2008). These skulls were plastered in a very individualistic style (Stordeur and Khawam 2007), but most of them were reburied in groups (Kuijt 1996). Personal relations were underlined by the association of infant burials with reburied skulls (Benz 2012).

As Ian Kuijt (2008) has argued, the so-called skull-cult represents cyclical thinking. The exhibition of the skulls stressed continuity. Some of them were even replastered several times (Goren et al. 2001). As long as the skulls were physically present, they were possibly considered members of the communities, granting that old traditions were respected. However, as evidenced by the children burials with which the skulls were reburied and their individuality, there is at least some linear thinking too (Benz 2012). The focus was thus not only on an eternal presence of the past, but also on creating transgenerational relations to and memory of specific individuals.

FIGURE 3.4 Increasing social differentiation manifested by differentiation in burial rituals and elaborate grave constructions beside trash burials and collective burials. Special burial (Loc. 408) from the LPPNB site of Ba'ja, Southern Jordan. (Foto: Ba'ja Neolithic Project, H. G. K. Gebel)

Evidence for Linear Concepts of Time

Evidence for linear concepts of time might come from storage, from the obvious importance of genealogical relations and from the close familial ties in combination with the individualistic style of skull plastering.

Furthermore, communities interacted in exchange of local and exotic commodities. Various commodities were produced for social needs, exchange and/or as recording devices ("coupons") (Hermansen 2004; Gebel 2010:59, figure 19; Purschwitz 2017). The exclusivity of some of these objects indicates restricted access, strong territorial claims and circumscribed identities. The red sand stone rings from Ba'ja are the most famous of these objects: they were produced in almost every household at Ba'ja, but at about 20 km to the southeast, at the contemporary site of Basta, these rings were made of oil-schist and coloured red to make them resemble the Ba'ja rings (Gebel 2010:59; Purschwitz 2017:266). This example of early *product piracy* illustrates what happens when groups start to segregate.

As outlined in the neurobiological section, people tend to assimilate with other group members. In 2016 an elaborate burial was discovered at Ba'ja with an individual who wore two composite arm rings and other jewellery. The grave was clearly delimited by large stones (Gebel et al. 2017) (Figure 3.4). According to the efforts for the construction and the "grave goods", the buried person must have been considered exceptional. At the other end of this hierarchy were individuals buried in so-called trash burials (Gebel et al. 2006b:18; Rollefson 2000:184; see also Price and Bar Yosef 2017:155–159). The higher status of the Ba'ja individual may have instigated the wish of others to get such arm rings too. In case of popularisation of the product, new diacritical means had to be found when status should be represented by objects. As long as this vicious circle was not broken through by ideological concepts that naturalized or legitimized social differences, the production of commodities as diacritical means would never end. It would lead to the continuous production of seemingly "new" objects. With cyclical concepts of time, this vicious circle can be broken by, e.g., proclaiming the status quo as the given order. However, with linear concepts of time, which aim at progress, it is more difficult to counteract the wish to achieve a higher status.

Linear thinking might also be indicated by hiding objects. Such deposits may have served to claim certain spaces, avoiding risks or creating loci of commemoration (Gebel 2002). For our argument it is of relevance that this act represents some kind of contract relating the past, present and future.

The examples from the Levant have shown that the archaeological records can be ambivalent. One and the same context can comprise instances of cyclical and linear concepts of time. Despite this fuzziness, it became clear that with the emergence of "productive milieus" (Gebel 2010, 2017) and hierarchisation episodic concepts were marginalized, whereas cyclical and linear concepts gained in importance. Exchange, accumulation and the storing of goods, exclusive mating systems are means to increase social commitment and lower future risks. The emerging social differentiation probably needed some kind of legitimisation either by territorial or genealogical claims. Both reasoning recur to the past with respect to the future (Assmann 2002:70–71; Müller 2005:44).

Before closing this section, both case studies should be briefly compared. In the Levant, familial relationships were of great importance with mating rules and segregation of sites or "familial shrines" (Rollefson 2000:186). There were common practices such as the exhumation of skulls of selected individuals, but how this ritual was practised varied considerably. Moreover, there is no standardization of symbols or of monumental architecture as in Northern Mesopotamia. This lack of an overarching symbolic system is one of the major differences between both areas and periods (Benz 2012; Benz and Bauer 2013; Gebel 2013, 2017). The prime advantage of such a common symbolic system is its integrative strength irrespective of time or any other criteria (Cohen 1985). This is in contrast to unilineal descent groups, which might represent a "most effective means of maintaining social order" (Rollefson 2017:108), but they run the risk of segregation, competition, inequality and of being unable to integrate heterogeneous groups. In the worst case they perish with the last heir.[8] Their boundedness and the changing personal relations due to death made these communities vulnerable. From this perspective, skull plastering might be interpreted as an effort to overcome time and secure continuity of the *family*.

Hypothesis 5: *With the production and commodification of things an investment into the future becomes a necessity. Creating commitment and loyalties were important aspects to plan the future. Linear and cyclical concepts of time allow such planning.*

Hypothesis 6: *The standardization of a symbolic repertoire (Northern Mesopotamia) with a mainly cyclical concept of time or the legitimation of social groups by genealogical means (Levant) with a more linear concept of time were two different means to promote the shift from flexible networks to durable and fixed group identities.*

Hypothesis 7: *The circumscription of social groups and increasing social differentiation enhanced the need for symbolic display of group/individual identities. Sedentism promoted the objectification of identities. With the increase of linear concepts of time and increasing hierarchisation, assimilation and imitation led to a vicious circle with the need for ever new diacritical means.*

DISCUSSION

This investigation on time concepts in early Neolithic communities has shown that the conception of the past, present and future was of vital importance for the stability of early sedentary groups. The results of socioneuro-biological research underline the decisive role of collective memories for the coherence and identities of larger groups. The possibility to influence memory so that it matches collective ideas (Hirst et al. 2018) turns "history making" (Hodder 2016) into an important sociopolitical tool.

Both case studies have demonstrated that all three concepts of time existed, but that they differed in importance with significantly different effects on social and spatial structures. The main difference was not necessarily between cyclical and linear concepts of time. On the contrary: one context can comprise aspects of linear and cyclical thinking (Assmann 2003:29). The main difference occurred between episodic and linear/cyclical concepts of time. Whereas linear and cyclical concepts operate with circumscribed concepts of space and social identities, episodic concepts of time are characterised by open network structures. Cyclical and linear concepts of time recur to the past, even though they use it in different ways for dealing with the present and future.

The stability of cyclical concepts with an integrative symbolic system has been demonstrated for Northern Mesopotamia. The monumental buildings created networks and feelings of belonging on several levels: during building through communal work and during rituals through emotionally charged art, extraordinary locations and monumentality. They negated time and served as visible, enduring objectifications of that communality. The reduced reflexivity during rituals contrasted with rather flexible space concepts in daily routines.

The communities of the Levant created more instances of linear concepts of time with confined concepts of space in daily life. *Genealogical* ties to specific ancestors probably hint at linear concepts of time. However, as Assmann (2005:132) has pointed out, genealogies can also lose their relevance for linear time concepts, when "dynasties" become petrified and the individual only assumes a role. The high individuality of the plastered skulls indicates that this was not the case during the Neolithic. Increasing segmentation and the lack of an integrative social system may have contributed to the collapse of the mega-sites of the late PPNB (Gebel 2017). The differences in concepts of time between both case studies cannot be ascribed solely to differences between productive and foraging milieus or to differences in population size, as an outlook to the Early Neolithic site of Çatalhöyük might illustrate (Hodder 2006).

Despite similarities in settlement and economy between Çatalhöyük and the PPNB sites, at Çatalhöyük, the rather balanced combination of linear and cyclical concepts of time formed a stable system for more than a millennium. Evidence for linear concepts might come from a plastered skull reburied with a female person, retrieval of objects from earlier houses and the burials beneath house floors and their reopening (Hodder 2016; Hodder and Pels 2010; cf. Carleton et al. 2013). However, biological affinity was not an essential criterion for being buried inside a house, but larger social networks were obviously sustained by subfloor burials (Pilloud and Larsen 2011). Archaeobotanical remains also hint at cooperative structures between households (Bogaard 2017). In contrast to the PPNB of the Levant with emerging hierarchies (Gebel et al. 2017;

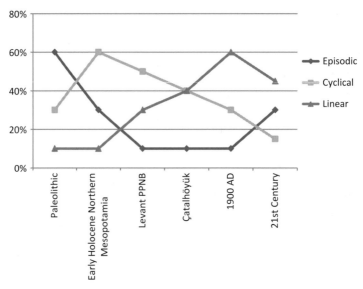

FIGURE 3.5 Hypothetical proportions of episodic, cyclical and linear concepts of time. Percentages are only rough estimates. According to context, social groups and culture, these may vary considerably even within one community.

Rollefson 2017), Ian Hodder (2006:98) described Çatalhöyük as an "egalitarian village". Cyclical concepts of time may be reflected by the constant and almost identical renovation and rebuilding of houses and wall paintings/reliefs.

CONCLUSION

Comparing the different cultural concepts of time provides good evidence that there was not a linear development from episodic to cyclical and linear concepts of time (cf. Assmann and Müller 2005; Wendorf 1985) (Figure 3.5). Linear concepts of time, inherent in all communities, had gained in importance with early sedentary communities, but it took a long time until they dominated in the nineteenth and twentieth centuries. In the long run, it seems that episodic concepts of time reemerge due to their openness and flexibility, whereas cyclical and linear concepts of

time with circumscribed spatial and social identities lead to major contradictions between an ideal state and reality (Connerton 2009).

This does not mean that the innovations achieved since and thanks to the Neolithic are ignored. However, due to the external storage of knowledge, information could be accumulated. Population increase contributed to an accelerated rate of innovations and enhanced collective cognition. It is well known that large and heterogeneous groups perform better than small homogenous groups (Phillips 2015; van Leuwen et al. 2015:1). With agriculture and living in houses, preconceived behaviour increased, guiding the individual but also limiting creativity. Individuals probably perceived themselves first and foremost as part of the group (Rollefson 2017). Planning of the future became an indispensible precondition to stabilize social commitment, trust and economic prosperity (Gintis 2006:397). Whereas people of the tenth millennium BCE still seemed to consider themselves as part of nature, farmers created bounded identities with enhanced emphasis on familial relations, objectified by the accumulation of things. Segregation, commodification and linear concepts of time contributed to the idea that new objects meant progress and innovation per se. However, Neolithic farmers neither had higher capacities of cognition, nor were they more creative or more innovative than Paleolithic hunter-gatherers. Living in larger communities, building on long traditions and having other concepts of time and space altered but did not enhance cognitive capacities of Neolithic people. Above all it made them ever more dependent on things.

ACKNOWLEDGEMENTS

I am grateful to Ian Hodder for the invitation to contribute to this book. Special thanks are due to Hans Georg K. Gebel for inspiring discussions and to Andrew Lawrence for his thoughtful language editing.

REFERENCES

Abbès, F. 2014. The Bal'as Mountains. A different scenario of the Near Eastern Neolithization. In: *La transition néolithique en Méditerranée*, eds. C. Manen, T. Perrin and J. Guilaine. Aix en Provence: Errance. 13–26.

Alexander, B. C. 1991. *Victor Turner Revisited: Ritual as Social Change. Academy Series 74.* Atlanta: Scholars Press.

Alt, K. W., Benz, M., Müller, W., Berner, M. E., Schultz, M., Schmidt-Schultz, T. H., Knipper, C., Gebel, H. G. K., Nissen, H. J. and Vach, W. 2013. Earliest evidence for social endogamy in the 9,000-year-old-population of Basta, Jordan. *PLoS ONE* 8(6):e65649. doi: 10.1371/journal. pone.0065649 PMID: 23776517B.

Alt, K. W., Benz, M., Vach, W., Simmons, T. L. and Goring-Morris, A. N. 2015. Insights into the social structure of the PPNB Site of Kfar HaHoresh, Israel, based on dental remains. *PLoS ONE* 10(9): e0134528. doi:10.1371/journal.pone.0134528.

Arbuckle, B. and Özkaya, V. 2006. Animal exploitation at Körtik Tepe: An early Aceramic Neolithic site in southeastern Turkey. *Paléorient* 32 (2):113–136.

Assmann, J. 2002. *Das kulturelle Gedächtnis. Schrift, Erinnerung und politische Identität in frühen Hochkulturen*, 4th ed. Munich: Beck.

Assmann, J. 2003. *Ägypten, eine Sinngeschichte.* Frankfurt am Main: Fischer.

Assmann, J. 2005. Einführung: Zeit und Geschichte. In: *Der Ursprung der Geschichte. Archaische Kulturen, das Alte Ägypten und das Frühe Griechenland*, eds. J. Assmann and K. E. Müller. Stuttgart: Klett Cotta, 7–16.

Assmann, J. and Müller, K. E., eds., 2005. *Der Ursprung der Geschichte. Archaische Kulturen, das Alte Ägypten und das Frühe Griechenland.* Stuttgart: Klett Cotta.

Baird, D., Fairbairn, A., Martin, L. and Middleton, C. 2012. The Boncuklu Project: The origins of sedentism, cultivation and herding in Central Anatolia. In: *Central Anatolia. The Neolithic in Turkey 3*, eds. M. Özdoğan, N. Başgelen and P. Kuniholm. Istanbul: Archaeology and Art, 219–244.

Bar-Yosef, O. and Valla, F. R., eds. 2013. *Natufian Foragers in the Levant.* International Monographs in Prehistory Archaeological Series 19. Ann Arbor, MI: International Monographs in Prehistory.

Bauer, J. 2013. *Das Gedächtnis des Körpers.* München: Piper.

Becker, C. 2004. On the Identification of sheep and goats: The evidence from Basta. In: *Basta I. The human ecology.* Bibliotheca neolithica Asiae meridionalis et occidentalis & Yamouk University, Monograph of the Faculty of Archaeology and Anthropology 4, eds. H. J. Nissen, M. Muheisen, and H. G. K. Gebel. Berlin: ex oriente, 219–310.

Belfer-Cohen, A. and Goring-Morris, A. N. 2017. "Moving around" and the evolution of corporate identities in the Late Epipalaeolithic Natufian of the Levant. In: *Neolithic Corporate Identities. Studies in Early Near Eastern Production, Subsistence, and Environment 20*, eds. M. Benz, H. G. K. Gebel and T. Watkins. Berlin: ex oriente, 81–90.

Benz, M. 2000. *Die Neolithisierung im Vorderen Orient. Theorien, archäologische Daten und ein ethnologisches Modell*. Studies in Early Near Eastern Production, Subsistence, and Environment 7. Berlin: ex oriente.

Benz, M. 2010. The principle of sharing – an introduction. In: *The Principle of Sharing. Segregation and Construction of Social Identities at the Transition from Foraging to Farming*. Studies in Early Near Eastern Production, Subsistence, and Environment 14, ed. M. Benz. Berlin: ex oriente, 1–17.

Benz, M. 2012. "Little poor babies" – creation of history through death at the transition from foraging to farming. In: *Beyond Elites. Alternatives to Hierarchical Systems in Modelling Social Formations*. Universitätsforschungen zur Prähistorischen Archäologie 215, eds. T. L. Kienlin and A. Zimmermann. Bonn: Habelt, 169–182.

Benz, M. 2017. Changing medialities. Symbols of Neolithic corporate identities. In: *Neolithic Corporate Identities*. Studies in Early Near Eastern Production, Subsistence, and Environment 20, eds. M. Benz, H. G. K. Gebel and T. Watkins. Berlin: ex oriente, 135–156.

Benz, M. and Bauer, J. 2013. Symbols of power – symbols of crisis? A psycho-social approach to Early Neolithic symbol systems. *Neo-Lithics* 2/13:11–24.

Benz, M. and Bauer, J. 2015. On scorpions, birds, and snakes: Evidence for shamanism in Northern Mesopotamia during the Early Holocene. *Journal of Ritual Studies* 29(2):1–24.

Benz, M. and Gramsch, A. 2006. Zur soziopolitischen Bedeutung von Festen. Eine Einführung anhand von Beispielen aus dem Alten Orient und Europa. *Ethnographisch Archäologische Zeitschrift* 47:417–437.

Benz, M., Alt, K. W., Erdal, Y. S., Şahin, F. S. and Özkaya, V. 2017a. Re-presenting the past. Evidence from daily practices and rituals at Körtik Tepe. In: *Religion, History and Place in the Origin*

of Settled Life, ed. I. Hodder. Boulder: The University Press of Colorado, Utah State University Press.

Benz, M., Deckers, K., Rößner, C., Alexandrovskiy, A., Pustovoytov, K., Scheeres, M., Fecher, M., Coşkun, A., Riehl, S., Alt, K. W. and Özkaya, V. 2015. Prelude to village life. Environmental data and building traditions of the Epipalaeolithic settlement at Körtik Tepe, Southeast Turkey. *Paléorient* 41(2):9–30.

Benz, M., Erdal, Y. S., Şahin, F. S., Özkaya, V. and Alt, K. W. 2016. The equality of inequality. Social differentiation among the hunter-fisher-gatherer community of Körtik Tepe, Southeastern Turkey. In: *Rich and Poor – Competing for Resources in Prehistory*. Tagungen des Landesmuseums für Vorgeschichte Halle 13, eds. H. Mellart, H. P. Hahn, R. Jung and R. Risch. Halle: Landesamt für Denkmalpflege und Archäologie Sachsen Anhalt, Landesmuseum für Vorgeschichte Halle (Saale), 147–164.

Benz, M., Willmy, A., Doğan, F., Šahin, F. S. and Özkaya, V. 2017b. A burnt pit house, large scale roasting, and enigmatic Epipaleolithic structures at Körtik Tepe. Southeastern Turkey. *Neo-Lithics* 1/17:3–12.

Bienert, H.-D., Gebel, H. G. K. and Neef, R., eds. 2004. *Central Settlements in Neolithic Jordan*. Studies in Early Near Eastern Production, Subsistence, and Environment 5. Berlin: ex oriente.

Bloch, M. 2010. Is there religion at Çatalhöyük … or are there just houses? In: *Religion in the Emergence of Civilization. Çatalhöyük as a Case Study*, ed. I. Hodder. Cambridge, UK: Cambridge University Press, 146–62.

Blumler, H. 2013. *Symbolischer Interaktionismus. Aufsätze zu einer Wissenschaft der Interpretation*. Berlin: Suhrkamp.

Bogaard, A. 2017. Neolithic "cooperatives": Assessing supra-household cooperation in crop production at Çatalhöyük and beyond. In: *Neolithic Corporate Identities*. Studies in Early Near Eastern Production, Subsistence, and Environment 20, eds. M. Benz, H. G. K. Gebel and T. Watkins. Berlin: ex oriente, 119–133.

Bradley, R. 2002. *The Past in Prehistoric Societies*. London/New York: Springer.

Brewer, M. B. 1991. The social self: On being the same and different at the same time. *Personality and Social Psychology Bulletin* 17(5):475–482.

Byrd, B. 2005. *Early Village Life at Beidha, Jordan: Neolithic Spatial Organization and Vernacular Architecture*. British Academy Monographs in Archaeology 14. Oxford, UK: Oxford University Press.

Carleton, C., Conolly, J. and Collard, M. 2013. Corporate kin-groups, social memory, and "history houses"? A quantitative test of recent reconstructions of social organization and building function at Çatalhöyük during the PPNB. *Journal of Archaeological Science* 40(4):1816–1822.

Carter, T., Grant, S., Kartal, M., Coşkun, A. and Özkaya, V. 2013. Networks and Neolithisation: Sourcing obsidian from Körtik Tepe (SE Anatolia). *Journal of Archaeological Science* 40(1):556–569.

Cauvin, J. 1997. *Naissance des divinités. Naissance de l'agriculture*. Paris: CNRS.

Chapman, J. 2000. *Fragmentation in Archaeology. People, Places and Broken Objects in the Prehistory of South-eastern Europe*. New York: Routledge.

Cohen, A. P. 1985. *The Symbolic Construction of Community*. Chichester, UK: Ellis Horwood.

Connerton, P. 2009. *How Modernity Forgets*. Cambridge, UK: University Press.

Coqueugniot, E. 2014. Dja'de (Syrie) et les représentations symboliques au IXe millénaire cal BC. In: *La transition néolithique en Méditerranée*, eds. C. Manen, T. Perrin and J. Guilaine. Aix en Provence: Errance, 91–108.

Dietrich, O., Notroff, J. and Dietrich, L. 2018. Masks and masquerade in Early Neolithic: A view from Upper Mesopotamia. *Time and Mind* 11(1):3–21.

Dunbar, R. I. M. 1992. Coevolution of neocortex size, group size and language in humans. *Behavioral and Brain Sciences* 16:681–735.

Dunbar, R. I. M. 2013. What makes the Neolithic so special? *Neo-Lithics* 2/13:25–29.

Dunbar, R. I. M., Gamble, C. and Gowlett, J. 2010. The social brain and the distributed mind. *Proceedings of the British Academy* 158:3–15.

Edelson, M., Sharot, T., Dolan, R. J. and Dudai, Y. 2011. Following the crowd: Brain substrates of long-term memory conformity. *Science* 333(6038):108–111.

Gebel, H. G. K. 2002. Walls. Loci of forces. In: *Magic Practices and Ritual in the Near Eastern Neolithic*. Studies of Early Near Eastern Production, Subsistence and Environment 8, eds. H. G. K. Gebel, B. D. Hermansen and C. H. Jensen. Berlin: ex oriente, 119–132.

Gebel, H. G. K. 2010. Commodification and the formation of Early Neolithic social identity. The issues as seen from the Jordanian Highlands. In: *The Principle of Sharing and Construction of Social Identities at the Transition from Foraging to Farming*. Studies of Early Near Eastern Production, Subsistence and Environment 14, ed. M. Benz. Berlin: ex oriente, 35–80.

Gebel, H. G. K. 2013. The territoriality of Early Neolithic symbols and ideocracy. *Neo-Lithics* 2/13:39–41.

Gebel, H. G. K. 2014. Territoriality in early Near Eastern sedentism. *Neo-Lithics* 14/2:23–44.

Gebel, H. G. K. 2017. Neolithic corporate identities in the Near East. In: *Neolithic Corporate Identities*. Studies of Early Near Eastern Production, Subsistence and Environment 20, eds. M. Benz, H. G. K. Gebel and T. Watkins. Berlin: ex oriente, 57–80.

Gebel, H. G. K, Benz, M., Purschwitz, C., Kubíková, B., Stefaniško, D., al-Souliman, A. S., Tucker, K., Gresky, J. and Abuhelaleh, B. 2017. Household and death: Preliminary results of the 11th Season (2016) at Late PPNB Ba'ja, Southern Jordan. *Neo-Lithics* 17/1:18–36.

Gebel, H. G. K, Hermansen, B. D. and Kinzel, M. 2006b. Ba'ja 2005: A two-storied building and collective burials. Results of the 6th season of excavation. *Neo-Lithics* 1/06:12–19.

Gebel, H. G. K., Nissen, H. J. and Zaid, Z., eds. 2006a. *Basta II. The Architecture and Stratigraphy*. Bibliotheca neolithica Asiae meridionalis et occidentalis & Yamouk University, Monograph of the Faculty of Archaeology and Anthropology 5. Berlin: ex oriente.

Gintis, H. 2006. Moral sense and material interests. *Social Research* 73(2):377–404.

Goren, Y., Goring-Morris, A. N. and Segal, I. 2001. The technology of skull modelling in the Pre-Pottery Neolithic B (PPNB): Regional variability, the relation of technology and iconography and their archaeological implications. *Journal of Archaeological Science* 28:671–690.

Guenther, M. 2010. Sharing among the San, today, yesterday and in the past. In: *The Principle of Sharing – Segregation and Construction of Social Identities at the Transition from Foraging to Farming*. Studies in Near Eastern Production, Subsistence, and Environment 14, ed. M. Benz. Berlin: ex oriente, 105–135.

Haun, D. B. M., van Leeuwen, E. J. C. and Edelson, M. G. 2013. Majority influence in children and other animals. *Developmental Cognitive Neuroscience* 3:61–71.

Haun, D. B. M., Rekers, Y. and Tomasello, M. 2014. Children conform to the behavior of peers; other great apes stick with what they know. *Psychological Science* 25(12):2160–2167.

Hayden, B. 2014. *The Power of Feasts. From Prehistory to the Present*. Cambridge, UK: Cambridge University Press.

Helfrich, H. 1996. Psychology of time from a cross-cultural perspective. In: *Time and Mind*, ed. H. Helfrich. Seattle, WA: Hogrefe & Huber, 105–120.

Helfrich, H. 2011. Kultur und Zeit. In: *Perspektiven interkultureller Kompetenz*, eds. W. Dreyer and U. Hößler. Göttingen: Vandenhoeck & Ruprecht. 125–136.

Hermansen, B. D. 2004. *Raw material of the small finds industries*. In: *Basta I. The Human Ecology*, eds. Nissen, H. J., Muheisen, M. and Gebel, H. G. K. Bibliotheca neolithica Asiae meridionalis et occidnetalis & Yamouk University, Monograph of the Faculty of Archaeology and Anthropology 4. Berlin: ex oriente, 117–128.

Hirst, W., Yamashiro, J. K. and Coman, A. 2018. Review. Collective memory from a psychological perspective. *Trends in Cognitive Sciences* 22 (5):438–451.

Hodder, I. 2016. More on history houses at Çatalhöyük: A response to Carleton et al. *Journal of Archaeological Science* 67:1–6.

Hodder, I. 2006. *The Leopard's Tale. Revealing the Mysteries of Çatalhöyük*. London: Thames & Hudson.

Hodder, I. 1990. *The Domestication of Europe*. Oxford [etc.], UK: Basil Blackwell.

Hodder, I. and Pels, P. 2010. History houses: A new interpretation of architectural elaboration at Çatalhöyük. In: *Religion in the Emergence of Civilization. Çatalhöyük as a Case Study*, ed. I. Hodder. Cambridge, UK: Cambridge University Press, 163–186.

Hodder, I. and Meskell, L. 2011. A 'Curious and Sometimes a Trifle Macabre Artistry'. *Current Anthropology* 52(2):235–263.

Holtorf, C. 2005. Geschichtskultur in ur- und frühgeschichtlichen Kulturen Europs. In: *Der Ursprung der Geschichte. Archaische Kulturen, das Alte Ägypten und das Frühe Griechenland*, eds. J. Assmann and K. E. Müller. Stuttgart: Klett Cotta, 87–111.

Hornsey, M. J. and Jetten, J. 2004. The Individual within the group: Balancing the need to belong with the need to be different. *Personality and Social Psychology Review* 8(3):248–264.

Itahashi, Y., Miyake, Y., Maeda, O., Kondo, O., Hongo, H., Van Neer, W., Chikaraishi, Y., Ohkouchi, N. and Yoneda, M. 2017. Preference for fish in a Neolithic hunter-gatherer community of the upper Tigris, elucidated by amino acid δ 15 N analysis. *Journal of Archaeological Science* 82. DOI: 10.1016/j.jas.2017.05.001.

John, E. 2010. The fixed versus the flexible – Or how space for rituals is created. In: *The Principle of Sharing and Construction of Social Identities at the Transition from Foraging to Farming*. Studies of Early Near Eastern Production, Subsistence and Environment 14, ed. M. Benz. Berlin: ex oriente, 203–212.

Kinzel, M. 2013. *Am Beginn des Hausbaus. Studien zur PPNB Architektur von Shkārat Msaied und Ba'ja in der Petra-Region, Südjordanien*. Studies in Early Near Eastern Production, Subsistence, and Environment 17. Berlin: ex oriente.

Koruyucu, M. M., Şahin, F. S., Delibaş, D., Erdal, Ö. D., Benz, M., Özkaya, V. and Erdal, Y. 2018. Auditory exostosis: Exploring the daily life at an early sedentary population (Körtik Tepe, Turkey). *Journal of Osteoarchaeology* 1–11.

Kretzer, D. I. 2013. Ritual, Politik und Macht. In: *Ritualtheorien. Ein einführendes Handbuch*, eds. A. Belliger and D. J. Krieger. Wiesbaden: Springer, 361–386.

Kuijt, I. 1996 *New Perspectives on Old Territories: Ritual Practices and the Emergence of Social Complexity in the Levantine Neolithic.* UMI Microform.

Kuijt, I., ed., 2000. *Life in Neolithic Farming Communities: Social Organisation, Identity and Differentiation.* New York: Academic/Plenum Publishers.

Kuijt, I. 2008. The regeneration of life. Neolithic structures of symbolic remembering and forgetting. *Current Anthropology* 49:171–197.

Kuijt, I. and Goring-Morris, A. N. 2002. Foraging, farming, and social complexity in the Pre-Pottery Neolithic of the Southern Levant: A review and synthesis. *Journal of World Prehistory* 16(4):361–440.

Lakin, J. L., Chartrand, T. L. and Arkin, R.M. 2008. I am too just like you: Nonconscious behavioral response to social exclusion. *Psychological Science* 19(8):816–822.

Lang, C., Peters, J., Pöllath, N., Schmidt, K. and Grupe, G. 2013. Gazelle behaviour and human presence at early Neolithic Göbekli Tepe, southeast Anatolia. *World Archaeology* 45(3):410–429.

Maher, L. A., Richter, T., Macdonald, D., Jones, M. D., Martin, L. and Stock, J. T. 2012. Twenty thousand-year-old huts at a hunter-gatherer settlement in Eastern Jordan. *PLoS ONE* 7(2):e31447.

Mazurowski, R. F. and Kanjou, Y., eds. 2012. *Tell Qaramel 1999–2007. Protoneolithic and Early Pre-Pottery Neolithic Settlement in Northern Syria.* Polish Center of Mediterranean Archaeology Excavation Series 2. Warsaw: University of Warsaw.

Miyake, Y., Maeda, O., Tanno, K., Hongo, H. and Gündem, C. Y. 2012. New excavations at Hasankeyf Höyük: A 10th millennium cal. BC site on the Upper Tigris, Southeast Anatolia. *Neo-Lithics* 1/12: 3–7.

Morenz, L. D. 2014. *Medienrevolution und die Gewinnung neuer Denkräume. Das frühneolithische Zeichensystem (10./9. Jt. v. Chr.) und seine Folgen. Studia Euphratica 1.* Berlin: EB Verlag.

Müller, K. E. 2005. Der Usprung der Geschichte. In: *Der Ursprung der Geschichte. Archaische Kulturen, das Alte Ägypten und das Frühe Griechenland,* eds. J. Assmann and K. E. Müller. Stuttgart: Klett Cotta, 17–86.

Neef, R. 2004. Vegetation and plant husbandry. In: *Basta I. The Human Ecology.* Bibliotheca neolithica Asiae meridionalis et occidnetalis & Yamouk University, Monograph of the Faculty of Archaeology and Anthropology 4, eds. Nissen, H. J., Muheisen, M. and Gebel H. G. K. Berlin: ex oriente, 187–218.

Over, H. 2015. The origins of belonging: Social motivation in infants and young children. *Philosophical Transactions of the Royal Society B* 371:20150072. https://dx.doi.org/10.1098/rstb./2015.0072.

Özdoğan, M. and Özdoğan, A. 1998. Buildings of cult and the cult of buildings. In: *Light on Top of the Black Hill: Studies Presented to Halet Cambel,* eds. G. Arsebük, M. Mellink and W. Schirmer. Istanbul: Ege Yayinlari, 581–601.

Özdoğan, M., Başgelen, N. and Kuniholm, P., eds., 2011. *The Neolithic in Turkey 1. The Tigris Basin.* Istanbul: Archaeology & Art.

Özkaya, V. and Coşkun, A. 2011. Körtik Tepe. In: *The Neolithic in Turkey 1, The Tigris Basin,* eds. M. Özdoğan, N. Başgelen and P. Kuniholm. Istanbul: Archaeology & Art, 89–127.

Phillips, K. W. 2015. Der Vorteil sozialer Vielfalt. *Spektrum der Wissenschaft* 7:63–66.

Pilloud, M. A. and Larsen, C. S. 2011. "Official" and "practical" kin: Inferring social and community structure from dental phenotype at Neolithic Çatalhöyük, Turkey. *American Journal of Physical Anthropology* 145:519–530.

Price, T. D. and Bar-Yosef, O. 2017. Traces of inequality at the origins of agriculture in the ancient Near East. In: *Pathways to Power. New Perspectives on the Emergence of Social Inequality,* eds. T. D. Price and G. M. Feinman. New York: Springer, 147–168.

Purschwitz, C. 2017. *Die lithische Ökonomie von Feuerstein im Frühneolithikum der Größeren Petra Region.* Studies in Early Near Eastern Production, Subsistence, and Environment 19. Berlin: ex oriente.

Purschwitz, C. and Kinzel, M. 2007. Ba'ja 2007: Two room and ground floor fills: Reconstructed house-life scenarios. *Neo-Lithics* 2/07: 22–35.

Renfrew, C. 2005. Mind and matter: Cognitive archaeology and external symbolic storage. In: *Cognition and Material Culture: The Archaeology of Symbolic Storage,* eds. C. Renfrew and C. Scarre.

Oxford, UK: Oxbow Books, McDonald Institute Monographs. 1–6.

Riehl, S., Benz, M., Conard, N., Darabi H., Deckers, K., Našlı H. F. and Zeidi-Kulehparcheh, M. 2012. Plant use in three Pre-Pottery Neolithic sites of the northern and eastern Fertile Crescent – A preliminary report. *Vegetation History and Archaeobotany* 21(2):95–106.

Rizzolatti, G. and Sinigaglia, C. 2008. *Empathie und Spiegelneurone. Die biologische Basis des Mitgefühls.* Edition unseld. Frankfurt am Main: Suhrkamp.

Rössner, C., Deckers, K., Benz, M., Özkaya, V. and Riehl, S. 2018. Subsistence strategies and vegetation development at Aceramic Neolithic Körtik Tepe, Southeastern Anatolia. *Vegetation History and Archaeobotany*, 27(1):15–29. doi.org/10.1007/s00334-017-0641-z.

Rollefson, G. O. 2017. "I am we": The display of socioeconomic politics of Neolithic commodification. In: *Neolithic Corporate Identities.* Studies in Early Near Eastern Production, Subsistence, and Environment 20, eds. M. Benz, H. G. K. Gebel and T. Watkins. Berlin: ex oriente. 107–116.

Rollefson, G. O. 2000. Ritual and social structure at Neolithic 'Ain Ghazal. In: *Life in Neolithic Farming Communities: Social Organisation, Identity and Differentiation,* ed. I. Kuijt. New York: Academic/Plenum Publishers, 165–190.

Rollefson, G. O. and Köhler-Rollefson, I. 1989. The collapse of early Neolithic settlements in the Southern Levant. In: *People and Culture in Change. Proceedings of the Second Symposium on Upper Palaeolithic, Mesolithic and Neolithic Populations of Europe and the Mediterranean Basin.* BAR International Series 508:1–2, ed. I. Hershkovitz. Oxford, UK: BAR, 73–89.

Rosenberg, M., Nesbitt, R., Redding, R. W. and Peasnall, B. L. 1998. Hallan Çemi, pig husbandry, and post-Pleistocene adaptations along the Taurus-Zagros Arc (Turkey). *Paléorient* 24(1): 25–41.

Safranski, R. 2017. *Zeit. Was sie mit uns macht und was wir aus ihr machen,* 2nd ed. Frankfurt am Main: Fischer.

Savard, M., Nesbitt, M. and Jones, M. K. 2006. The role of wild grasses in subsistence and sedentism: New evidence from the northern Fertile Crescent. *World Archaeology* 38(2):179–196.

Schmidt, K. 2011. Göbekli Tepe. In: *The Neolithic in Turkey 2. The Euphrates Basin,* eds. M. Özdoğan, N. Başgelen and P. Kuniholm. Istanbul: Archaeology & Art, 41–83.

Schreiber, F., Coşkun, A., Benz, M., Alt, K. W. and Özkaya, V., with contributions from Reifarth N. and Völling, E. 2014. Multilayer floors in the Early Holocene houses at Körtik Tepe, Turkey – an example from House Y98. *Neo-Lithics 2/14:13–22.*

Simon, U. 2011. Reflexivity and discourse on ritual. Introductory reflexions. In: *Ritual Dynamics and the Science of Ritual IV. Reflexivity, Media, and Visuality,* ed. A. Michaels. Wiesbaden: Harrassowitz, 3–23.

Steets, S. 2015. *Der sinnhafte Aufbau der gebauten Welt. Eine Architektursoziologie.* Berlin: Suhrkamp.

Stordeur, D. 2015. *Le village de Jerf el Ahmar (Syrie, 9500–8700 av. J.-C.). L'architecture, miroir d'une société néolithique complexe.* Paris: CNRS Editions.

Stordeur, D. and Ibáñez, J. J. 2008. Stratigraphie et répartition des architectures à Mureybet. In: *Le site néolithique de Tell Mureybet (Syrie du Nord) I.* British Archaeological Reports. International Series 1843 (2), ed. J. J. Ibáñez. Oxford: Archaeopress, 33–95.

Stordeur, D. and Khawam, R. 2007. Les crânes surmodelés de Tell Aswad (PPNB, Syrie). Première regard sur l'ensemble, premières réflexions. *Syria* 84:5–32.

Sütterlin, C. 2013. *Urbilder, Suchbilder, Trugbilder. Inszenierungen und Rituale des Sehens. Kunst zwischen Kultur und Evolution.* Historisch-anthropologische Studien. Frankfurt am Main: Peter Lang.

Tambini, A., Rimmele, U., Phelps, E. A. and Dvachi, L. 2017. Emotional brain states carry over and enhance future memory formation. *Nature Neuroscience* 20(2):271–278.

Tarr, B., Launay, J., Cohen, E. and Dunbar, R. 2015. Synchrony and exertion during dance independently raise pain threshold and encourage social bonding. *Biology Letters* 11:20150767. http://dx.doi.org/10.1098/rsbl.2015.0767.

Theweleit, K. 2013. An entirely new interaction with the animal world? *Neo-Lithics* 2/13:57–60.

Thomas, N. 1998. Foreword. In: *Art and Agency. An Anthropological Theory*. A. Gell. Oxford, UK: Clarendon Press, vii–xiii.

Van Leeuwen, E. J. C., Kendal, R. L., Tennie, C. and Haun D. B. M. 2015. Conformity and its look-a-likes. *Animal Behaviour* 2015 e1–e4. http://dx.doi.org/10/j.anbehav.2015.07.030.

Van Leeuwen, E. J. C., Cohen, E., Collier-Baker, E., Rapold, C. J., Schäfer, M., Schütte, S. and Haun D. B. M. 2018. The development of human social learning across seven societies. *Nature Communications* 9(2076):1–7. DOI: 10.1038/s41467-018-04468-2.

Von den Driesch, A., Cartajena, I. and Manhart, H. 2004. The late PPNB site of Ba'ja, Jordan: The faunal remains (1997 season). In: *Central Settlements in Neolithic Jordan*. Studies in Early Near Eastern Production, Subsistence, and Environment 5, eds. H.-D. Bienert, G. H. K. Gebel and R. Neef. Berlin: ex oriente. 271–288.

Watkins, T. 2004. Architecture and 'theatres of memory' in the Neolithic South West Asia. In: *Rethinking Materiality: The Engagement of Mind with the Material World*, eds. E. DeMarrais, C. Gosden and C. Renfrew. Cambridge, UK: McDonald Institute of Archaeological Research, 97–106.

Watkins, T. 2010. Changing people, changing environments: How hunter-gatherers became communities that changed the world. In: *Landscapes in Transition: Understanding Hunter-Gatherer and Farming Landscapes in the Early Holocene of Europe and the Levant*. Levant Supplementary Series 8, eds. B. Finlayson and G. Warren. Oxford, Oakville: CBRL and Oxbow Books, 104–112.

Watkins, T. 2012. Household, community, and social landscape: Maintaining social memory in the Early Neolithic of Southwest Asia. In: *'As time goes by?' — Monumentality, Landscapes and the Temporal Perspective*. Universitätsforschungen zur Prähistorischen Archäologie 206, eds. M. Furholt, M. Hinz and D. Mischka. Bonn: Habelt, 23–44.

Weidenhaus, G. 2015. *Soziale Raumzeit*. Berlin: Suhrkamp.

Weiss, E., Wetterstrom, W., Nadel, D., Bar-Yosef, O. and Smith, B. D. 2004. The Broad Spectrum revisited: Evidence from plant remains. *PNAS* 101/26:9551–9555.

Wendorf, R. 1985. *Zeit und Kultur. Geschichte des Zeitbewusstseins in Europa*, 3rd ed. Opladen: Westdeutscher Verlag.

Whitehouse, H. 2000. *Arguments and Icons: Divergent Modes of Religiosity*. Oxford, UK: University Press.

Widlok, T. 2013. Ritualökonomie. In: *Ritual und Ritualdynamik*, eds. C. Brosius, A. Michaels and P. Schrode. Göttingen: UTB. Vandehoek & Ruprecht, 171–179.

Widlok, T. 2017. *Anthropology and the Economy of Sharing*. London: Routledge.

Willcox, G. and Stordeur, D. 2012. Large-scale cereal processing before domestication during the tenth millennium cal BC in northern Syria. *Antiquity* 86 (331): 99–114.

Winkelman, M. 2002. Shamanism and cognitive evolution. *Cambridge Archaeological Journal* 12 (1):71–101.

Wittmann, M. 2013. The inner sense of time. *Nature Reviews Neuroscience* 14(3):217–223.

Woodburn, J. 1988. African hunter-gatherer social organization: Is it best understood as a product of encapsulation? In: *Hunter and Gatherers 1. History, Evolution and Social Change*, eds. T. Ingold, J. Woodburn and D. Riches. Oxford, UK: Berg, 31–64.

Wulf, C. 2005. *Zur Genese des Sozialen: Mimesis, Performativität, Ritual*. Bielefeld: transcript.

Yartah, T. 2013. *Vie quotidienne, vie communautaire et symbolique à Tell 'Abr 3 – Syrie du Nord. Données nouvelles et nouvelles réflexions sur l'horizon PPNA au nord du Levant. 10 000–9000 BP*. PhD Thesis. Lyon: University of Lyon.

4

COGNITIVE CHANGE AND MATERIAL CULTURE

A Distributed Perspective

Michael Wheeler

Whichever way one looks at it, studying ancient minds is a challenge. This is largely because the main investigative strategies that have proven to be so successful in unravelling the secrets of modern minds are rendered unavailable. Long-dead subjects cannot sign up for reaction time laboratory experiments, and decomposed brains aren't suitable for neuroimaging. Call this epistemological quandary 'the problem of ancient minds'. Given that the questions addressed by this volume concern the existence and character of changes in consciousness and cognition at the Neolithic site of Çatalhöyük, there seems little doubt that the problem of ancient minds will be prowling the pages of the various chapters, just itching to make a nuisance of itself.

Of course, human ingenuity knows no bounds, and various canny tactics have been deployed to make progress against the problem, in its general form. For example, in one branch of so-called neuroarchaeology, living human beings have their brains scanned while performing the same tasks as were performed by our ancient ancestors (e.g. making certain tools). On the strength of preexisting hypotheses from cognitive neuroscience about the psychological functions of the neural areas thereby activated, these experiments generate inferences about which cognitive capacities are required for the execution of the tasks in question, and thereby about the cognitive capacities that must have been present in ancient minds (for a paradigmatic example of this research programme in action, see e.g. Putt et al. 2017).

One way of thinking about what's going on in such neuroarchaeological experiments is to note that the physical machinery whose contribution forms the ultimate target of the investigation is (was) located inside the skull and skin of the cognitive agent. Of course, there are relevant elements located outside the skull and skin too – e.g. tools, artefacts and the other constituents of material culture – and these form part of the traditional, routine business of archaeological research.

On the face of things, however, the difficulty, when one's topic is ancient *minds*, is that such external elements are not themselves constituents of our ancestors' psychological machinery. They are 'merely' the products of that machinery and/or items with which the ancient inner psychological machinery of interest once interacted. So, for the archaeologist interested in ancient minds, the struggle, it might seem, is to find reliable ways of using what evidence and resources we do have to uncover the character and structure of the missing ancient inner, *because that's where the minds in question were.*

For some (although not all) readers, the idea that ancient minds were located inside ancient heads will seem to follow pretty much directly from the undeniable thought that ancient brains were located inside ancient heads, on the grounds that, to the extent that it makes sense to talk about minds being located at all, minds are always located where brains are. Fuelled most recently by the excitement surrounding contemporary brain-imaging techniques, there is no doubt that, right now, this neuro-centric conception of mind is the default view in cognitive psychology, developmental psychology, cognitive-science-friendly philosophy, and indeed in many other intellectual disciplines that concern themselves in one way or another with psychological phenomena. Importantly, in the present context, the reach of such neuro-centrism extends not only to neuroarchaeology, but also to cognitive archaeology in general, understood as the broader endeavour to study the minds of our human ancestors, based upon the surviving material archaeological remains and by drawing on the theories and concepts deployed by contemporary cognitive science. (For just one pioneering example of the broader endeavour, see Mithen 1996.)

Notwithstanding the overall dominance of neuro-centrism, however, the fact remains that, even within cognitive science itself, there is an increasingly prominent alternative. According to the *distributed* view (often traced first to Hutchins 1995), cognition (understood liberally as encompassing mind, thought, intelligence, reasoning, emotions, feelings and experience – in short, the psychological) is, at least sometimes, in some way, spread out over the brain, the non-neural body and, in many paradigm cases, an environment consisting of objects, tools, other artefacts, texts, individuals and/or social/institutional structures. The phrase 'in some way' introduces a deliberate vagueness into the specification of the distributed view. As we shall see later, how one fills in the details of the 'spreading' at issue will determine whether the distributed view is, at a fundamental (one might even say 'metaphysical') level, an illuminating modulation of the neuro-centric view or an altogether more surprising position. For now, however, what's important is this: in both of the forms in which we shall consider it later, the distributed perspective highlights the important roles that external elements routinely play in experience, thought, reason and so on, but it does so without seeking to marginalize the manifest importance of the brain in the generation of these phenomena. Rather, it aims to place proper emphasis on the point that, to understand what the brain actually does, one needs to take account of the subtle, complex and often surprising ways in which that organ is enmeshed with non-neural bodily and environmental factors.

To give the flavour of distributed cognition, here's a brief description of what is now a canonical example. Early modern theatre companies performed an astonishing number of plays (as many as six different plays a week), with relatively infrequent repetition, very little group rehearsal, each actor playing multiple roles, and in the face of mounting a new play roughly every fortnight. If we imagine a scenario in which each actor was required to store each of these plays in his brain, it seems that we would be forced to conclude that early modern actors possessed super-human organic memory capacities. This seems unlikely, so how did they do it? Adopting a distributed perspective, Tribble (2005, 2011) argues that a number of tricks and ploys resulted in the seemingly prohibitive information processing required being spread out over the individual actor and the physical and social environments of the early modern theatre, thus rendering it manageable. For example, stripped-down manuscript parts that excised all unnecessary information (including the other parts, save for sparse line cues) were used in conjunction with what were called 'plots' – sheets of paper containing scene-by-scene accounts of entrances and exits, casting, and sound and music cues. This external scaffolding worked by assuming both the particular three-dimensional organization of the physical theatrical space (e.g. the door arrangements on the early modern stage) and certain conventions of movement that were operative in theatre at the time (meaning that the door through which an actor is to enter or exit is hardly ever specified in the aforementioned plots). Finally, various guild-like social structures and protocols supported the development of apprentice actors, enabling them to perform progressively more complex roles.

How does the distributed cognition paradigm bear on our present, archaeological concerns? Given that the environmental factors highlighted by the distributed perspective include items of material culture, it is tempting to see a symbiotic connection between that cognitive-scientific approach and archaeology, especially in contexts where archaeologists seek to draw conclusions about the human mind from material-cultural evidence. The background picture at work in the distributed perspective is of 'our distinctive universal human nature, insofar as it exists at all, [as] a nature of biologically determined openness to deep, learning- and development-mediated, change' (Wheeler and Clark 2008, 3572) and thus, given a technologically saturated environment, of human organisms as what Clark (2003) calls *natural born cyborgs*, creatures who are naturally evolved, both now and in the ancient past, to seek out intimate couplings with the non-biological resources of material culture. Crucially, as should be clear already, such couplings extend to the achievement of psychological feats such as, for example, memory and reasoning. Moreover, in a process that Clark has dubbed *cognitive niche construction* (e.g. Clark 2008; see also Wheeler and Clark 2008), which is nicely illustrated by the foregoing example of distributed memory in the early modern theatre, human beings design and build external structures that, often in combination with culturally transmitted practices, transform problem spaces in ways that typically promote, but sometimes (when things go wrong) obstruct, thinking and reasoning.

It is tempting to propose that when the problem of ancient minds is approached from the distributed perspective, that problem will lose much of its bite. After all, the idea that human cognition is shaped fundamentally by organic-technological hybridization might reasonably indicate that we ought to be able to say quite a lot about ancient minds from the archaeological evidence provided by the technology and material culture with which those minds were, by hypothesis, intimately coupled. Indeed, within recent archaeological theorizing, it might seem to be the explicitly distributed dimension of Malafouris's increasingly influential *material engagement theory* that enables him to use material culture as a productive bridge between experiential, conceptual, and social aspects of the self (Malafouris 2013). And one can feel the same putatively beneficial mutuality bubbling away just beneath the surface in the argument by Hodder in Chapter 1 regarding, specifically, cognition in the Neolithic period that, given the notion of a contextually distributed and plastic mind, it is reasonable to expect that the Neolithic, with its panoply of new techniques and ways of life, would be associated with cognitive change.

In this chapter, I shall interrogate the apparent symbiosis between the archaeology of cognition and the distributed perspective. I shall argue that, once one accepts that cognition is distributed, settling the nature of ancient thought, and, more particularly, determining whether cognitive change has occurred, on the basis of material-cultural

evidence, is a rather more complicated business than one might have imagined. My case study will be the alleged emergence of higher levels of cognition and consciousness in the Neolithic, as indicated by the material-cultural evidence at Çatalhöyük.

Before we start our investigation proper, two clarifications are in order. First, in the spirit of cross-disciplinary fertilization, this chapter approaches the question of changes in consciousness and cognition at Çatalhöyük from the perspective of the philosophy of cognitive science. As a consequence, the focus of discussion will be on the underlying assumptions and the general structure of certain considerations and inferences, rather than on the detailed interpretation of specific pieces of material evidence. That said, and as will become clear, the arguments of this chapter, if correct, will have repercussions for how we interpret the material evidence, and, in particular, for the conclusions that we might draw, from the archaeological data at Çatalhöyük, regarding changes in the Neolithic mind. Put another way, the goal of this investigation is not merely to draw some theoretical conclusions about the relationship between distributed cognition and archaeology, but to extract some lessons about what we are entitled to say about changes in consciousness and cognition at Çatalhöyük, on the basis of the available material-cultural evidence, once we allow our hypotheses about ancient minds to be shaped by certain general accounts of the basic character of psychological phenomena that are operative in cognitive science.

Second, although the intention here is to argue that which theory of mind an archaeologist selects, from the available options in cognitive science, will have implications for what precisely can and cannot be said about ancient consciousness and cognition on the basis of the material record, that argument, even if successful, in no way blocks off the other direction of potential cross-disciplinary travel, that is, a situation in which what we learn from the material record leads us to say something different about our scientific theories of mind. We might discover, for example, that certain elements that we would expect to observe in ancient material culture, if a particular scientific theory of mind applies to that context, simply can't be found, thereby casting doubt on the applicability of that theory, at least as it stands. But that direction of travel is not what is at issue here. With those two clarifications in place, it is time for the real work of this chapter to begin.

MATERIAL SYMBOLS AND COGNITIVE CHANGE

It is, of course, an immensely plausible thought that historical changes in habitation, agriculture, technology or trade indicate the introduction of new techniques and ways of life that will be associated with cognitive change. But that's a pretty 'big-picture' thought, and things are not so obvious when we turn our attention to more detailed hypotheses about which particular changes or innovations in which particular practices drove, were driven by, or were at least correlated with, which particular cognitive changes. Here we will be taking our cues from one such detailed hypothesis.

Small geometric clay objects (spheres, discs, cones) are common finds in all occupational levels at Çatalhöyük. So what, precisely, are these objects? One prominent proposal is that they are 'tokens', or what (drawing on terminology from the distributed cognition literature) I shall call 'material symbols'. In other words, by functioning within a structured system of representational relationships, such physical objects become material resources for symbolic information storage. Bennison-Chapman, who, as we shall see, proceeds to question this interpretation of the objects concerned, characterizes 'tokens' (material symbols) as: 'small tools acting as mnemonic aids, used to hold and transmit information. They are utilised within the sphere of administration, to store and communicate information' (Bennison-Chapman, this volume, Chapter 5). So, if the small geometric clay objects recovered at Çatalhöyük are indeed material symbols, they should be interpretable as the physical realizers of recombinable symbols within a standardized system in which simple geometric shapes in different sizes are used to represent units of, for example, animals, crops, processed foods and raw materials.

So far, so good, but how does the claim that there are material symbols at Çatalhöyük bear on the question of cognitive change? According to thinkers such as Schmandt-Besserat (1992), Renfrew (1998, 2012) and Watkins (2010), the appearance of material symbols in the archaeological record is evidence of a shift in cognitive capacities because only a more 'advanced' mind has the 'higher' cognitive abilities that are required to invent and operate a symbolic system, where the candidates for such 'higher' abilities include objectification, abstraction (taking a particular shape to represent, say, an animal) and metrication. With Neolithic village life in general (not just at Çatalhöyük) identified by the aforementioned thinkers as a source for such evidence, the precise historical drivers for the transition in question are a matter of debate, with some (e.g. Schmandt-Besserat, Renfrew) tending to favour something like a shift from a mobile hunter-gatherer lifestyle to one of sedentary agriculture, and thus from a form of community in which the counting of resources was not necessary to one in which it was, and others (e.g. Watkins) favouring factors such as the possibilities for expressing and storing more complex concepts opened up by the new built environment and the cognitive challenges posed by the social fact that the members of the community were now living alongside one another on a more permanent basis. This debate over the historical drivers of cognitive change (and it is important to note that the views I have just canvassed do not exhaust the available options) provides part of the backdrop to the archaeological research project explored in this volume, in which Çatalhöyük, with its large amount of data, is used as a laboratory for testing hypotheses about the causes of cognitive change (Hodder, this volume, Chapter 1). More specifically, one line of investigation is to agree that material symbols exist at the site and then to interrogate the archaeological data with the aim of revealing the cause of their emergence and thus of the associated cognitive change (Chapter 1). But it is the shared, motivating idea that sits behind the search for the specific historical drivers that concerns us here. That idea is that the deployment of material symbols requires certain sophisticated forms of cognition and consciousness, so the appearance of such symbols in material culture marks the emergence of new psychological capacities.

To help us explore this theoretical territory, and concentrating specifically on Çatalhöyük, we can express the central line of reasoning just traversed in the form of an explicit argument.

Premise 1: The appearance of material symbols in the archaeological record at a site constitutes evidence of cognitive change, in that period, at that site. More specifically, it constitutes evidence of a shift to certain sophisticated forms of cognition and consciousness.

Premise 2: The small geometric clay objects found at the Neolithic site of Çatalhöyük are material symbols.

Conclusion: There is evidence of cognitive change at the Neolithic site of Çatalhöyük and, more specifically, of a shift to certain sophisticated forms of cognition and consciousness.

Now, if someone wanted to reject this argument, and thus the claim that there was a shift to sophisticated levels of cognition and consciousness at Çatalhöyük evidenced by the discovery of material symbols at the site (there might, of course, be an alternative basis for the conclusion that such a shift has taken place), one strategy would be to reject the second premise, that is, to argue that the small geometric clay objects found at Çatalhöyük are not material symbols. This is precisely what Bennison-Chapman (this volume, Chapter 5) does. First, she identifies a suite of conditions that would plausibly need to be met if the clay objects in question really did function as material symbols in the manner required. Among these conditions are things like being crafted into a range of standardized shapes and sizes consistent with the range of goods present in the Çatalhöyük economy, being used in groups, and being retained for later information retrieval. Then she presents detailed archaeological evidence from the site that strongly suggests the conditions in question are not met. For example, there is no evidence of development in the range or homogeneity of form of the clay objects. In addition, the objects in question are usually recovered alone and often within disposal contexts. Finally, she presents considerations in favour of certain alternative hypotheses regarding the function of the objects, such as that they were gaming pieces or that they were simple counting (as opposed to accounting or recording) tools, used in a one-to-one correspondence with individual items in particular counting events (and thus not as part of a symbolic system).

As fascinating and as important as this dispute is, it does not matter, for our purposes here, whether Bennison-Chapman is right that the small geometric clay objects found at Çatalhöyük are not material symbols. What's more significant is that the conclusion, which constitutes the denial of premise 2 in our highlighted argument, leaves premise 1 of that argument intact. Put another way, Bennison-Chapman is, as far as I can tell, happy to believe, along with her opponents, that the appearance of material symbols in the archaeological record at a site constitutes evidence of cognitive change – and more specifically of a shift to certain sophisticated forms of cognition and consciousness – in that period, at that site. Thus, for Bennison-Chapman and her opponents, *if* the geometric clay objects found at Çatalhöyük are material

symbols, that would be good evidence of the emergence of certain advanced cognitive capacities there; it's just that, for Bennison-Chapman, those objects aren't material symbols, whereas, for her opponents, they are. But now what about the shared premise itself? Is *that* correct? If it isn't, then the link between material symbols and sophisticated levels of consciousness and cognition is broken, and the recovery of material symbols at some site would not be evidence of cognitive change. Under these circumstances, even if Bennison-Chapman is wrong, and the small geometric clay objects recovered at Çatalhöyük are indeed material symbols, that would not be evidence of the proposed emergence of sophisticated levels of consciousness and cognition in the Neolithic mind.

The remainder of this chapter will focus on premise 1 of the target argument, on, that is, the claim that the appearance of material symbols in the archaeological record at a site constitutes evidence of cognitive change, in that period, at that site, and more specifically of a shift to certain sophisticated forms of cognition and consciousness. Facing up to the problem of ancient minds, what we really want to know is what went on in the minds of our ancient ancestors when they interacted with external symbol systems, and whether the introduction of such systems heralded a radical shift in the fundamental nature of their cognitive resources. In an attempt to meet these challenges, we can pursue a strategy that is, in truth, a close neighbour of the neuroarchaeologist's appeal to what we know about the psychological states and processes that are present when contemporary human beings perform certain kinds of tasks (see earlier). That is, we can find out what contemporary cognitive science tells us about what goes on in people's minds when they interact with modern external symbol systems. More specifically, given that the distributed perspective looks like it's the archaeologist's friend, we can find out what that particular perspective in contemporary cognitive science tells us about the psychological states and processes in play. Then we can extrapolate to the case of ancient material symbols and ancient minds. So, it is by seeing if/how the distributed perspective provides a theoretical bridge from ancient material symbols to ancient cognition – a connection that is at the centre of the highlighted research on Çatalhöyük – that the alleged symbiosis between the archaeological investigation of the ancient mind and distributed cognition may be assessed.

DISTRIBUTED COGNITION I: EMBEDDED MINDS

In a series of compelling cognitive-scientific treatments that combine philosophical reflection with empirical modelling studies, Bechtel (1994, 1996; see also Bechtel and Abrahamsen 1991) develops and defends the view that certain 'advanced' cognitive achievements, such as mathematical reasoning, natural language processing and natural deduction, are the result of sensorimotor-mediated embodied interactions between in-the-head connectionist networks and external symbol systems. In cognitive science, the term 'connectionist network' picks out a class of systems in which a (typically) large number of interconnected units process information in parallel. Inasmuch as the brain too is made up of a large number of interconnected units (neurons) that process information in parallel, connectionist networks are 'neurally inspired', although usually at a massive level of abstraction. At the heart of connectionist theorizing is the concept of a distributed representation – a pattern of activation spread out across a group of processing units (analogous to a pattern of neural activity in a brain). One feature of connectionist networks that has made them popular with many cognitive theorists is that, as a by-product of their basic processing architecture and form of information storage, properties that endow them with a powerful line in statistical pattern completion, these systems 'naturally' demonstrate a range of intelligence-related capabilities that plausibly underlie the distinctive psychological profile of biological thinkers. Such capacities include flexible generalization from existing data, default reasoning, and the graceful degradation of performance in the face of restricted damage or noisy/inaccurate input information. What's striking about Bechtel's explanation of our sophisticated cognitive achievements in (roughly) mathematics, language and formal logic is that the genuinely psychological contribution at work is exhausted by these sorts of biologically realistic capabilities. The rest is a matter of embodied interaction with, and environmental scaffolding by, external material symbols. But why, exactly, is this striking? To answer that question, and to understand more precisely, from a distributed perspective, what's going on in Bechtel's explanation, we need to make contact with one of the most famous quarrels in cognitive-scientific history.

In contrast to connectionism, the classical form of cognitive science denies that the abstract structure of the brain is a good model for the nature of mind. Rather, it demands, we should pay attention to the abstract structure of human language. Such language (on one popular account anyway) is at root a finite storehouse of atomic symbols (words), which are combined into complex expressions (phrases, sentences and so on) according to certain formal-syntactic rules (grammar). The meaning of some complex expression is a function of the meaning of each atomic symbol that figures as a constituent in that expression, plus the syntactic structure of the expression (as determined by the rules of the grammar). In short, human language features a combinatorial (equivalently, compositional) syntax and semantics. And, for the classical cognitive scientist, so it goes for our inner psychology. That too is based on a finite storehouse of atomic symbols (concepts) that are combined into complex expressions (thoughts) according to a set of syntactic rules. In short, thinking, like language, features a combinatorial syntax and semantics. Thus Fodor famously speaks of our inner psychological system as a *language of thought* (Fodor 1975).

One much-discussed argument for the classical view (and thus against connectionism) hails from Fodor and Pylyshyn (1988), who claim that connectionist theorizing about the mind is, at best, no more than a good explanation of how classical states and processes may be implemented in neural systems. In brief, Fodor and Pylyshyn argue as follows. It's an empirical observation that thought is systematic. In other words, the ability to have some thoughts (e.g. that Elsie loves Murray) is intrinsically connected to the ability to have certain other thoughts (e.g.

that Murray loves Elsie). If we adopt a classical vision of mind, the systematicity of thought is straightforwardly explained by the combinatorial syntax and semantics of the cognitive representational system.

The intrinsic connectedness of the different thoughts in question results from the fact that the processing architecture contains a set of atomic symbols alongside certain syntactic rules for recombining those symbols into different molecular expressions. Now, Fodor and Pylyshyn argue that although there is a sense in which connectionist networks instantiate structured states (e.g. distributed connectionist representations have active units as parts), specifically combinatorial structure is not an essential or a fundamental property of those states. This ultimately renders connectionist networks inherently incapable of explaining the systematicity of thought, and thus of explaining thinking. What such systems might do, however, is explain how a classical computational architecture may be implemented in an organic brain.

Bechtel explicitly develops his account in opposition to Fodor and Pylyshyn's deflationary conclusions regarding connectionism. That said, he agrees with Fodor and Pylyshyn on two key points, first, that where systematicity is present, it is to be explained by combinatorially structured representations, and second, that connectionist networks fail to instantiate combinatorial structure as an essential property of their internal organization. He does not need to endorse Fodor and Pylyshyn's claim that all thought is systematic, however. For his purposes, all that is required is that some cognitive activities (e.g. linguistic behaviour, natural deduction, mathematical reasoning) exhibit systematicity. Bechtel's distinctive (anti-Fodor-and-Pylyshyn) move is to locate the necessary combinatorial structure in systems of symbolic representations that remain *external* to the connectionist network itself (e.g. in written or spoken language, or in mathematical/logical notations). Given the idea that our inner psychology should be conceived in connectionist terms, this is tantamount to saying that the necessary combinatorial structure resides not in our internal processing engine, but rather in the environment. For this solution to work, it must be possible for the natural sensitivity to statistical patterns that we find in connectionist networks generally to be deployed in such a way that some of those networks, when in interaction with specific external symbol systems, may come to respect the constraints of a combinatorial syntax, even though their own inner representations are not so structured. Bechtel's studies suggest that this may be achieved by exploiting factors such as the capacity of connectionist networks to recognize and generalize from patterns in bodies of training data (e.g. large numbers of correct derivations in sentential arguments), plus the temporal constraints that characterize real embodied engagements with stretches of external symbol structures (e.g. different parts of the input will be available to the network at different times, due to the restrictions imposed by temporal processing windows). The conclusion is that 'by dividing the labor between external symbols which must conform to syntactical principles and a cognitive system which is sensitive to those constraints without itself employing syntactically structured representations, one can perhaps explain the systematicity . . . of cognitive performance' (Bechtel 1994, 438).

As defined earlier, cognition is distributed when it is, in some way, spread out over the brain, the non-neural body and (in many paradigm cases) an environment consisting of objects, tools, other artefacts, texts, individuals and/or social/institutional structures. Bechtel's model of an inner connectionist network in embodied interaction with material symbols, where the external symbol system explains the systematicity of cognitive performance, fits the bill. Moreover, it's an example of the distributed perspective at work that speaks directly to the issue of what goes on in people's minds when they interact with external symbol systems. But now we need to be more specific about the precise form of distributed cognition that's on the table because it turns out that, despite the shared, paradigm-defining emphasis on bodily engagement and environment-involving processing, the term 'distributed cognition' is actually an umbrella concept that encompasses a number of distinct theoretical views. Two modulations of the core idea will be relevant here, modulations that are generated by different conceptions of what is involved in cognition *spreading out* over brain, body and world.

According to the hypothesis of *embedded* cognition, the distinctive adaptive richness and/or flexibility of intelligent thought and action is regularly, and perhaps sometimes necessarily, causally dependent on the bodily exploitation of certain environmental props or scaffolds. (For philosophical elucidations and explorations of this idea, see e.g. Clark 1997; Wheeler 2005.) What's important about this approach, for present purposes, is that although the embedded theorist seeks to register the routinely performance-boosting, often transformative, and sometimes necessary causal contributions made by environmental elements to many cognitive outcomes (witness the role of Bechtel's external symbols in explaining systematicity), she continues to hold that the actual thinking going on in such cases remains brain-bound. (There is a less common, more radical iteration of the view according to which cognition is distributed through the brain *and* the non-neural body, although not the environment. I shall ignore this option.) It's the embedded version of distributed cognition that Bechtel seems to prefer. Thus his claim that the 'property of systematicity, and the compositional syntax and semantics that underlie that property, might best be attributed to natural languages themselves but not to the mental mechanisms involved in language use' (Bechtel 1994, 436) is plausibly explained by the fact that he takes the only genuinely cognitive elements in the nexus of neural, bodily and environmental factors to be inside the head: systematicity and combinatorial structure are features of the external symbol systems, but not the mental mechanisms involved, because the only mental mechanisms involved are the inner connectionist networks that do not themselves exhibit systematicity or combinatorial structure.

Re-entering the archaeological context, if the embedded interpretation of Bechtel's model is correct, what we confront is an infuriating resuscitation of the problem of ancient minds. To see why, notice that, on that interpretation, the cognitive mechanisms implicated in navigating and exploiting the sorts of external material symbol system under consideration (material realizations of symbolic logical notation, say) do not involve

sophisticated cognitive capacities, over and above those that were already operative in the non-symbolic context. So, by extrapolation, the same natural sensitivity to statistical patterns that we find in connectionist networks generally, a sensitivity that underlies capacities for generalization, default reasoning and graceful degradation that surely will have been central to all kinds of adaptive thought and experience in prior hunter-gatherer communities, may continue to characterize cognition in the new Neolithic environment of (we are currently assuming) material symbols, simply by becoming targeted on patterns in the external symbolic systems in question. So, if, from the perspective of the embedded version of distributed cognition, we ask ourselves the question, 'Does the presence of an external material symbol system require, or at least strongly indicate, cognitive change, in the sense of the installation of a revolutionary package of more sophisticated psychological capacities?', our answer should be 'no'. This is because, on the basis of Bechtel's model, the increased sophistication of the observed psychological *performance* may have been purchased using the same old connectionist currency of statistical pattern completion that was already operative, but that is now newly allied with some powerful external scaffolding (the material symbol system) that allowed the Neolithic mind, including that mind as realized at Çatalhöyük, to buy more for its psychological money.

These thoughts find additional support in some reflections by Clark (1997) on what happens to the brain with the advent of language. Clark's proposal – which we can interpret for the moment as an example of embedded theorizing – is that language should be thought of as 'an external resource that complements but does not profoundly alter the brain's own basic modes of representation and computation' (198). In other words, the biological brain has certain generic forms of inner state and mechanism ('the brain's own basic modes of representation and computation') that, from both an evolutionary and a developmental perspective, precede linguistic competence. When language comes onto the cognitive scene, it heralds not a transformation in those generic types of inner resource, but rather an external augmentation of them. Indeed, buying into a broadly connectionist approach to cognitive science, Clark takes the human brain to be essentially a device for pattern-association, pattern-completion and pattern-manipulation. So Clark's recognizably Bechtelian claim is that our language-involving behaviour is to be explained by an all-conquering partnership between, on the one hand, a pattern-sensitive brain and, on the other, an external storehouse of rich symbolic structures.

To bring Clark's position into proper view, it is worth pausing to compare it with a related account that, tentatively, Clark himself attributes to Dennett (Dennett 1991; Clark 1997, 197). Dennett argues that our innate neural hardware may differ from that of our nonlinguistic evolutionary near-neighbours (such as chimpanzees) in only relatively minor ways. Nevertheless, it is precisely these relatively minor hardware differences that constitute the evolutionary source of the human ability to create, learn and use public language. According to Clark, this part of Dennett's story is correct: there is no mandate to attribute human beings with the kind of innate language processing mechanism whose design would mean that our brains, compared with those of our evolutionary near-neighbours, contain a fundamentally different kind of neural device. However, Dennett's further proposal, as Clark explains it, is that developmental exposure to a linguistic environment results in a subtle reprogramming of the computational resources of the human brain, such that our innate pattern-completing neural architecture comes to simulate a kind of logic-like serial processing device. Clark, by contrast, resists the idea of any extensive ontogenetic reprogramming phase driven by language. Thus, we are told, developmental exposure to and use of language brings about no significant reorganization of the brain's basic processing architecture. If this is true for our linguistic capabilities, the same points can surely be made regarding the psychological capacities required to create, learn and use the material symbol systems that predate writing.

The foregoing considerations cast doubt on the inference from the appearance of material symbols in the archaeological record to the occurrence of significant cognitive change. They also indicate that distributed cognition may not be quite the friend that the archaeologist interested in ancient minds needs. After all, so far anyway, our foray into distributed cognition suggests that, with the explanatory weight spread over brain, body and world, plus, crucially, the intimate causal couplings between these different but complementary elements, there is no secure inferential bridge from what we recover in the form of material culture to changes in the nature of cognition. Old brains don't necessarily need to learn substantially new cognitive tricks in order to deliver more sophisticated psychological achievements following innovations in material culture.

Perhaps we are not being radical enough in our adoption of a distributed perspective. Despite all its exciting talk of embodied interaction and environmental scaffolding, the fact remains that the embedded version of distributed cognition shares a central traditional assumption with the neuro-centric orthodoxy, namely that psychological states and processes are instantiated in physical machinery that is *always* inside the skull and skin. Thus certain external elements act as non-cognitive factors that support and augment the wholly internal cognitive states and processes. Looking at this aspect of the embedded view from a different angle, and borrowing a way of putting things from Adams and Aizawa (2008), a key feature of embedded cognition is that the dependence of cognition on external elements is causal – or, to bring out what really matters, *merely* causal – rather than *constitutive*. If the dependence in question were constitutive in character, then the external elements of interest would not be non-cognitive causal scaffolds for cognition; they would count as genuine *parts of* the cognitive process or architecture.

This is the view endorsed by the second version of the distributed perspective to be canvassed here. Thus, according to the hypothesis of *extended* cognition, the physical machinery of mind sometimes extends beyond the skull and skin (see Clark and Chalmers 1998 and Clark 2008 for canonical

treatments, and for a more recent collection that contains criticisms, defences and developments of the view, see Menary 2010). More precisely, the advocate of extended cognition holds that there are actual (in this world) cases of intelligent thought and action, in which the material vehicles that realize the thinking and thoughts concerned are spatially distributed over brain, body and world, in such a way that certain external elements are rightly accorded fundamentally the same cognitive status as would ordinarily be accorded to a subset of your neurons. If this view is right, then, under certain circumstances, your phone-number-storing mobile device literally counts as part of your mind, in the sense that it's part of your mnemonic machinery.

Here is not the place to develop and defend a detailed account of when some external element, such as a material symbol, qualifies as a constituent part of one's psychological machinery, that is, in the relevant sense, as part of one's extended mind. As we might expect, there are several proposals for delivering this result, and a sometimes bad-tempered debate surrounds them. (Menary 2010 is a good place to make contact with the debate. For my own favoured way of arguing for extended cognition, see e.g. Wheeler 2010a, 2010b, 2011.) However, it's important to note that the transition to approaching things in terms of extended, rather than embedded, cognition does not necessarily require any associated change in the underlying causal structure of the distributed system under consideration. Rather, it may be based on an acknowledgement that some of the causal structures present in that system meet the conditions for cognitive status. To see how this might work, consider, once again, the Bechtelian connectionist-network-plus-symbol-system architecture described earlier, which so far, and in line with Bechtel's own approach, has been treated as an instance of embedded cognition. For the sake of argument, let's simply assume that we have been convinced by various considerations that where one finds a suitably organized material system in which atomic symbols are automatically combined and manipulated, according to the principles of a compositional syntax and semantics, so as to meet Fodor and Pylyshyn's systematicity requirement, one finds a cognitive system. (Something like this view is endorsed by Newell and Simon's physical symbol system hypothesis, one of the canonical statements of classical cognitive science; Newell and Simon 1976.) Under these circumstances, one might be moved to claim that Bechtel's distributed architecture, comprising an inner connectionist network and external symbols coupled together via embodied sensorimotor interactions, itself qualifies as just such an automatic, material, compositional symbol system, and thus as a cognitive system. In other words, in this distributed architecture, the genuinely cognitive machinery includes not only the connectionist network, but also the embodied interface and the external material symbols themselves. Conceived this way, a Bechtelian architecture for doing mathematics, natural language processing or natural deduction is a case of extended cognition.

If the extended interpretation of Bechtel's model is correct, things certainly look a little better for the archaeologist interested in ancient minds. After all, whether we are working from within neuro-centrism or from within an embedded distributed perspective, material culture is condemned to a life outside cognition proper, and so the objects and artefacts studied by archaeology are (roughly) things that ancient minds made and/or used. The cognitive states and processes concerned are not themselves simply on show in those things, although certain inferences about the nature of those states and processes might be ventured. (Enter the problem of ancient minds.) However, with the cognitive architecture concerned now conceptualized as *including* the external material symbols, past ways of thought are not just *expressed in* material culture but are often partly *constituted by* material culture. So the archaeologist gets to study past minds in a rather more direct manner. Indeed, some of the things studied by archaeology are literally parts of (no longer functioning) ancient minds (Wheeler 2010b). So, if, from the vantage point afforded by the extended interpretation of Bechtel's architecture, we ask ourselves the question, 'Does the presence of an external material symbol system require, or at least strongly indicate, cognitive change, in the sense of the installation of a revolutionary package of more sophisticated psychological capacities?', then our answer should be 'yes'. This is because the appearance of material symbols to which certain internal mechanisms are coupled via embodied sensorimotor interactions is itself (it is not merely evidence of) cognitive change. It is the emergence of new and more sophisticated cognitive structures. This remains true even if (and we cannot be sure about this) the inner part of the extended ancient mind instantiates nothing more than the old connectionist currency of statistical pattern completion that was already operative in the presymbolic context. So, for fans of the extended cognition hypothesis, if the small geometric clay objects at Çatalhöyük are in fact material symbols, then the Neolithic mind at that site did undergo significant cognitive change.

It might seem as if our extended-mind-based argument for the conclusion that cognitive change has occurred has the unhappy effect of rendering that conclusion empty or trivial. The complaint here would go as follows: if material symbols routinely count as cognitive elements, and if the notion of the 'symbolic' applies generally to many elements in material culture, then a very large number of the changes in material culture will count straightforwardly as cognitive changes. So the conclusion that cognitive change has occurred says nothing – or at least nothing interesting or illuminating. Fortunately, the specific extended-mind-based argument outlined earlier does not fall prey to this particular objection because that argument is developed in the context of (i) material elements that are symbolic in a restricted and demanding sense, in that they function as recombinable constituents within standardized systems of representational structures and relationships, and (ii) a related, and equally restricted and demanding, account of 'cognition', according to which certain outcomes in human performance are underpinned by atomic symbols that are exploited and manipulated according to the principles of a compositional syntax and semantics, thus enabling the systematicity condition for thought to be met in those domains. As Bennison-Chapman nicely shows (see earlier), not all material-cultural elements will be material symbols *in the sense of* (i). Building on this, we can now add, given (ii), that

the kinds of exploitation and manipulation to which the (by our current criterion) non-symbolic elements will be subjected will be of the *wrong kind* to count as cognitive. That should be enough to alleviate the trivialization concern, because a large number of the changes that take place in material culture will not count as cognitive changes. In other words, if one concludes, on the basis of the extended-mind-based argument offered earlier, that cognitive change has occurred, one is saying something with genuine content.

CONCLUSIONS

In this chapter, I have used the example of the alleged emergence of higher levels of cognition and consciousness in the Neolithic, as indicated by the material-cultural evidence at Çatalhöyük, to explore the relationship that exists between the archaeology of the ancient mind and distributed cognitive science. I have argued that the conclusions that should be drawn regarding the occurrence of cognitive change, based on the material-cultural evidence, will be different (indeed, diametrically opposed) depending on which version of distributed cognition is embraced. Adopting the embedded version, one cannot know whether there has been cognitive change on the basis of the appearance of material symbols in the archeological record because such change may not be required to explain our successful deployment of those symbols. Adopting the extended version, one may be able to conclude that cognitive change has occurred because the material symbols themselves may have cognitive status, but that conclusion would still leave one unsure about the character of the inner contribution to the overall cognitive process. So, although there may be good reason to think that the distributed perspective is the archaeologist's friend, that enthusiasm needs to be matched by an understanding of the challenges, as well as the advantages, of such an alliance.

ACKNOWLEDGEMENTS

Some passages in Section 3 of this chapter were adapted from passages in (Wheeler 2004, 2005, 2015). For discussion of the ideas presented here, many thanks to the participants at the conference, Consciousness and Creativity at the Dawn of Settled Life, McDonald Institute for Archaeological Research, University of Cambridge, July 2017, and especially to Ian Hodder and John Sutton.

REFERENCES

Adams, F. and Aizawa, K. (2008), *The Bounds of Cognition*, Malden, MA: Blackwell.

Bechtel, W. (1994), "Natural Deduction in Connectionist Systems", *Synthese* vol. 101, pp. 433–463.

Bechtel, W. (1996), "What Knowledge Must Be in the Head in Order to Acquire Language', in *Communicating Meaning: The Evolution and Development of Language*, eds. B. Velichkovsky and D. M. Rumbaugh, Hillsdale, NJ: Lawrence Erlbaum Associates.

Bechtel, W. and Abrahamsen, A. (1991), *Connectionism and the Mind: An Introduction to Parallel Processing in Networks*, Oxford, UK: Basil Blackwell.

Clark, A. (1997), *Being There: Putting Brain, Body, and World Together Again*, Cambridge, MA: MIT Press.

Clark, A. (2003), *Natural-Born Cyborgs: Minds, Technologies, and the Future of Human Intelligence*, New York: Oxford University Press.

Clark, A. (2008), *Supersizing the Mind: Embodiment, Action and Cognitive Extension*, Oxford, UK: Oxford University Press.

Clark, A. and Chalmers, D. (1998), "The Extended Mind", *Analysis*, Vol. 58, no. 1, pp. 7–19.

Dennett, D. C. (1991), *Consciousness Explained*, Boston: Little, Brown & Co.

Fodor, J. A. (1975), *The Language of Thought*, Cambridge, MA: Harvard University Press.

Fodor, J. A. and Pylyshyn, Z. (1988), "Connectionism and Cognitive Architecture: A Critical Analysis", *Cognition*, Vol. 28, pp. 3–71.

Hutchins, E. (1995), *Cognition in the Wild*, Cambridge, MA: MIT Press.

Malafouris, L. (2013), *How Things Shape the Mind*, Cambridge, MA: MIT Press.

Menary, R. (ed.) (2010), *The Extended Mind*, Cambridge, MA: MIT Press.

Mithen, S. (1996), *The Prehistory of the Mind: A Search for the Origins of Art, Religion and Science*, London: Thames and Hudson.

Newell, A. and Simon, H. A. (1976), "Computer Science as Empirical Inquiry: Symbols and Search", *Communications of the Association for Computing Machinery*, vol. 19, no. 3, pp. 113–126.

Putt, S. S., Wijeakumar, S., Franciscus, R. G. and Spencer, J. P. (2017), "The Functional Brain Networks That Underlie Early Stone Age Tool Manufacture", *Nature Human Behaviour*, vol. 1, Article number: 0102, doi:10.1038/s41562-017-0102.

Renfrew, C. (1998), "Mind and Matter: Cognitive Archaeology and External Symbolic Storage", in *Cognition and Material Culture: The Archaeology of Symbolic Storage*, eds. C. Renfrew & C. Scarre, Cambridge, UK: McDonald Institute for Archaeological Research, pp. 1–6.

Renfrew, C. (2012), "Towards a Cognitive Archaeology: Material Engagement and the Early Development of Society", in *Archaeological Theory Today*, ed. I. Hodder. Cambridge, MA: Polity Press, pp. 124–145.

Schmandt-Besserat, D. (1992), *Before Writing (Vol. 1): From Counting to Cuneiform*, Austin: University of Texas Press.

Tribble, E. B. (2005), "Distributing Cognition in the Globe", *Shakespeare Quarterly*, vol. 56, no. 2, pp. 135–155.

Tribble, E. B. (2011), *Cognition in the Globe: Attention and Memory in Shakespeare's Theatre*, New York: Palgrave Macmillan.

Watkins, T. (2010), "New Light on Neolithic Revolution in South-West Asia", *Antiquity*, vol. 84, no. 325, pp. 621–634.

Wheeler, M. (2004), "Is Language the Ultimate Artefact?", *Language Sciences*, vol. 26, no. 6, pp. 693–715.

Wheeler, M. (2005), *Reconstructing the Cognitive World: The Next Step*, Cambridge, MA: MIT Press.

Wheeler, M. (2010a), "In Defense of Extended Functionalism", in *The Extended Mind*, ed. R. Menary, Cambridge, MA: MIT Press, pp. 245–270.

Wheeler, M. (2010b), "Minds, Things and Materiality", in *The Cognitive Life of Things: Recasting the Boundaries of the Mind*, eds. C. Renfrew and L. Malafouris, Cambridge, UK: McDonald Institute for Archaeological Research, pp. 29–37.

Wheeler, M. (2011), "Embodied Cognition and the Extended Mind", in *The Continuum Companion to Philosophy of Mind*, ed. J. Garvey, London: Continuum, pp. 220–238.

Wheeler, M. (2015), "A Tale of Two Dilemmas: Cognitive Kinds and the Extended Mind", in *Natural Kinds and Classification in Scientific Practice*, ed. C. Kendig, London: Routledge, pp. 175–185.

Wheeler, M. and Clark, A. (2008), "Culture, Embodiment and Genes: Unravelling the Triple Helix', *Philosophical Transactions of the Royal Society*, vol. 363, pp. 3563–3575.

5

CONSCIOUS TOKENS?

Lucy Ebony Bennison-Chapman

SMALL, GEOMETRIC-SHAPED CLAY OBJECTS (spheres, discs cones, etc.) are a common feature of all occupational levels at Çatalhöyük. Crudely manufactured in the context of the site's material culture, clay objects are generally disposed of after little use, in middens. Clay objects appear at the start of the Neolithic across the wider Near East. They are the most prevalent artefact at neighbouring ninth to eight millennium BC Boncuklu Höyük, for example, and remain common across Anatolia and the Near East into the first millennium BC. It is largely assumed that from their inception, clay objects acted as "tokens", used as part of a formal, settlement wide and intersettlement mnemonic record-keeping system, consistent across the entire Near East for millennia. Their sudden appearance in the Neolithic was necessitated by the simultaneous shift in lifestyle from mobile hunter-gather to sedentary farming communities. It is further argued (Schmandt-Besserat 1992a, 1992b, 1996) that it is only after the cognitive shift into the modern, civilised mind that humans become capable of counting, recording and conceiving of abstract numbers. In this theoretical context, the presence of "tokens" at a settlement is clear evidence for the presence of a highly organised, intelligent, cognitively "advanced" population.

Systematic analysis of over 700 clay objects, considering object form, use-wear, immediate contextual deposition and broader spatial and temporal patterning, finds no support for the interpretation of these items as information storage tools at Çatalhöyük. Furthermore, the study of the distribution of clay objects across the wider Neolithic Near East, reveals little indication of correlations between site type, size, complexity and lifestyle, as would be expected (Bennison-Chapman 2013). At Çatalhöyük, there is no evidence for the use of small geometric clay objects as "tokens" – symbols used to represent goods or produce, and to retain information for retrieval at a later point in time. Clay objects held no intrinsic value, nor did they have a single, solid, universal role transcending households, occupational areas or levels of settlement at Çatalhöyük. They are just as likely to have been utilised as simple counting tools, as they were in gaming or ritual activities. The presence of clay objects therefore provides little evidence for higher levels of consciousness at Neolithic Çatalhöyük.

INTRODUCTION

It is often claimed that higher levels of consciousness were essential for Neolithic village life. This is evidenced by an apparent increase in abstract thought, leading to metrication and objectification in the Neolithic (e.g. Donald 1991; Renfew 1998, 2007, 2012; Watkins 2010). Small, geometric clay objects, interpreted as "tokens" are presumed to be the material culture evidence for such cognitive abilities (Schmandt-Besserat 1992a, 1996). Aside from the many associated issues such as definitions of cognition, environmental factors, and the ability of material culture to influence and inform us on the mind (see Wheeler, this volume, Chapter 4), we must first look at the evidence for the existence of "tokens" at all in the archaeological record of the Neolithic Near East. Do we really have "tokens" at Çatalhöyük? If so, how, when and where were they used?

Small geometric clay objects appear in the archaeological record of the Near East at the start of the Neolithic, in the tenth millennium cal. BC (e.g. PPNA Jericho, Sheikh-e Abad and Çayönü) (Broman Morales 1990; Kenyon & Holland 1983: 815, fig. 367.6 p. 356; Matthews et al. 2013: 140, 141, table 11.5 p. 142). Commonly referred to as "tokens", they are found across the entire Near East region and are also the most prevalent artefact at neighbouring ninth to eight millennium BC Boncuklu Höyük. Clay objects remain common across Anatolia and the Near East into the first millennium BC. It is largely assumed that from their inception, clay objects functioned as "tokens": symbolic, mnemonic information storage tools (Schmandt-Besserat 1992a, 1996). Acting as a symbolic code, their function, it is argued, was consistent across the Near East, remaining unchanged into historic times (Schmandt-Besserat 1992a, 1996). Necessitated by the shift in lifestyle from mobile hunter-gather to sedentary farming communities, Schmandt-Besserat claims that it is only after a cognitive shift into the modern, civilised mind that humans become capable of counting, recording and conceiving of abstract numbers and using mnemonic devices.

Small geometric-shaped clay objects are a common feature of all occupational levels at Çatalhöyük. Present in a basic range of shapes (spheres, discs, cones, etc.), Çatalhöyük's clay objects are crudely manufactured in the context of the site's material culture and are generally disposed of, after little use, in middens (Figure 5.1). In the theoretical context of this volume (see especially Chapter 1, this volume), the presence of "tokens" at a Neolithic settlement is clear evidence of a highly organised, intelligent, cognitively "advanced" population, one exhibiting higher levels of consciousness with small geometric clay objects of basic shapes used to symbolise abstract notions of specific and varied commodities (specific animals, crops, processed food-stuffs and raw materials for craft production). However, this interpretation rests upon the assumption that these small geometric clay objects functioned as "tokens" at Çatalhöyük: abstract, symbolic, mnemonic, information storage devices.

FIGURE 5.1 Examples of the types of small geometric clay objects recovered from Çatalhöyük East. (Photos: author's own)

Are small geometric clay objects at Neolithic Çatalhöyük "tokens" and thus evidence of abstraction, metrication and higher levels of consciousness? I define "tokens" as small tools acting as mnemonic aids, used to hold and transmit information. They are utilised within the sphere of administration, to store and communicate information. In this chapter I argue that systematic analysis of hundreds of clay objects from Çatalhöyük finds no support for the interpretation of these items as "tokens" in the traditional sense at Çatalhöyük. Evidence for other interpretive functions including simple counting aids, children's toys, gaming pieces and items of divination or lots will be discussed alongside evidence for their use in the symbolic, record keeping sphere.

RESEARCH CONTEXT

Early Research

Clay objects are small (generally <5 cm maximum dimension), portable objects, which are intentionally crafted into a geometric form (sphere, cone, disc, etc.) (Figure 5.1). The nonfunctional term "clay object" is used here, yet due to their uncertain function, identical and similar objects are referred to in archaeological literature as "tokens", "jetons", "counters", "gaming pieces" and the like (examples of diverse terminology from

Neolithic sites in the Near East include: "jeton": Costello 2000, 2002: "discs or jet-ons". "Gaming piece": Verhoeven & Akkermans 2000: fig. 4.7.3, pp. 117, 108; Kenyon & Holland 1983: p. 815, fig. 367.1-16 p. 560; Kenyon & Holland 1982: pp. 557–558, fig. 226.1-4 p. 557. "Abstract stalk": Broman Morales 1990: pp. 64–65, 71–72, 74, pl. 5.h & I p. 84. "Tally": Tekin 2007: fig.14 p. 51; Verhoeven & Akkermans 2000: fig. 4.7.4, pp. 117, 108. "Cone", "disc", cylinder" or other simple geometric-shape label: Duru & Umurtak 2005: various shape terms used including "rectangular prisms", "clay lumps", "cylindrical shaped objects" & "disc shaped objects" see pp. 109–110, 174, pl. 130–131, 172; Mahasneh & Gebel 1998: terms used include "cone", "cylinder", "disc", "sphere" 108, fig. 1 p. 108; Esin et al. 1991: "cones" 134; Broman Morales 1990: "cone" pp. 387–388 & fig. 168: 3–4, "abstract cone" pp. 66, 71–72, 74, pl. 5. j p. 84, "ball" p. 389; fig. 169: 1, 2, 3, 4, 10, "disc" pp. 66–67, 71–72, 75 & pl. 6.d p. 85, "ball" pp. 66, 71–72, 75, pl. 6.e p. 85; Voight 1983: "small cones" fig. 102.a–b p. 183 & pl. 27.i–q; Çambel & Braidwood 1979: "pawn-shaped" p. 149 lower illus-tration b. "Miscellaneous geometrics" [no further shape classification given]: Voight 1983: fig. 102.c–e p. 183 & pl. 27.g–h and "token": Iceland 2010; Özbal et al. 2004: fig. 13.15–22 p. 104 & fig. 15.8–10 p. 106; Nilhamn 2002; Akkermans 1996b: fig. 8.4 p. 465, fig. 8.5 p. 466). Clay objects can be plain or decorated with markings and incisions. For the purposes of this study, small ("miniature") vessels are excluded from this definition, as are any miniature version of a naturalistic form such as zoomorphic figurines.

An abundance of small geometric clay objects has long been acknowledged throughout the Near East. However, it was not until clay bullae, hollow spherical clay envelopes, marked with impressions on the outside and containing small clay objects, were first excavated at Near Eastern sites of the late fourth to second millennium BC that attention focused for the first time on the small clay objects themselves. The earliest publication of clay objects comes from archaeologist J. de Morgan (de Morgan et al. 1905), a catalogue of objects, including those classified as "tokens" and "counters" from numerous Near Eastern sites of the "Early Periods". The first study of *Neolithic* clay objects concerned Jarmo's late Neolithic (sixth millennium) artefacts, completed by Broman in 1958. Since this study, others have focused on clay objects and associated hollow envelopes (bullae), from the late fourth and third millennia BC (proto- and early historic) leaving Neolithic clay objects largely ignored.

The earliest interpretative study is by Leo Oppenheim (1959). His work was crucial in linking clay objects to counting and adminis-tration. This also cemented the link between clay objects, bullae and sealing practices in the early historic Near East (Leo Oppenheim 1959). The publication sparked a renewed research interest into early administrative technologies and their relationship to the appearance of writing, forming the basis for all subsequent interpretations of clay objects across all periods of Near Eastern archaeology. Leo Oppenheim's interpretation of nonlite-rate accounting systems in the Near East centres on the discussion of Text 449, a cuneiform administrative text published in the Harvard Semitic Series volume XVI

(Leo Oppenheim 1959). The "text" is in fact a clay envelope or "bulla", referred to as an "egg-shaped tablet", largely intact and with detailed markings on the outer surface (Leo Oppenheim 1959: 123). Recovered from second millennium BC Nuzi (ancient Yorghan Tepe) upon excavation, it contained 48 items recorded as "little stones" (Leo Oppenheim 1959: 122–123). The outer surface of the bulla records eight lines of cuneiform inscription (see following) and a seal impression (not published). The text, when translated, was found to be a count of 48 animals, along with details of their age, sex and reproductive maturity (Leo Oppenheim 1959: 124). With the number of animals in the inscription exactly matching the number of "stones" contained inside the "egg-shaped tablet", Leo Oppenheim is certain the artefact is administrative in function (Leo Oppenheim 1959: 123). Notably, the text opens with the line "Stones [referring] to sheep and goats. . ." The Akkadian word *abnu* being translated as "stone", therefore describing the containing items as mere pebbles acting as "counters, markers, or something of the sort" (Leo Oppenheim 1959: 123–124).

Leo Oppenheim's work was important in bringing attention to small, geometric clay objects. It led to subsequent research into early administrative systems in the Near East, clearly linking clay objects, bullae, the use of seals and writing. Leo Oppenheim's work suggests two crucial things. First, the small objects inside the bulla all served a single function, their appearance (shape, colour, size) unimportant. Second, they performed a role alongside and not instead of writing. Yet large urban centres of south Mesopotamia of the late fourth millennium BC onwards and small Neolithic agrarian communities are far removed in time and nature.

DENISE SCHMANDT-BESSERAT

Denise Schmandt-Besserat is the most prominent academic in the investigation of Near Eastern clay objects. Since the late 1970s she advanced detailed theories as to why geometric clay objects initially appeared in the Neolithic, the evolution of their use and form through time, and their supposed decline with the advent of writing in the third millennium BC (Schmandt-Besserat 1977, 1978a, 1978b, 1979, 1980, 1988, 1992a, 1992b, 1994, 1996, 1999). Schmandt-Besserat's theory stems from extensive study of 10,000 clay objects, mostly previously unpublished material (Schmandt-Besserat 1992a: 10, 1992b). The artefacts are dominated by small, geometric clay objects, but also include geometric-shaped stone objects, miniature vessels and anthropomorphic and zoomorphic figurines in clay (Schmandt-Besserat 1992a, 1992b, 1996). The material covers a long chronology, spanning mid-Neolithic (c. 8,000 BC) to Early Bronze Age (c. 3,000 BC). It hails from 116 sites across Southwest Asia, from modern Iran, Iraq, Syria, Turkey, Israel and Jordan (Schmandt-Besserat 1992a: 7, 1992b: vii–viii).

Inspired by the work of Leo Oppenheim, from the start of the Neolithic, "tokens", she claims, were invented by farmers, acting as mnemonic devices to meet administrative needs. Shape, size and elaboration symbolised a specific quantity of a set commodity. "Tokens" acted as a nonverbal, nonwritten "code". This code was understood and used consistently throughout the Near East, directly evolving into cuneiform (the world's earliest known written script) around the mid-to-late fourth millennium BC (Schmandt-Besserat 1977, 1978a, 1980, 1992a, 1996). At all times, tokens were used in groups. Initially kept together in organic containers (wooden boxes, leather pouches, etc.), an increase in bureaucracy in the fourth millennium led to new methods of organisation, storage and archiving with bullae invented specifically to contain "tokens", acting as a permanent archive (Schmandt-Besserat 1992a: 108; 1996: 7).

Schmandt-Besserat's theory is complex, linking to the many social, economic and cognitive developments taking place from the Palaeolithic into the start of the early historic period of the late fourth millennium BC. "Tokens", she claims, appear simultaneously with animal and plant domestication and food production in the Neolithic. Their appearance becomes more elaborate with the "rise of social structures" and "rank leadership", peaking in use at the time of state formation c. 4,000 BC (Schmandt-Besserat 1992a: 99; 1996: 7). Schmandt-Besserat argues that that clay objects do not appear in the archaeological record until the Neolithic as mobile hunter-gather communities had neither need nor cognitive ability to count resources (Schmandt-Besserat 1992a: 157–159). Agriculture, the hallmark of sedentary Neolithic village life was what made accounting necessary (1992a: 161, 166–168, 170, 172, 1996: 102). At this point in time, a cognitive shift allowed the first framers to use abstract symbols, abstract number and thus utilise small clay objects as symbolic accounting tools (Schmandt-Besserat 1988, 1992a, 1996, 1999).

Upon the publication of her two-volume book (1992a, 1992b), Schmandt-Besserat's work became widely accepted. As such, her ideas have profoundly influenced the interpretation of small, geometric clay objects found at Neolithic, as well as later prehistoric and historic sites in the Near East. "Token" became the word used to identify such objects when found at Near Eastern sites. Neolithic archaeologists have been heavily influenced by Schmandt-Besserat's ideas in their interpretations of the role of clay objects (Akkermans & Duistermaat 1996; Costello 2000, 2002, 2011 in addition to archaeologists mentioned at the opening of the introduction). Researchers from secondary disciplines have been even more accepting of her theory (for example, Bottéro, Herrenschmidt & Vernant 2000; Coulmas 2003; Fischer 2001; Malafouris 2013; Netz 2002). The one exception is the early historic community, represented Peter Damerow, Robert Englund, Jöran Friberg and Hans Nissen. The group, comprised of linguistic scholars specialising in the origins of writing and counting, has been outspoken in its opposition to Schmandt-Besserat's "token" theory, citing many problems with her research (Brown 1996; Damerow 1993; Englund 1993, 1998; Friberg 1994; Michalowski 1993) and concluding that her 1992 work was an unsuccessful, "sprawling and highly speculative piece of research" (Brown 1996: 37, 42).

From the fourth millennium BC onwards, small clay objects are commonly recovered sealed inside hollow clay spheres or "bullae" acting as envelopes. These bullae often contained the impressions of the small items they contained along with cylinder seal impressions (see, for example, Leo

Oppenheim 1959: fig. 1 & 2 p. 122; Nissen et al. 1993: pp. 12–13; Pitman 1996: fig. 18a p. 231; Woods 2010: no. 32 & 33 p. 66, no. 35–36 p. 68). Soon writing also appeared on the surface of bullae and on flat clay tablets. Thus from the mid-fourth millennium BC onwards, small clay objects were almost certainly used alongside bullae, seals and writing as part of the administrative package. Though covering a vast geographic area and time period, Schmandt-Besserat's argument rests almost entirely on evidence from south Mesopotamia and Susa, likewise from urban sites of the fourth millennium BC onwards (1992b). One cannot assume a similar or identical function of material culture across such distant societies, distances and time periods (Bennison-Chapman 2014: ch. 2). To her credit, and in part due to the lack of an alternative theory, when recovered at Neolithic sites, clay objects were until very recently, attributed with the same administrative function as their fourth-millennium Sumerian counterparts. Geometric clay objects have been catalogued as "counters", "geometrics", "figurines", "gaming pieces", "tallies" and "misc. items" in addition to their interpretation as recording devices usually with no analysis of their form or regard to their find context.

AIMS, RESEARCH QUESTIONS AND HYPOTHESIS

Small geometric clay objects are assumed to have functioned as "tokens", symbolic tools used in the administration of agricultural produce within Neolithic communities. With different shapes and sizes seemingly representing exact units of specific commodities, in a standardised and universal symbolic system,

Neolithic "tokens" were therefore mnemonic, information storage devices. If the dominant interpretation of clay objects within the Neolithic context is true, their presence at a site is unequivocal evidence of the existence of higher levels of consciousness. Their presence as "tokens" suggests villages at Çatalhöyük were capable of abstract thought, distant thought and metrication. Yet despite often being presented as fact, evidence for the use of clay objects as "tokens" within the Neolithic Near East is far from straightforward, as seen earlier.

This chapter scrutinises small geometric clay objects from Neolithic Çatalhöyük and independently assesses the evidence in support of their use as "tokens" as outlined earlier. If clay objects functioned as tokens in the way Schmandt-Besserat (1992a, 1992b, 1996) claims, it would be expected that they would be present in a range of standardised shapes and sizes, be recovered in groups, and show an increased diversity and distribution throughout Çatalhöyük's long occupation. Evidence fitting this interpretation is sought, alongside evidence for other common functional interpretations such as their use in administration but as simple counters, nonadministrative roles such as gaming pieces, children's toys, and the possibility that clay objects were indeed nonartefacts (waste products, accidently formed or "doodles" in clay). Specifically, if clay objects were used as "tokens", we would expect the following: (1) a range of objects definitely and intentionally crafted into a range of clear, geometric shapes; (2) little variation within specific three-dimensional shape categories; (3) a correlation between their presence at a site and specific features including sedentism, agriculture, a range of crops and other materials in circulation; (4) a set repertoire of shapes, consistent with the range and type of goods and commodities in circulation at the site; and (5) regional and temporal correlation across the entire Neolithic of the Near East.

MATERIALS AND METHODS

Data for this chapter stems from extensive research into the classification, form, context and function of clay objects from sites across the Neolithic of the Near East. The methodology is a three-stage approach, (1) studying individual objects, (2) their contextual distribution at Çatalhöyük and (3) interpreting this data within the broader regional context of Neolithic Anatolia and the Near East. Due to the duration and scale of excavations, along with a thorough retrieval process and finds policy, thousands of artefacts crafted from clay have been recovered from Çatalhöyük over the many decades of excavations. Aside from generally identifiable artefacts including large "clay [cooking] balls", stamp seals and figurines, there are many crates of miscellaneous clay objects of unidentified function containing well over one thousand small, intentionally shaped clay objects in addition to nonartefactual pieces of clay such as remnants of structural material. A wide variety of clay materials and artefacts were viewed and assessed at Çatalhöyük in order to identify artefacts fitting the definition of clay object. Over 1,500 artefacts fitting the classification criteria were selected and studied in two phases, almost 700 in the initial phase and a further 800 in the second phase of analysis. Various features and characteristics of individual clay objects were assessed related to their

appearance (e.g. colour, shape, dimensions), manufacture (e.g. clay type, finish, presence of fingerprints) and postdeposition processes (e.g. presence of burning, condition). This data was used to characterise and compare clay objects and establish the degree of similarity within and across specific three-dimensional shapes and thus identify groups of clay objects potentially capable of conveying the same symbolic meaning.

The contextual distribution of every single individual clay object was assessed, recording for each object the site area (North, South or TP), broad occupational phase (early, middle, late or final), exact stratigraphic level and the immediate find context and location (e.g. pit fill, pit within domestic structure). Analysis of the nature of the clay objects from different context types was undertaken, to track any changes in the nature or use of clay objects through time, across different areas of site, according to which features and/or artefacts and materials clay objects were found in association with and so on. One major downfall of past "token" studies is the lack of consideration of the contextual distribution of clay objects within a site as well as the use of these details to seek correlation between the range and nature of on-site activities and the presence and nature of clay objects. Consequently, data from Çatalhöyük's clay objects were considered in the wider context of Neolithic Anatolia and the Near East. Data from Çatalhöyük was compared to similarly detailed clay object studies of neighbouring Boncuklu Höyük (mid-ninth to mid-eight millennia BC) and Tell Sabi Abyad (north Syria, mid-eighth to early sixth millennia BC) in addition to data from the examination of 20 less complete assemblages along with a broader level survey charting the presence, relative number or absence of clay objects at an additional 56 sites (Bennison-Chapman 2014; 2019a; 20019b). The aim was to evaluate the evidence for an intersite system of symbolic token accounting during the Neolithic.

RESULTS: OBJECT CHARACTERISTICS

Çatalhöyük's clay objects occur in a range of three-dimensional shapes. The objects are classified into seven *basic* three-dimensional shapes including a category for miscellaneous/other. Spheres (including semispheres) constitute over half of all studied objects (55%) with discs forming the second largest broad shape category, representing almost one-quarter of the total (23%). Cones are the next most numerous shaped clay object (8%). All other shapes (ovoid, cube/cuboid,

cone, cylinder and miscellaneous) occur in far smaller proportions. Subdivisions occur within some of the basic shapes, leading to a total of 14 *detailed* three-dimensional shapes represented within the Çatalhöyük clay object assemblage. Spheres, for example, are split into true spheres and semi- or flattened spheres. The cones are divided into five sub-categories dependent on the shape of the base and straightness of the sides, for example. Spheres still dominate the assemblage, with *true* spheres comprising 46 per cent of the assemblage. All other detailed three-dimensional shapes are represented in far smaller proportions with type 2 discs (flat base, 14%), flattened/semispheres (9%) and type 1 cones (round base, straight sides, 5%) the next most numerous (Figure 5.2).

The overwhelming majority of studied clay objects were complete and intact (64%), although methodology did not account for

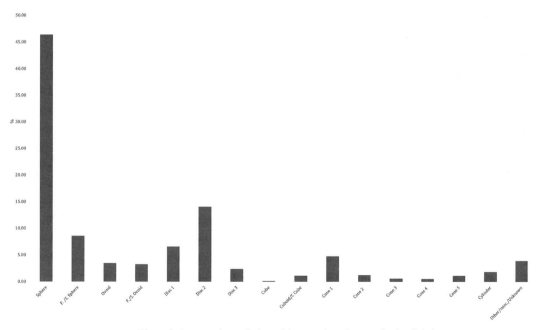

FIGURE 5.2 The relative number of clay objects assigned to each *detailed* three-dimensional shape category used in the study (*n* = 1,057).

heavily fragmented artefacts. Eighteen per cent of Çatalhöyük's clay objects assemblage are characterised as being damaged to the extent that the remaining artefact is less than 75 per cent complete. For the overwhelming majority of clay objects, weight and dimensions can be compared against one another, within and across three-dimensional shape categories. The selection strategy characterises clay objects as small and portable artefacts. The majority of objects weigh less than 3.00 g (50%), and 10 per cent of studied clay objects weigh over 10.00 g. Equally small in size, the maximum dimension of Çatalhöyük's clay objects as measured from three angles falls between 1.22 cm and 2.06 cm. Few objects stand out from the assemblage as a whole for being small or large variations of a common form. Yet size and weight data show there was no standardized weight or size overall or within any particular three-dimensional shape. The clay objects do not fall within any particular grouping, with a graduated increase and decrease in size, peaking within the average ranges listed earlier. In short, no correlation is evidenced in terms of object shape and size. This is not true of later, proto-historic (mid-late fourth millennium) clay objects. Recent research on the clay objects found within bullae Chogha Mish (Susiana plain), for example (Woods 2010), shows that when recovered in caches (as was the norm), clay objects tend to be grouped with others of the same shape, and furthermore, they are of identical proportions, size and therefore overall appearance (Delougaz & Kantor 1996: table 11 pp. 121–122 & table 12 p. 123; Woods 2010: pp. 7, 15–28, 3–85, fig. 21 p. 61). A contemporary example from Hacinebi

Tepe (north Mesopotamia) demonstrates similar object shape and size standardization. Amongst other shapes were 10 spheres created in two distinct size groupings (Pitman 1996: p. 230, bulla HN1100 fig. 18a p. 231).

Like other small clay artefacts at Çatalhöyük (figurines and larger "clay balls"), the site's clay objects comprise a limited range of natural colours, most likely made from locally sourced, naturally occurring clays (Avis 2010; Doherty 2013, 2017: ch. 2). No evidence for tempering is attested. The use of pigment is documented on one or two examples only (faint traces of a red pigment), meaning the majority of clay objects exist in their natural colour. Practically all of Çatalhöyük's clay objects are intentionally hardened (85%), yet this was carefully undertaken, as the presence of blacked surfaces, the result of high temperature exposure is extremely low (<10%).

Fourteen different colour shades were defined and identified, ranging from jet black, through to grey and bright white, dark brown, lighter brown, orange and beige, with red and yellow less commonly found. These colours reflect the full range of naturally occurring, locally available clay sources in Çatalhöyük's immediate surrounds (Doherty 2017: 75, fig. 4.1 p. 68, fig. 4.3 p. 74). Differences in clay colour reflect distinctions in the landscape where the clays are formed. The Konya plain displays a wide variety of clay colours, each reflecting the immediate conditions under which it developed. Black and dark clays were formed under very moist conditions, where high levels of dark organic matter could persist. In contrast, the white and pale green marls found across the entire extent of the Konya plain were created in lakes and at lake margins; areas with little or no alluvial sediment, very low iron and organic matter in combination with very high calcium carbonate content (Doherty 2017: 75–79). Thus in colour, Çatalhöyük's clay objects are present in a diverse range of colours, though the majority can be classified amongst the mid-tone ranges of the basic colours (mid-greys and browns). There is diversity in the type and range of clay objects colours according to three-dimensional shape categories. Spheres, for example, are present in a wide range of colour shades reflecting all 14 identified tones. Cones (all subtypes combined) are equally diverse in colour. Discs in contrast are presented in a far more limited range of colours, with just four to six shades represented according to exact colour-shade.

The assemblage is homogenous in finish with almost all objects described as having a "smooth" or "very smooth" outer surface finish (97%), along with a "fine" clay texture (99%). This shows a clear care and intentionally of craft and attentional to detail. This followed through in the relative lack of fingerprint impressions with just 9 per cent of clay objects displaying finger or palm prints on the clay surface (as viewed with a hand lens, 21 mm loupe, ×30 magnification). Likewise the presence of incidental impressions, most commonly basketry/matting, leather and plants are found on the surfaces of clay objects, yet in negligible proportions (5%; Bennison-Chapman 2013: fig. 15.6 p. 258). The generally faint nature, limited surface coverage (one or part of one surface only) along with their presence only on shapes that need to be manufactured using a flat surface (spheres, made by rolling the clay in the hands, for example, evidence such impressions, in contrast to their dominance on flat base discs).

A small, yet distinctive number of clay objects display intentional, decorative markings (7%), such as those far more common in the proto- and rarely historic period clay objects of the fourth millennium BC onwards (Schmandt-Besserat's "complex tokens"; see, for example, Delougaz & Kantor 1996: pl. 40. B, C, E, G & H; Jasim & Oates 1986: fig. 3 row 2 p. 356; Nisan et al. 1993: fig. 9 p. 13; Schmandt Besserat 1992a: 102, 107; Woods 2010: fig. 24-6 p. 62, fig. 27 p. 63 & fig. 30 p. 64). The markings most commonly appear on either the top or both the top and base of the objects; most are highly visible against the otherwise plain and smooth clay surface, with straight lines; either single or pairs of parallel lines prevail. Though clay objects of certain shapes are more likely to display decorative markings than others, there is no direct correlation between marking forms and objects of specific three-dimensional shape. Spheres do not come in a plain form along with the occasional occurrence of spheres with a single linear incision. Discs do not occur in both plain forms and those with a set of parallel lines incised on one surface. Therefore, though sometimes *marked*, evidence for the clear, consistent, symbolic meaning is lacking in the presence of the decorated clay objects from Çatalhöyük.

A small number of sets of clay objects are distinctive due to the level of homogeneity of three-dimensional shape along with additional characteristics of appearance and manufacture. One example is a group of three squat cylindrical-shaped objects (CO#s 396, 431 and 441, recorded as "other/ miscellaneous" shape) (Bennison-Chapman 2013: fig. 15.15 p. 270). They share similarities in the degree of detail, finish, craft and decoration, which hints at a defined, uniform function (summarised in Bennison-Chapman 2014: ch. 7 fig. 7.13). Near identical in dimensions and proportions, each has a concave base, perfectly rounded shape in plan view, tall straight sides and a pointed tip. Each is highly crafted from a fine clay.

SUMMARY

In comparison to the slightly earlier, neighbouring Neolithic village of Boncuklu Höyük (Bennison-Chapman 2014; 2019a), increased standardization is evidenced in all aspects of clay objects manufacture and appearance at Çatalhöyük. Yet overall, the clay object assemblage of Çatalhöyük is represented by a divergent range of simply manufactured artefacts. Though a varied selection of three-dimensional shapes is present, there is little evidence for the intentional, conscious standardisation of sets of artefacts, uniting them not only by shape category, but also according to other aspects such a size, colour, level of finish or the presence of markings, characteristics that when combined could have been used to represent specific, and distinctive commodities with the objects therefore acting as symbolic mnemonic tools. This is not the case at Late Neolithic Tell Sabi Abyad in Upper Mesopotamia, for example, where within certain limited occupational horizons and site areas, clay objects are far more standardized within their shape categories (Bennison-Chapman 2014, 2019b). At Çatalhöyük, there are, however, a very small number of distinctive sets of clay objects, yet as seen later, all come from disparate site areas and therefore could not have been utilised together as a set of tools.

RESULTS: OBJECT CONTEXT

The function of Çatalhöyük's clay objects cannot be understood if studied in isolation. The exact find-spot, activities carried out within it, the presence or absence of associated clay objects and/or other artefacts and activities all need to be taken into account when making any assessment of the presence of clay objects as indicators of potential Neolithic cognitive abilities. This is especially true when evaluating evidence for the possible presence, evolution and operation of clay objects as an aspect of material culture capable of symbolising, retaining and transmitting information.

BASIC CONTEXT

Occupation at Neolithic Çatalhöyük East can be divided in three main excavation areas, North, South and TP (Hodder, Chapter 1, this volume). North and South areas have similarly large clay object counts. Almost half (49%) of studied clay objects come from the North area, with a further 42 per cent excavated in the south. TP has yielded just 9 per cent of Çatalhöyük's clay objects, yet when the density of objects rather than count is considered, TP has a significantly higher clay object density compared to the other site areas at 0.0028 objects per litre (Figure 5.3). The temporal occupation of Çatalhöyük can broadly be divided into four phases (Hodder, Chapter 1, this volume). Overall, there is an increase in the density of clay objects at Çatalhöyük through time. This is true of both of the two main occupation areas, North and South, where there is a more than twofold increase in the density of clay objects in *Late*

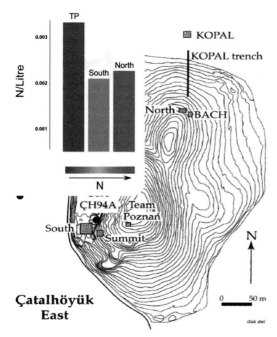

FIGURE 5.3 Plan of Çatalhöyük East Mound showing the three main excavation areas, North, South and TP. Insert: the number (reflected by colour) and the density (height of the columns) of clay objects at Çatalhöyük's main excavation areas. (Plan courtesy of the Çatalhöyük Research Project; thanks to Dr M. Milella)

and *Final Neolithic Occupation* phases compared to the *Early* and *Middle Occupation* phases. This patterning seems, at first, to support Renfrew's (1998, 2007, 2012) argument that an increasing quantity of material culture from the onset and throughout the Neolithic, along with greater engagement with material culture due to the needs of sedentary life resulted in and is evidence of cognitive change. However, when assessed in greater, occupational level by occupational level detail within North and South areas separately, it is clear that rather than a steady, gradual increase in the density of clay objects throughout the Çatalhöyük's occupation, the frequency of clay objects peaks and falls haphazardly

(Figure 5.4). Although this is not evidence against the theory of cognitive change, it does not support the more common theory held by Renfrew (1998, 2007, 2012) and others (i.e. Donald 1991; Watkins 2010).

NATURE OF CONTEXT

If clay objects were utilised as commonly assumed, they may have been retained in order for the information they symbolically held to be checked and verified upon the conclusion of a transaction or at a longer interval – a stock take, end of season or annual audit-type activity. The large proportion of clay objects recovered from midden contexts does not directly indicate such meaning or activity. Forty-two per cent of Çatalhöyük's clay objects come from broad "midden" contexts (open-air disposal zones and activity areas), with a further 8 per cent from "construction/make-up/packing layer" context types representing the re-use of soil and other materials containing refuge including disposed of clay objects. This type of context indicates clay objects were readily disposed of and held no intrinsic value (not a surprise, considering their ease of craft and low value, abundant raw material). The vast majority of broad "midden" context clay objects (83%) come from common, open midden areas; however, a smaller proportion comes from more distinctive contexts *within* middens, including "fire spots", "room fill" and "pit fill". Aside from midden context objects, 21 per cent of Çatalhöyük's clay objects come from the broad category of "fill", which includes depositions such as pit fill, room fill, building fill and burial fill. However, in almost all instances, when examined closely,

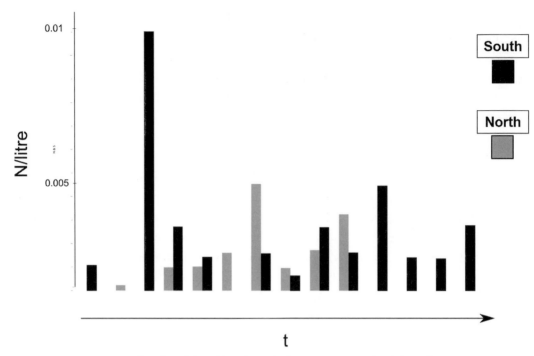

FIGURE 5.4 Density of clay objects in each discrete excavation level through time (across the *Early, Middle* and *Late Occupation* phases); North compared to South excavation areas.

the fill clay objects are included as part of the general soil makeup, and not included as intentional depositions (found in situ with other artefacts within a pit, on cache on a floor surface, nor in a specific, meaningful placement within a grave for example).

From the study of the broad contextual distribution of both the "midden" and "fill" context clay objects, no support for the notion that clay objects were used in groups, retained or cached for later information retrieval is attested. Nor is there evidence of a set symbolic system. The *nature* of clay objects within and across select detailed context types (pits within buildings, open-air middens, burials and room fill, for example) was assessed, and no correlation between the shape, size, colour, finish or any other aspect of an object's appearance according to

context type was apparent. However, "cluster" objects, though rare, do indicate the presence of potentially interesting object associations along with nondisposal contexts.

CLUSTER OBJECTS

Cluster clay objects are defined as clay objects recovered in immediate and definite association with at least two other artefacts, either additional clay objects, artefacts of another classification or cultural objects. Differentiation is seen in the three-dimensional shape of cluster clay objects, the overwhelming majority of which are spheres, found alongside, and exclusively with large numbers (into the hundreds) of other spheres (Atalay 2013: 247, 248–252; 2001, 2005; Bennison-Chapman 2014: ch. 7, appx. D; 2013:

fig. 15.14 p. 270). Previously extensively studied under the term "mini-ball", spheres recovered in clusters are united by a number of other shared characteristics. (a) They are recovered alongside almost exclusively or only alongside other alike artefacts. (b) The spherical cluster clay objects are all are manufactured from unbaked clay of a white, pale beige to cream hue. (c) Clusters of "mini-balls" are most often recovered, intentionally placed inside buildings (57%), mostly within the main room. This differs from the contextual patterning of not only all clay objects combined, but all spherical-shaped clay objects overall (all colours and finishes) (Bennison-Chapman 2014: appx. D, tbl. A.D-1). Though occasionally recovered singly inside a building, the "mini-balls" recovered from inside buildings are mostly recovered in large caches running into the hundreds. Building 44, for example, has 29 "mini balls", Building 3 has 64, Building 63 has 63, and Building 75 has 485 "mini balls" (Bennison-Chapman 2014: fig. A.D-3, tbl. A.D-2). (d) Temporally, more than three-quarters (567) of "mini-balls" occur in Çatalhöyük's *Late* and *Final Occupation* phases (as opposed to just 99 from the *Early* and *Middle* phases) (Atalay 2013: 248–250; 2012: 14/4–14/7; 2000; Bennison-Chapman 2014: ch. 7, appx. D). There is no steady increase in their numbers through time, but "mini-ball" counts peak in certain occupational phases; South.P and North.I (Bennison-Chapman 2014: fig. A.D-2).

Aside from spheres, cluster clay objects are rare, with just nine other examples (1% all studied clay objects) documented within the present study at Çatalhöyük (Bennison-Chapman 2014: ch. 7). These differ in nature entirely, and nothing distinctive regarding the nature of the nine, nonspherical cluster clay objects can be discerned. These dense clusters of occupational deposits primarily consist of concentrated groupings of animal bones (i.e. unit 17070, CO#s 1066, 1067), stones, refuse (interpreted as "feasting deposits" alongside single, up to two or three geometric clay objects only; Bennison-Chapman 2014: ch. 7 tbl. 7.11). A unique example comes from Building 42, where three clay objects were recovered in direct association with a complete ceramic pot, which had in turn been set into the floor of the main room (CO#'s 1314, 1315 and 1317, associated with oven F. 828 and platform).

CONTEXT SUMMARY

In summary, the contextual evidence for Çatalhöyük's clay objects does not support the theory of their use as symbolic, mnemonic devoices, nor as tools used for long-term information storage and retrieval. In quantity they mostly occur in the site's largest two excavation areas, North and South yet are most *dense* within the smaller TP excavation zone. Clay objects are most commonly recovered alone, as single objects within disposal or secondary deposit contexts. Temporally, they do increase through time in number, yet this is not a gradual nor steady increase within any of the site's excavation areas. No patterning can be identified in terms of the nature and level of homogeneity/diversity of clay objects when comparing sets from specific temporal phases, site areas or context types. Spatially, clay objects are not, for example, deposited mostly in open-air middens within certain sectors of the village, and within buildings in others. In the *Early* and *Middle Occupation* phases, the proportion of clay objects recovered in middens, as compared to fill, and the nature of the midden and fill contexts types differs little. Likewise, no increase in clay objects diversity in terms of three-dimensional shape is apparent, nor an increase in manufacture homogeneity, if the objects were used as symbols, increasingly so, with differences in basic appearance (shape, size, colour, elaboration) all important in terms of the information they held is seen. Almost half of Çatalhöyük's clay objects come from broad midden contexts, in which basic open-air middens dominate. The 21 per cent of clay objects recovered from fill contexts are dominated by the incidental inclusion of clay objects into the fill of daily activities such as the in-filling of pits, fire-spots and burials. As seen earlier, Çatalhöyük has a small number of distinctive sets of extremely homogenous clay objects, sharing many similarities in addition to basic three-dimensional shape. Many, yet far from all, of the spheres share similar contexts, recovered with identical objects in internal clusters within buildings. Aside from these, the sets of small numbers of homogenous cones and squat cylinders, for example, derive from divergent context types showing that despite a uniform appearance, they were neither manufactured nor used together.

DISCUSSION

The results presented allow us to return to the questions posed at the beginning of this chapter. How common were the geometric clay objects, how were they used, and what does this allow us to say about changing levels of consciousness at Neolithic Çatalhöyük?

NONADMINISTRATIVE POSSIBILITIES

Evaluating the potential nonadministrative explanations for the function of Neolithic clay objects, some seem more likely than others. Clay objects are intentionally manufactured artefacts that cannot be dismissed as "doodles", clay "blanks" or simply compacted dirt. Their use in gaming at some sites is a strong possibility. Gaming is generally a leisure activity. With more than one type of game common within any community, the overall diversity seen within Çatalhöyük's clay object assemblage is easily explained by this interpretation. Board-based games are just one of many types of games evidenced from at least the Neolithic of the Near East (Becker 2007; Freed 1982; Hoerth 2007; Kendall 2007; Lorenzi 2013; Simpson 2007; Vandier 1964: fig. 1–3 p. 494). Of approximately 13 Neolithic examples, the holes on the surfaces of the boards measure 3–4 cm – the correct size for the overwhelming majority of clay objects to fit within (Bartl, Ramadan & Al-Hafian 2011: fig. 28 p. 72; Simmons & Najjar 2006: fig. 7 p. 88; Simpson 2007: 6–7). The timing of the appearance of clay objects coincides with sedentism. Early village communities likely needed activities to enhance and maintain community bonds, and gaming could have promoted community cohesion. Limited evidence for caches of clay objects suggest otherwise – when disposed of in middens, they appear to have been disposed of singly. In gaming they would have been utilised in sets.

Children's Toys?

It is difficult to prove whether clay objects may or may not have been used as children's toys. Aside from gaming – a pastime open to people of all ages – the idea of clay objects being specifically entertainment items for the very young is in itself problematic. The notion of "toys" implies a notion of "childhood" – a modern concept, not overtly attested at Çatalhöyük or other Neolithic sites in the Near East. Neonates receive special postmortuary treatment at Çatalhöyük, yet little else suggests children were considered "different" (Andrews et al. 2005; Boz & Hager 2013; Hodder 2006: 62, 117, 128, 159, 163, 175, 199). Therefore this possible interpretation is irrelevant in this context.

Ritual Objects?

Çatalhöyük and the Neolithic Near East in general has an abundantly rich record of evidence related to ritual and spiritual beliefs (see, for example, Hodder 2010). Neolithic beliefs were complex, and ritual varied. Though overall, evidence of Neolithic ritual is rich, the evidence we have relates to only certain elements of ritual practice. Confirmation of activities from many significant spheres of ritual activity: dance, singing, changing, processions, masks, costume, makeup and body paint is extremely sparse or absent in the Neolithic archaeological record. The category of "ritual" is often assigned to items where no other definitive function can be proved. Yet, Çatalhöyük has many lines of evidence and practices indicative of ritual activities. Therefore use of clay objects as part of normal ritual activity is not unrealistic, yet also, not likely to have been their main purpose.

Decision-Making Tools?

Small geometric clay objects may have been used in divination; for decision making and to foretell future events. Clay objects could have been used as "lots"; being thrown or drawn from a container to make a choice or decision. The outcome of decisions may have been dependent on how objects fell (for example, the distribution of the objects, or the angle or location of a specific objects within the group), as commonly evidenced ethnographically (Peek 1991). Evidence for this function at Neolithic Çatalhöyük is again inconclusive. The number, size and variety of appearance of the case-study assemblages certainly suggest the possibility of the use of their clay objects as lots. They are small enough for a few to be placed into a container or cupped in the hand, ready to be tossed or selected by an agent. Agriculturalists would certainly be in need of decision-making tools and lots may have been useful in making fair, undisputable and unbiased decisions. Many decisions would need to be made related to hunting and animal herding, plant and animal cultivation, the distribution of resources (including meat, cereals, land and animals) and the distribution of labour roles. "Lots" could have been a way to make difficult decisions, to ease tension and competition and to avoid confrontation between individuals and families within the new and growing village settlements of the Neolithic. Yet direct evidence of this function, like that of ritual in general is absent at Çatalhöyük.

ADMINISTRATIVE FUNCTIONS

The three basic ways in which small clay objects could have been used as administrative tools are (1) as aids in simple counting, (2) as nonsymbolic information storage devices and (3) as symbolic, mnemonic record keeping and information retention and transmission tools.

(1) Simple Counting Aids

One of the simplest functions for small, geometric clay objects proposed is their use in counting. A distinction must be made here between pure counting and recording or accounting: the latter distinguished by the use of the objects to retain and transmit information. As nonsymbolic, noninformation holding tools, clay objects certainly could have been useful counting tools. They may have been used in simple one-to-one correspondence to count a number of individual items or sets of items. A clay object would be moved from one place to another, counted side by side with each item. This could be advantageous if large numbers of items were being counted. The use of clay objects as counting aids could prevent people from losing count, which could easily happen, especially when performing large counts, undertaking counting in a busy or chaotic situation, and if there was a delay, however small, in the completion of a count. One-to-one counting with clay objects would also serve to increase the accuracy of counts, and such a system would also enable people with limited numeracy skills to perform simple counting tasks with ease. At the end, the new pile created would visually represent the number of items or units that had been counted (Herskovits 1932). Additionally, if, as the absence of abstract numbers in the earliest written records of south Mesopotamia for the first 1,000 years of writing (until the end of the third millennium cal. BC.) can be taken as evidence of the lack of a concept of abstract numbers (Brown 1996: 39; Englund 1993: 1671; Friberg 1994: 482, 483; Michalowski 1993: 998; Nissen et al. 1993: 130, 131–151),

and correspondingly the absence of number vocabulary, abstract counting would be an impossibility. This is not to say that Neolithic communities lacked the cognitive ability of abstract counting and had no number words; however, the use of clay objects to aid counting in a one-to-one method makes the question of whether nor not these early village communities had the ability to conceive of abstract numbers irrelevant.

Assemblages of small, geometric clay and stone objects could have been used to aid simple counting. As a wide variety of people, animals and commodities might have been counted, the context of the clay objects within sites of the Neolithic would not be informative with regards to their exact counting function. They may be left scattered in fields or buildings or swept into midden areas as it would be likely they were disposed of after being used – or kept to be reused for a further count. Therefore, single clay objects, broad clay object scatters or caches of clay objects in a variety of find spots are all likely scenarios for the disposition of these objects if used in simple counting. The contextual evidence from Çatalhöyük largely supports the simple counting theory.

(2) Nonsymbolic Information Storage Devices

Adding to the complexity of counting involves using the position of "counters" on a board or abacus, for example, as indicators of values (as evidenced historically in other cultures; see, for example, Netz 2002). The position of clay objects (or other items) on a board or abacus could indicate further meaning, to change the value of a single "counter" from a single to multiple unit (from 1 to 10 to 100, for example, in the metric system, or from 1 to 6 to 60 in the sexigesimal system of the earliest written records from south Mesopotamia) (Nissen et al. 1993: 131–151). In this scenario, clay objects may perform complex counts, their appearance being irrelevant as the information related to value is symbolised by their relative positions rather than in the objects themselves. Though possible, the use of Çatalhöyük's clay objects in the manner just described is not supported by the evidence, as their multiple, elaborate and varied shapes do not support the theory that appearance was unimportant. Likewise, contextual evidence does not support this scenario, as groups of clay objects would be simultaneously used, equally manipulated, thus equally ready to be disposed of at the same time. Why, therefore, are the overwhelming majority of clay objects disposed of singly? Neither option one nor two incorporate the *symbolic* element, crucial to most arguments that interpret the presence of "tokens" in the Neolithic as a sign of higher cognitive functioning. The operation of clay objects as advanced counters in the latter part of scenario two, however, could certainly be argued as evidence of significant intelligence.

(3) Symbolic Tools and Recording Devices

Dominant thought interprets "tokens" as evidence of increased cognitive abilities for two reasons: first, they are interpreted as evidence for humans to conceive of abstract ideas – a sphere standing for a sheep being evidence for abstraction. Yet why not just use a zoomorphic figurine to stand for the animal it represents (no evidence of such a system is seen at Çatalhöyük)? Clay objects at Çatalhöyük could potentially, as an extension to the counting system outlined earlier, be assigned a short-term, ad hoc symbolic value. Objects of a similar appearance could be used to count one specific item and counters of a different colour, size or shape, for example, used to count a second. This would prevent errors in the overlap of counts, or if the counters were accidently mixed. With objects given meaning at a single place in time, the meaning was lost once the count had been made, yet providing the ability to simultaneously count different things side by side. This concept cannot be proven or disproved, as the objects were not retained at all, nor the meaning held within their similarities permanent. This simple symbolic system is not supported by the contextual evidence, yet the diverse nature of the clay objects at Çatalhöyük means it could have potentially operated. Second, the "token" theory takes the "token" argument to a higher level, claiming the simple geometric shapes have consistent symbolic meaning, not only locally, but also regionally from the Neolithic to the fourth millennium BC (Schmandt-Besserat 1992a, 1996). In this system, clay objects were a method of communication, the shape representing a word relating to a specific, nonchanging community in a singular form or set unit (a single animal or a sack of grain, for example). The "code" was understood and used by all, and therefore "tokens" were retained, carried on the body and once transactions completed, archives were created by the storage of sets of "tokens" (Schmandt-Besserat 1992a, 1996). This represents a sophisticated method of information storage and communication distinct from both spoken and written word (Watkins 2010: 631). The value held within the shape of the "token" was universal, and therefore their function was also singular and universal.

SUMMARY

The evidence from Çatalhöyük does not support the notion of their use, either exclusively, or at times in conjunction with other functions, as symbolic, information storage and information transmission tools. Their infrequent recovery in caches is evidence against this. The singular shape of the clay objects most commonly cached together (the spherical "mini-balls") would suggest that in this system, the residents of Çatalhöyük were using the advanced administration system of scenario three only for the management of a single commodity represented by the sphere. In this case, all other clay objects must have functioned outside of the realm of administration. Furthermore, small spheres could not have acted as "tokens" alone. Though commonly cached together in large numbers, small clay spheres are equally as numerous in other contexts, recovered as lone artefacts in middens most commonly (identical to the dominant contextual deposition of all clay objects at Çatalhöyük). Therefore, even the spheres must have had a dual purpose. The interpretation of sphere caches as administrative archives brings to light other problems – why utilise an advanced, highly efficient and tightly managed system of control for one single commodity, and leave no evidence for the administration of any other commodity at the site? This suggests that clay sphere caches at Çatalhöyük, though distinct, do not represent archives.

The form of the other-shaped clay objects at Çatalhöyük and the overall degree of assemblage homogeneity again points away from the symbolic record keeping interpretation. Not all three-dimensional shape categories are overtly and immediately uniform, a necessity in the scenario in question. Many shapes are also only represented in very small proportions. Only a limited number of highly homogenous object sets have been identified in the Çatalhöyük assemblage, not enough for a site-wide, universal symbolic information storage and communication system to have been in operation. As seen in the contextual analysis earlier, not even within a discrete time period or smaller areas of the site is there evidence for the existence of a small number of highly distinct (across shape categories) and homogenous (within three-dimensional shape) clay objects, those homogenous sets identified as coming from diverse temporal and geographic parts of Çatalhöyük. If Çatalhöyük's clay objects were part of a set symbolic code, strong correlation across the Neolithic Near East would be expected. The same limited range of clearly defined and well-made shapes would be expected, evenly distributed across the geographic and temporal span of each settlement. With correlation of their presence, absence and range of shapes according to the nature of the site (e.g. temporary/seasonal, permanent, residential, ritual, agricultural, hunter gather, mixed subsistence), the evidence in this respect is lacking (Bennison-Chapman 2014: ch. 10, appx. J). Last, one must consider that a singular, consistent functional role for the use of clay objects is not the only feasible interpretation at Çatalhöyük or elsewhere.

CONCLUSION

This research proves the common misconceptions about Neolithic "tokens" to be untrue. Clay objects are certainly intentionally made artefacts and not naturally formed clumps of clay or "doodles". There is no evidence for a singular and consistent function at Çatalhöyük nor across the wider Neolithic of the Near East. Nor does the evidence suggest clay objects were invented by the first farmers in the Near East, to keep track of agricultural produce. At Çatalhöyük along with neighbouring sites such as Boncuklu Höyük, and those further afield, clay objects are crafted into a clear range of geometric shapes, yet at Çatalhöyük, along with many other sites, the level of object standardization is limited. No correlation can be seen between the presence and relative number of clay objects and any specific site feature such as, most crucially, the appearance of farming. This is to be expected if clay objects acted as "tokens" and were introduced by farmers to administer their produce.

No variability is evidenced at Çatalhöyük in terms of the type and range of shapes or object standardization. Both temporally and according to context type little changes in the *nature* of Çatalhöyük's clay objects. They are more common in later phases of occupation; however, this is an overall pattern, and when examining the density of clay objects, level by level across all four phases, changes in density can be stark, yet do not correlate to any major events. With reference to object shape, no change in the range or homogeneity of form

is seen at all. The dominant obsidian source slowly changes from one to another throughout Çatalhöyük's occupation, for instance, yet no difference in clay object form (the disappearance of one shape, replaced with a different shape, for example) is seen. Likewise, the *Later Occupation* phases demonstrate the transition to a heavy investment in sheep and cattle, yet no increase in the count or density of a "token" representing sheep or cattle, for example, occurs. From the middle of the occupational sequence (South N-O and North G) major developments occur across various spheres of life at Çatalhöyük, including the widespread use of pottery and the introduction of milk and domestic cattle. Yet no new "token" shapes occur, nor do increase in count or density during this or subsequent occupation phases.

No set "token" repertoire is suggested, as other sites studied in addition to Çatalhöyük display a similar lack of correlation between major events and the presence or absence of features (e.g. strong ritual evidence, the appearance of domestication) (Bennison-Chapman 2014: ch. 10, appx. J). Nor can any regional, or temporal correlation be seen according to the presence, relative number or type and range of shapes in circulation within a given site – suggestive of the invention and spread of an administrative technology and symbolic code. With no set repertoire of shapes, consistent with the range and/or types of goods and commodities in circulation at Çatalhöyük and other Neolithic sites, little variability is evidenced in all expected aspects of clay objects. This is evidence *against* the idea of as singular role and consistent function within Çatalhöyük and the wider Neolithic Near East. Variability is evidence not only in the distribution of clay objects across the Neolithic Near East, but also in the nature of those sites and the immediate contexts in which clay objects are found.

Clay objects likely fulfilled multiple roles at Çatalhöyük, across different households, areas of site and phases of settlement. Their large numbers at Çatalhöyük and at other sites where present, the variability of deposition, the high proportion recovered from disposal contexts along with the simple range of shapes, their quick manufacture, crude appearance and the accessibility of clay proves that "tokens", at Çatalhöyük, were quickly and easily made and disposed of as readily. All evidence points to Çatalhöyük's clay objects having acted as multifunctional artefacts, their accessibility and ease of craft affording them fluidity of function and interpretation with imbued value and meaning. This is not to say clay objects were never used in administration. As discussed in the Discussion section, one of their likely roles at Çatalhöyük was as simple counters. Tell Sabi Abyad, a large, multitelled site in upper Mesopotamia, also has clear evidence for the use of clay objects in administration (Akkermans 1996a, 1996b; Akkermans et al. 2012, 2014; Akkermans & Duistermaat 1996; Verhoeven 1999; Verhoeven & Akkermans 2000). Again it seems likely that though found through its one-and-a-half millennia occupation history (c. 7,550–5,700 cal. B.C.), clay objects acted mainly or solely as counting tools retained for a limited time period, in two discrete site areas only, before being disposed of in groups, alongside other artefacts made of clay (Bennison-Chapman 2019b).

Despite much research, Çatalhöyük's small, geometric-shaped clay objects provide no definitive evidence for the existence of higher levels of consciousness of its inhabitants. The evidence for clay objects acting as "tokens" at Çatalhöyük is negligible. There is no evidence for what Renfrew (1998, 2007, 2012) or Donald (1991) or Watkins (2010) describe as the external storage of information with clay objects acting as material in Çatalhöyük's clay objects. Nor is there evidence of clay objects possessing a widely understood symbolic value thus acting as a form of communication, as a symbolic nonverbal communication system (Watkins 2010). Indeed, Çatalhöyük provides very little evidence to uphold the interpretation of its clay objects as tokens: symbolic, mnemonic information storage and transmission devices and thus indicative of increased cognitive abilities as Schmandt-Besserat (1977, 1978a, 1980, 1992a, 1992b, 1996) and others (including Mithen 2004; Renfrew 1998, 2007, 2012; Watkins 2010) so commonly suggest.

REFERENCES

Akkermans, P. M. M. G. ed. (1996a) *Tell Sabi Abyad, The Late Neolithic Settlement: Report on the Excavations of the University of Amsterdam 1988 and the National Museum of Antiquities Leiden 1991–1993 in Syria-Volume I*, Istanbul: Nederlands Historisch-Archaeologisch Instituut te Istanbul.

Akkermans, P. M. M. G. ed. (1996b) *Tell Sabi Abyad, the Late Neolithic Settlement: Report on the Excavations of the University of Amsterdam 1988 and the National Museum of Antiquities Leiden 1991–1993 in Syria-Volume II*, Istanbul: Nederlands Historisch-Archaeologisch Instituut te Istanbul.

Akkermans, P. M. M. G., Brüning, M., Hammers, N., Huigens, H., Kruijer, L., Meens, A., Nieuwenhuyse, O., Raat, A., Rogmans, E. F., Slappendel, C., Taipale, S., Tews, S. & Visser, E. (2012) "Burning Down the

House: The Burnt Building V6 at Late Neolithic Tell Sabi Abyad, Syria", *Analecta Praehistorica Leidensia*, vol. 43, no. 44, pp. 307–324.

Akkermans, P. M. M. G., Brüning, M., Huigens, H. & Nieuwenhuyse, O. eds. (2014) *Excavations at Late Neolithic Tell Sabi Abyad, Syria: The 1994–1999 Field Seasons*, Turnholt, Belgium: Brepolis.

Akkermans, P. M. M. G. & Duistermaat, K. (1996) "Of Storage and Nomads. The Sealings from Late Neolithic, Sabi Abyad, Syria [with comments and reply]", *Paléorient*, vol. 22, no. 2, pp. 17–44.

Andrews, P., Molleson, T. & Boz, B. (2005) "The Human Burials at Çatalhöyük" in *Inhabiting Çatalhöyük: reports from the 1995–99 seasons (Çatalhöyük Research Project Volume 4)*, ed. I. Hodder, Monograph No. 38, Cambridge, UK: McDonald Institute for Archaeological Research / British Institute of Archaeology at Ankara, pp. 261–278.

Atalay, S. (2000) "Clay Balls and Objects" in *Çatalhöyük Archive Report 2000*. Available at: www.catalhoyuk.com/archive_reports/2000/ar00_15.html.

Atalay, S. (2001) "BACH Area Clay Balls, Mini Balls and Geometric Objects" in *Çatalhöyük Archive Report 2001*. Available at: www.catalhoyuk.com/archive_reports/2001/index.html.

Atalay, S. (2005) "Domesticating Clay: The Role of Clay Balls, Mini Balls and Geometric Objects in Daily Life at Çatalhöyük" in *Changing Materialities at Çatalhöyük: Reports from the 1995–99 Seasons (Çatalhöyük Research Project Volume 5)*, ed. I. Hodder, Monograph No. 39, Cambridge, UK: McDonald Institute for Archaeological Research/British Institute at Ankara, pp. 139–168.

Atalay, S. (2012) "Analysis of Clay Balls from the BACH Area" in *Last House on the Hill: BACH Area Reports from Çatalhöyük, Turkey*, ed. R. Tringham & M. Stevanovic, Monumenta Archaeologica 27, Los Angeles: Cotsen Institute of Archaeology at UCLA, pp. 14/1–14/9.

Atalay, S. (2013) "Clay Balls, Mini Balls and Geometric Objects" in *Substantive Technologies at Çatalhöyük: Reports from the 2000–2008 seasons (Çatalhöyük Research Project Volume 9)*, ed. I. Hodder, London & Los Angeles: British Institute at Ankara & Cotsen Institute of Archaeology at UCLA, pp. 247–252.

Avis, J. (2010) "Figurines Clay Composition Report" in *Çatalhöyük Archive Report 2010*, pp. 94–103. Available at: www.catalhoyuk.com/downloads/Archive_Report_2010.pdf.

Bartl, K., Ramadan, J. & Al-Hafian, W. (2011) "Shir/West Syria Results of the Sixth and Seventh Seasons of Excavations in 2009" in *Chronique Archéologique en Syrie: Special Issue Documenting the Annual Excavation Reports Concerning the Archaeological Activities in Syria*, vol. V. Damascus, Syria: Press of the Ministry of Culture.

Becker, A. (2007) "The Royal Game of Ur" in *Ancient Board Games in Perspective: Papers from the 1990 British Museum Colloquium, with Additional Contributions*, ed. I. L. Finkel, London: The British Museum Press, pp. 11–15.

Bennison-Chapman, L. E. (2013) "Geometric Clay Objects" in *Substantive Technologies at Çatalhöyük: Reports from the 2000–2008 Seasons (Çatalhöyük Research Project Volume 9)*, ed. I. Hodder, Los Angeles, CA: British Institute at Ankara & Cotsen Institute of Archaeology at UCLA, pp. 253–276.

Bennison-Chapman, L. E. (2014) *The Role and Function of "Tokens" and Sealing Practices in the Neolithic of the Near East: The Question of Early Recording Systems, Symbolic Storage, Precursors to Writing, Gaming, or Monitoring Devices in the World's First Villages*, PhD, submitted to the Department of Archaeology, Classics and Egyptology; part of the School of Histories, Languages and Cultures, University of Liverpool, UK.

Bennison-Chapman, L. E. (2019a) "Reconsidering 'tokens': Neolithic origins of accounting or multifunctional, utilitarian tools?" *Cambridge Archaeological Journal*, vol. 29.2, pp. 233–259. https://doi.org/10.1017/S0959774318000513.

Bennison-Chapman, L. E. (2019b) "Clay Objects as 'Tokens'? Evidence for early counting and administration at Late Neolithic Tell Sabi Abyad, Mesopotamia".

Bottéro, J., Herrenschmidt, C. & Vernant, J. P. (2000) *Ancestor of the West: Writing, Reasoning, and Religion in Mesopotamia, Elam, and Greece*, Chicago: University of Chicago Press.

Boz, B. & Hager, L. (2013) "Intramural Burial Practices at Çatalhöyük" in *Humans and Landscapes of*

Çatalhöyük: Reports from the 2000–2008 Seasons (Çatalhöyük Research Project Volume 8), ed. I. Hodder, Los Angeles, CA: British Institute at Ankara & Cotsen Institute of Archaeology at UCLA, pp. 413–440.

Broman Morales, V. (1990) *Figurines and Other Clay Objects from Sarab and Çayönü*, Chicago: The Oriental Institute of the University of Chicago.

Brown, S. (1996) "Review of Schmandt-Besserat, D. *Before* Writing, Volumes I & II, 1992", *Canadian Society for Mesopotamian Studies Bulletin*, 31, pp. 35–43.

Çambel, H. & Braidwood, R. J. (1979) "An Early Farming Village in Turkey (originally published in *Scientific American*, March 1970)" in *Readings from Scientific American. Hunters, Farmers, and Civilizations: Old World Archaeology with Introductions by C. C. Lamberg-Karlovsky*, San Francisco, CA: W. H. Freeman and Company, pp. 145–151.

Costello, S. K. (2000) "Memory Tools in Early Mesopotamia", *Antiquity*, vol. 74, no. 285, pp. 475–476.

Costello, S. K. (2002) *Tools of Memory: Investigation of the Context of Information Storage in the Halaf Period*, PhD, Binghamton University.

Costello, S. K. (2011) "Image, Memory and Ritual: Re-viewing the Antecedents of Writing", *Cambridge Archaeological Journal*, vol. 21, no. 2, pp. 247–262.

Coulmas, F. (2003) *Writing Systems: An Introduction to Their Linguistic Analysis*, Cambridge, UK: Cambridge University Press.

Damerow, P. (1993) "Bookkeepers Invented Scripture: Review of Schmandt-Besserat's *Before Writing* 1992", *Rechtshistorisches Journal*, vol. 12, no. VI, pp. 9–35.

Delougaz, P. & Kantor, H. (1996) *Chogha Mish, Volume 1: The First Five Seasons of Excavations, 1961–1971*. Abbas Alizadeh, ed. Oriental Institute Publications 101. Chicago: The Oriental Institute.

Doherty, C. (2013) "Sourcing Çatalhöyük's Clays" in *Substantive Technologies at Çatalhöyük: Reports from the 2000–2008 Seasons (Çatalhöyük Research Project Volume 9)*, ed. I. Hodder, Los Angeles, CA: British Institute at Ankara & Cotsen Institute of Archaeology at UCLA, pp. 51–66.

Doherty, C. (2017) *Living with Clay: Materials, Technology, Resources and Landscape at Çatalhöyük*, PhD, submitted to the School of Archaeology and Ancient History, University of Leicester, UK.

Donald, M. (1991) *Origins of the Modern Mind: Three Stages in the Evolution of Culture and Cognition*, Cambridge, MA: Harvard University Press.

Duru, R. & Umurtak, G. (2005) *Höyücek. 1989–1992 Yılları Arasında Yapılan Kazıların Sonuçları 2005 (Höyücek. Results of the Excavations 1988–1992)*, Ankara, Turkey: Türk Tarih Kurumu Yayınları.

Englund, R. K. (1993) "The Origins of Script. Review of *Before Writing* by Denise Schmandt-Besserat", *Science*, 260(5114), pp. 1670–1671.

Englund, R. K. (1998) "Review of D. Schmandt-Besserat, 'How Writing Came About'", *Written Language and Literacy*, vol. 1, pp. 257–261.

Esin, U., Bıçakçı, E., Özbaşaran, M., Balkan-Atlı, N., Berker, D., Yağmur, İ. & Atlı, K. (1991) "Salvage Excavations at the Pre-Pottery Site of Aşıklı Höyük in Central Anatolia", *Anatolica*, vol. 17, pp. 123–174.

Fischer, S. R. (2001) *A History of Writing*, London: Reaktion Books.

Freed, R. E. (1982) "Games" in *Egypt's Golden Age: The Art of Living in the New Kingdom, 1558–1085 BC*, ed. R. E. Freed, Boston: Museum of Fine Arts-Boston, pp. 54–55.

Friberg, J. (1994) "Preliterate Counting and Accounting in the Middle East: A Constructively Critical Review of Schmandt-Besserat's *Before Writing*", *Orientalistische Literaturzeitung*, vol. 89, no. 5–6, pp. 477–502.

Herskovits, M. J. (1932) "Population Statistics in the Kingdom of Dahomey", *Human Biology*, vol. 4, no. 2, pp. 252–261.

Hodder, I. (2006) *Çatalhöyük: The Leopard's Tale: Revealing the Mysteries of Turkey's Ancient 'Town'*, London: Thames & Hudson.

Hodder, I. (2010) *Religion in the Emergence of Civilisation: Çatalhöyük as a Case Study*, Cambridge, UK: Cambridge University Press.

Hoerth, A. J. (2007) "The Game of Hounds and Jackals" in *Ancient Board Games in Perspective: Papers from the 1990 British Museum Colloquium, with Additional Contributions*, ed. I. L. Finkel, London: The British Museum Press, pp. 64–68.

Iceland, H. (2010) "Chapter 1: Token Finds at Pre-Pottery Neolithic 'Ain Ghazal, Jordan: A Formal and Technological Analysis" in *'Ain Ghazal Excavation Reports Volume 2: Symbols at 'Ain Ghazal*. Ed. D. Schmandt-Besserat. Published under the direction of Gary O. Rollefson and Zeidan Kafafi (visited on 14 April 2012). Available at: www.laits.utexas.edu/ghazal/Chap1/chapter1.html. [Last updated on 31 October 2010].

Jasim, S. A. & Oates, J. (1986) "Early Tokens and Tablets in Mesopotamia: New Information from Tell Abada and Tell Brak", *World Archaeology*, vol. 17, no. 3, pp. 348–362.

Kendall, T. (2007) "Mehen: The Ancient Egyptian Game of the Serpent" in *Ancient Board Games in Perspective: Papers from the 1990 British Museum Colloquium, with Additional Contributions*, ed. I. L. Finkel, London: The British Museum Press, pp. 33–45.

Kenyon, K. M., & Holland, T. A. (1982) *Excavations at Jericho Volume Four: The Pottery Type Series and Other Finds*, London: British School of Archaeology in Jerusalem.

Kenyon, K. M. & Holland, T. A. (1983) *Excavations at Jericho Volume 5: The Pottery Phases of the Tell and Other Finds*, London: British School of Archaeology in Jerusalem c/o The British Academy.

Leo Oppenheim, A. (1959) "On an Operational Device in Mesopotamian Bureaucracy", *Journal of Near Eastern Studies*, vol. 18, no. 2, pp. 121–128.

Lorenzi, R. (2013) "Oldest Gaming Tokens Found in Turkey" in *Discovery News* (last updated on 14 August 2013). Available at: http://news.discovery.com/history/archaeology/oldest-gaming-tokens-found-130814.htm. [Site visited on 14 August 2013].

Mahasneh, H. M. & Gebel, H. G. (1998) "Geometric Objects from LPPNB Es-Sifiya, Wadi Mujib, Jordan", *Paléorient*, vol. 24, no. 2, pp. 105–110.

Malafouris, L. (2013) *How Things Shape the Mind: A Theory of Material Engagement*, Cambridge, MA: MIT Press.

Matthews, R., Matthews, W. & Mohammadifar, Y. (eds.) (2013) *The Earliest Neolithic of Iran: 2008 Excavations at Sheikh-E Abad and Jani*, Oxford, UK: Oxbow Books.

Michalowski, P. (1993) "Review: Tokenism: *Before Writing*, Volume 1: From Counting to Cuneiform by Denise Schmandt-Besserat; *Before Writing*, Volume 2: A Catalog of Near Eastern Tokens by Denise Schmandt-Besserat", *American Anthropologist*, 95(4), pp. 996–999.

Mithen, S. (2004) *After the Ice: A Global Human History, 20,000–5000 BC*, London: Phoenix.

de Morgan, J., Jéquier, G., de Mecquenem, R., Haussoulier, B. & Graat van Roggen, D.-L. (1905) *Mémoires de la Délégation en Perse, vol. 7, Recherches archéologiques, zème série*, Paris: Editions Ernst Le Roux.

Netz, R. (2002) "Counter Culture: Towards a History of Greek Numeracy", *History of Science*, vol. 40, no. 3, pp. 321–352.

Nilhamn, B. (2002) *Tokens of Identity? Small Clay Objects in Near Eastern Archaeology*, Uppsala Universitet: Institutionen för Arkeologioch Antik Historia.

Nissen, H. J., Damerow, P. & Englund, R. K. (1993) *Archaic Bookkeeping: Early Writing and Techniques of Economic Administration in the Ancient Near East*, Chicago: University of Chicago Press.

Özbal, R., Gerritsen, F., Diebold, B., Healey, E., Aydin, N., Loyette, M., Nardulli, F., Reese, D., Ekstrom, H. & Sholts & S. (2004) "Tell Kurdu Excavations 2001", *Anatolica*, vol. 30, pp. 37–107.

Peek, M. (1991) *African Divination Systems: Ways of Knowing*, Bloomington: Indiana University Press.

Pitman, H. (1996) "Preliminary Report on the Glyptic Art: Hacinebi, 1993. In Gil Stein et al. Uruk Colonies and Mesopotamian Communities: An Interim Report on the 1992–3 Excavations at Hacinebi, Turkey", *American Journal of Archaeology*, vol. 100, no. 2, pp. 230–233.

Renfrew, C. (1998) "Mind and Matter: Cognitive Archaeology and External Symbolic Storage" in *Cognition and Material Culture: The Archaeology of Symbolic Storage*, ed. C. Renfrew & C. Scarre, Cambridge, UK: McDonald Institute for Archaeological Research, pp. 1–6.

Renfrew, C. (2007) *Prehistory – The Making of the Human Mind*, London: Phoenix.

Renfrew, C. (2012) "Towards a Cognitive Archaeology: Material Engagement and the Early

Development of Society" in *Archaeological Theory Today*, ed. I. Hodder, Malden, MA: Polity Press, pp. 124–145.

Schmandt-Besserat, D. (1977) *An Archaic Recording System and the Origin of Writing*, Malibu, CA: Undena.

Schmandt-Besserat, D. (1978a) "The Earliest Precursor of Writing", *Scientific American*, vol. 238, no. 6, pp. 50–59.

Schmandt-Besserat, D. (1978b) "Reckoning Before Writing", *Archaeology*, vol. 32, no. 3, pp. 22–31.

Schmandt-Besserat, D. (1979) "An Archaic Recording System in the Uruk-Jemdet Nasr Period", *American Journal of Archaeology*, vol. 83, no. 1, pp. 19–48.

Schmandt-Besserat, D. (1980) "The Envelopes That Bear the First Writing", *Technology and Culture*, vol. 21, no. 3, pp. 357–385.

Schmandt-Besserat, D. (1988) "From Accounting to Written Language: The Role of Abstract Counting in the Invention of Writing", *The Social Construction of Written Communication*, pp. 119–130.

Schmandt-Besserat, D. (1992a) *Before Writing, Volume I: From Counting to Cuneiform*, Austin: University of Texas Press.

Schmandt-Besserat, D. (1992b) *Before Writing, Volume II: A Catalogue of Near Eastern Tokens*, Austin: University of Texas Press.

Schmandt-Besserat, D. (1994) "Before Numerals", *Visible Language*, vol. 18, no. 1, pp. 48–60.

Schmandt-Besserat, D. (1996) *How Writing Came About*, Austin: University of Texas Press.

Schmandt-Besserat, D. (1999) "Tokens: The Cognitive Significance", *Documenta Praehistorica*, vol. 26, pp. 21–27.

Simmons, A. H. & Najjar, M. (2006) "Ghwair I: A Small, Complex Neolithic Community in Southern Jordan", *Journal of Field Archaeology*, vol. 31, no. 1, pp. 77–95.

Simpson, S. J. (2007) "Homo Ludens: The Earliest Board Games in the Near East" in *Ancient Board Games in Perspective: Papers from the 1990 British Museum Colloquium, with Additional Contributions*, ed. I. L. Finkel, London: The British Museum Press, pp. 5–10.

Tekin, H. (2007) "Hakemi Use: Güneydoğu Anadolu'da Son Neolitik Döneme Ait Yeni Bir Merkez" in *Anadolu'da Uygarligin Dogusu ve Avrupa'ya Yayilimi: Türkiye'de Neolitik Dönem: Yeni Kazılar, Yeni Bulgular. Vol. 2: Levhalar*, eds. M. Özdoğan & N. Başgelen, Istanbul: Arkeoloji ve sanat Yayınları, pp. 41–52.

Vandier, J. (1964) *Manuel d'Archéologie Égyptienne IV: Bas-Reliefs et Peintures*, Paris: Picard.

Verhoeven, M. (1999) *An Archaeological Ethnography of a Neolithic Community: Space, Place and Social Relationships in the Burnt Village at Tell Sabi Abyad, Syria*, Istanbul: Nederlands Historisch – Archaeologisch Instituut te Istanbul.

Verhoeven, M. & Akkermans, P. M. M. G. ed. (2000) *Tell Sabi Abyad II: The Pre-Pottery Neolithic B Settlement*, Istanbul: Nederlands Historisch-Archaeologisch Instituut te Istanbul.

Watkins, T. (2010) "New Light on Neolithic Revolution in South-West Asia", *Antiquity*, vol. 84, no. 325, pp. 621–634.

Woods, C. (ed.) (2010) *Visible Language: Inventions of Writing in the Ancient Middle East and Beyond*, Chicago: The Oriental Institute of the University of Chicago.

6

BRICK SIZES AND ARCHITECTURAL REGULARITIES AT NEOLITHIC ÇATALHÖYÜK

Marek Z. Barański

INTRODUCTION

Central Anatolian Çatalhöyük (ca. 7,100–5,950 cal. BCE) is a rare example of a well-preserved Neolithic settlement that is considered one of the key sites for understanding changes in prehistoric ways of life, from the domestication of cattle and the adoption of a settled way of living, to the invention of pottery and metallurgy, and the appearance of long-distance trade (Hodder 2007; Hodder & Farid 2014). It is also an optimal site for the study of mudbrick architecture because of its continual habitation sequence, as well as the extensive exposure of architectural remains. This deeply stratified sequence, with houses built one upon another, provides a unique opportunity to document temporal changes both within and between the houses through all the main occupational phases spanning in total over 1,100 years.

This chapter is an attempt to investigate whether the changes in Çatalhöyük's construction techniques of walls and foundations, as well as the changes in mudbrick dimensions, could have been associated with a cognitive shift, namely higher levels of consciousness and greater innovation. Consequently, it will discuss possible reasons for moving towards new strategies or systems. In addition, this chapter will consider when, if at all, higher levels of consciousness and creativity can be observed. As consciousness is clearly embedded in mudbrick manufacture and house building, I will consider whether it was of practical or discursive (abstract) character (Lippuner & Werlen 2009; also Giddens 1984). I intend to examine whether the inhabitants of Neolithic Çatalhöyük, who possessed certain building knowledge and skills, were able to give an account of relevant architectural activities and explicitly express them with the use of an abstract system. In this regard, mudbrick sizes and bonds are examined to identify general directions of change in architecture at Çatalhöyük. The analysis also provides insights into a standardization process that seems to have characterized at least the final phases of settlement occupation (ca. 6,250–5,950 cal. BCE). Two directly succeeding buildings – B.74 and

B.95 – from these Late Neolithic phases are examined in detail in order to identify whether standardized units of measurements were used in mudbrick manufacture.

A BRIEF OVERVIEW OF EARLY MEASUREMENT SYSTEMS

The human body has provided the most convenient base for early linear measurements (Kenoyer 2010; Stone 2014; also Ifrah 2000). As such, the dimensions of body parts are perhaps the most relevant for understanding architectural regularities in ancient times. These dimensions include width of a finger or a hand, various types of hand spans, a foot, a pace, the length of a forearm, as well as the distance between tips of the fingers of both outstretched arms or the vertical distance from the feet to the tip of the hands stretched above the head.

Various research shows that many different systems based on body measurements were developed in ancient times, most of them being only used in a small locality (Stone 2014; Whitelaw 2007). Two of them, which gained a certain universal nature, were introduced within the Sumerian and the Egyptian civilizations during the fourth millennium BCE (Clagett 1999; Powell 1995; also Rottländer 1997). These systems were based on the cubit, which is a distance from the elbow to the extended fingertips. Because the length of the body parts varies due to different sizes of people, the cubits of various lengths were originally employed. However, the Egyptians are believed to be the first to introduce an attested standard measure, namely the royal cubit (long or architectural cubit), which was a standard cubit (short or anthropological cubit) extended by the width of a hand. This unit of measurement has survived in the form of rods made of hard stone, bronze or wood. It was against these kinds of devices that the cubit sticks or rulers in use in ancient Egypt were measured at regular intervals (Arnold 1991: 251–256; also Lepsius 1865; Petrie 1926). It is interesting to examine how some of these measurement sticks were divided. For example, the Egyptian royal cubit (ca. 52.4 cm) was subdivided into 28 digits (7 spans) each being the breadth of a finger. Consequently, there were 24 digits in a standard (small) cubit, 14 and 12 in a large and a small span, respectively, 5 in a hand and 4 in a palm. Also, the digit was subdivided into unit fractions. For example, the smallest division, $1/16$ of a digit, was equal to $1/448$ part of a royal cubit (Clagett 1999: 7–8). Interestingly, the names of all these divisions suggest anatomical origin. However, the way the cubit was subdivided indicates rather strong astrological associations as there are 7 days per lunar week as well as 28 days and 4 weeks per lunar month.

Similar tools were also developed by the early Mesopotamians as well as Indus Valley civilisations (e.g. Rottländer 1997; Whitelaw 2007: 14–15). There is strong evidence of the aforementioned measuring rods or knotted cords of rope having been used in brickmaking, constructing buildings and monuments as well as in surveying and planning of towns (Arnold 1991; Englebach 1930; Iwata 2008; Kenoyer 2006, 2010; Rossi 2007). The Babylonian cubit (ca. 53.0 cm) was, in turn, divided into 30 particles that were about a finger's breadth each; 20 of these subunits, or $2/3$ of the cubit, made up a foot. The preceding measures and subdivisions were closely related to the Babylonian number system, which was based on 60 (Høyrup 1994; Powell 1972). This presents a challenge when the developing systems of measurements are examined. Many early number systems tended to be based on 10, based on the number of fingers on a human hand. As Georges Ifrah (2000: 22) argues, 'traces of the anthropomorphic origin of counting systems can be found in many languages'. The Babylonians used a flexible system of base 60 that could have easily been related both to 5 fingers in one hand as well as 12 partitions of the 4 fingers, excluding the thumb. John J. O'Connor and Edmund F. Robertson (2003) explain this by saying that 'most early number systems were not positional systems, so the reason to use multiples of 10 in measurement subdivision was less strong'. Also, 10 is an unfortunate number into which a unit may be divided. Basing subdivisions on 12, allows for more natural subdivisions and consequently gives much more range for trading quantities. However, as O'Connor and Robertson (2003) mention, it should be borne in mind that because most measuring systems seem to have developed on the basis of a combination of different natural measures, no decision about a number to subdivide by would arise.

It's worth mentioning that sometimes two or more numeral systems could have been used in parallel. On the subject of Harrapan architecture, Ian Whitelaw (2007: 14–15) argues that the dimensions of bricks correspond with the units marked out on a ruler excavated from Mohenjodaro. For example, the Harrapan civilization, which emerged in the Indus Valley in the fourth millennium BCE, is believed to have been the first to

develop and use the decimal system. Yet, there is evidence that a binary system of length notation was also used, in which the counting goes: one, two and one, two and two, two and two and one, and so on. William J. LeVeque and David E. Smith (2017) notice that the pair system is still found among the ethnologically oldest tribes of Australia, Papua New Guinea, as well as among some African Pygmies and in various South American tribes. They also underline that some other indigenous people use other number systems, for example with base 3 and 4 or a scale with base 5. Therefore, despite the fact that the decimal system clearly has overshadowed all others throughout the course of history, we should be aware that the number sense is not the ability to count but the ability to recognize that something has changed into a small collection. Interestingly enough, it is something that not only human beings but also some animal species have (Dantzig 1930: 1–5). We are born with the sense of numbers, yet we still have to learn how to count and measure.

The diversity of number systems used in ancient times allows us to believe that the early concepts of measurement and proportion might not solely have been based on body measurements but could have also been linked to rituals or ideology and passed down from one generation of builders to the next (Kenoyer 2010: 118). However, following David G. Kendall (1974), 'the primary question is not how measurements were made, but whether they were made'. This statement is particularly important in regard to the Neolithic Çatalhöyük, which predates by a few thousand years the ancient civilizations of the Egyptians, the Sumerians and the Harrapans.

In this context, it is really intriguing to try to look for evidence of regularities in mudbrick architecture at Çatalhöyük. If the existence of a unit of length can be considered as possible, it is reasonable to ask whether it implies the use of any kind of abstract metric system.

DATA SET AND METHODS

Mudbrick studies at Çatalhöyük tend to focus either on technology of production (Love 2012; Matthews et al. 1996: 306; Tung 2013) and architectural constructional techniques (Barański 2014: 197; Barański et al. 2015; Matthews & Farid 1996; Mellaart 1967; Stevanović 2013) or contribute to environmental reconstructions (Boyer et al. 2006; Doherty 2013) and even dating programmes (Parish 1996). All these studies provide insights into various aspects of Neolithic social life through shared resources, production choices, organization of labour, construction, use and abandonment of a house, as well as residential identity or social expression. Important research by Serena Love (2013) studied the variation in the composition and sizes of bricks both within and between houses. These detailed analyses provide no proof for standardized units of measurements that might have been in use at the Neolithic Çatalhöyük. Serena Love's research follows the initial work by James Mellaart (1967: 55–56), who believed that bricks came in three sizes: standard, large and other. As he noted, more than one size was in use in each of the 12 occupational levels he distinguished (see Hodder & Farid 2014: 14–15; also Barański et al. (2015) on the problematic nature of the level scheme). However, there has been little or no attempt so far to fully include in the research the buildings and mudbricks from the final and late occupational phases. In view of changes in building techniques and strategies through time at Çatalhöyük, these structures may shed new light on the question of mudbrick standardization.

In this study, I refer to measurements of 585 mudbricks from foundations, foundation walls and load-bearing walls from 40 distinct buildings. As opposed to earlier research, these buildings and mudbricks are grouped into four main occupational phases and not levels. This purposeful departure from the level scheme allowed me to observe long-term changes in architecture at Çatalhöyük, including changes in the late and final phases. As such, 14 of the analysed houses are currently associated with the early phases, another 14 with the middle phases, 9 with the late phases and 3 with the final phases. This data set may appear very limited bearing in mind that the remnants of over 170 buildings were identified during Ian Hodder's excavations (Hodder & Farid 2014). However, it must be stressed that the number of samples per house and per mudbrick structure depends largely on preservation, the number of exposed courses, as well as dimensions of the wall or the foundation. For example, most of the exposed mudbrick structures are still covered with wall plaster as a means of conservation. A great number of bricks could only be studied in sections, as the relevant walls have not been excavated for safety reasons. Furthermore, remnants of buildings, particularly from the final phases, are heavily damaged and only partially preserved as a result of various postdepositional processes. All these issues pose significant difficulties in recording a statistically representative sample

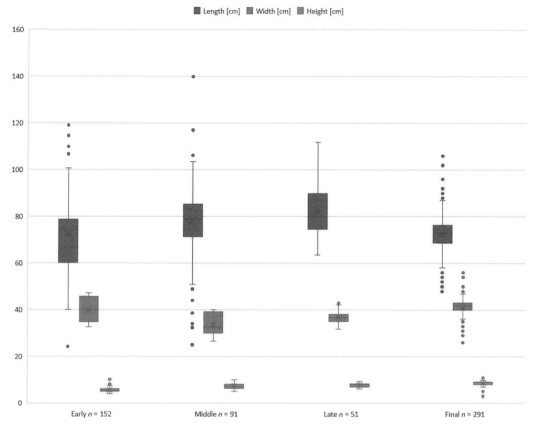

FIGURE 6.1 Mudbrick dimensions at Çatalhöyük by length, width and height as well as the occupational phases.

of mudbrick dimensions per building. As a result, in order to obtain reliable results, I decided to switch my focus from individual buildings to the main occupational phases. This phasing is based on stratigraphy, changes in material culture and, to some extent, radiocarbon dating (see Chapter 1, this volume).

As a part of this research, whenever possible the measurements of certain mudbrick structures were manually retaken on the site. This action was undertaken in order to provide more consistency in mudbrick documentation, as there has been a general tendency to: (1) document the most typical mudbrick measurements, (2) define only the range in brick sizes and not the size of the particular

brick or (3) record relevant dimensions in only full centimetres. Retaking some of the measurements ensured more reliable results in regard to statistical methods, which were used to evaluate whether brick sizes at Çatalhöyük had changed over time in any specific way. A Microsoft Excel spreadsheet and descriptive statistics were used in order to generate box plots in regard to mudbricks from each of the main occupational phases (Figure 6.1). More detailed analyses (with the use of the advanced analytics software package TIBICO Statistica) were undertaken in regard to mudbricks from compound foundations of two succeeding buildings, B.74 and B.95 from the TP Area (Marciniak & Czerniak 2012).

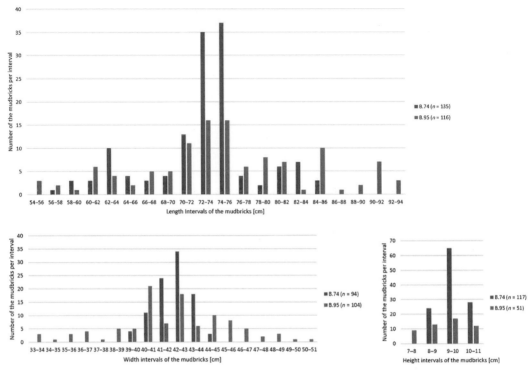

FIGURE 6.2 Collation of mudbrick dimensions from buildings B.74 and B.95 from the final phases of occupation.

These houses, both with an elaborate structure and building plan, characterize the final phases of the settlement occupation. The distribution of a single variable, including its central tendency (the arithmetic mean, median and mode) and dispersion (the range and quartiles of the data set, and measurements of spread such as the variance and standard deviation) were described. Next, the Lilliefors test was used in order to test the null hypothesis that all the brick measurements from either building B.75 or B.95 come from a normally distributed set of buildings from the final phases. As this hypothesis was rejected, the Mann-Whitney U test was used to determine whether mudbricks from the two buildings were selected from the data set having the same distribution, namely HO: $FB.74 = FB.95$ and HA: $FB74 \neq$ $FB95$ or HO: $MB74 = MB95$ and HA: $MB74$ $\neq MB95$ and $\alpha = 0.05$. Finally, the coefficient of variation (V_s) was defined in order to compare the data set from the two buildings. These results are presented in histograms (Figure 6.2). In addition, an approximate calculation of most typical (most repeated) brick sizes in regard to length, width and height is presented. These calculations are based on grouping of the data into intervals, which are characterized by a range of 4 cm ($\pm$ 2 cm).

As the mudbricks from buildings B.74 and B.95 appear to be similar, additional statistical techniques were used in an attempt to investigate whether brick sizes at Çatalhöyük show evidence of statistically significant units of measurements. These techniques were adopted from the early work on the existence of a 'megalithic yard', which had been subjected to statistical evaluation (Broadbent 1956; Kendall 1974; also Thom 1955, 1962). The preceding analyses of quantal models trace integral multiples of some unspecified basic unit. As there is a general problem with investigating multimodality (Çankaya & Fieller 2008), in addition to the methods implied by Simon R. Broadbent (1956) and David G. Kendall (1974), the *Quanta Survo* programme module has been applied. Unlike these early evaluations, two or more incommensurable basic units are traced in the same set of observations (Mustonen 2012). The relevant statistical analyses were based on the set of data that only included values (measurements) that appear at least fivefold. For example, the brick length of 86 cm was excluded, as it appeared only once, while the length of 74 cm appeared 28 times in the case of building B.74. The idea behind this selection was to exclude some of the outliers or potentially faulty data due to inaccuracy of the archive measurements.

RESULTS

Mudbricks at Çatalhöyük varied greatly in size between both buildings and phases (comp. Love 2013; also Matthews & Farid 1996: 289–290; Mellaart 1967: 54). In addition, there are examples of houses in which mudbricks of different sizes were used (Figure 6.1). In general, the length appears to be the dimension that is the most diversified. Based on that, Çatalhöyük's bricks can be grouped into four categories: small bricks (up to ca. 45 cm), medium bricks (from ca. 45 to 70 cm), large bricks (from ca. 70 to 95 cm) and very large bricks (over 95 cm) (comp. Mellaart 1967: 55–56; also Cessford 2007:

413). It seems that large bricks are the most common regardless of the occupational phase.

Mudbricks from the early phases vary the most in size. These blocks range in length from 39.3 to 100.8 cm, in width from 32.6 to 47.1 cm and in height from 3.8 to 7.4 cm. However, the most typical bricks seem to be between 60.3 and 78.7 cm long, between 34.7 and 45.6 cm thick and between 4.9 and 6.1 cm high. There are a few outliers present in the data set, in particular in regard to a brick's length. Taking into account the irregular shape and the relatively small height of bricks from the early phases, this situation can perhaps be explained by wall building techniques of the time, as some of the mudbricks tend to have been laid on the wall when wet (Matthews & Farid 1996: 289). However, Serena Love (2010: 154–155) considers mudbricks from all phases to have been mould made.

Mudbricks from the middle phases still appear to be largely diversified. These bricks seem to range in length from 50.8 to 103.5 cm, in width from 26.6 to 40.0 cm and in height from 5.0 to 10.0 cm. The most typical bricks are between 71.3 and 85.2 long, between 32.6 and 39.1 thick, and between 6.2 and 8.1 cm high. On the basis of the preceding, it can be concluded that the mudbricks from the middle phases are generally longer, less wide and significantly higher than the earlier bricks. With regard to quite a few outliers, one can argue (following on from Cessford 2007: 413) that the bricks of extremely long length are rejected probably due to an inability to distinguish two bricks that were most likely not separated by a vertical strip of mortar. Some short bricks are also excluded from the analyses, as these appear to

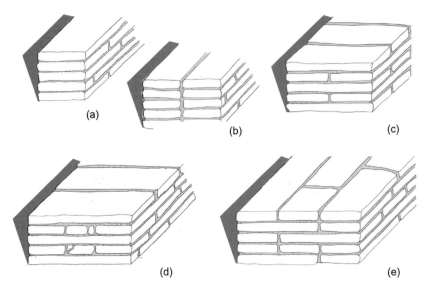

FIGURE 6.3 Types of mudbrick structures at Çatalhöyük: (a) a simple wall, (b) double wall, (c) a compound one-brick-thick foundation, (d) a compound one-and-a-half-brick-thick foundation with a rubble core and (e) a compound one-and-a-half-brick-thick foundation with a solid core (Barański 2017).

represent either cracked and truncated bricks or the bonding in of internal walls.

Mudbricks from the late phases range in length from 63.4 to 111.8 cm, in width from 31.7 to 43.0 cm and in height from 6.0 to 9.3 cm. However, the most typical bricks are between 74.6 and 89.9 cm long, between 35.0 and 38.1 cm thick and between 7.0 and 8.2 cm high. These bricks are slightly longer and less diversified in width and height than the bricks from the early and the middle phases. Interestingly, no outliers were detected.

Mudbricks from the final phases appear to range in length from 58.0 to 87.0 cm, in width from 36.0 to 47.0 cm and in height from 7.0 to 10.0 cm. The measurements of the most typical bricks are between 68.8 and 76.2 cm in length, between 40.0 and 43.0 cm in width and between 8.0 and 9.0 cm in height. These bricks seem to be the least diversified in length, width and height. In addition, the aforementioned mudbricks are the thickest and the highest from the entire data set. Despite the small number of buildings analysed, I would argue that these results may be considered as a sign of an ongoing standardization process. It needs to be stressed that mudbrick foundations or foundation walls of all these houses are characterized by a new bonding technique that was first introduced in the late phases and became very common in the final phases. This new brick arrangement is reminiscent of English bond, where one course has the short sides of the bricks (headers) facing outwards, and the next course has the long sides of the bricks (stretchers) facing outwards (Figure 6.3c). As such, the total width of two bricks and mortar between them corresponds with the length of a single brick. English bond produced a solid structure that was rather easy to lay and is believed to be the strongest bond for one-brick-thick structures

TABLE 6.1 Collation of basic statistical measures in regard to the mudbrick dimensions from buildings B.74 and B.95

Measures	Values					
	Length		Width		Height	
	B.74	B.95	B.74	B.95	B.74	B.95
Arithmetic mean	72.10	74.23	41.64	41.46	9.03	8.63
Median	73	74	42	42	9	9
Mode	74	72	42	40	9	9
First quartile	70	70	41	40	9	8
Third quartile	74	80	42	44	9	9
Standard deviation	5.79	9.13	1.14	3.52	0.67	1.04
Coefficient of variation	8.03	12.30	2.75	8.50	7.40	12.04
Coefficient curve	−0.36	−0.02	−0.30	−0.20	−0.03	−0.19
Number of observations	135	116	94	104	117	51

TABLE 6.2 Most typical mudbrick dimensions in regard to buildings B.74 and B.95; percentages calculated as the number of mudbricks of a particular dimension (either length, width or height) from a particular building

Length [cm]			Width [cm]			Height [cm]		
B.74 <70	70–74	>74	<41	41–42	>42	<9	9	>9
(20.7%)	(55.6%)	(23.7%)	(16.0%)	(61.7%)	(22.3%)	(79.5%)	(55.6%)	(23.9%)
B.95 <70	70–80	>80	<40	40–44	>44	<8	8–9	>9
(19.9%)	(53.4%)	(26.7%)	(21.2%)	(59.6%)	(19.2%)	(17.7%)	(58.8%)	(23.5%)

providing a stable base for simple load-bearing walls.

When two buildings B.74 and B.95 with compound foundations are compared, the mudbrick dimensions appear to be rather similar (Table 6.1). Admittedly, there are statistically relevant differences in dispersion and arithmetic mean in regard to length and height. Bearing in mind the general nature of sun-dried mudbricks and the issues with regard to archive measurements, these differences can still be seen as very small (Figure 6.2).

With regard to width, the mudbricks of building B.74 appear to range from 39.0 to 44.0 cm. However, the most typical bricks are between 41.0 and 42.0 cm thick. At the same time, there are more mudbricks that are wider than the average $(\bar{x})$ = 41.64 cm (M = 42.0 cm; D = 42.0 cm). In the case of B.95, mudbricks range in width from 33.0 to 50.0 cm in width. The most typical bricks are between 40.0 and 44.0 cm thick (Table 6.2; Figure 6.2). Interestingly, slightly more than half of the B.95 bricks are less wide than the average $(\bar{x})$ = 41.46 cm.

With regard to height, the mudbricks of building B.74 range from 8.0 to 10.0 cm. However, the most typical bricks are 9.0 cm high (($\bar{x}$) = 9.03 cm; M = 9.0 cm; D = 9.0 cm). The height of mudbricks of building B.95 are between 7.0 and 10.0 cm high in turn (Table 6.2; Figure 6.2). However, the most typical bricks appear to range in height between 8.0 and 9.0 cm (($\bar{x}$) = 8.63 cm; M = 9.0 cm; D = 9.0 cm).

The length of the mudbricks of buildings B.74 and B.95 are also similar. However, when compared to the width and height, there is a slightly larger variety among the data set, in particular in regard to building B.95. The mudbricks of building B.74 appear to range in length from 58.0 to 85.0 cm. However, the most typical bricks are between 70.0 and 74.0 cm long. In the case of building B.95, the mudbricks are between 54.0 and 93.0 cm long, and the most typical bricks are between 70.0 and 80.0 cm long (Table 6.2; Figure 6.2). Interestingly, the majority of bricks from both buildings are longer than the average, which is ($\bar{x}$) = 72.10 and ($\bar{x}$) = 74.23 cm for B.74 and B.95, respectively. The central tendency of distribution of the values in regard to the brick's length suggests that there was more than one type of mudbrick used to build these houses. Indeed, one can observe a few concentrations of data when analysing the histogram (Figure 6.2). As mudbricks tend to be quite uniform in width and thickness but vary in their length, it is likely that some sort of technique was being used to constrain the width but not the length. Two techniques to mould the length of a brick are shuttering and planking, where the mud paste is poured between two planks to control the lateral spread and cut at irregular intervals (Houben & Guillaud 1994). Given the general irregularity of Çatalhöyük bricks, Serena Love (2010: 159–160) suggests that it is likely that this sort of technique may have been used, rather than a rectangular mould that would have produced uniform shapes.

Based on the data grouping, the most typical mudbrick dimensions for B.74 appear to be 72 × 41 × 9 (± 2 cm) and 82 × 41 × 9 (± 2 cm). These bricks make up about 37 per cent and 8 per cent of the data set which include only bricks with known length, width and height. In the case of B.95, the most typical mudbrick dimensions seem to be 73 × 43 × 9 (± 2 cm) and 89 × 43 × 9 (± 2 cm). These bricks make up about 23 per cent and 6 per cent of the relevant data set. However, all these calculations are estimates for various reasons that were discussed earlier. Furthermore, experiments with mudbrick manufacture show that wet clay shrinks around 0.5 cm in thickness and width and up to 2.0 cm in overall length (Kenoyer 2010: 118). Mudbrick shrinkage as well as compression due to static loads are not taken into account in this study. Still, an attempt to search for a reasonable basic unit of length giving the observations as integer multiples of the basic unit was undertaken. The results of these statistical evaluations are as follows:

B.74
DATA X: 8 9 10 40 41 43 62 70 72 73 74 75 80 82 END
RANGE=2(0.1)25 Q_MIN=2
QUANTA X,X,2,CUR+1
Data: X Variable: X N=14 ss=0.108742

	quantum	# matches
1	2.275053	5
2	2.000000	9

METHOD=Kendall RANGE=2(0.1)25 SCORE_
  MIN=2
QUANTA X,X,0,CUR+1
Data: X Variable: X N=14
GPLOT COSQUANT,quant,score / LINE=1
  MODE=SVGA Plot the quantogram!
Peaks of Kendall's Cosine Quantogram:

quantum	score
10.30000	3.195071
8.100000	2.248122

B.95
DATA X: 7 8 9 10 38 39 40 41 42 43 44 45 46 60
  70 72 74 75 76 78 80 84 85 90 END
RANGE=2(0.1)25 Q_MIN=2
QUANTA X,X,2,CUR+1
Data: X Variable: X N=24 ss=1.02852

	quantum	# matches
1	2.280270	8
2	2.000000	16

METHOD=Kendall   RANGE=2(0.1)25
  SCORE_MIN=2
QUANTA X,X,0,CUR+1
Data: X Variable: X N=24
GPLOT COSQUANT,quant,score / LINE=1
  MODE=SVGA Plot the quantogram!
Peaks of Kendall's Cosine Quantogram:

quantum	score
2.00000	2.309401

Despite the use of advanced statistics the existence of a basic unit of measurement could not be demonstrated. Quantum 2.0 (cm) should not be considered due to the nature of the archive measurements, which were only recorded in full centimetres. The other values have rather a low number of matches. If any regularities can be observed at all, these are most likely due to the fact that the measurement system at Çatalhöyük must have been related to proportions based on body parts rather than absolute measurements. For example, the width or length of hands would not have varied excessively throughout the settlement, and consequently the measures derived from them would have been relatively uniform.

DISCUSSION

Changes in mudbrick sizes seem to have been associated with the introduction of new building techniques and strategies. These developments went hand-in-hand with essential and long-term processes of a social, cultural, economic and environmental nature. In this context, previous excavation results allow us to believe that within the late and final phases the population of the Neolithic Çatalhöyük was decreasing slowly (Cessford 2005; Hillson et al. 2013). At the same time the settlement was characterized by a gradually diminishing density of housing, which was connected with the growing number of open or enclosed spaces (Düring 2001; Farid 2014; Mellaart 1967). However, the buildings gradually covered more and more area and were characterized by a greater level of complexity. In addition, it is very likely that some of the buildings were two-storey and perhaps had a cellar, as there are examples of buildings that were at least partially dug into the slope of the mound (Barański et al. 2015).

I would like to argue that some of these processes of remodeling and transforming the built environment of Çatalhöyük were influenced by changes in ground conditions. Numerous evidence of damage, deformation and repair of structural elements of buildings come from all the excavation areas and are characteristic of different settlement phases (Barański et al. 2015; Farid 2014). Even though the ground conditions were never favourable on the mound, they must have been decreasingly favorable after the middle phases. Many of the late and final buildings at the Neolithic Çatalhöyük had to be erected entirely or to much of an extent on made-up ground that consisted of midden-like deposits. Surfaces of this type are characterised by low strength parameters and as a result make up a weak load-bearing layer (comp. Drągowski 2010). At a tell-site like Çatalhöyük, there must have been unstable slopes that were exposed to a loss of stability due to gravitational and hydrodynamic loads. The conditions in which these loads were present were most probably related to erosion and loosening of soil or undercutting of the mound, to uncontrolled growth in inclination of an embankment, to the load implied on the mound slope or soil above it by structures built as well as to water absorption of the ground and swelling of soil. All these factors might have occurred both separately and simultaneously.

The preceding situation must have required a search for the best technical solutions with regard to both construction and maintaining of a building. At first, a gradual growth in general wall thickness or building of retaining mudbrick structures next to external walls of the buildings can be documented (Figure 6.3b). Interestingly, these practices were initially observed in the case of the walls that were abutted by midden deposits (Farid 2014). The unfavourable ground conditions would have required some kind of planned excavations in order to create safe conditions of land and building use. Partial levelling of particular areas, the creation of terraces, as well as digging of

foundation ditches can be seen as a subsequent solution in regard to building construction that was implemented by the inhabitants of the Neolithic Çatalhöyük (Barański et al. 2015; Özbaşaran & Duru 2014; Regan 2014). This method provided more safety for the structural elements and better conditions for the use of the buildings. The general lack of evidence of this kind of practice in the early and the middle phases may be partly explained by the fact that the walls of the earlier buildings were situated directly over the remnants of walls of preceding buildings (Farid 2014; Mellaart 1967). Additionally, the high density of housing encouraged the stability of individual buildings necessary to provide safe conditions of use. With the growing number of courtyards and midden areas as well as changes in building plans, this solution must have proved to be partly insufficient and caused more damage and deformation, e.g. transverse and longitudinal cracking, buckling and deviation of mudbrick walls defining these structures were observed.

The building strategies that included construction of retaining walls and digging of foundation ditches seem to precede the introduction of compound mudbrick foundations. The latter are typical of buildings of the late and the final phases (Figure 6.3) (Barański 2014: 196–197). The process of progressive development towards these structures is most apparent in the case of the succeeding houses B.56, B.44 and B.10 (Regan 2014). The walls of the first of these buildings were situated within a foundation ditch, in which the bottom part was intentionally filled with rubble. With the next building, B.44, a sandwiched footing of mudbrick was documented between the rubble at the bottom and the wall that was laid on top. This foundation was built with reused mudbricks coming from building B.56 and supported the walls of building B.44, which were narrower by a dozen centimetres. Finally, the preserved one-brick-thick foundations of the last building in the sequence, B.10, were characterized by a more complicated brickwork bond made up of alternating courses of bricks. This new bonding technique seems to have been most likely further developed in the final phases as can be seen in the case of massive one-and-a-half-brick-thick mudbrick structures of a few buildings of the time (Figure 6.3d and –e) (Barański 2017).

CONCLUSION

The architecture at Çatalhöyük can be described as a complex and multidimensional process of change. This change was partly reflected in the introduction of new building techniques and strategies as well as a considerable decrease in the diversity of mudbrick sizes. Consequently, bricks are clearly the most uniform in the late and particularly final phases of occupation. This is when a new arrangement of bricks that is reminiscent of English bond was practised. This bond has alternating stretching and heading courses, and as such, it requires bricks that are uniform in size throughout the wall. In other words, the wall thickness, which in the case of Çatalhöyük was equivalent to the length of one or one-and-a-half bricks, is a multiple of the brick width. As much as this bonding technique was common in the final phases, there is no strong evidence for a uniform or abstract general measurement system. The analyzed

mudbricks from compound foundations of two buildings B.74 and B.95 turned out to be quite uniform but still varied, particularly in length that was also different within each of these houses. As such, the total width of two bricks and mortar between them rarely corresponded with the length of a single brick. Furthermore, statistical evaluations of mudbrick data from these two buildings failed to prove any reasonable basic unit of length.

By way of conclusion, it is beyond doubt that the inhabitants of the Neolithic Çatalhöyük possessed complex building knowledge that was passed on and developed over time. It is, however, unlikely that it involved an abstract system that could be seen as a higher and discursive consciousness. It seems that the minds of the men of this Late Neolithic society were, above all, shaped by practical things in regards to building strategies and techniques. Much of the standardization seen in the late and the final phases could have been related to proportions based on certain body parts.

Further studies of mudbricks from buildings from the late and the final phases of occupation might shed more light on the issues of standardization and systems of measurements with the use of body parts at the Neolithic Çatalhöyük. Given the fact that bricks are based on specific proportions, it would not be surprising that similar proportions are reflected in the plan of the houses. However, the direct proximity of buildings within the settlement must have considerably limited the possibilities to plan and erect new buildings. Therefore, the analyses of internal architectural features, e.g. raised platforms, might prove more fruitful.

ACKNOWLEDGEMENTS

I sincerely thank Ian Hodder for his invitation to contribute to this volume. Thanks are also extended to members of the Çatalhöyük Research Project, particularly Katarzyna Regulska for on-site assistance, Serena Love for thoughtful comments on earlier versions of this chapter, Dominik Lukas and Milena Vasić for help with data computing, as well as Lucy Bennison-Chapman, Sean Doyle, Arkadiusz Klimowicz, Christopher Knüsel, Scott Haddow and Milena Vasić for stimulating discussions on consciousness and creativity at the Near Eastern Neolithic. I am also indebted to Zygmunta Barańska and Teresa Plenikowska for invaluable guides on statistical analyses, and Kyle Alexander and Justyna Gabriel for help in reaching some of the early papers listed in the bibliography.

This chapter was initially presented at the Templeton Foundation-funded conference, 'Consciousness and Creativity at the Dawn of Settled Life', in Cambridge in 2017. Some of the ideas, which are discussed here, are further developed in the doctoral thesis, 'Late Neolithic Architecture at Çatalhöyük: Continuity and Change at the End of 7th Millennium BCE' (Barański 2017). My research on architecture at Çatalhöyük, in particular in regard to the final phases of occupation, was made possible thanks to funding from the National Science Centre in Poland as a part of the project 'Çatalhöyük in the Late Neolithic (6,500–5,900 BCE): Reconstruction of the Settlement Layout Based on Architectural and Structural Aspects of Buildings" (PRELUDIUM 6: DEC-2013/11/N/HS3/04889).

REFERENCES

Arnold D., 1991. *Building in Egypt: Pharaonic Stone Masonry*. Oxford, UK: Oxford University Press.

Barański M. Z., 2014. Late Neolithic Architecture. In *Çatalhöyük 2014 Archive Report*, www.catalh oyuk.com/downloads/Archive_Report_2014.pdf, 194–202.

Barański M. Z., 2017. *Późnoneolityczna architektura Çatalhöyük, Turcja: kontynuacja i zmiana u schyłku 7. tysiąclecia p.n.e. (Late Neolithic Architecture at Çatalhöyük: Continuity and Change at the End of 7th Millennium BC)*. Unpublished doctoral thesis, defended February 2018 at Gdańsk University of Technology in Gdańsk, Poland.

Barański M. Z., García-Suárez A., Klimowicz A., Love S., Pawłowska K., 2015. Complexity in Apparent Simplicity: The Architecture of Neolithic Çatalhöyük as a Process. In I. Hodder, A. Marciniak (eds.), *Assembling Çatalhöyük*. Leeds: Maney Publishing, 111–126.

Boyer P., Roberts N., Baird D., 2006. Holocene Environment and Settlement on the Çarşamba Alluvial Fan, South Central Turkey: Integrating Geoarchaeology and Archaeological Field Survey. *Geoarchaeology* 21 (7), 675–698.

Broadbent S. R., 1956. Examination of a Quantum Hypothesis Based on a Single Set of Data. *Biometrika* 43, 32–44.

Çankaya, E., Fieller, N. R. J., 2008. Quantal Models: A Review with Additional Methodological Development. *Journal of Applied Statistics*, 1–16.

Cessford C., 2005. Estimating the Neolithic Population at Çatalhöyük. In I. Hodder (ed.), *Inhabiting Çatalhöyük: Reports from the 1995–99 Seasons*. Cambridge, UK: McDonald Institute for Archaeological Research/London: British Institute of Archaeology at Ankara, 323–326.

Cessford C., 2007. Building 1. In I. Hodder (ed.), *Excavating Çatalhöyük: South, North and KOPAL Area Reports from the 1995–99 Seasons*. Cambridge, UK: McDonald Institute for Archaeological Research/London: British Institute of Archaeology at Ankara, 405–530.

Clagett M., 1999. *Ancient Egyptian Science: A Source Book, Vol. III: Ancient Egyptian Mathematics.*

Memoirs of the APS, Vol. 232. Philadelphia: American Philosophical Society.

Dantzig T., 1930. *Number: The Language of Science.* London: Macmillan Company.

de Garis Davis N., 1935. *Paintings from the Tomb of Rekh-mi-Rē at Thebes.* New York: The Metropolitan Museum of Art Egyptian Expedition Publications.

de Garis Davis N., 1943. *The Tomb of Rekh-Mi-Rē at Thebes, (t. I-II).* New York: The Metropolitan Museum of Art Egyptian Expedition Publications.

Doherty C., 2013. Sourcing Çatalhöyük's Clay. In I. Hodder (ed.), *Substantive Technologies at Çatalhöyük: Reports from the 2000–2008 Seasons.* London: British Institute at Ankara/Los Angeles, CA: Cotsen Institute of Archaeology Press, 51–66.

Drągowski A., 2010. Charakterystyka i klasyfikacja gruntów antropogenicznych (Characteristics and Classification of Anthropogenic Soils). *Przegląd Geologiczny* 58 (9/2), 868–872.

Düring B. S., 2001. Social Dimensions in the Architecture of Neolithic Çatalhöyük. *Anatolian Studies* 51, 1–18.

Englebach C., 1930. *Ancient Egyptian Construction and Architecture.* Mineola, NY: Dover Publications.

Farid S., 2014. Timelines: Phasing Neolithic Çatalhöyük. In I. Hodder (ed.), *Çatalhöyük Excavations: The 2000–2008 Seasons.* London: British Institute of Archaeology at Ankara/Los Angeles, CA: Cotsen Institute of Archaeology Press, 91–130.

Giddens A., 1984. *The Constitution of Society: Outline of the Theory of Structuration.* Oakland: University of California Press.

Hillson S. W., Spencer Lasen C., Boz B., Pilloud M. A., Sadvari J. W., Agarwal S. C., Glencross B., Beauchesne P., Pearson J. A., Ruff C. B., Garofalo E. M., Hager L. D., Haddow S. D., 2013. The Human Remains I: Interpreting Community Structure, Health and Diet in Neolithic Çatalhöyük. In I. Hodder (ed.), *Humans and Landscapes of Çatalhöyük: Reports from the 2000–2008 Seasons.* London: British Institute of Archaeology at Ankara/Los Angeles, CA: Cotsen Institute of Archaeology Press, 339–396.

Hodder I., 2007. Çatalhöyük in the Context of the Middle Eastern Neolithic. *Annual Review of Anthropology* 36: 105–120.

Hodder I., Farid S., 2014. Questions, History of Work and Summary of Results. In I. Hodder (ed.), *Çatalhöyük Excavations: The 2000–2008 Seasons.* London: British Institute of Archaeology at Ankara/Los Angeles, CA: Cotsen Institute of Archaeology Press, 1–34.

Houben H., Guillaud H., 1994. *Earth Construction: A Comprehensive Guide.* Ann Arbor, MI: Intermediate Technology Publications.

Høyrup J., 1994. Babylonian Mathematics. In I. Grattan-Guinness (ed.), *Companion Encyclopedia for the History and Philosophy of the Mathematical Sciences* (vol. I). Abingdon, UK: Routledge, 21–29.

Ifrah G., 2000. *The Universal History of Numbers: From Prehistory to the Invention of the Computer.* Hoboken, NJ: John Wiley & Sons. (First published in France with the title: Histoire universelle des chiffres by Editions Robert Laffont, Paris, in 1994)

Iwata S., 2008. Weights and Measures in the Indus Valley. In H. Selin (ed.), *Encyclopaedia of the History of Science, Technology, and Medicine in Non-Western Cultures* (2nd ed.). New York: Springer, 2254–2255.

Kendall D. G., 1974. *Hunting Quanta. Philosophical Transactions of the Royal Society London A* 276, 231–266.

Kenoyer J. M., 2006. Indus Valley Civilization. In S. Wolpert (ed.), *Encyclopedia of India* (vol. 2). Farmington Hills, MI: Thomson Gale, 258–266.

Kenoyer J. M., 2010. Measuring the Harappan World: Insights into the Indus Order and Cosmology. In I. Morley & C. Renfrew (eds.), *The Archaeology of Measurement: Comprehending Heaven, Earth and Time in Ancient Societies.* Cambridge, UK: Cambridge University Press, 106–121.

Lepsius R., 1865. *Die Alt-Aegyptische Elle und Ihre Eintheilung.* Berlin: Königlichen Akademie der Wissenchaften.

LeVeque W. J. & Smith, D. E., 2017. Numerals and Numeral Systems. www.britannica.com/topic/numeral

Lippuner R., Werlen B., 2009. Structuration Theory. In R. Kitchin, N. Thrift (eds.), *International Encyclopedia for Human Geography*. Amsterdam: Elsevier.

Love, S., 2010. How Houses Build People: An Archaeology of Mudbrick Houses from Çatalhöyük, Turkey. Unpublished PhD Thesis, Department of Anthropology, Stanford University.

Love S., 2012. The Geoarchaeology of Mudbricks in Architecture: A Methodological Study from Çatalhöyük, Turkey. *Geoarchaeology: An International Journal* 27, 140–156.

Love S., 2013. An Archaeology of Mudbrick Houses from Çatalhöyük. In I. Hodder (ed.), *Substantive Technologies at Çatalhöyük: Reports from the 2000–2008 Seasons*. London: British Institute of Archaeology at Ankara/Los Angeles, CA: Cotsen Institute of Archaeology Press, 81–96.

Marciniak A., Czerniak L., 2012. Çatalhöyük Unknown: The Late Sequence on the East Mound. In R. Matthews, J. Curtis (eds.), *Proceedings of the 7th International Congress on the Archaeology of the Ancient Near East*. Volume I: *Mega-Cities and Mega-Sites. The Archaeology of Consumption and Disposal, Landscape, Transport and Communication*. Wiesbaden: Harrassowitz, 3–16.

Matthews W., Farid S., 1996. Exploring the 1960's Surface: The Stratigraphy of Çatalhöyük. In I. Hodder (ed.), *On the Surface: Çatalhöyük 1993–95*. Cambridge, UK: McDonald Institute for Archaeological Research, 271–300.

Matthews W., French C., Lawrence T., Cutler D., 1996. Multiple Surfaces: The Micromorphology. In I. Hodder (ed.), *On the Surface: Çatalhöyük 1993–95*. Cambridge, UK: McDonald Institute for Archaeological Research, 301–347.

Mellaart J., 1967. *Çatal Hüyük: A Neolithic Town in Anatolia*. London: Thames & Hudson.

Mustonen S., 2012. *Hunting Multiple Quanta by Selective Least Squares*. www.survo.fi/papers/Hunting Quanta2012.pdf

O'Connor J. J., Robertson E. F., 2003. *The History of Measurement*. www.history.mcs.st-andrews.ac.uk/HistTopics/Measurement.html.

Özbaşaran M., Duru G., 2014. Istanbul (IST) Area of the East Mound. In I. Hodder (ed.), *Çatalhöyük Excavations: The 2000–2008 Seasons*. London: British Institute of Archaeology at Ankara/Los Angeles, CA: Cotsen Institute of Archaeology Press, 621–658.

Parish R., 1996. Luminescence Dating of Mud Brick from Çatalhöyük. In I. Hodder (ed.), *On the Surface: Çatalhöyük 1993–95*. Cambridge, UK: McDonald Institute for Archaeological Research, 343–344.

Petrie W. M. F., 1926. *Ancient Weights and Measures*. British School of Archaeology in Egypt Series. London: University College, Department of Egyptology.

Powell M. A., 1972. The Origin of the Sexagesimal System: The Interaction of Language and Writing. *Visible Language* 6: 5–18.

Powell M. A., 1995. Metrology and Mathematics in Ancient Mesopotamia. In J. M. Sasson (ed.), *Civilizations of the Ancient Near East*. New York: Scribner's, 1941–1958.

Regan R., 2014. The Sequence of Buildings 75, 65, 56, 69, 44 and 10 and External Spaces 119, 129, 130, 144, 299, 314, 319, 329, 333, 339, 367, 371 and 427. In I. Hodder (ed.), *Çatalhöyük Excavations: The 2000–2008 Seasons*. London: British Institute of Archaeology at Ankara/Los Angeles, CA: Cotsen Institute of Archaeology Press, 131–189.

Rossi C., 2007. *Architecture and Mathematics in Ancient Egypt*. Cambridge, UK: Cambridge University Press.

Rottländer R. C. A., 1997. *Die Entwicklung der Antiken Längeneinheiten aus der Nippur-Elle*. PTB- Mitteilungen 107 (4): 247–256.

Stevanović M., 2013. New discoveries in House Construction at Çatalhöyük. In I. Hodder (ed.), *Substantive Technologies at Çatalhöyük: Reports from the 2000–2008 Seasons*. London: British Institute of Archaeology at Ankara/Los Angeles, CA: Cotsen Institute of Archaeology Press, 97–114.

Stone M. H., 2014. The Cubit: A History and Measurement Commentary. *Journal of Anthropology*, Vol. 2014 (489757): 1–11. http://dx.doi.org/10.1155/2014/489757.

Thom A., 1955. A Statistical Examination of the Megalithic Sites in Britain. *Journal of the Royal Statistical Society* 118 (3), 275–295.

Thom A., 1962. The Megalithic Unit of Length. *Journal of the Royal Statistical Society* 125 (2), 243–251.

Tung B., 2013. Building with Mud: An Analysis of Architectural Materials at Çatalhöyük. In I. Hodder (ed.), *Substantive Technologies at Çatalhöyük: Reports from the 2000–2008 Seasons*. London: British Institute of Archaeology at Ankara/Los Angeles, CA: Cotsen Institute of Archaeology Press, 67–80.

Whitelaw I., 2007. *A Measure of All Things: The Story of Man and Measurement*. London: Macmillan.

PART III

GREATER INNOVATION AND CREATIVITY

THE MERONOMIC MODEL OF COGNITIVE CHANGE AND ITS APPLICATION TO NEOLITHIC ÇATALHÖYÜK

Chris Thornton

THERE IS A NATURAL DESIRE TO EXPLAIN the development of cognitive phenomena that seem particularly characteristic of the human mind. Creativity is a case in point, consciousness another. A recent archaeological project has attempted to understand evidence from the Neolithic site of Çatalhöyük in relation to the emergence of both consciousness and creativity at the dawn of settled life. This project faces the need to settle on a precise understanding of what is meant by the terms in question. But theorists differ as to what this understanding should be. And there are deeper disputes relating to cognition in general. What the term 'cognitive' signifies continues to be debated, with some arguing that it has no precise meaning that would differentiate it from terms such as 'adaptive' and 'intelligent'.

A major aim of the project is to understand the degree to which cognitive *change* underlies behaviors that seem to have occurred at this site. This necessitates adopting a model of cognitive change. What is argued here is that a meronomic model is well suited to this purpose. Meronomic analysis allows cognitive change (by conceptual innovation) to be modeled in a precise way. It also allows conceptual creativity to be quantitatively assessed. This is subject to some reservations, however. Given the hope of the approach being of use in an archaeological setting, it is worth examining the pros and cons in more detail.

Functionalities of the human mind, cognitive or otherwise, remain relatively mysterious at this time. Proposals are forthcoming (e.g. Gärdenfors, 2004; Clark, 2016), but consensus remains elusive. The lack of agreement obstructs any project that seeks to make reference to mental phenomena in an instrumental way (e.g. to explain archaeological evidence). Ventures in this direction can be made. But as they are forced to adopt a specific view of cognition, their fate is bound up with the view in question. Mithen's (1996) original approach in cognitive archaeology, for example, adopted Fodor's (1983) proposal for a modular mental architecture and was bound to it for that reason.

With cognitive science unable to settle on a received view of cognition, the prospects for a robust cognitive archaeology may seem limited. But a meronomic approach gets around this to some degree. The framework makes no assumptions about the mind, other than that it trades in the identification of categories. That this capacity exists is universally agreed; the use of mental concepts is accepted by all theorists (Machery, 2009). (The cognitive science view of a concept as a mental representation of a category is assumed throughout.) In practice, the existence of mental concepts can hardly be denied because without them there can be no language, and without language, there can be no denials.

How is this of use? The starting point in the meronomic approach is recognition that concepts are inherently accommodative. Due to the way one concept may be able to accommodate others in combination, they can be assembled into hierarchical structures. We can conceptualize a combination of food and water as sustenance, for example. What this reveals is that the concept of sustenance has the capacity to accommodate the concepts of food and water taken in combination. These three concepts can be assembled in a hierarchical structure, with the concept of sustenance in the accommodative role. Other hierarchical arrangements of these three concepts are semantically illegitimate. We cannot conceptualize water to be a combination of food and sustenance, for example.

This capacity for accommodation endows concepts with mathematical properties. Specifically, it renders them inherently generative. Any set of concepts gives rise to a (possibly empty) set of accommodative structures. These can be derived in a purely analytic way by identifying all legitimate accommodations.

This becomes of interest from the cognitive point of view, as it provides a way of analyzing the compositional conceptualizations that a particular endowment of concepts enables. The degree to which a construction is novel can be measured in a formal way. This leads on to a way of modeling conceptual change and creativity that is essentially mathematical in nature.

This does not solve the problem that we do not know with any certainty what cognition is, or how it works. It does not provide archaeologists with what is required for truly robust projects in cognitive archaeology. Due to its minimal supposition, and its reliance on formal analysis, it does provide leverage, however. To undertake meronomic analysis, we only have to specify the endowment of concepts that is assumed to exist initially. Any results obtained are of cognitive significance if the mind (or more specifically the conceptual system) can utilize conceptual accommodation. This is not to assume very much, given our self-evident capacity to compose accommodative constructions by means of language (as illustrated earlier).

A meronomic brand of cognitive archaeology retains some degree of immunity from changing fashions in cognitive science, then. A particular proposal must assume some endowment of concepts, and it has the potential to be criticised or invalidated thereby. The award of cognitive significance to the results obtained also requires the assumption that conceptual accommodation is within the repertoire of the mind. Otherwise, the approach is an exercise in purely formal analysis, and no less secure as such than any mathematical calculation.

It is useful to be clear about how this relates to the general issue of conceptualization, however. Interpretation of materials and activities is obviously something archaeologists have great interest in. To interpret evidence of human activity in the past, it is necessary to make assumptions about the meanings, interpretations, categories, etc. that underpinned those activities. There has to be some understanding of how worldly phenomena were 'chunked' by the people in question. Vigorous debate on this issue is the natural result. An important theme is the danger of overextending the modern mindset. The temptation to apply a modern conceptual apparatus to settings in which it may have played little or no role is strengthened by the necessity to use modern language in stating any proposal. As modern language is saturated with the modern mindset, expressing ideas that deviate from it is less than straightforward.

This gives rise to cautionary notes, such as Keane's assertion that 'language should not be the privileged theoretical model for a semiotics of material things' (Keane, 2003, p. 422). The need to resist specific emphases is also highlighted. Pauketat notes (with approval) the increasing tendency in archaeology to reject traditional 'dualisms that separate thought and action' (Pauketat, 2013, p. 35), while Keane acknowledges (with disapproval) the lingering tendency 'to divide our attention between things and ideas' (Keane, 2005, p. 182).

Specific proposals for new forms of conceptualization are made. Keane and Pauketat both favour the idea of a 'bundle' as a fundamental unit of conceptualization (Keane, 2005; Pauketat, 2013).[1] It is argued that, in addition to other benefits, viewing things in this way can overcome the modern tendency to separate continuity and change. In Pauketat's opinion, 'Using the metaphorical language of a bundle ... we might begin to see continuity and change as one and the same phenomenon' (Pauketat, 2013, p. 55). Such proposals inevitably face the difficulty that meaningful exchange 'requires a shared language and a medium of communication' (Keane, 2005, p. 200). To the extent that this necessitates sharing a conceptual apparatus, ventures towards significantly different interpretations of the world are inherently problematic.

As it involves assuming an initial endowment of concepts, a meronomic approach is, to some extent, subject to these concerns. At the same time, it can claim some degree of independence. Which concepts are assumed to be endowed is not the critical issue, as they may form only a small subset of the concepts that can be generatively derived. The commitment to an initial conceptual endowment is not a commitment to a whole conceptual apparatus – only to its seeds. The conceptual apparatus is a potentially large derivation from the initial endowment. The natural objective in a meronomic approach is to assume a minimal number of concepts of maximal generative capacity, then. The conceptual apparatus then derived has the potential to depart from the modern mindset to an arbitrary extent. Any meronomic approach should aim to restrict the assumed endowment in this way.

The remainder of the chapter sets out the approach in more detail and examines how it can be used to model cognitive change and conceptual creativity. The eventual aim is to road test the method as a way of assessing evidence from Çatalhöyük. The section immediately following examines the mechanics of meronomic composition, taking particular account of its less obvious aspects. The role potentially played by singular accommodations and abstract concepts is highlighted. The chapter then explores the ways in which the meronomic model lends itself to quantitative assessment of conceptual creativity. Finally, the chapter considers application of the model to evidence of human behavior at Neolithic Çatalhöyük.

MERONOMIC CONCEPTUAL CHANGE

As noted, the ability of concepts to compose meronomically derives from their capacity for accommodation. Suppose the combination of an X and a Y can be conceptualized as a Z (where X, Y and Z are concepts). This establishes that concept Z is able to accommodate the concept combination $X + Y$. The three concepts are potentially organized in a hierarchical structure, with Z as parent (or *holonym*), and X and Y as children (or *meronyms*). To illustrate: the combination of a lawn and flowerbed can be conceptualized as a garden. This establishes that GARDEN can accommodate the combination LAWN + FLOWERBED. There is a valid meronomic arrangement of concepts in which GARDEN is the parent[2] (holonym), and LAWN and FLOWERBED are the children (meronyms). Using the terminology of Artificial Intelligence, the structure consists of two *has-a* links: one from GARDEN to LAWN, and another from GARDEN to FLOWERBED (Brachman, 1983).

The structure is drawn out in Figure 7.1 in the conventional way, with root pointing upwards. There are two ways to describe what is expressed. The hierarchy can be seen as the construction of a concept. Putting the

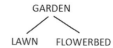

GARDEN

LAWN   FLOWERBED

FIGURE 7.1 Meronomic organization of GARDEN, LAWN and FLOWERBED reflecting the capacity to conceptualize the combination of a lawn and flowerbed as a garden.

cited concepts together in this hierarchical way has the effect of constructing a specialization of the garden concept; namely, the concept of a garden comprising a lawn and flowerbed. Viewed this way, the hierarchy is a compositional construction. Alternatively, we can view it in a decompositional way. The structure can be seen to express a way of decomposing the concept of garden. On this view, what is specified is the potential for a garden to have a lawn and flowerbed as *parts*.

It will be seen that the two views are two sides of the same coin. In one case, we focus on how a complex idea can be put together; in the other, on how it can be broken down. Historically, the decompositional interpretation has been particularly prominent, however. Dubbing meronomies 'part–whole hierarchies' or even 'partonomies' (Tversky, 1989, p. 983), theorists have seen them primarily as a way of representing knowledge about how concepts of wholes decompose into concepts of parts (e.g. Winston and Herrmann, 1987). In some cases, theorists have taken the step of viewing the meronomy as a type of conceptual analysis (e.g. Gerstl and Pribbenow, 1995). The structure has been seen as the ontological counterpart of the taxonomy – a way of using hierarchical structure to show necessary conceptual relationships. According to this view, taxonomic organization of concepts expresses relations of subsumption, while meronomic organization expresses relations of 'parthood' (Tversky, 2005).[3]

The analytic view of the meronomy has proved problematic, however, due to the inherent subjectivity of meronomic composition. The fact that the combination of a lawn and flowerbed *can* be conceptualized as a garden falls short of being an analytic truth. This is just one of many – perhaps *infinitely* many – ways to conceptualize the constitution of a garden. As Tversky points out, concepts 'can be decomposed in many different ways' (Tversky, 2005, p. 9).

Furthermore, parts can 'be optional; in the sense, they might or might not appear in the whole to which they relate' (Fiorini and Gärdenfors, 2014, p. 138). This and other problems affecting the analytic view of the meronomy have been widely debated in the field of ontology (Cruse, 1979; Johansson, 2006).[4]

VARIATIONS IN CONSTRUCTIVE FORM

The construction discussed earlier – a lawn and flowerbed conceptualized as a garden – is typical in its use of concrete concepts and two-way branching. A meronomic unit can have any number of branches, however. The structure can be of any depth, and the concepts featured can be arbitrarily abstract. The structures of Figure 7.2 illustrate some of the possibilities. Consider the top left hierarchy. A journey can be conceptualized as combining a flight and a drive. Hence, there is a valid meronomic unit with JOURNEY as parent and FLIGHT and DRIVE as children. This is the structure shown. Its meaning is the concept we started with: a

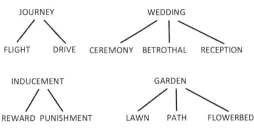

FIGURE 7.2 Meronomies illustrating variation in accommodative inclusivity and conceptual abstraction.

journey involving a flight and drive.[5] The top right hierarchy illustrates the use of three-way branching. A ceremony, betrothal and reception taken together can be conceptualized as a wedding. Hence there is a valid meronomic structure as shown. What is constructed is the concept of a wedding with this makeup.

The bottom left structure illustrates the potential for accommodation to be noticeably inclusive. The combination of a bribe and fine can be conceptualized as an inducement. Hence, INDUCEMENT can be the parent of a meronomic unit that has BRIBE and FINE as children. The meaning obtained is the idea we started with: a bribe and fine conceptualized as an inducement. As well as using abstract concepts, this structure exploits accommodation that is rather general relative to what is accommodated. An inducement can have many other constitutions, of many different kinds. The effect of the construction is thus to specialize the accommodating concept's meaning quite considerably. The existence of many alternatives is implied. (This harks back to Tversky's [2005] point, that concepts can be decomposed in many different ways. The more general the accommodating concept is, the more ways it can be (de)composed.)

The potential for use of singular accommodations is also of note. A lawn by itself can be conceptualized as a garden. Hence there is a valid hierarchical construction that has GARDEN as parent and LAWN as child. What is obtained is the idea of a lawn conceptualized as a garden (i.e., the idea of a garden consisting solely of a lawn). Other examples of singular accommodation can be visualized. A disagreement can be conceptualized as a battle: BATTLE can accommodate DISAGREEMENT. Fishing can be conceptualized as a pastime: PASTIME can accommodate FISHING. With these singular constructions, it becomes natural to use the phrase 'classified as' instead of 'conceptualized as'. The three preceding constructions can be considered to stem from the fact that a lawn can be classified as a garden, that a disagreement can be classified as a battle, and that fishing can be classified as a pastime. This style of description will be used wherever possible.

With the potential for singular accommodations taken into account, it is possible to identify one way in which meronomy is related to taxonomy. Imagine a singular accommodation in which the accommodated concept is subsumed by the accommodating concept (i.e., where the extension of the latter is within that of the former). Given a fine can be classified as a penalty, we might have a structure with PENALTY as parent, and FINE as child, for example. As a fine is a special case of a penalty, this is, in fact, ordinary class subsumption. The construction is an *is-a* link in effect. Taxonomy can be seen as a limiting case of meronomy in this situation. For all practical purposes, a meronomy passes muster as a taxonomy if all accommodations are singular, and all are class-subsumptive.

Another special case occurs if the accommodating concept in a meronomic unit is COMBINATION itself. A new concept is then composed, but in a redundant way. What is accommodated is a combination by definition. Accommodation using COMBINATION, or any equivalent, is redundant.[6]

Making full use of the meronomic repertoire, and exploiting the potential for multi-level constructions, conceptual meanings of considerable complexity can be built up. Singular accommodations provide a way of expressing basic attributes and properties. A chair can be classified as red (RED can accommodate CHAIR). Children can be classified as young (YOUNG can accommodate CHILDREN). Snow can be classified as deep (DEEP can accommodate SNOW).

Constructions like these can also be used to assemble concepts of role. Children can be classified as the agent of an action. Snow can be classified as the target of an action, and so on.

Concepts constructed by singular accommodations can be incorporated into more complex structures to obtain meanings not unlike those we encounter in language. Consider the idea of a rock blocking a stream. A blockage can be conceptualized as having an agent in the form of a rock (a rock classified as agent), and an object in the form of a stream (a stream classified as object). Hence there is a valid meronomic construction that has BLOCKAGE as parent, and ROCK classified as AGENT as one child, and STREAM classified as OBJECT as the other. This hierarchical arrangement of concepts constructs the concept of a rock blocking a stream (see Figure 7.3).

This example illustrates that placing concepts into a meronomic hierarchy can

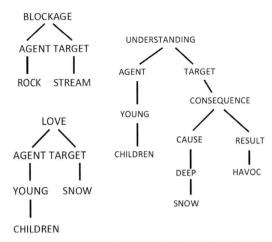

FIGURE 7.3 Meronomic construction of ideas involving agents and targets.

produce ideas involving agents and objects, taking roles in specific types of action. The semantic possibilities can be further illustrated by making minor changes to the structure. Say we change ROCK to CHILDREN. The structure now yields the idea of children blocking a stream. Say we also change BLOCKAGE to LOVE, and STREAM to FRUIT. This idea obtained is now that children love fruit. Changing LOVE to FEAR, FRUIT to SNAKES, and CHILDREN to PEOPLE produces the idea that people fear snakes, and so on.

These examples also highlight use of recursion. The output of any meronomic construction is a new concept; new concepts are the ingredients for new constructions. Meronomic construction is a fully recursive procedure. In principle, the depth of a meronomic hierarchy is unbounded for this reason. An example showcasing three levels of construction appears in the bottom left of Figure 7.3. This is the top left structure with BLOCKAGE changed to LOVE, and ROCK changed to CHILDREN. The

additional structural element has the effect of classifying CHILDREN as YOUNG. As a result of these changes, what is obtained is the idea that *young* children in particular love snow.

A more complex case is illustrated on the right. This hierarchy embeds one three-level construction within another. A consequence can be conceptualized as having a cause in the form of deep snow and a result in the form of havoc. This reveals the potential for a two-child arrangement of concepts in which CONSEQUENCE is the parent. Assuming HAVOC is made the child of RESULT, and CAUSE is made the parent of a subconstruction, which has DEEP as the parent of SNOW, what is obtained is the idea of havoc being a consequence of deep snow.

The meaning of the enclosing construction can then be established. An understanding can be conceptualized as having an agent in the form of young children, and an object in the form of the consequence in question. There is a valid hierarchical arrangement, which makes UNDERSTANDING the parent of the relevant structures. One of the structures builds the idea of an agent in the form of young children. The other, the idea of the consequence just described. The overall meaning is then that young children understand that deep snow causes havoc. Again, variations can be envisaged. Changing UNDERSTANDING to LOVE yields the idea that young children love the idea that deep snow causes havoc. Changing SNOW to RAIN, and DEEP to HEAVY produces that idea that young children understand that heavy rain causes havoc.

With abstract concepts, singular accommodation and recursion all brought into play, conceptual accommodation is found to have considerable semantic fertility, then. The ability that concepts have to fit together meronomically allows complex ideas to be assembled. Semantic precision is always retained, however. The meaning of any complex derives directly from the meaning of its components: it is the meaning of the accommodating element conceptualized as accommodating the meanings of the accommodated elements (taken together). A meronomic structure always defines its meaning in this compositional way, directly expressing the compositionality principle (Szabó, 2012). The capacity of concepts to compose meronomically is found to be inherent to their capacity for accommodation.

How does this model of conceptual construction relate to the general issue of conceptualization, as viewed from the archaeological point of view? Understanding the meanings, signs, concepts, categories, etc. salient to a particular time and place is a matter of great importance in archaeology. Reference has already been made to Pauketat's (2013) proposal to do this by means of the notion of a 'bundle', where this construct can assemble phenomena *as, of* or *in* time. Pauketat envisages entire networks of 'sacred objects, ceremonial buildings, human bodies, celestial bodies, and unseen spirits [being] seamlessly bundled, connected, embodied, and emplaced' (Pauketat, 2013, p. 44). This way of conceptualizing phenomena departs from the modern way of thinking and may or may not be archaeologically useful accordingly. The meronomic model of conceptualization has no implications either way. Its only supposition is that cognition involves the grouping (chunking) of phenomena.

Bundling being a way of grouping phenomena, there is no inconsistency. Proposals of this nature can sit alongside the meronomic model of conceptual construction.

QUANTIFYING CREATIVITY

An advantage of meronomic analysis is its potential use for quantifying conceptual creativity. On the face of it, all meronomic constructions are alike in terms of novelty. Every construction accommodates a certain combination of concepts within another concept. The procedure never varies. Constructions may differ considerably, however, in the degree to which they create extensional novelty.

The extension (or, more formally, extensional meaning) of a concept is the set of entities to which it refers (Carnap, 1947). The extension of RED is the set of all red things. The extension of BRIBE is the set of all bribes, and so on. A meronomic construction produces a new concept by combining concepts hierarchically. What is the extensional meaning of a concept constructed in this way? As extensional meanings are sets, we know that accommodation of one extensional meaning within another entails the accommodation of one *set* within another. This is the operation that we call set intersection. But it is important to recognize that what is accommodated – and thus intersected – is the *joint* extension of the combination. The rule that applies is as follows:

• The extensional meaning of a meronomic construction is the joint extension of the accommodated combination *intersected* with the extension of the accommodating concept.

Consider the example of a bribe and fine jointly conceptualized as an inducement. The extensional meaning is the set of all inducements intersected with the set of all bribe + fine combinations. Contrast this with the case of a grate, hearth and chimney jointly conceptualized as a fireplace. In the latter case, the extensional meaning is the set of all fireplaces intersected with the set of all grate + hearth + chimney combinations. The two examples differ considerably in terms of extensional novelty. The combination of a grate, hearth and chimney is a fireplace almost by definition: virtually all fireplaces have this makeup. The intersection differs little from the two sets from which it is derived. The extensional meaning derived has little if any novelty.

In the case of a bribe and fine conceptualized as an inducement, the derived intersection is more novel. As inducements can take many other forms than bribe + fine combinations, and as a bribe + fine combination can be many things other than an inducement, the intersection deviates more significantly from its two sources. Accordingly, the outcome is a more novel extensional meaning. An effective way to understand novelty in the context of meronomic conceptualization, then, is in terms of extensional innovation. In what follows, constructions will be termed *inventive* if the associated extension differs significantly from the two sets from which it is derived, and *derivative* otherwise.

In an extreme case of inventive construction, the derived intersection may be empty, but potentially filled in by application of background knowledge.

Consider, for example, a lake and river jointly conceptualized as a warrior. The intersection of the set of all warriors with the set of all lake + river combinations would seem to be empty. But it is not impossible to imagine a phenomenon that might be characterised in this way. (Imagine, for example: rainfall causes the lake to expand and the river to flood, resulting in the action of the river destroying dwellings.) Cases of this type will be termed *radically inventive*.

A second aspect of novelty involves productivity. As every meronomic construction creates a new concept, and as new concepts are the ingredients of new meronomic constructions, any construction has the potential to give rise to (i.e., enable) others. Constructions can have knock-on effects. If we take the position that concepts of greater novelty are likely to be more productive, this becomes a second way of quantifying conceptual creativity. The more a construction provides the means of making further constructions, the more it can be described as novel. The terms *potent* and *inert* will be used to characterize this. The former term will designate a construction that is especially productive; the latter, one that is not. Equipped with this basic, quantitative terminology, the meronomic model can be used to explore creative aspects of cognitive conceptual change, in relation to archaeological evidence.

APPLICATION TO ARCHAEOLOGICAL EVIDENCE

As an initial exploration of how the model can be applied to archaeological data, it is useful to focus on some evidence reported by Gebel (2002, 2013). Gebel records that, at the Neolithic site of Ba'ja, small stone tools seem to have been inserted into walls as a method of symbolic reinforcement. In his words,

the hidden objects used in the walls and floors most likely served as a forceful "medicine" against evil influence; hammerstones and celts, but also grinders, all representing heavy-duty tools, could have been understood as practical instruments to strengthen a wall ... Strength was added to the structure, especially necessary with the terraced architecture of Ba'ja.

(Gebel, 2002, p. 131)

Gebel sees the introduction of heavy-duty tools to reinforce weak walls as application of a 'forceful medicine'. It is possible to look at this from a meronomic point of view. The starting point is to define the conceptual endowment people are assumed to possess in advance. Given Gebel's interpretation, it seems reasonable to suppose a repertoire of basic concepts would have been in currency. Assume that at least the following were included: WALL, TOOL, STONE, EARTH, HARD OBJECT, LIFE and SOURCE. A concept of the IMPLANTING (of an object) also seems to be implied, along with something like a concept of HARVESTING (of power).

With these concepts assumed to be possessed, it is possible to consider the conceptual innovations that might have precipitated the behavior of placing heavy-duty tools into walls. One scheme focuses on the materials from which a wall can be constructed. A wall is potentially conceptualized as a combination of stone and earth. Assuming a stone can be classified as a hard object, there is a potential analogy between stones and heavy-duty tools, traced through the hardness that they have in common. Given one meronomic

construction featuring HARD OBJECT as parent of STONE, and another featuring HARD OBJECT as parent of TOOL, an association between the two children is formed, potentially enabling the former to substitute for the latter. On this account, the conceptual process is not complex. But the innovations involved do seem to entail some element of creativity. Both the enabling conceptualizations would appear to be towards the inventive end of the inventive/derivative spectrum.

An alternative scheme focuses on the potential role of IMPLANTING. Being users of agriculture, people of this time may have conceptualized implanting as life making (in the sense that planting a seed has this effect). This could set the stage for a cognitive sequence in which the placement of a tool into a wall is conceptualized as implanting, and hence as life making. On this interpretation, a heavy-duty tool might be understood to be placed into a wall as a way of giving the wall the strength of life specifically. In a variation on the theme, the wall might be conceptualized as an extension of the ground, rather than as a structure placed over it. This could potentially reinforce conceptualization of the act as a form of implanting.

The latter of these two schemes may be closer to what Gebel has in mind when he speaks of 'forceful medicine'. The meronomic structures involved seem not to be implausible, at least not from a modern perspective. The indications of conceptual creativity are perhaps slightly stronger in the latter of the two accounts. In both cases, the enabling constructions are towards the inventive end of the inventive/derivative spectrum. But, in the latter case, the conceptual connection established between implanting and agriculture has a potential potency extending beyond the immediate context of wall construction.

EVIDENCE FROM ÇATALHÖYÜK

Archaeological evidence from the site of Çatalhöyük is particularly intriguing from the conceptual point of view. Of the activities the occupants of the site engaged in, much is known. How these activities were conceptualized is far less clear. There is considerable scope for framing hypotheses of a meronomic nature. The aim here will be to look for evidence of creativity in ordinary day-to-day activities, building in particular. This is not to deny there is considerable evidence of seemingly artistic creative activities, such as wall painting, figurine making, body adornment, bead making, and so on. It simply reflects the degree to which the creative implications of those activities have been examined elsewhere (see other chapters in this volume). The following review of the archaeological evidence draws primarily on Ian Hodder's introductory presentation to the 'Consciousness and Creativity at the Dawn of Settled Life' conference at the McDonald Institute; information is also taken from (Hodder, 2006a, 2006b, 2012), and from the Çatalhöyük Research Project website. The assumed initial endowment of concepts remains as given earlier.

The starting point in the interpretation of Neolithic Çatalhöyük is generally Mellaart's (1967) conception of the site as a town. The site is known to consist of a large number of rectangular brick buildings, and these are generally interpreted as the dwellings of a settlement, spread over multiple levels. It has

emerged, however, that the site lacks many of the features one would expect to find in a settlement, and the extent to which houses were used as places of burial has also become apparent. This raises a basic question of interpretation. Were the buildings of Çatalhöyük conceptualized as houses for the living, or houses for the dead? In meronomic terms, the question is whether the conceptualization of a building was more akin to a construct with DWELLING or TOMB as parent. The two possibilities can be compared for the degree that they imply acts of conceptual creativity. The buildings of Çatalhöyük have ovens and hearths and show unequivocal evidence of cooking and food consumption. On the basis that cooking facilities play a vital part in any human dwelling, a conceptualization based on DWELLING is surely not unrealistic. Meronomically, it would seem to be towards the derivative end of the inventive/derivative dimension.

Not all the evidence points in this direction, however. Many facilities that would seem to play an important role in a structure conceptualized as a dwelling are found to be missing. It is now recognized that the buildings had no windows, for example. Apparently, this does not reflect a lack of window-making know-how, as lintels were used internally (for doors). Mellaart (1967) assumed the buildings must have had windows and took the step of visualizing them pictorially. But hard evidence of their existence has not been obtained. As well as having no windows, the buildings lack external doors. In place of external doors, they have roof hatches, allowing descent by ladder. Internal arrangements are also seemingly at odds with the purpose of a dwelling. Where internal doors exist, they may be too low to walk through, necessitating the use of crawling. Most striking of all, buildings were used for burying the dead, with the siting of graves within buildings being highly organized and systematic. The extent to which this activity existed is also of note. Buildings have been found to contain more than 60 graves.

Some of the infrastructural evidence also seems antithetical with the settlement interpretation. The buildings are crammed together wall-to-wall, meaning that moving from the bottom to the top of the settlement would have involved clambering over a series of roofs, all at different elevations (Hodder, 2006b). Transporting heavy objects or building materials from one location to another would presumably have been nightmarishly difficult. There are no streets or communal spaces, and scant evidence of neighbourhoods.[7] At its peak, it is thought the site would have involved the lives of as many as eight thousand people. Yet evidence of the non-house-based industrial and commercial activities such a substantial population would imply is lacking. Signs of communal gathering are detected, but only some way away from the site.

The archaeological data reveal that at some point in the life of a building, it would be dismantled/demolished and possibly burned as well. It would then be replaced with a construction immediately above, and essentially *identical* to the one demolished. There are indications of this activity having a mortuary purpose. The layout of graves (including what are described as 'bone nests') at one level would be replicated in the building above, suggesting an attempt to connect the dead together by physical alignment.

From the meronomic point of view, there are various ways to approach this puzzling evidence. Conceptualization of the buildings as dwellings might represent a meronomic construction of *extreme* inventiveness; i.e., accommodation within DWELLING of a combination of phenomena that would fail most tests of dwelling-hood. On this view, the act can be seen as considerably creative, at least in terms of extensional innovation. At the same time, it is difficult to see how it could lead on to others, on which basis it would also appear to be of low potency. The indications for conceptual creativity are contradictory in this sense. Conceptualization of the buildings as dwellings suggests considerable creativity on the inventive/derivative dimension, but less so on the potent/inert dimension.

An alternative scheme is more along the lines of the IMPLANTATION interpretation of Gebel's heavy-tool example. The starting point, in this case, is the assumption of the buildings being, not houses for the living, but houses for the dead. The main construction is envisaged to have something like TOMB, rather than DWELLING as its parent. Again, there are suggestions that any such structure would be conceptually inventive. All the buildings at Çatalhöyük incorporate ovens and cooking areas, and there is evidence of these being used for normal daily consumption of food. To the extent that cooking and eating seem not to be constitutive of tomb-hood, a conceptualization based on TOMB would seem to be inventive necessarily.

On the other hand, even in the modern world, eating and burial-making can be combined, as in a wake. So accommodation of these activities within the concept of a tomb may not be entirely ruled out. Again, the concept of IMPLANTATION could play a connective role. If placement of the dead into carefully sculpted graves is assumed to be conceptualized as entombment, this might imply a conceptual connection with the idea of implantation into a life source (i.e., the ground). In light of the evidence of dwellings being systematically dismantled and burned, conceptualization of the buildings might then deviate significantly from the modern idea of a tomb. It might refer to an 'elaborate mortuary ceremonialism' more generally (Pauketat, 2013, p. 47), in which demolition and burning of a tomb is used to convey the dead back into what is conceptualized as the source of life.

This scheme assumes several interlocking constructions, some of which might be inventive. Conceptualization of a brick construction as a vehicle would certainly count as such if it were made in the face of extensional meanings with no intersection. Similarly, with the combination of burial-making and feast-making conceptualized as an implantation. Given the range of possible accommodations of IMPLANTATION, this particular construction would seem especially inventive. Also of interest is the conceptualization of physical alignment as a means of securing a physical connection. This also suggests inventive processes of conceptualization.

There are, in addition, indications of constructive potency, however. If we assume the dismantling and burning of buildings was conceptualized as a way of consolidating the transmission of dead occupants into the ground, this might imply conceptual connections with other cases of deliberate breakage.

Gebel records the finding of an intentionally broken 'flint dagger found in a collective burial' (Gebel, 2013, p. 200). If deliberate breakage of a weapon can be related to deliberate destruction of buildings at Çatalhöyük, this might imply the existence of a very potent originating conceptualization dealing with breakage and its capacity to connect life and death. It is not impossible to see in this signs of substantive conceptual creativity on the inert/potent dimension.

Generally, then, meronomic assessment of the evidence from Çatalhöyük can be developed in at least two ways. Which version is preferred depends on whether the buildings are interpreted as houses for the living, or houses for the dead. It depends, ultimately, on whether archaeologists come to interpret the site as a settlement of dwellings distributed over multiple levels, or as one or more mounds of composited tombs. In either case, it is possible to interpret the behaviours that seem to be implied as showing evidence of conceptual creativity on the inventive/derivative dimension. But the interpretation of the site in terms of tomb-mounds seems to open the way for richer interpretations of creativity on the inert/potent dimension.

The final conclusion of the present approach, then, has to be that the building activities evidenced at Çatalhöyük can certainly be interpreted as expressing *conceptual* creativity. But it seems such interpretations are developed more easily, and to a greater extent, if the site is viewed as a compositing of tombs, than as a settlement. To the extent that cognitive change can be modeled as conceptual creativity, the case for detecting manifestations of cognitive change at the site is not lacking in foundation. Analysis to see if this result can be taken forward and made precise might pay dividends. The fabulously rich data emerging from the excavation of Çatalhöyük is surely a treasure trove for cognitive science, no less than for archaeology. It is hoped that future applications of meronomic analysis will be able to contribute to understanding what the people of this time and place really had in mind.

REFERENCES

Brachman, R. J. (1983). What IS-A Is and Isn't: An Analysis of Taxonomic Links in Semantic Networks. *IEEE Computer, 16*, No. 10.

Carnap, R. (1947). *Meaning and Necessity: A Study in Semantics and Modal Logic*, Chicago, IL: University of Chicago Press.

Clark, A. (2016). *Surfing Uncertainty: Prediction, Action, and the Embodied Mind*, Oxford, UK: Oxford University Press.

Cruse, D. A. (1979). On the Transitivity of the Part-Whole Relation. *Journal of Linguistics, 15* (pp. 29–38).

Fiorini, S. R. and Gärdenfors, P. (2014). Representing Part-Whole Relations in Conceptual Spaces. *Cognitive Processing, 15*, No. 2 (pp. 127–142).

Fodor, J. A. (1983). *The Modularity of Mind*, Cambridge, MA: MIT Press.

Gärdenfors, P. (2004). *Conceptual Spaces: The Geometry of Thought (paperback edition)*, Cambridge, MA: MIT Press.

Gebel, H. G. K. (2002). Walls. Loci of Forces. In Gebel, H. G., Hermansen, B. D., and Jensen, C. H. (Eds.), *Magic Practices in the Near Eastern Neolithic: Studies in Early Near Eastern Production, Subsistence and Environment 8* (pp. 119–132), Berlin: Ex Oriente.

Gebel, H. G. K. (2013). The Neolithic Commodification of Stone. In Borrell, F., Ibanez, J. J., and Molist, M. (Eds.), *Stone Tools in Transition: From Hunter-Gatherers to Farming Societies in the Near East 1* (pp. 191–206), Barcelona: Universidad Autónoma de Barcelona.

Gerstl, P. and Pribbenow, S. (1995). Midwinters, End Games, and Body Parts: A Classification of Part-Whole Relations. *International Journal of Human- Computer Studies, 43* (pp. 865–889).

Habel, C., Pribbenow, S. and Simmons, G. (1995). Partonomies and Depictions: A Hybrid Approach. In Glasgow, J., Narayanan, N. H., and Chandrasekaran, B. (Eds.), *Diagrammatic Reasoning: Cognitive and Computational Perspectives* (pp. 627–653), Cambridge, MA: MIT Press.

Hodder, I. (2006a). *The Leopard's Tale: Revealing the Mysteries of Çatalhöyük*, London: Thames & Hudson.

Hodder, I. (2006b). This Old House. *Natural History Magazine*.

Hodder, I. (2012). *Entangled: An Archaeology of the Relationships between Humans and Things*, Wiley-Blackwell.

Johansson, I. (2006). Formal Mereology and Ordinary Language – Reply to Varzi. *Applied Ontology, 1* (pp. 157–161).

Keane, W. (2003). Semiotics and the Social Analysis of Material Things. *Language and Communication, 23* (pp. 409–425).

Keane, W. (2005). Signs Are Not the Garb of Meaning: On the Social Analysis of Material Things. In Miller, D. (Ed.), *Materiality* (pp. 182–205), Durham, NC: Duke University Press.

Machery, E. (2009). *Doing without Concepts*, Oxford, UK: Oxford University Press.

Mellaart, J. (1967). *Çatalhöyük: A Neolithic Town in Anatolia*, London: Thames & Hudson.

Mill, J. S. (1843/1965). *On the Logic of Moral Sciences*, New York: Bobbs-Merrill.

Mithen, S. (1996). *The Prehistory of the Mind: A Search for the Origins of Art, Religion and Science*. London: Thames and Hudson.

Pauketat, T. R. (2013). Bundles of/in/as Time. In Robb, I. and Pauketat, T. R. (Eds.), *Big Histories, Human Lives. Tackling Problems of Scale in Archaeology* (pp. 35–56), Santa Fe, NM: SAR Press.

Ross, W. E. (1924). *Aristotle's Metaphysics*, Oxford, UK: Clarendon Press.

Szabó, Z. G. (2012). The Case for Compositionality. In Werning, M., Hinzen, W., and Machery, E. (Eds.), *The Oxford Handbook of Compositionality* (pp. 64–80), Oxford, UK: Oxford University Press.

Tversky, B. (1989). Parts, Partonomies, and Taxonomies. *Developmental Psychology*, 25, No. 6 (pp. 983–995).

Tversky, B. (2005). On Exploring Parts and Wholes. In Gero, J. S. and Maher, M. L. (Eds.), *Computational and Cognitive Models of Creative Design VI* (pp. 3–16), Sydney, Australia: Key Centre of Design Computing and Cognition, University of Sydney.

Winston, M. E., Chaffin, R., and Herrmann, D. (1987). A Taxonomy of Part-Whole Relations. *Cognitive Science*, 11, No. 4 (pp. 417–444).

CONTAINERS AND CREATIVITY IN THE LATE NEOLITHIC UPPER MESOPOTAMIAN

Olivier Nieuwenhuyse

STIMULATED BY MY READING OF MERLIN Donald (1991, 1998), I shall explore the notions of 'consciousness' and 'creativity' through the concept of the extended mind. The crux of my argument is that the expanding material world in the Neolithic can be seen as an expansion of the extended, or distributed, mind. I shall leave aside what actually constitutes human cognition or how it is modularly organized (see Wheeler, Chapter 4, this volume). Rather, being an archaeologist, I shall concentrate on the 'extended' part of the hybrid, working from the broad notion that the human cognitive world and the (material) environment in which humans socialize are dialectically related (Boivin 2008; Clark 1997; Dunbar et al. 2010; Malafouris 2016; Renfrew 1998, 2004, 2012).

For Donald (1991), later Palaeolithic humans reached the cognitive level of what he called 'theoretic' thought when for the first time they developed symbolic external storage in the form of visuographic expression; to many scholars this crucial innovation turned 'us' into real humans. Donald went on to describe subsequent stages of cognitive development with the further elaboration of external storage during the 'ideographic', 'phonologic' and 'global electronics' stages, associated with the introduction of cuneiform, alphabetic writing, and the internet, respectively (Donald 1991: 285ff). But this account left an immense temporal gap between the Late Palaeolithic and the first literate societies unexplored. Subsequent studies have filled this gap by identifying the Neolithic as the key intermediary stage (Cauvin 1994; Hodder 1990; Mithen 2002; Renfrew 1998, 2001, 2012; Watkins 2004, 2010, 2017). Sedentism and domestication were associated with unprecedented investments in a denser material world and an expanding exchange of goods, people and ideas. These in turn spurred, and were simultaneously facilitated by, cognitive change.

These inspiring studies lead me to make several points. First, I wish to caution against the widespread notion of a unified Neolithic as prevalent in several accounts of human cognitive change. 'The Neolithic' never existed; this helpful abstraction remains a figment of contemporary scholarly imagination

(Finlayson 2013). This is not just to emphasize the dramatic regional diversity in the ways the Neolithic unfolded in the ancient Near East (Akkermans and Schwartz 2003), but more pointedly to underscore the quantitative and qualitative gulf that separates the initial stages of the Neolithic from its later stages (Bernbeck and Nieuwenhuyse 2013). I will make my point by discussing the use of Çatalhöyük as a case study for the Neolithic. Further, to put this extraordinary site into a comparative perspective I will discuss aspects of reflexive potential and creativity in the later Neolithic of Upper Mesopotamia, mainly focussing on the case study of Tell Sabi Abyad in northern Syria.

In contemporary Western culture, notions of creativity often concern its commodification value, typically shrouded in myth. 'Creativity' either refers to idealized forms of individual self-expression in producing items for elite consumption (Bourdieu 1984; Veblen 1899) or to technological innovation to streamline industrial production (Bernbeck 2017). As Sofaer (2015: 2) observed, this modern, capitalist take on creativity leaves little room for its useful extrapolation into the pre-modern past. For archaeologists, creativity can be seen more neutrally as a social cognitive phenomenon, something that emerges in specific social settings that stimulated individuals to establish conceptual connections and crossovers between components that previously were kept apart (Carruthers 2002: 226; Liep 2001; Sofaer 2015: 2). Creativity involves reconfiguring the familiar; hence it is always culturally specific (Sofaer 2015: 2).

This is certainly not to argue that creativity is entirely a cultural construct. The capacity emerged as part of human cognition during the long evolution of our ancestors, and it belongs to the human condition similar to language (Mithen 2002). But as this chapter is concerned with the Neolithic rather than with human origins, I situate creative activity in the material elaboration that characterized the Upper Mesopotamian Late Neolithic in particular (ca. 7,000–5,300 cal BC). Similar to the development of abstract thought in the Palaeolithic (Mithen 2002; Renfrew 1998), Late Neolithic creativity came about through embodied engagements with the material world (Renfrew 2001: 129; Sofaer 2015: 15). I seek to explore increased reflexive potential and creativity as dialectically related to the dramatic increases in material dependencies (Hodder 2012; 2016a, 2016b) that changed the world so profoundly during the Late Neolithic.

Given the vast scope of the topic I shall limit the discussion of materials and objects to just one generic object category, that of the Container (Klose 2015). In the form of durable, mobile receptacles for holding stuff, containers date back to the earliest manifestations of our species (Gamble 2007). They became especially prominent during the Late Neolithic period. I shall focus on three fields – 'container situations' (Klose 2015) – in which I argue container-innovations stimulated creative, reflective thought: crossovers between separate technologies for making containers, the manipulation of biographical potential, and finally, the emergence of reflective notions of quantities.[1]

ÇATALHÖYÜK IN PERSPECTIVE

Çatalhöyük (the East Mound) is usually phrased as the major type site for the Near

Eastern Neolithic. Given the breathtaking conceptual scope of the project, the extensive fieldwork and the enviable publication record, it certainly is. However, as a Neolithic type site, it is a curious one.

First, it appears to be historically unique, a one-off. Within the broader setting of the Konya Plain, intensive surveys have identified no counterparts (Baird 2005). Nor does this Neolithic community appear to have had any identifiable Anatolian neighbors with a comparable archaeological constitution. This concentration of efforts and resources on a single, permanent location is an intriguing aspect of the Central Anatolian Neolithic. It puts Central Anatolia apart from other parts of the ancient Near East such as Upper Mesopotamia, where Neolithic communities distributed themselves over the wider landscape (Bernbeck 2013). This translated in distinctive material-cultural horizons typically spread over vast geographic distances. The Halaf culture is a famous Upper Mesopotamian case in point (Akkermans 1993; Hijara 1997; Nieuwenhuyse 2007), but complex networks of overlapping, supra-local distributions of material expressions and cultural practices already characterized much earlier stages of the Neolithic. These provided a series of linkages connecting culturally heterogeneous groups from the Levant through Upper Mesopotamian well into the Zagros (Akkermans and Schwartz 2003; Fazeli Nashli and Matthews 2013; Nieuwenhuyse 2017a). From a contextual-archaeology perspective, such regionally distinct configurations of the human–material hybrid almost certainly facilitated different cognitive outcomes in the Neolithic. Creativity may have meant something different to people

inhabiting different ecological and material landscapes.

More profoundly, the perception of Çatalhöyük as a *Neolithic* site sits somewhat uneasily with recent insights on the Neolithic period elsewhere in the Middle East. Obviously, this is to a large extent a matter of terminology, and I do not wish to be splitting hairs. However, it has recently dawned that at least in Upper Mesopotamia a vast gulf in cognitive potential separated the later Neolithic, also known as the Pottery Neolithic (ca. 7,000–5,300 cal BC), from the earlier stages characterized by incipient sedentism and domestication (Marciniak in press; Nieuwenhuyse et al. 2013). While the long-term evolutionary importance of the early Holocene innovations can hardly be overstated, the archaeological record shows that their initial impact was not as dramatic as implied in terms such as the Neolithic 'revolution'. The Neolithic 'package' never arrived as such; it emerged over the (very) long term (Akkermans and Schwartz 2003; Finlayson 2013).

For the Upper Mesopotamian region specifically, key innovations that many archaeologists would now ascribe to the *Late* Neolithic would include the domestication of cattle (Cavallo 2000; Russell 2010), the intensification of secondary products exploitation including wool and dairy products (Evershed et al. 2008; Nieuwenhuyse et al. 2015; Roffet-Salque et al. 2018; Rooijakkers 2012; Russell 2010), and the spread of village-type settlements away from the earlier nuclei of settlement, fanning out into the vast expanses of steppe (Nieuwenhuyse and Akkermans in press). As outlined later, especially relevant for studies of consciousness and creativity is the much denser material entanglement emerging in the Late Neolithic (Nieuwenhuyse in press-a).

Ignoring these profound differences risks implying a cognitive unity in the Neolithic that at best may not be entirely warranted. Comparisons for the remarkable achievements of the inhabitants of Neolithic Çatalhöyük are sometimes sought in galaxies far away and a really long time ago. For example, three millennia or more separate the hilltop buildings from Göbeklitepe near Şanlıurfa from the swampy village at Çatalhöyük East. Certainly, there are convincing continuities of some iconographic motifs and of the underlying religious concepts that may help understand these continuities (e.g. Hodder and Meskell 2010). But abstract, overarching dispositions framing long-term history are less relevant for grasping cognitive changes manifested at much more limited time spans. Donald himself (1991) argued for fast-paced cognitive shifts associated with spurs in the capacity of the external symbolic storage, as with the advent of writing in the later fourth millennium BC and most recently the internet.

Archaeologists have been careful to point out the marked cultural variability within the Neolithic (e.g. Hodder and Meskell 2010: 33), and the Çatalhöyük project is at the forefront of contextualizing specific cultural practices (Hodder and Meskell 2010: 47–50). But there is a distinct tendency in cognitive archaeology in particular to simply brush aside such issues and adopt the Neolithic as a unified analytical object defined primarily by the generalized phenomenon of sedentism and domestication (e.g. Mithen 2002; Renfrew 2001; Watkins 2017). This flatly contradicts the stated purpose of situating

human cognition in material engagement through external symbolic storage. As Malafouris put it (2016: 213), perhaps a bit poetically, creative agency emerges from the results that matter.

At issue here is scale: cognitive studies have tended to prioritize the grand sweeps of human history at the neglect of the small-scale embodied engagements in which creativity is embedded. A few millennia may well be utterly irrelevant to long-term, biological human evolution but to a relational perspective on changing human-material engagements *within* the Neolithic, they matter. A one-sided concern with large-scale structures and cognitive frameworks silences the tremendous variability of Neolithic experiences (Bernbeck and Nieuwenhuyse 2013: 29–30). I argue for a contextualized, rather than a generalized, cognition.

So, for present purposes I prefer to see Çatalhöyük East as a type site for the *Central Anatolian* region in the *Late Neolithic* period. In what follows I will draw attention to evidence for creativity from its closest neighbour: the Late Neolithic of Upper Mesopotamia.

CONTAINER ENTANGLEMENTS

Across Upper Mesopotamia, containers came to hold a central role in the orchestration of daily life in the Late Neolithic, as many if not most fields of activity one way or another came to depend on their availability. As captured by the equivalent term 'Pottery Neolithic', Near Eastern archaeologists have tended to focus most of their analytical attention on the ceramic traditions that emerged in the period. Indeed containers made of pottery ultimately became the proverbial numerically most ubiquitous artefact on Late Neolithic sites (perhaps after flint tools), as lamented by Orton and Hughes (2013: 3). But Late Neolithic peoples employed an extraordinary diversity of materials in addition to pottery for making containers, including unfired clay, basketry, gypsum and lime plaster, stone, and bitumen (Berghuijs 2018, 2019; Gibbs 2015; Nieuwenhuyse and Campbell 2017; Nilhamn and Koek 2013).

Although we remain very insufficiently informed on the actual uses and depositional associations of most of these artefact categories, they often seem to have held complementary, sometimes overlapping, roles. Collectively, they transformed long-established ways of doing beyond recognition, as for example in the fields of storage and administration (see following), and they facilitated the emergence of practices with no prior history, such as the introduction of pot-cooked food in the later seventh millennium BC (Nieuwenhuyse et al. 2015; Nieuwenhuyse 2018). Both at Çatalhöyük and at Tell Sabi Abyad, early evidence of human dairy consumption can be associated with the later seventh-millennium cooking pots (Evershed et al. 2008). At the close of the seventh millennium, Upper Mesopotamian societies gave concrete expression to the semiotic potential of pottery and the material affordances of Upper Mesopotamian clays for visual messaging – the 'painted pottery revolution' (Nieuwenhuyse 2007, 2009, 2017) – to form new, supra-local identities. This Mesopotamian phenomenon roughly coincides with the Central Anatolians moving from Çatalhöyük East to Çatalhöyük West, a move that was associated with intriguingly comparable

container developments (Biehl et al. 2012; Franz and Ostaptchouk 2012; Willet et al. 2016).

Processual archaeologists, of course, have always been keenly aware that the adoption of pottery must have had broad societal repercussions over the long term. After all, this generalizing, cross-cultural expectation finds good support in comparative studies of the ethnographic present (Arnold 1985). The analytical importance of pottery containers can be traced back to the nineteenth-century pioneers of social-evolutionary thinking such as Morgan (1877), for whom the introduction of pottery already formed an evolutionary watershed. In the 1970s, Charles Redman (1978) elaborated on the profoundly transformative power of pottery in the Near East. In his multifactor systems approach to long-term social evolution, the introduction of pottery was a major positive feedback factor that made the village farming economy the primary means of subsistence throughout the Near East, as it made movable, yet watertight containers available to all (Redman 1978: 178). Easy to produce in bulk, pottery made the transport and storage of agricultural products much more efficient, leading to a demographic surge and rising social complexities. So pottery is often seen as an essential part of the Neolithic 'package' (e.g. Zeder 2009).

However, implicit in many of these narratives was a rather deterministic, teleological view: pottery was assumed to have been adopted *because* it enabled Neolithic groups to do the many important things with which pottery would eventually become associated (Brown 1989; Gibbs 2015: 339; Hodder 2016b: 247). In contrast, we now know that these important later things took many centuries to manifest themselves. They were not foreseen when people first began the sustained production of pottery. Most if not all of the subsequent developments appear to have been unintentional knock-on effects unfolding over great swaths of time. Furthermore, while earlier approaches certainly acknowledged the existence of culture-historical variability in the form of different configurations of specific types of decorated pottery, flint tools, or house plans, they mostly took the Late Neolithic as a monolithic conceptual entity, a specific stage on the evolutionary ladder defined by the presence of 'pottery'.

As we now know, the sustained production of pottery in Upper Mesopotamia began around 7,000 cal BC in the form of tantalizingly limited quantities of visually conspicuous containers with very limited volume capacities. They were durable, portable, multifunctional tools (Odaka 2017; Tsuneki 2017), but they do not yet appear to have had a significant transformative power. The potentially socially erosive manifestation of such power may in fact have been socially resisted (Bernbeck 2017; Pollock and Bernbeck 2010); it can also be argued that these containers simply occupied a very specific, quantitatively limited 'seat in life' amongst Neolithic communities initially. At this initial stage, pottery may have held roles closely comparable to those of stone vessels, which they resembled in shape, size and outward appearance (Nieuwenhuyse and Campbell 2017).

The real breakthrough of ceramics, an 'emancipation' of sorts, occurred only in subsequent stages of the seventh millennium. At Tell Sabi Abyad ceramic sherd densities increased a factor of 20–40 between ca. 6,700 and ca. 6,300 cal BC (Figure 8.1a). At the very few Upper Mesopotamian sites where archaeologists have been able to collect ceramic sherd density measurements, the exact statistics differ, but a very similar pattern of massive increase is observed (Adams 1983; Nieuwenhuyse 2018; Nieuwenhuyse et al. 2018; Thuesen 1988). We can be sure this was not a localized phenomenon. In fact, it is closely comparable to the emergence of pottery as a ubiquitous craft at Çatalhöyük (Anvari et al. 2017; Rosenstock et al. in press).

As noted, several non-ceramic categories of containers were current in the Late Neolithic. In addition to pottery, containers made of light-coloured plaster or gypsum – the so-called White Ware, or *vaisselle blanche* – were important. Originating in much earlier Neolithic societies, in the seventh millennium the 'seat in life' of White Ware containers may have overlapped with those of ceramics in several ways (Nilhamn 2017; Nilhamn and Koek 2013). They became increasingly a part of everyday life as indicated by the rising density values (Figure 8.1b). In contrast, the role of stone for making containers appears to have become quantitatively restricted (Figure 8.1c). Stone vessels certainly remained important throughout later prehistory and well into the historical periods, but in the seventh millennium BC some of their previous roles appear to have been taken over by pottery (Adams 1983). So, how might all this relate to consciousness and creativity? The remainder of this chapter will argue that the increasing material entanglements with containers of all sorts provided an impetus to, and a need for, new and expressive forms of creativity.

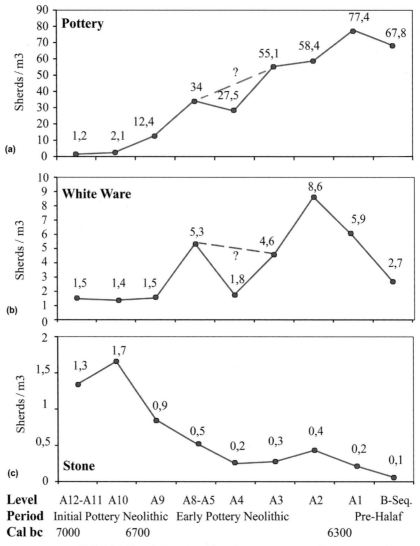

FIGURE 8.1 Tell Sabi Abyad. Density values for containers made in pottery (a), White Ware (b) and stone (c) in the seventh millennium BC (after Nieuwenhuyse 2018).

TINKERING WITH CRAFTS

In a sense, the Late Neolithic period as a whole was a highly 'creative' one, considering the versatility with which craftspersons were able to work with different materials and technologies. But the gradually changing densities of various materials by themselves would not argue for a more prominent role of (conscious) creativity. Analytically important as they may be to contemporary scholarship, actors in the past may have been blissfully unaware of the circumstance that their world was slowly filling up with new types of containers (e.g. pottery, plaster), or that others were becoming less prominent (e.g. stone). The progressive entanglements with containers certainly must have had far-reaching repercussions for the organization of production, which over time swallowed up more time and resources (Hodder 2012, 2016b). For the Upper Mesopotamian realm, such reorganizations have barely begun to be explored, but they may have come about in piecemeal fashion and may not have been perceived as very abrupt, if they were noticed at all.

Certainly, ceramic studies attest to ceramic-technological innovations in the production of pottery, which over time changed the final products from small-sized, relatively poorly crafted containers of which the practical uses remain fuzzy, into technologically advanced vessels made in an increasing range of shapes and sizes (see following). But the gradually accumulating ceramic expertise that we may infer from these developments may have existed largely as forms of tacit, practical knowledge. Contrary to the machinations of contemporary inventors, and contradicting the connotations of phrases such as the Neolithic 'revolution', the Late Neolithic under-standings of specific materials, impressive as they most certainly were, would mostly have constituted collective, normative guidelines. They may not have been amenable to much explicit comment or 'theoretical' discussion of why certain things were done the way they were or how they might be done differently.

Archaeologists have long struggled with explaining the giant step they perceived the 'invention' of pottery to be, and new discoveries are vigorously reinvigorating the debate (Gibbs 2015; Jordan et al. 2016; Le Mière 2017). Implicit in many earlier explanations has been the idea that pottery was superior to, and therefore more technologically advanced than, any of its predecessor container technologies. Given the minimalist presence

of ceramic containers in the initial stages of the Late Neolithic, Upper Mesopotamian archaeologists have recently questioned how much of a technological breakthrough this new material really was (Tsuneki et al. 2017). Pottery hitchhiked onto already existing container traditions. Multiple cases of localized 'invention' followed by abandon-ment of pottery have been documented across the wider region in the Pre-Pottery Neolithic period, showing that the craft formed part of practical knowledge systems long before some Neolithic groups favoured its sustained production.

In the Near East, it has often been suggested that the craft came about when Neolithic craftspersons were able to cre-atively exploit pre-existing technologies, re-arranging the constituent elements of their *chaîne opératoires* (Gibbs 2015: 341). Various contemporaneous 'stepping stones' have been pointed out, including the production of bread, plaster, architecture, and containers made of various organic materials (Nieuwen-huyse and Campbell 2017). As argued, the notion of a 'stepping stone' may assume a level of reflexive creativity that may not be entirely warranted by the data. As well, it leads archaeologists to expect hybrid forms of containers at archaeological contexts that document the transition into the Pottery Neolithic: these would evidence the first 'experiments' with making pottery. Here I would like to briefly highlight three cat-egories of hybrids that I argue do indeed demonstrate a reflexive, creative approach to container production: basketry – pottery, plaster – pottery, and pottery – painted plas-ter. Relevant to this discussion is their timing. Far from being associated with the magical moment of pottery 'invention', they occur much later in the archaeological sequence. Rather than the *cause* of increased container dependencies, they can be argued to be its *result*.

The relationships between basketry and ceramic in particular has always been thought to be self-evident. Scholars have long hypothesized how craftspeople in the Near Eastern Neolithic stepping-stoned from organic containers such as basketry to more durable, 'artificial' pottery (Berghuijs 2018). But convincing basketry–pottery hybrids remain to be demonstrated at the dawn of the Pottery Neolithic. Interestingly, recent work at sites with sequences spanning the seventh millennium show several examples of such hybrids appearing in the later parts of the millennium. In each of these cases, it can be argued that their appearance betrays in-depth understanding of the properties of unfired and fired clays, basketry, cordages and textiles.

For example, at several sites large containers have been documented that were shaped while standing on coiled basketry, leaving the imprints on the exterior base (Berghuijs 2018, 2019). To the potters this may have been a strategy to allow the heavy containers to be moved about during the shaping and drying (Figure 8.2a). Very occasionally the later seventh-millennium contexts yield coarse pottery vessels shaped *around* baskets. Far from being pristine 'experiments', these can be seen as a (short-lived) response to issues arising from the increasing scale of ceramic production. In the Northern Levant, mid-to-late seventh millennium Dark-Faced Burnished Ware cooking vessels were purposely, methodologically, covered with impressions

of cloth and cordage. This improved the heat conductivity of the vessels, turning them into advanced cooking utensils (Nieuwenhuyse et al. 2012).

The relationships between pottery and plaster are as old as pottery itself. Not only do they share parts of their *chaîne opératoire*, but also already very early in the Pottery Neolithic pots were occasionally plastered. Presumably this was done to improve the performance of the containers by reducing their porosity. Pots selected for plastering were larger than non-plastered ones, and they sometimes resembled White Ware containers. Initially the coating was little more than a thin layer applied to either surface. But in the later parts of the seventh millennium, more complicated contraptions were introduced. Some vessels gained a very thick interior coating, which sometimes was sculpted into an interior ledge. In subsequent stages of Upper Mesopotamia such interior ledges were made of pottery, as an inextricable part of the pottery vessel; in the later seventh millennium they were (occasionally) added after the firing and with different materials. One fine example of a large-hole-mouth pot with such a thick, post-firing interior coating was found in situ. This pottery-plaster hybrid had a lid in place, which consisted of a chipped block of limestone (Figure 8.2b).

Additional complexities are found with later seventh-millennium pottery containers that were plastered, then painted or slipped (Figure 8.2c). These may have been more common in the past than is apparent from the archaeological record, as the post-firing treatments are susceptible to erosion and sensitive to archaeological recovery methods

FIGURE 8.2 Tell Sabi Abyad and Shir. Later seventh-millennium BC crossovers between containers made in different materials. (a) basketry-impressed base of a large pottery vessel; (b) thickly plastered hole mouth pot; (c) plastered-and-painted pottery basin (after Nieuwenhuyse 2018, 2019).

(Nilhamn 2017). The containers selected tended to be relatively large, heavy and immobile; they would have been part of the stationary equipment of the house, 'fixtures' rather than 'portables' (Cribb 1991: 76). As such, it might not be too far-fetched to see them as semantically linked to the 'house', and to the plastered-painted walls occasionally found in later seventh-millennium buildings (e.g. at Bouqras or Umm Dabaghiyah). Speculating even further, their introduction perhaps offers yet another connection to Late Neolithic Çatalhöyük, where in the later

seventh millennium people moved from painting their houses to decorating their pottery (Hodder 2012: 151–156).

What these basketry-related, plastered and plastered-and-painted pottery hybrid examples have in common is the innovative rearrangement of raw materials, technologies and social representations in ways that reflect in-depth understanding, but also resulted in quite visible modifications of socially important aspects of the domestic environment. Late Neolithic people must have spoken openly on the functional possibilities of different types of hybrids and their individual material properties.

TINKERING WITH BIOGRAPHIES

It may seem almost self-evident that immediately after people in the ancient Near East adopted pottery, they would exploit the almost infinite possibilities of this versatile material for making whatever object they fancied. In fact, the archaeological record for Upper Mesopotamia suggests that during the first half millennium or so of sustained pottery production, communities limited their creative engagement with fired clay to the making of containers, in the quite literal sense of the word. Moreover, these small, morphologically still undifferentiated containers were simply abandoned after their use life had ended. Clay as a raw material had been employed for a wide range of craft products since time immemorial for making figurines, clay containers and buildings, which all continued into the Late Neolithic. Many of these unfired clay artefacts had a single phase of use after which they were discarded, and so, initially, were fired clay containers. But at the end of the seventh millennium a veritable 'explosion' can be identified in expanding the post-firing applications of pottery by way of repairing, reshaping and curating pottery containers or parts thereof.

At Tell Sabi Abyad, this took many forms. Pottery vessels began to be reused as containers with an altered functional use, usually in wholly different spatial settings. For example, large jars were occasionally reused as ovens, and bowls could end up as containers for the dead (Nieuwenhuyse 2007: 59; Plug and Nieuwenhuyse 2018). People also began to use *parts* of pottery containers for making new types of objects. With jars, the necks were sometimes separated from the bodies, after which both components were reused: the necks became stoves or 'pot stands', the bodies hole-mouth cooking pots (Campbell 2012: 308; Nieuwenhuyse 2007: 127–129). In particular, the later seventh millennium saw the emergence of the 'sherd' as a basic raw material for making objects. Pottery sherds were adopted for constructing floors of kilns, as a supporting skeleton for shaping plaster containers, and for making small artefacts including discs, scrapers, spindle whorls, lids, and scoops for removing fleshy body parts in burial rites (Akkermans 2008; Brüning et al. 2014; Nieuwenhuyse 2007: 59; Nilhamn and Koek 2013; Plug and Nieuwenhuyse 2018; Spoor and Collet 1996: 440–441). Intriguingly, pottery sherds appear to have been ritually deposited in large numbers inside buildings that were deliberately burned (Akkermans et al. 2012; Verhoeven 1999).

Finally, at the end of the seventh millennium, more than half a millennium after the introduction of sustained pottery production, the first pottery repairs are recorded (Nieuwenhuyse and Dooijes 2018). Several methods for mending pottery have been identified. White plaster (in all likelihood gypsum) was adopted for filling cracks and gaps in porous, plant-tempered wares. In contrast, the finer wares, made of more compact, dense clay fabrics that resulted in sharp breaks, were repaired by drilling perforations on either side of the break and using a piece of cloth, leather or rope to bind the fragments together. Often a dark-coloured, organic glue was additionally used to cement the joins.

Perforations and glue are also found on their own, one without the other.

Archaeologists have proposed several explanations for repaired or curated containers. Such practices may be adopted for the pragmatic purpose of maintaining the functional integrity of the objects, and they may reflect conditions of temporary scarcity. At an ideological level, they can suggest collective notions of thrift or taboos against 'waste' (Bernbeck 1994: 263–265; Dooijes and Nieuwenhuyse 2007, 2009; Hsieh 2016; Sofaer 2015: 40–43; Tomkins 2007). They can also point to notions of value and a role of (curated) artefacts in negotiating social identities and networking (Campbell 2012; Chapman and Gaydarska 2007; Maeir 2016). At prehistoric Tell Sabi Abyad these explanations do not appear to have been mutually exclusive, and types of repair or reuse can be argued to have carried different social and economic meanings (Nieuwenhuyse and Dooijes 2018).

For present purposes, these practices have several aspects in common. First, they effectively prolonged the use life of the object, by creating a new phase of use of the object or parts of objects. They comprised a deliberate de-contextualizing followed by re-contextualizing in new settings. In a word, they extended the *biography* (Kopytoff 1986) of the objects. Further, they did so in ways that were in many cases quite visible to the community at large. The plaster-repaired large storage jars may have been deposited inside dark, poorly accessible storage buildings (Nieuwenhuyse and Dooijes 2018), but the elaborately-painted serving-and-display vessels were meant to be seen and used in collective commensality (Hole 2017; Pollock 2013); almost certainly they continued their social lives after their repair. As well, importantly, the objects affected parts of daily life that were socially and economically relevant: they facilitated practices crucial to social reproduction and biological survival.

These circumstances make it unlikely that these practices were non-discursive, part of long-established, tacit collective knowledge that did not require verbal comments. They show the emergence of a discursive, reflective attitude to the materials and containers at hand. Late Neolithic people must have spoken openly on the possibilities associated with specific sorts of makeover. The new practices comprised a purposeful, highly creative tinkering with the biographical potential of artefacts. For the first time containers were provided with histories; some became, literally, 'history containers'. The timing of the appearance of these practices long after the adoption of sustained ceramic production – more than half a millennium earlier – is quite relevant. Repairing, reshaping and curating are possible by virtue of a sound understanding of the limitations and affordances of the available materials and objects (Knappett 2005; Sofaer 2015: 40–41). Such understandings would have accumulated over many generations in the earlier stages of the Late Neolithic before 'coming out' in new forms of creativity.

CONTAINERS AND VOLUME

The potential to store stuff in advanced containers has long been assumed to have been a primary incentive for Near Eastern peoples, luring them into making the quantum leap towards sustained pottery production. For long this tacit understanding found support in the tantalizingly few excavated 'early' Pottery Neolithic sites available, such as the basal levels of Tell Hassuna in northern Iraq, which indeed yielded domestic contexts loaded with pottery storage containers (Lloyd and Safar 1945). Recent work on earlier contexts in Upper Mesopotamia shows that, indeed, a concern with adapting pottery containers for efficient storage formed a major thread running through the development of ceramic industries in the seventh millennium. At the same time, it has become clear that the new craft far from immediately afforded storage in any significant way. It took Late Neolithic societies over half a millennium of slow and incremental change before efficient ceramic storage had been fully incorporated (Nieuwenhuyse 2018).

At Tell Sabi Abyad, Shir, Tell Haloula, Mezraa Teleilat, Tell el-Kerkh, and several other seventh-millennium sites, archaeologists may now chart the manifold, interrelated innovations and strategies adopted by successive generations of skilled craftspersons that slowly enhanced the storage potential of pottery vessels. They included coating the vessels with plaster, discussed earlier. They involved changes in the preparation of raw materials and in shaping techniques to make vessels stronger. They are apparent in morphological changes leading from undifferentiated shapes to S-shaped forms, to, ultimately, the 'invention' of the neck in the later seventh millennium (Bader and Le Mière 2013). Here I wish to highlight one particularly important aspect: the gradually rising capacities.

Pottery containers initially were small and unable to hold significant volumes. In the earliest few centuries of the Pottery Neolithic

they contained (much) less than five litres. Between ca 6,500 and 6,350 cal BC at Tell Sabi Abyad some vessels already gained over fifty litres (average 3.2 litre). This was followed by a rapidly expanding volume diversity as some pots became bigger and taller. By ca. 6,250 cal BC some pots reached over 75 litres (average 6.7 litre). At Late Neolithic Shir some vessels held up to 190 litres (Nieuwenhuyse 2018, 2019). People could store significantly much more stuff inside pots. The rising pottery volumes are especially prominent in the typological categories of closed shapes: 'pots' and 'jars' (Figure 8.3). Pottery jars began to reach the capacities of some of the other, pre-existing storage technologies using bins and plastered clay silos.

At one level, this will have contributed to changes in the social organization of Late Neolithic groups. The more private storage mode enabled by durable, flexible pottery

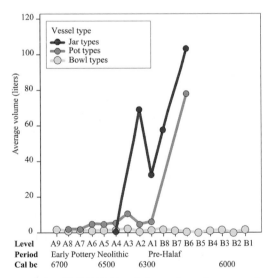

FIGURE 8.3 Tell Sabi Abyad. Increasing volume capacities of pottery containers in the seventh millennium (after Nieuwenhuyse 2018).

containers may have stimulated the autonomy of emerging extended households (Bogaard et al. 2009; Flannery 2002). For present purposes, however, I argue that the embodied engagement with increasingly variable container volumes stimulated reflective thought on the social usages and potentials of such variability. This is because this variability in container volume was not simply a feature only archaeologists can identify retrospectively. Rather, it was fully, and conspicuously, enmeshed with vital aspects of prehistoric domestic, economic and political life. Obviously, voluminous objects and the attendant experience of volume were nothing new to the Late Neolithic, but in the much denser, 'containerized' world of the later seventh millennium, volume almost became a guiding principle.

For instance, different types of repair (see earlier) were associated with vessels differing in size, use and deposition: whereas gypsum repairs were made on large, heavy storage vessels found in buildings, perforations-glue were featured on small bowls and jugs recovered from open areas. Later seventh-millennium to early sixth-millennium communities produced their larger, bulkier containers locally, but amongst the smaller, non-voluminous types there is clear evidence for ceramic exchange (Le Mière and Picon 2008; Spataro and Fletcher 2010). Adult burials sometimes contained a few *small* vessels (Plug and Nieuwenhuyse 2018). Decorative style, too, became associated with vessels of different sizes. Larger, relatively immobile types were treated with applied decoration. These bulky, closed shapes were often kept inside in dark, shady rooms (Nieuwenhuyse in press-b). In contrast,

smaller, lightweight vessels suitable for serving and display were usually painted or slipped. These figured in bouts of commensality, both at the domestic level and in public events (Nieuwenhuyse 2007). In short, various ceramic volumes figured in different sorts of activities; held different social, ideological and religious meanings; and may even have appealed to different bodily senses.

It is emphasized that later seventh-millennium engagements with volume did *not* rely on abstract quantitative concepts. Abstract counting emerged much later in Mesopotamian prehistory (Benison-Chapman, Chapter 5 this volume; Nissen et al. 1993). The associations cited earlier do not yield clear-cut, discrete groups nor do they suggest standardized quantities, let alone numbers. The patterns are clear but operate at the level of statistical associations, yielding diffuse and overlapping categories. Nonetheless, a more overt, discursive recognition of (differential) volume in terms of 'big' or 'small', 'more' or 'less', can be argued to have come to the fore in the Late Neolithic, changing the cognitive apparatus – the 'extended' part of the hybrid mind – with which people engaged with the world. If so, this would have guided further reflection and changes in practice.

To return to storage, no sooner had pottery storage containers emerged than they became part of a series of important changes in the administration of stored goods. These are still poorly understood, but are generally thought to reflect the emergence of new concepts of private and collective property. These concepts may have responded to a need to monitor access to goods in an increasingly mobile society (Akkermans and Duistermaat 1996; Duistermaat 2013). Neolithic societies had long made use of a concrete system of controlling the flow of goods that had involved containers and small geometric objects that may have been used as simple counting aids. Previously, these clay items had mostly occurred as isolated, singular specimens, but by the later seventh millennium they began to be deposited in complex configurations of multiple items and other objects (Chapman-Benison, Chapter 5 this volume; Verhoeven 1999). At the same time the first unequivocal stamp seals appear (Duistermaat 2013).

Container volume figured as a relevant framing factor in these new administrative configurations. The practice of sealing selectively prioritized containers of small size, or more to the point, of limited volume. No door sealings have so far been identified that might have secured capacious bins, silos or storage rooms. People selected baskets, leather bags or polished stone vessels. At Tell Sabi Abyad, no less than about one-third of all sealed items in the Burnt Village were pottery vessels (Duistermaat 1996: 345–347, table 5.1). These were all *small* vessels (Duistermaat 1996: 350). In terms of the formal ceramic typology established at the site, they would be categorized as 'Small Jars', containing a few litres at the most. So, the increased variability in pottery container size, in tandem with increased overall availability of pottery containers in daily life, contributed to a reorganization of pre-existing administrative systems in ways that more openly acknowledged the existence of volume differentials.

CONCLUDING REMARKS

When Donald argued that explanations of human thinking skills should account for the

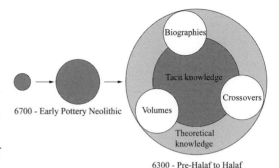

FIGURE 8.4 Representation of increasing container dependencies in the Upper Mesopotamian Late Neolithic, starting out as largely tacit knowledge in the Early Pottery Neolithic but stimulating discursive thought by the later seventh millennium BC.

historical order in which symbolic inventions unfolded (1991: 356–357), he had the long-term development of extended cognition in mind. Applying the concept of external symbolic storage to the Neolithic of the ancient Near East, but arguing for contextualized cognition, leads me to emphasize the distinctiveness of the *later* Neolithic. I situate creativity in the increasing dependencies on containers from about 6,700 cal BC (Figure 8.4). In the opening stages of the Late Neolithic, creativity mainly lay in the gradually accumulating knowledge base as increasingly sophisticated containers more and more became part of daily life. I argue that much of this knowledge was tacit understanding of the properties of the raw materials, their transformations, and the final products. By the later seventh millennium BC this became more explicit. I have briefly sketched three fields in which more discursive creativity may be argued: crossovers, biographies and volumes. The latter engagements may qualify as examples of theoretic thinking.

This chapter does not argue that humans became 'smarter' in the (later) Neolithic, nor necessarily that they became more self-conscious overall. Rather, it explores how increased reflexivity can be observed in the *specific field* of containers. The later seventh millennium was distinctive because containers became quantitatively available as never before, because they transformed and enabled activities crucially important to the community, and, finally, because many of these transformations were visible and thereby inviting to verbal comment.

I have offered the archaeology of Upper Mesopotamia as an alternative test case for exploring cognitive (and other) changes in the Neolithic. Comparing and contrasting regionally specific developments can offer a vital counterweight against misguided notions of a unified Neolithic. As we have seen, while the Upper Mesopotamian Late Neolithic was different from the Neolithic to Early Chalcolithic sequence at Çatalhöyük, several intriguing commonalities can be pointed out. As in Central Anatolia, the Upper Mesopotamian container-related developments sketched earlier did not occur in a cultural vacuum but were an integral part of far-reaching transformations of social life at the turn of the seventh to early sixth millennia BC (locally known as the Pre-Halaf to Early Halaf period). Explanations have tended to either prioritize containers (especially pottery) as a primary causal factor (as in processual archaeology), climate change as an external systemic push (the 8.2 ka abrupt climate event), or the role of humans as meaning-giving creatures forming new identities, religions and ideologies (Mottram 2016; Nieuwenhuyse and Akkermans in press; Nieuwenhuyse et al. 2016). The attractiveness of current approaches emphasizing the co-constitution of humans and the material world lies in acknowledging the importance of exploring the mutual dependencies.

While this chapter has selectively focused on just one material culture category – containers – future studies may therefore explore how a higher level of reflexivity with containers became transformative in its own right to 'act back' on other, less tangible aspects of society in the Upper Mesopotamian Late Neolithic. These may include social-political ideologies, notions of property or concepts of the body. The heightened awareness of a personal self that many have argued was associated with the rise of elaborately decorated pottery styles in the later seventh-millennium (Nieuwenhuyse 2007) or with the emergence of a self-conscious 'attitude of care' in a world increasingly filled-up with fragile containers (Bernbeck 2017) are just two examples. Long after the dawn of settled life in the ancient Near East, containers had come to occupy a central place in framing human endeavour.

REFERENCES

Adams, R. M. 1983. The Jarmo stone and pottery vessel industries. In Braidwood, L. S., Braidwood, R. J., Howe, B., Reed, C. and Watson, P. J. (eds.), *Prehistoric Archaeology along the Zagros Flanks*. Chicago: Oriental Institute (OIP 105), 209–232.

Akkermans, P. M. M. G. 1993. *Villages in the Steppe*. Ann Arbor, Michigan: University Monographs in Prehistory.

Akkermans, P. M. M. G. 2008. Burying the dead in Late Neolithic Syria. In Cordoba, J., Molist, M., Perez, C., Rubio, I. and Martínez, S. (eds.), *Proceedings of the Fifth International Congress on the Archaeology of the Ancient Near East*. Madrid: Universidad Autonoma de Madrid, 621–645.

Akkermans, P. M. M. G., Bruning, M., Hammers, N., Huigens, H., Kruijer, L., Meens, A.,

Nieuwenhuyse, O. P., Raat, A., Rogmans, E. F., Slappendel, C., Taipale, S., Tews, S. and Visser, E. 2012. Burning down the house: The burnt building V6 at Late Neolithic Tell Sabi Abyad. *Syria. Analecta Praehistorica Leidensia* 43/44, 307–324.

Akkermans, P. M. M. G. and Duistermaat, K. 1996. Of storage and nomads. The sealings from Late Neolithic Tell Sabi Abyad, Syria. *Paléorient* 22, 17–44.

Akkermans, P. M. M. G. and Schwartz, G. 2003. *The Archaeology of Syria*. Cambridge, UK: Cambridge University Press.

Anvari, J., Franz, I., Naumov, G., Willet, P. T. and Rosenstock, E. 2017. Continuous change: Venturing into the Early Chalcolithic at Çatalhöyük. In Steadman, S. R. and McMahon, G. (eds.), *The Archaeology of Anatolia: Recent Discoveries (Volume 2)*. Cambridge, UK: Cambridge Scholar Press, 6–39.

Arnold, D. 1985. *Ceramic Theory and Cultural Process*. Cambridge, UK: Cambridge University Press.

Bader, N. O. and Le Mière, M. 2013. From Pre-Pottery Neolithic to Pottery Neolithic in the Sinjar. In Nieuwenhuyse, O. P., Bernbeck, R., Akkermans, P. M. M. G. and Rogasch, J., (eds.), *Interpreting the Late Neolithic of Upper Mesopotamia*. Turnhout: Brepols (PALMA 9), 513–520.

Baird, D. 2005. The history of settlement and social landscapes in the Early Holocene in the Çatalhöyük area. In Hodder, I. (ed.), *Çatalhöyük Perspectives. Reports from the 1995–99 Seasons*. Cambridge, UK: McDonald Institute, 55–74.

Berghuijs, K. 2018. Basketry-impressed pottery from Late Neolithic Tell Sabi Abyad. In Nieuwenhuyse, O. P. (ed.), *Relentlessly Plain. Seventh Millennium Ceramics at Tell Sabi Abyad, Syria*. Oxford, UK: Oxbow, 277–282.

Berghuijs, K. 2019. Cordage, basketry, and textile impressions. In Bartl, K. (ed.), *The Late Neolithic Site of Shir/Syria. Volume I. The Excavations at the South Area 2006–2009*. Darmstadt: Damaszener Forschungen 18, WBG Philipp von Zabern, 424–431.

Bernbeck, R. 1994. *Die Auflosung der häuslichen Produktionsweise*. Berlin: Dietrich Reimer Verlag.

Bernbeck, R. 2013. Multisited and modular sites in the Halaf tradition. In Nieuwenhuyse, O. P., Bernbeck, R., Akkermans, P. M. M. G. and Rogasch, J., (eds.), *Interpreting the Late Neolithic of Upper Mesopotamia*. Turnhout: Brepols (PALMA Series 9), 51–62.

Bernbeck, R. 2017. Merging clay and fire: Earliest evidence from the Zagros. In Tsuneki, A., Nieuwenhuyse, O. P. and Campbell, S. (eds.), *The Emergence of Pottery in West Asia*. Oxford: Oxbow, 97–117.

Bernbeck, R., and Nieuwenhuyse, O. 2013. Established paradigms, current disputes and emerging themes: The state of research on the Late Neolithic in Upper Mesopotamia. In O. P. Nieuwenhuyse, R. Bernbeck, P. M. M. G. Akkermans, and J. Rogasch (eds.), *Interpreting the Late Neolithic of Upper Mesopotamia*. Turnhout: Brepols (PALMA 9), 17–37.

Biehl, P. F., Franz, I., Ostaptchouk, S., Orton, D., Rogasch, J. and Rosenstock, E. 2012. One community and two tells: The phenomenon of relocating tell settlements at the turn of the 7th and 6th millennia in Central Anatolia. In Hofmann, R., Moetz, F.-K. and Müller, J. (eds.), *Tells: Social and Environmental Space*. Bonn: Rudolf Habelt Verlag, 53–66.

Bogaard, A., Charles, M., Twiss, K. C., Fairbairn, A., Yalman, N., Filipović, D., Arzu Demirergi, G., Ertuğ, F., Russell, N. and Henecke, J. 2009. Private pantries and celebrated surplus: Storing and sharing food at Neolithic Çatalhöyük, Central Anatolia. *Antiquity* 83, 649–668.

Boivin, N. 2008. *Material Cultures, Material Minds*. Cambridge, UK: Cambridge University Press.

Bourdieu, P. 1984. *Distinction: A Social Critique of the Judgement of Taste*. Harvard, MA: Harvard University Press.

Brown, J. A. 1989. The beginnings of pottery as a socio-economic process. In van der Leeuw, S. E. and Torrence, R. (eds.), *What's New? A Closer Look at the Process of Innovation*. London: Unwin Hyman, 203–224.

Brüning, M. L., van Exel, V., van Kesteren, C., Nilhamn, B., Rooijakkers, T., Schuitema, K. and de Wit, T. 2014. The other small finds. In

Akkermans, P. M. M. G., Brüning, M. L., Huigens, H. O. and Nieuwenhuyse, O. P. (eds.), *Excavations at Late Neolithic Tell Sabi Abyad, Syria. The 1994–1999 Field Seasons*. Turnhout: Brepols (PALMA 11), 165–216.

Campbell, S. 2012. Rhythms of the past: Time and memory at Late Neolithic Domuztepe. In Borrell Tena, F., Bouso Garcie, M., Gómez-Bach, A., Tornero Dacasa, C. and Vicente Campos, O. (eds.), *Broadening Horizons 3. Conference of Young Researchers Working in the Ancient Near East*. Barcelona: Universitat Autonoma de Barcelona, 305–323.

Carruthers, P. 2002. Human creativity: Its cognitive basis, its evolution, and its connections with childhood pretence. *British Journal for the Philosophy of Science* 53, 225–249.

Cauvin, J. 1994. *Naissance des divinités, naissance de l'agriculture. La Révolution des symboles au Néolithique*. Paris: CNRS.

Cavallo, C. 2000. *Animals in the Steppe – A Zooarchaeological Analysis of Later Neolithic Tell Sabi Abyad, Syria*. Oxford, UK: Archaeopress (BAR International 891).

Chapman, J. C. and Gaydarska, B. I. 2007. *Parts and Wholes. Fragmentation in Prehistoric Context*. Oxford, UK: Oxbow.

Clark, A. 1997. *Being There. Putting Brain, Body, and World Together Again*. Cambridge, MA: MIT Press.

Cribb, R. 1991. *Nomads in Archaeology*. Cambridge, UK: Cambridge University Press.

Donald, M. 1991. *Origins of the Modern Mind*. Cambridge, MA: Harvard University Press.

Donald, M. 1998. Hominid enculturation and cognitive evolution. In Renfrew, C. and Scarre, C. (eds.), *Cognition and Material Culture: The Archaeology of Symbolic Storage*. Cambridge, UK: McDonald Institute for Archaeological Research, 7–17.

Dooijes, R. and Nieuwenhuyse, O. P. 2007. Ancient repairs: Techniques and social meaning. In Bentz, M. and Kästner, U. (eds.), *Konservieren oder Restaurieren. Die Restaurierung griechischer Vasen von der Antike bis heute*. Munich: Beck (Beihefte zu Corpus Vasorum Antiquorum 3), 15–20.

Dooijes, R. and Nieuwenhuyse, O. P. 2009. Ancient repairs in archaeological research; a Near Eastern perspective. In Ambers, J., Higgit, C., Harrison, L. and Saunders, D. (eds.), *Holding It All Together*. London: Archetype, 8–12.

Dunbar, R., Gamble, C. & Gowlett, J. 2010. *Social Brain, Distributed Mind*. Oxford, UK: Oxford University Press.

Duistermaat, K. 1996. The seals and sealings. In Akkermans, P. M. M. G. (ed.), *Tell Sabi Abyad: The Late Neolithic Settlement, Leiden and Istanbul*. Nederlands Historisch-Archaeologisch Instituut, 339–401.

Duistermaat, K. 2013. Private matters: The emergence of sealing practices in Neolithic Syria. In Nieuwenhuyse, O. P., Bernbeck, R., Akkermans, P. M. M. G. and Rogasch, J., (eds.), *Interpreting the Late Neolithic of Upper Mesopotamia*. Turnhout: Brepols (PALMA Series 9), 513–520.

Evershed, R. P., Payne, S., Sherratt, A. G., Copley, M. S., Coolidge, J., Urem-Kotsu, D., Kotsakis, K., Özdoğan, M., Erim-Özdoğan, A., Nieuwenhuyse, O. P., Akkermans, P. M. M. G., Bailey, D., Andeescu, R. R., Campbell, S., Farid, S., Hodder, I., Yalman, N., Özbaşaran, M., Bıcakcı, E., Garfinkel, Y., Levy, T. and Burton, M. M. 2008. Earliest date for milk use in the Near East and southeastern Europe linked to cattle herding. *Nature* 455, 528–531.

Fazeli Nashli, H. and Matthews, R. 2013. The Neolitisation of Iran: Patterns of change and continuity. In Matthews, R. and Fazeli Nashli, H. (eds.), *The Neolitisation of Iran. The Formation of New Societies*. Oxford, UK: Oxbow, 1–13.

Finlayson, B. 2013. Imposing the Neolithic on the past. *Levant* 45/2, 133–148.

Flannery, K. V. 2002. The origins of the village revisited: From nuclear to extended households. *American Antiquity* 67, 417–433.

Franz, I. and Ostaptchouk, S. 2012. Illuminating the pottery production process at Çatalhöyük West Mound (Turkey) around 8000 cal. BP. In Ramminger, B. and Stilborg, O. (eds.), *Naturwissenschaftliche Analysen vor-und frühgeschichtlicher Keramik II. Methoden, Anwendungsbereiche, Auswertungsmöglichkeiten*. Bonn: Rudolf Habelt Verlag, 97–129.

Gamble, C. 2007. *Origins and Revolutions. Human Identity in Earliest Prehistory*. Cambridge, UK: Cambridge University Press.

Gibbs, K. 2015. Pottery invention and innovation in East Asia and the Near East. *Cambridge Archaeological Journal* 251, 339–351.

Hijara, I. 1997: *The Halaf Period in Northern Mesopotamia*. London: NABU Publications (Edubba 6).

Hodder, I. 1990. *The Domestication of Europe*. Oxford, UK: Basil Blackwell.

Hodder, I. 2012. *Entangled: An Archaeology of the Relationships between Humans and Things*. Oxford, UK: Wiley-Blackwell.

Hodder, I. 2016a. *Studies in Human-Thing Entanglement*. Published online.

Hodder, I. 2016b. Degrees of dependence. The example of the introduction of pottery in the Middle East and at Çatalhöyük. In Der, L. and Fernandini, F. (eds.), *Archaeology of Entanglement*. Walnut Creek, CA: Left Coast Press, 235–250.

Hodder, I. and Meskell, L. 2010. The symbolism of Çatalhöyük in its regional context. In Hodder, I. (ed.), *Religion in the Emergence of Civilization*. Cambridge, UK: Cambridge University Press, 32–72.

Hole, F. 2017. Exploring the data: The pottery of Umm Qseir. In Mateiciucová, I., Cruells, W. and Nieuwenhuyse, O. P. (eds.), *Painting Pots – Painting People. Late Neolithic Ceramics in Ancient Mesopotamia*. Oxford, UK: Oxbow, 186–200.

Hsieh, J. 2016. The practice of repairing vessels in ancient Egypt: Methods of repair and anthropological implications. *Near Eastern Archaeology* 79/4, 280–283.

Jordan, P., Gibbs, K., Hommel, P., Piezonka, H., Silva, F. and Steele, J. 2016. Modelling the diffusion of pottery technologies across Afro-Eurasia: Emerging insights and future research. *Antiquity* 90, 590–603.

Klose, A. 2015. *The Container Principle. How a Box Changes the Way We Think*. Cambridge MA: MIT Press.

Knappett, C. 2005. *Thinking through Material Culture*. Philadelphia: University of Pennsylvania Press.

Kopytoff, I. 1986. The cultural biography of things: Commoditization as process. In Appadurai, A. (ed.), *The Social Life of Things: Commodities in Cultural Perspective*. Cambridge, UK: Cambridge University Press, 64–91.

Le Mière, M. 2017. The earliest pottery in West Asia: Some disputable questions around causes and consequences. In Tsuneki, A., Nieuwenhuyse, O. P. and Campbell, S. (eds.), *The Emergence of Pottery in West Asia*. Oxford, UK: Oxbow, 9–16.

Le Mière, M. and Picon, M. 2008. A contribution to the discussion on the origins of the Halaf Culture from chemical analyses of pottery. In Córdoba, J., Molist, M. Carmen Pérez, M., Rubio, I. and Martínez, S. (eds.), *Proceedings of the 5th International Congress on the Archaeology of the Ancient Near East, Universidad Autónoma de Madrid, April 3–8, 2006*. Madrid: Universidad Autònoma de Madrid, 729–734.

Liep, J. (ed.). 2001. *Locating Cultural Creativity*. London: Pluto Press.

Lloyd, S. and Safar, F. 1945. Tell Hassuna – excavations by the Iraq Government General of Antiquities in 1943 and 1944. *Journal of Near Eastern Studies* 4, 255–289.

Maeir, A. M. 2016. "There is nothing so whole as a broken hearth": Reflections on "The practice of repairing vessels in Ancient Egypt" (NEA 79.4 [2016] by Julia Hsieh). *Near Eastern Archaeology* 80/3, 202–203.

Malafouris, L. 2016. *How Things Shape the Mind*. Cambridge MA: MIT Press (paperback edition).

Marciniak, A. (ed.). in press. *Concluding the Neolithic. The Near East in the Second Half of the Seventh Millennium BC*. Atlanta, GA: Lockwood Press.

Mithen, S. J. 2002. Human evolution and the cognitive basis of science. In Carruthers, P., Stich, S. and Siegal, M. (eds.), *The Cognitive Basis of Science*. Cambridge, UK: Cambridge University Press, 23–40.

Morgan, L. H. 1877. *Ancient Society*. New York: Holt.

Mottram, M. 2016. When the going gets tough: Risk minimisation responses to the 8.2.ka event in the Near East and their role in the emergence of the Halaf cultural phenomenon. In Biehl, P. and Nieuwenhuyse, O. P. (eds.), *Climate and Cultural Change in Prehistoric Europe and the Near East*. Buffalo: SUNY Press, 37–65.

Nieuwenhuyse, O. P. 2007. *Plain and Painted Pottery. The Rise of Regional Ceramic Styles on the Syrian and*

Northern Mesopotamian Plains. Turnhout: Brepols (PALMA 3).

Nieuwenhuyse, O. P. 2009. The 'painted pottery revolution': Emulation, ceramic innovation and the Early Halaf in northern Syria. In Astruc, L., Gaulon, A. and Salanova, L. (eds.), *Méthodes d'approche des premières productions céramiques: étude de cas dans les Balkans et au Levant.* Rahden: Marie Leidorf, 81–91.

Nieuwenhuyse, O. P. 2017a. Globalizing the Halaf. In Hodos, T. (ed.), *The Routledge Handbook of Archaeology and Globalization.* London: Routledge, 839–854.

Nieuwenhuyse, O. P. 2017b. Pots to be seen. In Cruells, W., Mateiciucová, I. and Nieuwenhuyse, O. P. (eds.), *Painting Pots Painting People. Late Neolithic Ceramics in Ancient Mesopotamia.* Oxford, UK: Oxbow, 115–128.

Nieuwenhuyse, O. P. (ed.). 2018. *Relentlessly Plain. Seventh Millennium Ceramics at Tell Sabi Abyad.* Oxford, UK: Oxbow.

Nieuwenhuyse, O. P. 2019. The pottery from the South Area. In Bartl, K. (ed.), *The Late Neolithic site of Shir/Syria. Volume I: The Excavation of the South Area 2006–2009.* Darmstadt: Philipp von Zabern (Damaszener Forschungen), 263–423.

Nieuwenhuyse, O. P. in press-a. Containers of change: Social and material innovation in Late Neolithic Upper Mesopotamia. In Biehl, P. and Rosenstock, E. (eds.), *6,000 BC – Transformations and Change in the Near East and Europe.* Cambridge, UK: Cambridge University Press.

Nieuwenhuyse, O. P. in press-b. See or touch? Applied humanoid imagery from Late Neolithic Upper Mesopotamia. In Becker, J., Beuger, C. and Müller-Neuhof, B. *Iconography and Symbolic Meaning of the Humans in Near Eastern Prehistory, Oriental and European Archaeology.* Wien: Institut Orientalische und Europäische Archäologie (OREA).

Nieuwenhuyse, O. P. and Akkermans, P. M. M. G. in press. Transforming the Upper Mesopotamian landscape in the Late Neolithic. In Marciniak, A. (ed.), *Concluding the Neolithic. The Near East in the Second Half of the Seventh Millennium BC.* Atlanta, GA: Lockwood Press.

Nieuwenhuyse, O. P., Akkermans, P. M. M. G., van der Plicht, J., Russell, A. and Kaneda, A. 2016. The 8.2 ka event in Upper Mesopotamia: Climate and cultural change. In Biehl, P. and Nieuwenhuyse, O. P. (eds.), *Climate Change and Cultural Change in Prehistoric Europe and the Near East.* Buffalo: State University of New York Press, 67–94.

Nieuwenhuyse, O.P., Bartl, K., Berghuijs, K. and Vogelsang-Eastwood, G. 2012. The cord-impressed pottery from the Late Neolithic Northern Levant: Case-study Shir (Syria). *Paléorient* 38/1–2, 65–77.

Nieuwenhuyse, O. P., Bernbeck, R., Akkermans, P. M. M. G. and Rogasch, J. (eds.). 2013. *Interpreting the Late Neolithic of Upper Mesopotamia.* Turnhout: Brepols (PALMA 9).

Nieuwenhuyse, O. P. and Campbell, S. 2017. Synthesis: The emergence of pottery in West Asia. In Tsuneki, A., Nieuwenhuyse, O. P. and Campbell, S. (eds.), *The Emergence of Pottery in West Asia.* Oxford, UK: Oxbow, 167–192.

Nieuwenhuyse, O. P., Daskiewicz, M. and Schneider, G. 2018. Investigating Late Neolithic ceramics in the Northern Levant: The view from Shir. *Levant* Special Issue, 1–19. DOI:10.1080/00758914.2018.1453213.

Nieuwenhuyse, O. P. and Dooijes, R. 2018. Early pottery repairs at Tell Sabi Abyad. In Nieuwenhuyse, O. P. (ed.), *Relentlessly Plain. Seventh Millennium Ceramics at Tell Sabi Abyad.* Oxford, UK: Oxbow, 258–266.

Nieuwenhuyse, O. P., Roffet-Salque, M., Evershed, R. P., Akkermans, P. M. M. G. and Russell, A. 2015. Tracing pottery use and the emergence of secondary product exploitation through lipid residue analysis at Late Neolithic Tell Sabi Abyad (Syria). *Journal of Archaeological Science* 64, 54–66.

Nilhamn, B. 2017. Was White Ware always white? Looking into the world of painted plaster. In Mateiciucová, I., Cruells, W. and Nieuwenhuyse, O. P. (eds.), *Painting Pots – Painting People. Late Neolithic Ceramics in Ancient Mesopotamia.* Oxford, UK: Oxbow, 201–212.

Nilhamn, B. and Koek, E. 2013. Early pottery Neolithic White Ware from Tell Sabi Abyad. In Nieuwenhuyse, O. P., Bernbeck, R., Akkermans, P.

M. M. G. and Rogasch, J. (eds.), *Interpreting the Late Neolithic of Upper Mesopotamia*. Turnhout: Brepols (PALMA 9), 289–296.

Nissen, H. J., Damerow, P. and Englund, R. E. 1993. *Archaic Bookkeeping. Early Writing and Techniques of Economic Administration in the Ancient Near East*. Chicago: University of Chicago Press.

Odaka, T. 2017. The emergence of pottery in the Northern Levant: A recent view from Tell el-Kerkh. In Tsuneki, A., Nieuwenhuyse, O. P. and Campbell, S. (eds.), *The Emergence of Pottery in West Asia*. Oxford, UK: Oxbow, 61–72.

Orton, C. and Hughes, M. 2013. *Pottery in Archaeology*, 2nd ed. Cambridge, UK: Cambridge University Press.

Plug, J. and Nieuwenhuyse, O. P. 2018. Ceramics from the cemeteries. In Nieuwenhuyse, O. P. (ed.), *Relentlessly Plain. Seventh Millennium Ceramics at Tell Sabi Abyad*. Oxford, UK: Oxbow, 336–353.

Pollock, S. 2013. Defining a Halaf tradition: The construction and use of space. In Nieuwenhuyse, O. P., Bernbeck, R., Akkermans, P. M. M. G. and Rogasch, J. (eds.), *Interpreting the Late Neolithic of Upper Mesopotamia*. Turnhout: Brepols (PALMA 9), 171–182.

Pollock, S. and Bernbeck, R. 2010. Neolithic worlds at Tol-e Baši. In Pollock, S., Bernbeck, R. and Abdi, K. (eds.), *The 2003 Excavations at Tol-e Baši. Social Life in a Neolithic Village*. Mainz: Philipp von Zabern (Archäologie in Iran und Turan 10), 274–287.

Redman, C. L. 1978. *The Rise of Civilization: From Early Farmers to Urban Society in the Ancient Near East*. San Francisco: Freeman and Co.

Renfrew, C. 1998. Mind and matter: Cognitive archaeology and external symbolic storage. In Renfrew, C. and Scarre, C. (eds.), *Cognition and Material Culture: The Archaeology of Symbolic Storage*. Cambridge, UK: McDonald Institute for Archaeological Research, 1–6.

Renfrew, C. 2001. Symbol before concept. Material engagement and the early development of society. In Hodder, I. (ed.), *Archaeological Theory Today*. Cambridge, UK: Cambridge University Press, 122–140.

Renfrew, C. 2004. Towards a theory of material engagement. In DeMarrais, E., Gosden, C. and Renfrew, C. (eds.), *Rethinking Materiality*. Cambridge, UK: McDonald Archaeological Institute, 23–32.

Renfrew, C. 2012. Towards a cognitive archaeology: material engagement and the early development of society. In Hodder I. (ed.), *Archaeological Theory Today*. Cambridge, UK: Polity Press, 124–145.

Roffet-Salque, M., Evershed, R. P. and Russell, A. 2018. Tracing pottery use through lipid residue analysis. In Nieuwenhuyse, O. P. (ed.), *Relentlessly Plain. Seventh Millennium Ceramics at Tell Sabi Abyad, Syria*. Oxford, UK: Oxbow, 354–363.

Rooijakkers, C. T. 2012. Spinning animal fibres at Late Neolithic Tell Sabi Abyad, Syria? *Paléorient* 38, 93–109.

Rosenstock, Franz, I., Orton, D., Ostaptchouk, S., Rogasch, J., Stroud, E. and Biehl, P. F. in press. The transition between the East and West Mounds at Çatalhöyük around 6000 cal B.C.: A view from the West. In Marciniak, A. (ed.), *Concluding the Neolithic. The Near East in the Second Half of the Seventh Millennium BC*. Atlanta, GA: Lockwood Press.

Russell, A. 2010. *Retracing the Steppes. A Zooarchaeological Analysis of Changing Subsistence Patterns in the Late Neolithic at Tell Sabi Abyad, Northern Syria, c. 6900 to 5900 BC*. Leiden: PhD Thesis University of Leiden.

Schmandt-Besserat, D. 1992. *Before Writing. Volume I: From Counting to Cuneiform*. Austin: University of Texas Press.

Sofaer, J. 2015. *Clay in the Age of Bronze. Essays in the Archaeology of Prehistoric Creativity*. Cambridge, UK: Cambridge University Press.

Spataro, M. and Fletcher, A. 2010. Centralisation or regional identity in the Halaf period? Examining interactions within fine painted ware production. *Paléorient*, 36/2, 91–116.

Spoor, R. and Collet, P. 1996. The other small finds. In Akkermans, P. M. M. G. (ed.), *Tell Sabi Abyad. The Late Neolithic Settlement. Report on the Excavations of the University of Amsterdam (1988) and the National Museum of Antiquities Leiden (1991–1993) in*

Syria. Istanbul: Nederlands Historisch Archeologisch Instituut, 439–473.

Thuesen, I. 1988. *Hama. Fouilles et Récherches de la Fondation Carlsberg 1931–1938. I. The Pre- and Protohistoric Periods.* Copenhagen: Nationalmuseets.

Tomkins, P. 2007. Communality and competition: The social life of food and containers at Aceramic and Early Neolithic Knossos, Crete. In Mee, C. and Renard, J. (eds.), *Cooking up the Past. Food and Culinary Practices in the Neolithic and Bronze Age Aegean.* London: Oxbow, 174–199.

Tsuneki, A. 2017. The significance of research on the emergence of pottery in West Asia. In Tsuneki, A., Nieuwenhuyse, O. P. and Campbell, S. (eds.), *The Emergence of Pottery in West Asia.* Oxford, UK: Oxbow, 1–8.

Tsuneki, A., Nieuwenhuyse, O. P. and Campbell, S. (eds.). 2017. *The Emergence of Pottery in West Asia.* Oxford, UK: Oxbow.

Veblen, T. 1899. *The Theory of the Leisure Class: An Economic Study of Institutions.* New York: The Macmillan Company.

Verhoeven, M. 1999. *An Ethnographical Ethnography of a Late Neolithic Community. Space, Place and Social Relations at Tell Sabi Abyad, Syria.* Istanbul: Nederlands Historisch Archeologisch Instituut.

Watkins T. 2004. Building houses, framing concepts, constructing worlds. *Paléorient* 30, 5–24.

Watkins, T. 2010. Changing people, changing environments: How hunter-gatherers became communities that changed the world. In Finlayson B. and Warren, G. (eds.), *Landscapes in Transition.* Oxford, UK: Oxbow Books, 106–114.

Watkins T. 2017. From Pleistocene to Holocene: The Prehistory of southwest Asia in evolutionary context. *History and Philosophy of the Life Sciences* 39, 22.

Willett, P. T., Franz, I., Kabukcu, C., Orton, D., Rogasch, J., Stroud, E., Rosenstock, E. and Biehl, P. F. 2016. The aftermath of the 8.2 event. Cultural and environmental effects in the Anatolian Late Neolithic and Early Chalcolithic. In Biehl, P. F. and Nieuwenhuyse, O. P. (eds.), *Climate and Cultural Change in Prehistoric Europe and the Near East.* New York: SUNY Press, 95–115.

Zeder, M. 2009. The Neolithic macroevolution: Macroevolutionary theory and the study of culture change. *Journal of Archaeological Research* 17, 1–63.

CREATIVITY AND INNOVATION IN THE GEOMETRIC WALL PAINTINGS AT ÇATALHÖYÜK

Ian Hodder and Nazlı Gürlek

ONE OF THE PARADOXES OF ÇATALHÖYÜK is that every time we excavate a new house we know approximately what we will find: we know roughly where the hearth and oven will be, where the burials will be, where the ladder entry will be, how much plaster will be on the main room and side-room walls, where we will find obsidian caches, and so on. And as we empty out the fill and come down onto the floors we always do find more or less what we are expecting. The rules are always followed to some degree: the northern floors are clean and white, the southern mixed with residues of cooking and production, whole pots are never found in burials, neither are whole animals. And yet, at the same time, every house is different; we are always surprised by the specifics of how things are arranged. A human body is found sprawled on a house floor, with its head removed, a sheep is found in a burial (although not quite because separated from the human body by a mat), in some cases we find the oven moved to the north part of the main room. The paradox of Çatalhöyük is that it stands out from many other sites because of the strict rule-bound repetition of houses tightly packed together in apparent conformity and order, while at the same time the site stands out as one of the great early flowerings of human creativity.

One of the aims of this chapter is to examine this paradox through the lens of geometric wall paintings. As we will show, these are also in many ways very conformist and repetitive. There is an identifiable 'family of forms', but somehow this conformity seems to exist alongside enormous variation and individual creativity so that no two paintings are ever alike. The questions posed are: what is the relationship between conformity and creativity, and what causes the outpouring of creativity in geometric wall paintings at Çatalhöyük? The figurative and narrative paintings at the site are well known. But in fact the geometric wall paintings are far more common, and overall over 100 have been found. Yet they have as yet not been subject to systematic analysis. While such a fully developed analysis is not provided here, such work is being undertaken by Czeszewska (2014) and Busacca (2018).

A second aim of this chapter is to contribute to the question of whether increased cognitive complexity is suggested by the more elaborate and complex geometric wall paintings. There is, of course, a long tradition of research in which prehistoric art is used to infer cognitive and symbolic schemes. Evolutionary arguments have been based on engravings on Palaeolithic bone implements (Marshak 1991), and cave paintings have been subject to a variety of approaches (Whitley 1998) such as structuralist analyses (Leroi-Gourhan 1982) or comparison with images produced in shamanic trances (Lewis-Williams 2004a), or the handing down of ecological knowledge (Mithen 1996), or neuropsychology (Zaidel 2015). The figurative art at Çatalhöyük has been interpreted in terms of shamanic practices (Lewis-Williams 2004b). The rich symbolism at the site can certainly be understood in terms of external symbolic storage (Donald 1991; Renfrew and Scarre 1998; Turner 2006). So does the geometric wall art at Çatalhöyük include examples that suggest higher degrees of abstraction and greater complexity of objectification? And if so, what causes these changes?

THE CONTEXT OF THE GEOMETRIC WALL PAINTINGS

Neolithic wall paintings are found at a number of sites throughout the Middle East. Apart from panels of continuous red paint on floors and walls in Pre-Pottery Neolithic A (PPNA) contexts, the first geometric or figurative paintings are from Pre-Pottery Neolithic B (PPNB) contexts such as Djade al-Mughara (Cartwright 2008) and Tell

Halula (Molist 1998). There are also widely scattered examples at a number of Late Neolithic sites such as Ulucak Höyük, Hacılar, Bademağacı, Köşk Höyük, Tepecik-Çiftlik in Turkey, Tell Bouqras in Syria and 'Umm Dabaghiyah in Iraq. Apart from the latter case in which a good number of figurative and geometric paintings were found (Kirkbride 1975), the overall evidence is scarce and sparse. Certainly there is nothing to compare with the over 300 examples of wall paintings so far found at Çatalhöyük.

It is possible that the large numbers of wall paintings found at Çatalhöyük result from happenstances of survival. Certainly there are earlier sites such as Göbekli Tepe with elaborate figurative relief carvings on stone (Schmidt 2000). Paintings could have occurred on other materials such as cloths, mats and skins that have not survived. But there are also many sites with white plastered walls that could easily have been used to make multiple paintings, for example at Aşıklı Höyük in Cappadocia (Özbaşaran 2011), and indeed in the latter case red painting of floors does occur. It thus seems most likely that the concentration of wall paintings at Çatalhöyük results to some degree from a concentration of creativity in this medium.

In attempting to explain this particular concentration it is helpful to examine the specific context of geometric wall painting at the site. Of the 85 wall paintings available for study up to 2008 (Czeszewska 2014), the majority had been discovered by Mellaart in the 1960s, and of these 85 most were geometric and most geometric paintings occurred in the middle levels, with a drop-off in the later levels. In more recent work based mainly on over 250 paintings discovered by the current project, a general decrease in the frequency of paintings has been noted in the late levels (South P to T) in contrast to the high frequency found in the middle phases (South M to O) (Busacca 2018). However, no evidence could be found in the new data set of a concentration of geometric paintings in the middle levels. (For the categorization of levels, see Chapter 1.)

There does not appear, then, to be a specific context for geometric as opposed to other forms of painting (such as red panels and the much rarer figurative and narrative scenes). We need, therefore, to consider the context of paintings at the site as a class. The data indicate (Busacca 2018) that especially in the middle period, paintings are closely associated with burial and other ritual practices in the north and east part of houses, with a shift in the late levels to an association between burial and domestic contexts, hearths and bins in the southern domestic part of houses. The function of painting changes through time from being linked with the commemoration of burial to being linked to domestic activities. Painting is also more generally concentrated in the middle period.

The middle period (approximately 6,700–6,500 BCE) is the time of 'classic' Çatalhöyük in the sense that this is the time when there is most burial beneath the floors of houses, most evidence of bull horns and other animal parts installed in houses, and the time from which many of the most elaborate buildings have been discovered. During this middle phase, the sharp differences within houses between north and south, clean and dirty, ritual and secular are most clearly adhered to. This is also the time when the classic pattern of agglomerated housing is at its height,

with the greatest density of buildings and the least open space. This may well be the time when population density was at its height, and Hillson et al. (2013) identify clear evidence for higher levels of fertility in South M and North G. There is also most evidence at this time of stress on human bodies. The prevalence of osteoperiostitis among adult individuals is at its peak in South M to O and declines dramatically in the upper levels. This evidence suggests heightened conditions of non-specific stress, especially during the peak population (Hillson et al. 2013). Workload too seems to have been at its height in South M to O. Hillson et al. show that the prevalence of osteoarthritis decreases in the later levels relative to South M to O across all three age categories, although the results are only significant for older adults. This suggests that, at least for older adults, workload was highest during the middle levels and reduced in the later phases of occupation.

Throughout the sequence at Çatalhöyük there is a tension between collective sharing through complex networks and sodalities and the separate productive and ritual capacity of individual houses and house groups. The dead played a key role in dealing with this tension. On the one hand, the dead are buried beneath floors of houses and are used to create 'histories' through time through the retrieval and circulation of body parts. On the other hand, the circulation of body parts is used to create connections between houses. In the late levels this focus on secondary burial increases, but already in the middle levels some houses become ancestral or 'history' houses for larger groups than an individual house. Burial in these middle levels is thus caught up in the tension between house-based units and connections between them.

Given the strong link between painting and burial in the middle levels, it is in this context that the paintings must be understood. Is it possible that at this time the paintings helped in some way to work through the tensions between the mosaic of separate houses and the interconnections between them? Each house stored its own food, prepared its own meals, buried its own dead, conducted its own rituals. But houses were also involved in many cross-cutting sets of relationships with other houses. These relationships involved food sharing, sharing of burial location, affiliation to ritual and social networks, dispersal of genetic relations, communities of technological practice and so on (Hodder 2014).

Within the house, painting is most closely associated with the period in which categories are more clearly marked. Platforms are more clearly marked, and the paintings help to distinguish the northern part of the main room, associated with the dead, bull heads, and all the symbolism of violence and the sacred (Hodder 2019), from the southern parts of rooms. The non-geometric paintings at this time show the dead (headless bodies and flesh removal by vultures), and there are painted reliefs of leopards. Both vulture and leopard paintings are repeated when houses are rebuilt, referring backwards in time. Thus paintings as a general class in the middle period are associated with memory making and social distinction based on links to ancestors. They help to construct memories in place while at the same time creating stylistic links between houses because paintings of vultures and leopards, as well as specific

geometric designs are found in different, often widely separated houses.

In the later levels at Çatalhöyük, there is much archaeological evidence for two social and economic shifts. The first concerns a greater focus on the productive capacity of houses, which appear to be more self-sufficient in terms of production and consumption. Houses appear more independent and 'farm' like, and there is less focus on history making and decreasing burial in houses, with more of an emphasis on secondary burial and the movement of human remains. The second is a greater emphasis on mobility across the landscape. This same pattern of increased mobility is evident in a large number of data sets from human skeletal and sheep isotopic evidence to the exchange of pottery and obsidian. It is thus remarkable that the emphasis on painting in the house declines and becomes more concentrated in the southern part of the main room associated with domestic production, while geometric design also shifts to stamp seals and pottery. While we do not as yet know what was decorated or marked by the stamp seals (the most likely candidates seem to be human or animal skin or bread), the change from wall painting to stamp seals has long been recognized as important (Last 1998) and linked to a shift to mobiliary art and mobility in general.

It is clear, then, that the use of painting at Çatalhöyük, and in particular the use of geometric painting on wall paintings and stamp seals, is in a very direct way related to social and economic changes. In the middle, 'classic' levels at Çatalhöyük, wall painting is tied to the establishment of through-time histories and across-space sodalities. In the upper levels, there is more of a focus on movements and relationships between houses, and motifs occur on mobiliary art. How do these changes relate to degrees of creativity and innovation? And can a detailed examination of the geometric paintings reveal levels of cognitive abstraction and complexity that are linked to, even caused by, the social and economic changes? Clearly the paintings and designs were caught up in changing ways of seeing and engaging the world; can an analysis of the paintings provide an insight into cognitive change?

ANALYSIS OF THE GEOMETRIC WALL PAINTINGS

An important initial point concerns the production and reproduction of the paintings. It is widely recognized that Mellaart 'invented' many of the paintings from the site and 'touched up' many others (Balter 2005). It is therefore important only to use examples for which there is good photographic and other contextual evidence as in the examples used later. It is also important to inform the study of the Mellaart era paintings with the knowledge gained from the paintings discovered by the current project. Recent work on the geometric painting from Building 80 (Figure 9.1) has shown that it was not all produced at one time but that it was continually repaired and remade. The interpretation of what it looked like at any one moment in time is non-trivial. This point refers back to the contextual evidence that the paintings were involved in memory making. But it also makes the analysis of the paintings discovered by Mellaart difficult.

The geometric patterns in the Çatalhöyük corpus of paintings convey at first sight a high

FIGURE 9.1 Painting on east wall of Building 80 excavated by the current team.

degree of diversity. There is a great variety of designs, and very similar designs are often not found in adjacent buildings but scattered over the mound. For example, as shown in Figure 9.2, Building 80 and Building VI.A.50 are widely separated buildings, but they both have a very similar 'brick design'. In both cases the design consists of vertical lines with attached triangles, and with zigzags containing a 'brick' motif.

Within the diversity there appear to be repeated motifs and repeated organizational features or 'families of forms'. For example, the examples just described are similar to the paintings shown in Figure 9.3 in that there is an organization into vertical panels, with the vertical lines associated with triangles, lozenges and zigzags. Another family of forms is based around the spiral meander (Figure 9.4) also found in stamp seals. A further example consists of series of squares or blocks, often showing both squares and circles (Figure 9.5). There are numerous ways in which these families of forms can be defined (see Busacca 2018; Kamerman 2014), and indeed we will argue later that this intersection or slippage between categories is an important component of the geometric paintings. At the most

FIGURE 9.2 The Building 80 painting compared with Mellaart's drawing of wall painting from VI.A.50.

general level, all the paintings involve adjacencies between horizontal and vertical elements. At more detailed levels there are similarities and differences in motifs. There are also interesting links between the forms and material expression: for example the spiral meander forms, although occurring in paintings (as in Building 49), occur most commonly when incised in clay (as in a burial chamber in the TP Area, and in Building 77 and in stamp seals [Türkcan 2005]).

Many of the geometric paintings at first appear relatively simple in that they are difficult to read in contrasting or multilayered ways. But many have very complex patterns in which cross-cutting designs can be seen. We will argue that many of the latter can be interpreted as expressing a tension between separateness and connectivity.

For example, we have already seen that some paintings consist of a series of blocks and there does not seem to be much in the way of cross-cutting interactions between the blocks. This seems to be very much a repetitive, simple pattern. There does not appear to be much here that is

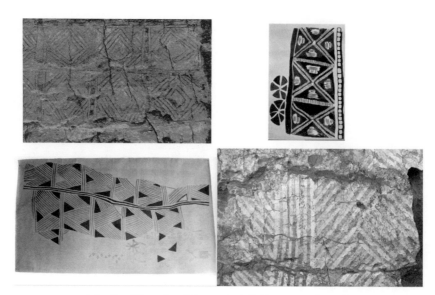

FIGURE 9.3 A family of forms involving vertical divisions, triangles and zigzags. Top left: wall painting from Mellaart's VII.1; top right: Mellaart's VII.8; lower left: drawing of wall painting from Mellaart's III.8; lower right: painting from TP Area excavated by the current team.

FIGURE 9.4 A family of forms involving spiral-meander designs. Top left: painting from Mellaart's VIII.14; top right: stamp seal excavated by the current team; lower left: painting from north platform in Building 49 excavated by the current team; lower right: incised panel from burial chamber in TP Area excavated by the current team.

cognitively multilevelled or complex. It is very tempting to see this in terms of the modular pattern of more-or-less identical houses at Çatalhöyük, and indeed the blocks in the lower image in Figure 9.5 from Mellaart's VII.14 have almost universally been

FIGURE 9.5 A family of forms involving blocks of squares and circles. Top: wall painting from Mellaart's VIII.25; lower: drawing of wall painting from north wall of Mellaart's VII.14.

FIGURE 9.6 Wall painting from north wall of Mellaart's VIII.14.

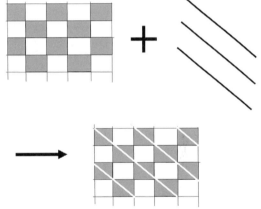

FIGURE 9.7 First analysis of painting in Figure 9.6.

interpreted in this way – this is often described as the first town plan.

But by way of contrast we can take the example of the painting in Figure 9.6. This is one in a sequence of paintings on the north wall of VIII.14. At one level this is just a chequer-board pattern (Figure 9.7) with cross-cutting diagonals. So it is just an example of the repetitive block pattern but with some diagonal lines linking the blocks. It is thus of

interest that this painting occurs directly below the 'town plan' painting of blocks described earlier. In both cases the paintings occur on the north wall of the main room. But there is more to the Figure 9.6 painting than a series of repeated blocks. Looked at more closely (Figure 9.6), it can be seen that the diagonal lines do not all join up. The modular blockiness is quite dominant, in that the diagonal lines are drawn separately for each dark square, and there are breaks in the diagonal lines at the corners of each square. So there seems a tension between the separateness of each block and the idea of an overall modular pattern linked by continuous diagonal lines. There are also two overall patterns already – the chequer board and the diagonal lines.

But we can also look at the pattern in a very different way. For example, we can focus on the diagonal lines (Figure 9.8). If we look at the areas between the diagonal lines we find triangles and lozenges. This is exactly

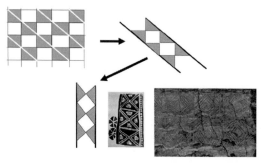

FIGURE 9.8 Second analysis of painting in Figure 9.6 and comparison with wall paintings from Mellaart's VII.8 and VII.1.

the pattern found in the vertically organized panels identified earlier as one of the families of forms. So the painting now refers to a different family of paintings – not those with blocks of squares but those with panels, lozenges, triangles, and zigzags.

So different patterns and associations are identified depending on how the VIII.14 painting is looked at. In particular, any given triangle has two possible affiliations – one to its square on the other side of a diagonal line, and one to its triangle within a pair of diagonal lines.

But the painting can be seen as yet more complex still. If looked at again (Figure 9.6), it can be seen that the diagonal lines are actually cigar-shaped within each dark square. The sides of the triangles against the diagonal lines are in fact arcs or curves, not straight lines.

So in fact the squares can be seen as cross cut by a series of circles (Figure 9.9) – and now the painting refers across to a different set of paintings consisting of series of circles.

There are several overall points here. The first is that some of these geometric paintings

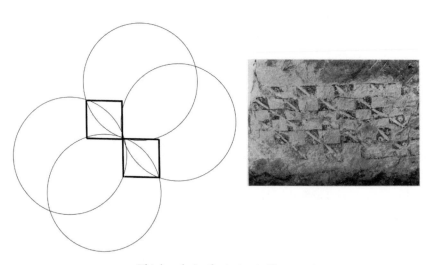

FIGURE 9.9 Third analysis of painting in Figure 9.6.

FIGURE 9.10 First analysis of Mellaart's drawing of wall painting from VIB.65.

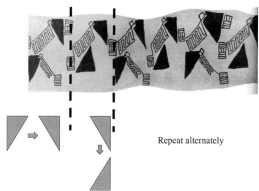

FIGURE 9.11 Second analysis of drawing in Figure 9.10.

contain complex cross-cutting patterns. The second is that within the painting any one entity, like a square, triangle, line or arc can be seen in relation to different other entities in different ways at the same time. Third, a painting may seem on first inspection to be in one category, but with closer scrutiny it appears to refer to many other categories at the same time. And fourth, in the case of Figure 9.6 anyway, there is a tension between separate entities or blocks and the relationships between them. What seem like separate distinct entities easily dissolve into relationships.

As a second example, we will take the painting in Figure 9.10 from Mellaart's VIB.65. We can talk of the entities in this painting as triangles, 'stairs' and 'barrels' all arranged according to various horizontal and vertical relations of adjacent units. The first thing to note is that the triangle entities themselves are elongated and asymmetrical. This allows one to see how one triangle shape is translated into other triangle shapes – for example, by repetition, mirror or rotational symmetry.

For example, the top row is a simple repetition of the triangle shape. But the bottom row is achieved by 180-degree rotational movements (Figure 9.10). We can also look at each vertical pairing of triangles (Figure 9.11). The first pairing on the left is produced by a horizontal mirror symmetry.

And the second pairing is produced by a vertical mirror symmetry.

Thus any one triangle can be looked at in relation to other triangles along different dimensions. One could describe the structure as in Figure 9.12. In addition, the 'stairs' and 'barrels' encourage the eye to look in both the horizontal and vertical directions. But they too have a related patterning: the 'stair' motif follows a more or less regular pattern of repetition (all the same repeated with alternating numbers of 'steps'). The barrels on the top row are combinations of horizontal and vertical units, but the barrels on the bottom row are composed of horizontal ones only.

As a third and final example, we would like to consider the painting in Figure 9.13, again from the north wall of VIII.14. In the case of this painting it is important to note that there are areas of damage and loss, and in making the interpretation in Figure 9.14 we were often uncertain of which lines to follow and reproduce.

Nevertheless, the main structure of the design appears fairly clear, and again an array of contrasting dimensions seemed evident. The overall design is constructed from a series of circles and 'sausages' or elongated ovoids.

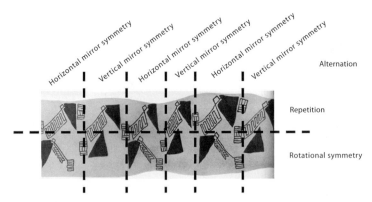

FIGURE 9.12 Summary analysis of drawing in Figure 9.10.

FIGURE 9.13 Wall painting from Mellaart's VIII.14.

FIGURE 9.14 Hodder and Gürlek's drawing of wall painting from Mellaart's VIII.14.

The result is a painting apparently very different and distinctive from any other at the site. And yet, the pairs of ovoids can be seen as being arranged in a zigzag pattern (Figure 9.15), thus making connections to the first family of forms identified earlier. Alternatively, as in Figure 9.16, the design can be seen as structured around the circles, with the ovoids arranged in a box (lozenge) or circle around them. As a yet further

interpretation (Figure 9.17), the circles and ovoids can be seen as arranged in forms very reminiscent of the rectilinear spiral-meander pattern prevalent in the later stamp seals (Figure 9.18).

These three examples of geometric wall paintings from the middle levels at Çatalhöyük can be seen as very 'fitting' (Hodder 2012) in the social and economic context of their time. The wall paintings can be

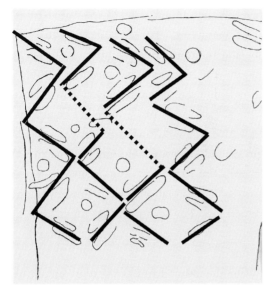

FIGURE 9.15 First analysis of drawing in Figure 9.14.

FIGURE 9.16 Second analysis of drawing in Figure 9.14.

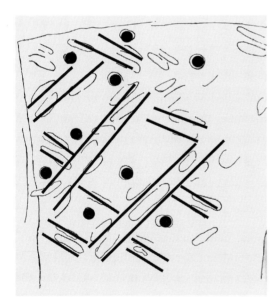

FIGURE 9.17 Third analysis of drawing in Figure 9.14.

FIGURE 9.18 Selection of stamp seals with spiral-meander designs including stamp seal of bear (top left).

interpreted as working through exactly the social and economic tensions of the middle levels. In specific terms, the paintings in the middle levels are related to the dead, to the construction of categories and memories in place in the house, but also to the connections between houses and social units. In more general terms, this tension between categories and connections, of the same thing being recombinable but according to rules and taboos, which are themselves open to reconfiguration, is very immediately recognized in the wall paintings. In the same way that each element in the more complex wall paintings can be put into different relations with other elements, depending on how one looks, so it can be argued that each person at Çatalhöyük was able to call on multiple overlapping and extended networks depending on which type of affiliation was put into play (such as food sharing, fictive and practical kinship, sodalities and societies and so on).

DISCUSSION

One might conclude from all this that there were no clear categories in the geometric wall paintings at Çatalhöyük and that motifs and forms were arranged in different ways so that different families of forms and relationships could be created; as a result each 'family' blurs into other families. There is just an endless play of transformation and connection between entities that change depending on how you look at them.

As noted in Chapter 1, definitions of consciousness have argued that it involves the dual processes of abstraction and object-ification (Bekaert 1998). Much human know-ledge is practical (know-how, savoir faire) and tied to motor habits, while more abstract levels of conscious and discursive thought involve representations, metaphors and codic oppositions. The abstractions thus depend on objectifications in the form of symbols or tokens. Archaeologically, the dual process of abstraction and objectification can be identified in material symbols and tokens (objectifications) that are generalized and recombinable (abstractions).

Certainly one could argue that the lines, zigzags, triangles, squares, lozenges, spirals and circles used in the wall paintings at Çatal-höyük constitute a set of abstract motifs that could be endlessly recombined. In the later

levels at the site we begin to see that relation-ships were made between these motifs and specific referents. For example, as shown in Figure 9.18, the spiral and meander pattern is shown in a stamp seal integrated into a bear. Other stamp seals make links between spiral meander and wild boar and between sets of circles and leopards. One might argue that at least in the later levels the geometric motifs had a representational and thus symbolic dimension. The wall paintings might thus be seen as resulting from abstract thought as defined.

On the other hand, such representational and symbolic components are rare, especially in the middle levels. We have already seen that the wall painting and other forms of art at Çatalhöyük are very closely tied to economic and social contexts. It is possible that the links between the art and context were very embodied. The art can be seen as an embodied working through of concerns at the time. In other words, the art can be seen as a complex visual system based on abstrac-tions resulting from the performance of everyday life. In the middle levels the wall paintings are embroiled in the construction of memories and categories materialized in the fabric of the house, while at the same time responding to the complex connections between houses, people and things. In the later levels society is more mobile, and the art is more mobile. This change is perhaps here too simply expressed, but we make the point in this simple way in order to draw attention to very stark and immediate con-nections. Of course it is widely recognized that 'art reflects society', but the directness and immediacy of this relationship at Çatal-höyük might suggest a very embodied and performative resonance rather than solely mental abstractions.

What, then, of the question of creativity and innovation? As discussed in Chapter 1, early village societies in the Middle East show a remarkable degree of continuity and are characterized by slow rates of change. This is particularly true of central Anatolia and Cappadocia, where Aşıklı Höyük has streets, houses and hearth locations that remain stable over hundreds of years (Özbaşaran 2011). Çatalhöyük is often described in similar terms, and indeed the continuity of houses and of the use of space is remarkable throughout the sequence (Düring 2006; Hodder and Cessford 2004). As noted earlier in this chapter, the bounding and marking of space within houses reaches its apogee in the middle levels. It is also in this middle phase that there is most evidence of the continuity of arrangements of space through time as houses are rebuilt on top of each other. There is most painting in these same middle phases, and we have seen that there is much evidence of the repetition of the same range of motifs and forms. One might have argued, then, that the geometric wall paintings show the same concern with conformity and stability as seen in house layout. But, as indeed was noted for houses at the start of this chapter, such an argument would be incorrect. In fact, the apparently simple geometric paintings conceal very elaborate variations and idiosyncratic versions. There is enormous 'play' with the same schemes and motifs. It is almost as if the very existence of a clear set of rules allows or promotes innovation and creativity.

It would be wrong, then, to assume an evolutionary development in wall painting from the less innovative early and middle phases at the site, to greater innovation in the later and latest levels. Superficially it would not be difficult to make such an argument. It is from South P (Mellaart's Level V) onwards that the much freer scenes of humans interacting with wild animals are found. These and the more naturalistic images in stone and clay of humans (also found in the upper levels) are often seen as the high-points of Çatalhöyük artistic skill and ingenuity. While these new forms of art are different, it is difficult to argue that they are more creative than the geometric wall paintings given the creativity of a different kind described in this chapter. The hunting scenes and the female figurines in the upper levels are again very repetitive, but they follow a different set of rules. As noted earlier, the paintings in the upper levels are associated more with domestic areas of the house, ovens and hearths. There is less painting and more mobiliary art (the stamp seals and increasingly on pottery). There is less association with the dead and more with production.

There is more mobility in the later and latest levels and more trade and exchange over longer distances. It could be argued that these interactions enhanced the potential for creativity and hence the 'flowering' of painted scenes. But while we can certainly identify changes in modes of creativity in the later levels, we have argued in this chapter that the geometric wall paintings also show a remarkable degree of creativity and ingenuity. The examples discussed in detail here all date to the middle levels. It is difficult to argue in the case of the wall paintings that there was an evolutionary development from less to more creativity.

There are many other shifts in the later levels of Çatalhöyük, including the greater reliance on domestic sheep and cattle, greater independence of houses, and greater differentiation between houses in terms of storage capacity. While all these factors may have influenced the changing modes of creativity in wall paintings and mobiliary art, it is difficult to argue for an overall increase in the amount of creativity. Many forms of creativity depend on the provisioning of resources, and it has long been argued (see Chapter 1) that the availability of surpluses resulting from agricultural intensification led to specialization of production and hence to greater innovation. At Çatalhöyük there is no good evidence for a high degree of specialization in wall painting production.

However, the shifting forms of power at Çatalhöyük, from a social power based on the control of ritual and ancestry to one based more on productive capacity, do seem to be related to the context of production of wall paintings. As has been widely studied using micromorphology techniques, the wall plasters in the middle levels of the site were finely produced and frequently resurfaced (Matthews 2005). There can be more than 250 separate layers of plaster placed on the walls. Because this frequent replastering occurs in main rooms rather than inside rooms where food is stored, this 'cleaning' has less to do with interrupting the breeding cycle of flies, mosquitos and small rodents, and more to do with the social context of the main room, with the emphasis there on social distinctions and memory making. In the later levels, while wall plastering continues, it becomes less frequent and increasingly coarse. In this sense the resources available for wall painting declined in the later levels, and as a result, as we have seen, the numbers of wall paintings decreased.

And yet the hunting scenes in the later levels are remarkably innovative, and in addition creative output shifted to various forms of mobiliary art, away from house walls. This trend reached its high point in the Chalcolithic West Mound at Çatalhöyük, where the painted pottery is exuberant in its originality and diversity. Overall it seems clear that it is difficult to argue that changing contexts increase or decrease the overall human cognitive capacity for creativity and innovation. Modes and avenues of creativity undoubtedly change. But it is far from clear that the social and economic changes in the Neolithic at Çatalhöyük had any impact on the degrees of creativity of which humans were capable.

CONCLUSION

Çatalhöyük is often described as a great flowering of artistry and creativity (e.g. Wheeler 1967, 10). It seems difficult to argue that this creativity was produced by any general cognitive change. After all, highly elaborate and accomplished wall paintings are known from earlier times in Cantabria and southwest France. Rather than changes in cognitive capacity, we see at Çatalhöyük a creativity very tightly tied to a highly complex social world. The densely packed village or town was cross-cut by social ties and identities of enormous complexity. Any one individual in any one house had a wide spread of connections or ties that could be drawn upon. Individuals were associated in houses with people they were related to by kinship, but also by practical kinship and ties of residence (Pilloud and Larsen 2011). They had associations with houses based on the circulation of the body parts of ancestors, the circulation of material items such as beads, groundstone, obsidian. They shared the preparation and consumption of food across houses. In addition there were sodalities that cut across houses, and there were associations built on history-making. In this complex world, the painting of walls punctuated daily life. Walls were often left unpainted. But on special occasions, especially related to the burial of the dead, they were used to contribute to the memory making and alliance building. They made a statement about respect for the dead; the creativity embellished and furthered the dead and promoted their involvement in social practices. In the later levels the artistry shifted to an embellishment of domestic production, exchange and interaction. Creativity changed its context, but it is difficult to argue for increases or decreases in creativity overall.

It is tempting to argue that the flowering of creativity in the wall paintings at Çatalhöyük is linked to the contradiction identified earlier between conformity and diversity. The establishment of a secure set of rules may allow a framework within which innovation and creativity can take place. But the Çatalhöyük evidence does not seem to fit this argument well. Certainly in the middle levels we have seen there is much evidence for stress, pressure and hard work. This is the time that boundaries are most clearly marked, and the wall painting seems to take its place in helping to mark out, create distinctions, establish difference. But at the same time, on the rare occasions when paintings were made,

individuals and households demonstrated their prowess at caring for and celebrating the dead, establishing their own distinction within the frames already set down. Through their individual performativity and ingenuity, individuals and households could establish new (and perhaps daring) new allegiances within the networks.

REFERENCES

Balter, M. 2005. *The Goddess and the Bull: Çatalhöyük: An Archaeological Journey to the Dawn of Civilization.* New York: Simon and Schuster.

Bekaert, S. 1998. Multiple levels of meaning and the tension of consciousness. *Archaeological Dialogues* 5 (1), 6–29.

Busacca, G. 2018. Painting as practice: spatial contexts and temporality of architectural paintings at Çatalhöyük. Paper presented to ANAMED Fellows' Symposium, Istanbul.

Cartwright, C. 2008. The world's oldest wall painting in Syria? *Palestine Exploration Quarterly,* 140, 3.

Czeszewska, A. 2014. Wall paintings at Çatalhöyük. In: Hodder, I. (ed.), *Integrating Çatalhöyük: Themes from the 2000–2008 Seasons.* Los Angeles, CA: Cotsen Institute of Archaeology Press/British Institute of Archaeology at Ankara.

Donald, M. 1991. *Origins of the Modern Mind: Three Stages in the Evolution of Culture and Cognition.* Cambridge, MA: Harvard University Press.

Düring, B. S. 2006. *Constructing Communities: Clustered Neighbourhood Settlements of the Central Anatolian Neolithic ca. 8500–5500 Cal. BC.* PhD thesis, Leiden University.

Hillson, S. W., Larsen, C. S., Boz, B., Pilloud, M. A., Sadvari, J. W., Agarwal, S. C., Glencross, B., Beauchesne, P., Pearson, J., Ruff, C. B., Garofalo, E. M., Hager, L. D. and Haddow, S. D. 2013: 'The human remains I: interpreting community structure, health and diet in Neolithic Çatalhöyük'. In: Hodder, I. (ed.), *Humans and Landscapes of Çatalhöyük: Reports from the 2000–2008*

Seasons. Los Angeles: Cotsen Institute of Archaeology Press, 339–96.

Hodder, I. 2012. *Entangled. An Archaeology of the Relationships between Humans and Things*. Oxford, UK: Wiley-Blackwell.

Hodder, I. 2014. Çatalhöyük: the leopard changes its spots. A summary of recent work. *Anatolian Studies*, *64*, 1–22.

Hodder, I. (ed.). 2019. *Violence and the Sacred in the Ancient Near East*. Cambridge, UK: Cambridge University Press.

Hodder, I. and Cessford, C. 2004. Daily practice and social memory at Çatalhöyük. *American Antiquity*, *69*(1), 17–40.

Kamerman, A. 2014. The use of spatial order in Çatalhöyük material culture. *In:* Hodder, I. (ed.), *Religion at Work in a Neolithic Society. Vital Matters*. Cambridge, UK: Cambridge University Press, 304–36.

Kirkbride, D. 1975. Umm Dabaghiyah 1974: A Fourth Preliminary Report. *Iraq*, 37, 3–10.

Last, J. 1998. A design for life: interpreting the art of Çatalhöyük. *Journal of Material Culture*, *3*(3), 355–78.

Leroi-Gourhan, A. 1982. *The Dawn of European Art: An Introduction to Palaeolithic Cave Painting*. Cambridge, UK: Cambridge University Press.

Lewis-Williams, D. 2004a. *The Mind in the Cave: Consciousness and the Origins of Art*. London: Thames & Hudson.

Lewis-Williams, D. 2004b. Constructing a cosmos: architecture, power and domestication at Çatalhöyük. *Journal of Social Archaeology*, *4*(1), 28–59.

Marshack, A. 1991. *The Roots of Civilization*. Mount Kisco, NY: Moyer Bell.

Matthews, W. 2005. Micromorphological and microstratigraphic traces of uses and concepts of space. *In:* Hodder, I. (ed.), *Inhabiting Çatalhöyük: Reports from the 1995–99 Seasons*. Cambridge, UK:

McDonald Institute for Archaeological Research, 355–98.

Mithen, S. J. 1996. *The Prehistory of the Mind. A Search for the Origins of Art, Religion and Science*. London: Thames and Hudson.

Molist, M. 1998. Des représentations humaines peintes au IXe millénaire BP sur le site de Tell Halula (Vallée de l'Euphrate, Syrie). *Paléorient*, 81–87.

Özbaşaran, M. 2011. Re-starting at Aşıklı. *Anatolia Antiqua*, 19, 27–37.

Pilloud, M. A. and Larsen, C. S. 2011. "Official" and "practical" kin: inferring social and community structure from dental phenotype at Neolithic Çatalhöyük, Turkey. *American Journal of Physical Anthropology*, *145*(4), 519–30.

Renfrew, C. and Scarre, C. (eds.). 1998. *Cognition and Material Culture: The Archaeology of Symbolic Storage*. Cambridge, UK: McDonald Institute for Archaeological Research.

Schmidt, K. 2000. Göbekli Tepe, southeastern Turkey: a preliminary report on the 1995–1999 excavations. *Paléorient*, 45–54.

Turner, M. (ed.). 2006. *The Artful Mind: Cognitive Science and the Riddle of Human Creativity*. Oxford, UK: Oxford University Press.

Türkcan, A. U. 2005. Some remarks on Çatalhöyük stamp seals. *In:* Hodder, I. (ed.), *Changing Materialities at Çatalhöyük: Reports from the 1995–1999 Seasons*. Cambridge, UK: McDonald Institute for Archaeological Research, 205–33.

Wheeler, M. 1967. Introduction. *In:* Mellaart, J. *Çatal Hüyük. A Neolithic Town in Anatolia*. London: Thames and Hudson.

Whitley, D. S. (ed.). 1998. *Reader in Archaeological Theory: Post-Processual and Cognitive Approaches*. New York: Psychology Press.

Zaidel, D. W. 2015. *Neuropsychology of Art: Neurological, Cognitive, and Evolutionary Perspectives*. New York: Psychology Press.

PART IV

GREATER AWARENESS OF AN INTEGRATED PERSONAL SELF

PERSONAL MEMORY, THE SCAFFOLDED MIND, AND COGNITIVE CHANGE IN THE NEOLITHIC

John Sutton

MEMORY, SELF AND COGNITIVE CHANGE IN THE NEOLITHIC

'The Çatalhöyük evidence as a whole', write Hodder and Pels, 'gives many indications that, indeed, people began to link themselves to specific pasts, by burying pots, tools, humans and hunting trophies in ways that indicate particular memories rather than a generic reference to a group' (2010, 182). Hodder draws on his multidisciplinary team's impressive studies of a wide range of artifacts and practices – household symbols, pit-digging, burial, figurines, tools, decoration, and more – to argue that forms of remembering emerged or consolidated at Çatalhöyük that were neither merely routinized and habitual, nor merely traditional and generic, and that took as their objects neither repeated activities nor widespread factual knowledge. Rather, the new forms of social memory being constructed at Çatalhöyük were 'conscious, specific, and commemorative', as household groups 'began to make specific connections between the present and the past' (Hodder & Cessford 2004, 35; Hodder 2006, 143).

Such striking claims about Neolithic cognitive change seem to chime neatly with the other ambitious hypotheses explored in this volume, intended to link measurable changes in the archaeological record to historical changes in consciousness, creativity, and self. Cognitive archaeology flourishes, confirming a wholehearted embrace of 'the murky subject of the human psyche' (Tattersall 2008, 121). Yet memory does not figure directly among the potential changes in cognitive capacities for abstraction, innovation, and integration with which this particular project began. It is not easy to pin down just what historical changes in memory practices and capacities might be in question, or to compare the forms of remembering under investigation with those featured in our current taxonomies of memory. Hodder's claims about Çatalhöyük do not directly concern possible changes in the capacity and operation of 'working memory' (Coolidge & Wynn 2005, 2008; Ambrose 2010). And in shifting archaeological attention away from embodied memory and collective memory, Hodder is probing the kind of precise recall of specific events, objects, or experiences that is now typically understood as episodic, autobiographical, or personal memory. In this chapter I return to memory as a test case for evaluating claims about cognitive change in the Neolithic, trying to flesh out and generalise Hodder's suggestive remarks about memory at Çatalhöyük by setting them in the context of a broad theoretical approach to personal memory that might both make sense of and in turn be buttressed and developed by the archaeological case study.

I use 'personal memory' as a usefully general label, less embedded than is 'episodic memory' in the current cognitive disciplines of psychology, neuroscience, philosophy, and psychiatry. It involves, roughly, our capacities to remember the particular events, episodes, or experiences of our own past. Typically, 'autobiographical memory' is a more complex construction, one of a number of ways in which more basic memory capacities can be deployed. Some theories of autobiographical remembering treat it as combining factual, semantic, or schematic knowledge of our past with sensory, imagistic, or affective episodic fragments to generate transient mental constructions that (in the ideal case) are partly caused by the events and experiences they are about (Conway & Pleydell-Pearce 2000; Conway 2005). Both the terms and these ways of dividing up the phenomena should be treated flexibly and as entirely compatible with strong further interests in embodied or collective memory: one point of identifying distinct forms of remembering is to be able to ask questions about how they interact (Sutton 2009). Approaches to episodic and autobiographical memory ramify and complicate (see

later) as we glimpse more of the neural dynamics, the developmental complexity, the social and contextual dependence, the functional diversity, and the cultural openness of these capacities. Pulling autobiographical memory apart, treating it as multiple, complex, variable, entangled, and open, may show how rich and uneven a developmental achievement it is and thus build a richer sense of the uneven historical tuning processes by which we came by it.

The aim is mutual or bidirectional illumination. On the one hand, theories of personal and autobiographical memory offer some help to cognitive archaeologists in interpreting features of their evidence base and their developing historical narratives. On the other hand, in reverse, the cognitive archaeology of specific periods helps other cognitive theorists in assessing the nature, functions, and components of episodic remembering. This hopeful picture contrasts with the baleful alternative possibility (considered later) that memory is not a proper topic of or for direct historical investigation and needs to be addressed with only the existing resources of biology, neuroscience, and experimental psychology.

I return to memory in the context of this project's aims in the hope that its challenges, in Neolithic settings, differ from those posed by investigating 'consciousness', 'creativity', and 'self'. Those terms – like 'cognition' and 'mind' themselves – drag with them such historical, cultural, and semantic variability and consequent scientific and theoretical uncertainty that further translation or mediating precision may be needed to begin identifying their traces. 'Memory' too is far from a likely natural kind (or whatever the nearest equivalent in the cognitive sciences might be), but despite its multiplicity may afford firmer grip on the kind of inferences needed.

In light of the extraordinarily detailed archaeological material found and integrated by the Çatalhöyük team (Hodder 2014, 2017a), Hodder enumerated factors that might correlate with or mark cognitive change in the Neolithic (2017b). With appropriate inferences, we might find signs of 'higher levels of consciousness' and/or 'greater creativity', in traces of (for example) intensified trade and exchange, new or increased patterns of metrication and standardisation, newly diverse technologies, or increased tendencies towards abstraction or towards recombination. With regard to any possible 'greater awareness of an integrated personal self', in particular, we might identify new practices or markers of self in the material record of patterns of domestication and property, or of privacy and self-sufficiency, and in evidence concerning certain artifacts and associated practices. Specifically, greater self-awareness might be *evidenced by* changing burial practices, which reveal different emerging attitudes to body parts, bodily integrity, and individuality; by related changes in the nature and treatment of figurines; and by increased personal adornment and novel patterns of wear, use, and repair of some personal artifacts such as pendants. And among the possible *causal factors* involved in such developing awareness of an integrated self, Hodder suggested examining a range of economic, demographic, and religious factors (Hodder 2017b).

These factors need not be either mutually exclusive or independent. There may be dependency relations or feedback loops between them in particular historical contexts. But there are difficulties in seeing how

to advance appropriately multicausal versions of these hypotheses. One reason it is challenging to interpret the notion of 'greater awareness of an integrated personal self' here is that for expository purposes Hodder retains a dichotomy inherited from anthropological theory between the distributed, fragmented, partible selves of societies which are focussed more firmly on the collective and on sharing, and more integrated individuals (Strathern 1988; Fowler 2004). Yet distinctive individuals can be the members and constituents of certain sorts of integrated collective groups, and conversely certain forms of distributed agency can flourish in more atomised and individualised societies. The striking evidence about houses and burials that Hodder has marshalled in addressing these topics might just as firmly indicate that forms of individualised agency long coexisted with transformable and unbounded selves as the former emerged clearly from the latter over a clean historical transition (Hodder 2011). Further, the looseness of fit between evidence and hypothesis that shadows cognitive archaeology is more troubling when the target is harder to catch and characterise. Historical facts about, say, beads, bricks, or bones may be clear enough without settling anything about which cognitive processes they indicate or what kind of 'self' they implicate.

So I add a further, compatible dimension to our investigation into the possibility of changing Neolithic awareness of an integrated personal self. Perhaps such changing awareness might also be *evidenced by* changes in forms and nature of personal or autobiographical remembering. And perhaps, in interaction with some of the factors mentioned earlier, further *causal factors* involved in such awareness of self in and over time might include new demands on more precisely tracking events and commitments, as well as the changing social and material memory practices and technologies that archaeologists have long studied.

I proceed by first explaining and defending the possibility of historical changes in autobiographical memory, anchoring this exercise in speculative cognitive archaeology and cognitive history in the picture of the 'scaffolded mind' suggested by the 'distributed cognition' framework. I discuss features of autobiographical memory and its components, which are highlighted in various domains of recent science and theory, and which taken together reveal personal remembering as a rich and complex set of learned and encultured skills. I then lay out the background conditions for the putative historical changes, in or before the Neolithic, before I go on to sketch a picture of the nature, causes, and implications of the hypothesised changes in memory capacities and practices.

MEMORY, DISTRIBUTED COGNITION AND COGNITIVE HISTORY

What would personal memory need to be, or to be like, to be the kind of psychological capacity that might undergo cognitive change in the Neolithic? Can we find conceptual and empirical space to allow for this possibility? I briefly consider the evolution and nature of the systems involved in personal memory, assessing implications for interdisciplinary cognitive historical research. I then back up to describe briefly the theoretical framework against which it makes sense to treat some changing sociomaterial settings as directly sculpting and retuning cognitive capacities like autobiographical memory.

Some ability to track what happened, when, and where is often ascribed to many non-human animals. Both the basic molecular mechanisms and the systemic neural circuitry of basic event memory may be 'fundamentally conserved across avian and mammalian species' (Allen & Fortin 2013, 10379). Lively experimental, methodological, and conceptual debates continue on how to characterise the exact ways in which non-human animals are sensitive to time (Hoerl & McCormack 2017). For current purposes, we can accept that much of our most basic memory capacity is deeply ancient, in place before the advent of anatomically modern humans.

Before, in, and soon after the emergence of *Homo sapiens,* these memory capacities developed further. Some stress an enhanced capacity for 'survival processing', by which it's natural and easier for us to remember concepts or scenarios that were more relevant for survival in our ancestral environments (Nairne & Pandeirada 2008). Others are cautious about postulating unique adaptive trajectories with direct survival or reproductive benefits, suggesting 1instead that episodic memory 'may just as well have evolved as a by-product of another capacity with benefits in other domains' (Redshaw & Suddendorf 2018). Among the related capacities often associated with potential developments in human episodic memory are changes in working memory and executive control, in theory of mind and social cognition and perspective-taking, perhaps in some forms of reasoning and metarepresentational capacities, and perhaps in some forms of narrative and language. There is insufficient evidence to settle questions about the historical and conceptual relationships between these various capacities, so that, for example, we just don't know whether recognisably modern basic human episodic memory capacities developed before, alongside, or after human language. Many also place at least some forms of human awareness of the location of self and events in time, often now labelled 'autonoesis' or 'mental time travel', around these early phases of *Homo sapiens,* and before or alongside the more dramatic changes in lifeways and social organisation of the last 50,000–70,000 years (Tulving 2002; Boyer 2009a; Suddendorf, Addis, & Corballis 2009; Michaelian 2016). The emerging suite of more flexible and integrative cognitive capacities in our ancestors at that stage likely included fairly sophisticated abilities to track events and sequences, to imagine and plan future actions, and to consider alternate possibilities, as well as involving the kind of rich links between emotion, imagery, and past or future experience with which we are now familiar (Boyer 2009a).

Though not perhaps impossible, it would therefore be difficult to base an argument for later, *Neolithic* changes in memory and cognition, long after any significant changes in brain size or structure, on a claim that the basic elements of episodic memory were not yet in play. But what lessons *should* we draw about the history and archaeology of episodic and autobiographical memory? One approach is to insist that while human memory has a biological history, of the kind sketched earlier, it has a cultural history in only a thin or minimal sense. If it was already fully formed before any of the signs of 'behavioural modernity', well before the Neolithic, then any historical changes in practices and activities of remembering, let alone in material or social supports for memory, are merely curious variation, ethnographic window-dressing or cultural froth on its real internal neural nature. On such a view, there are no genuinely *cognitive* ecologies of memory, shifting and varying across (pre)historical time, because memory and cognition are behind or outside culture. And in turn, archaeology will be of merely humanistic and casual interest to genuine memory scientists, who study the neurobiological capacities as they exist now and have since their biological evolution; while memory science can only help cognitive archaeology at the general level of specifying constraints on all human activity in history.

This is not the only or the right lesson. We can accept the consensus sketched earlier about the core elements of human memory while still allowing substantial variability in the development and deployment of those elements in cognitive practice. The first step here, before I deal with the nature of memory and with the specific historical changes in question, is to outline the way of thinking of memory as scaffolded and distributed across complex cognitive ecologies that provides the framework. Human brains are particularly plastic and incomplete, prone to construction and selection and pattern-transformation, deeply open to shaping by conditions, artifacts, places, and activities that we ourselves – individually and collectively – have partly created, shaped, and regulated. Our brains are situated and nested in wider cognitive ecologies of heterogeneous elements displaying 'webs of mutual dependence' (Hutchins 2010; Sutton 2010). As a result, just as there is a looseness of fit between cognition and material culture within which archaeological theory and inference must operate, so there is a looseness of fit between cognition and the brain, which is the space of psychology and cognitive theory.

In the language of distributed cognition, the *activities* or *practices* of remembering (as of feeling, sensing, problem solving, and so on) are often not located in the brain alone, but are hybrid and spread across brains, bodies, and worlds. In the language of niche construction, humans are epistemic engineers engaged in the iterative construction of cognitive niches, which are cultural and technological by nature. Compared to discussions of 'extended mind' in philosophy, we want to be less focussed on metaphysics and more on method, pointing to the cognitive activities and practices in which human minds tune themselves and identifying dimensions of variation that can be studied empirically across contexts (Sterelny 2010; Sutton, Harris, Keil, & Barnier 2010; Heersmink 2015). Where interactive scaffolding most strongly and specifically shapes ongoing cognitive processing, we will see some social and technological resources as playing unique and distinctive roles in differently balanced solutions to diverse, context-specific problems of managing the past and flourishing in present and future. Arguing that cognitive archaeology and ideas of embodied, scaffolded, and distributed cognition can be mutually beneficial, Kim Sterelny writes:

If thinking depends on doing, and on the world in which the agent is embedded, ancient thinking is more tightly linked to ancient activity. Much knowledge is know-how, and know-how is manifest in actions that leave physical traces ... To the extent we can reconstruct their social, technical, and ecological lifeways (admittedly, very partially) we can identify their cognitive and motivational capacities, as their lifeways are not just effects of hidden internal cognitive processes; they are causes, supports, and scaffolds of those processes.

(Sterelny 2017, 244–6)

So any cognitive ecology is a more or less integrated array, implicating embodied brains in meshed social and material settings. As intelligent agents, we are cultural and technological by nature, 'natural-born cyborgs' always adapting to cognitive niches that we have ourselves engineered (Donald 1991; Clark 2003; Sutton 2010). There is space and need for history and archaeology in cognitive science because mind and memory incorporate social and environmental techniques differently across distinctive contexts. We look for convergences between independently motivated debates or projects in history or archaeology, on the one hand, and cognitive theory and science on the other, like the productive parallel implementations of these ideas about distributed cognitive ecologies applied to the early modern cultural history of memory by Lyn Tribble (2011; compare Tribble & Keene 2011; Sutton & Keene 2017). In working our way back to Çatalhöyük, then, we want to hold neural, material, and social components of distributed memory systems equally in focus. By first probing harder on some of the features of rich modern human memory, we will then be able to identify some differential ways it is scaffolded across distinctive cognitive ecologies.

EPISODIC MEMORY AND AUTOBIOGRAPHICAL MEMORY

The basic capacities for remembering, imagining, and mental time travel, which were in place well before the Neolithic, have been, are, and can be deployed or knitted together in a range of ways. As children, we learn the skills of autobiographical remembering and of constructive episodic simulation in slow, multistaged, variable processes of enculturation, involving many cognitive, affective, interpersonal, and narrative resources. The ways that we come to remember the personal and shared past, and to imagine the future, are culturally and socially scaffolded. These processes of enculturation in turn transform some of our more basic inherited capacities to track isolated events and episodes. Along with other dimensions of cognitive development, social interaction shapes children's emerging capacity for joint attention to the shared past and the gradual emergence of richer temporal understanding. The norms, practices, and abilities grounding spontaneous personal memory soak in from and through the child's social and cultural setting (Sutton 2002; Nelson & Fivush 2004; Fivush 2011; Salmon & Reese 2016).

As a result, there is substantial variation, with regard to children's memory, in just what skills are learned and in the ways they are deployed. Cultural differences have been studied to date more thoroughly than gender, economic, and individual differences, but significant influences of all these kinds are likely. The mechanisms of this early scaffolding are diverse and go well beyond the child's interactive acquisition of language and local linguistic and narrative norms, although language socialization practices play a major role (Miller et al. 1990). Unique affective dynamics shape remembering from the start, as do the rhythms of embodied interaction and the live norms about interdependence, morality, and self-representation (Leichtman,

Wang, & Pillemer 2003; Wang 2013, 2018). Likewise, distinctive or privileged balances emerge among many distinct functions and uses of thinking and talking about past and future events (Harris, Rasmussen, & Berntsen 2014; Pasupathi & Wainryb 2018). Children come to acquire specific styles of reminiscence – more or less elaborative, more or less self-focussed, more or less emotionally involved, and so on – in complex interaction over time with their adult carers and their peers, as demonstrated by longitudinal studies of the mutual influences of parents and children on each other's memory practices (Reese 2014).

This rich sociocultural scaffolding of children's memory, which is there from the start across non-verbal as well as narrative modes of accessing the past, goes all the way down: in modern human memory there is no clear gulf between culturally mediated autobiographical memory and a more 'basic' or 'pure' episodic memory (Miller et al. 2014; Sutton 2015). The distributed cognition perspective helps us see that scaffolding does not fade or dismantle over time, but shifts and transforms: our adult memory remains entangled in multiple forms of scaffolding, even as we learn to transfer our habits and skills across contexts and to latch on to a wider array of assembled and systemic resources in our socially and technologically mediated worlds (Brown & Reavey 2015).

Adding to this sketch of the openness or porosity of our memory capacities in development and enculturation, as suggested by these robust, broadly Vygotskyan sociocultural traditions in developmental psychology, we can consider further widely accepted features of the neuroscience and psychology of episodic and autobiographical memory. At a neural level, some central dynamic circuits involving the medial temporal lobe and other parts of the 'core' or 'default mode network' may be necessary for binding or coordinating episodic memories (Addis 2018). Complexity is added not only in that significant redundancy or cognitive reserve is built in, but also in that other distinctive neural processes are involved in autobiographical remembering in practice, with sensory, spatial, scene-building, self-other, emotional, motivational, linguistic, narrative, and kinesthetic systems contributing to retrieval (Rubin 2005, 2006; Palombo et al. 2018). Memory processes are neatly bounded neither within the biological system, nor across its interfaces with the environment.

These are among the reasons that a focus on the *constructive* nature of remembering, imagining, and simulating past and future is ubiquitous in the contemporary cognitive sciences of memory. The same reasons underpin frequent claims that our fallible and imperfect ability to remember particular past events runs alongside or is subsidiary to broader capacities to imagine future and counterfactual events (Schacter, Addis, & Buckner 2007; de Brigard 2014; Addis 2018), such that on some views remembering is simply one way of imagining the past (Michaelian 2016).

Yet these shifts in scientific thinking about memory can seem to loosen our grip on the past. No matter how much overlap there is – neural, psychological, phenomenological – between constructive past and future thinking, or between remembering and imagining, personal memory still makes claims on the past, and despite its imperfections it is generally recognised as so doing (Campbell 2004; Poole

2008). Our peculiar human forms of autobiographical memory are also centrally implicated in constructing and maintaining identity over time, with self and memory in mutually sustaining and entangled relations, and in grounding temporally embedded emotions, which must be tracked over time (Sutton 2018). Taken together, these roles that memory is thought to play in connecting present and past, and in opening up access to past events, have – at least in the West – underwritten its cultural and moral importance within modern institutions, from promises and contracts to legal responsibility to our practices of loving and grieving. Even while we also deploy memory for many things other than tracking the past accurately, we want when necessary to be able to distinguish what happened from what was imagined or wished, what I experienced directly from what I learned through testimony, and what happened on one particular occasion from what typically used to happen.

On the one hand, then, the basic components of our memory systems or our 'constructive episodic simulation' capacities (Addis 2018) are constructive, social, and future-directed, to the extent that it becomes a little puzzling to work out whether, how, and why we can ever more or less accurately remember past events at all (Boyer 2009b). But on the other hand, much of modern life seems to depend, both personally and socially, on our capacities – fallible as they may be – to track the past more or less accurately. The developed, modern, mature, encultured autobiographical memory, in other words, is set up to achieve or to approximate forms of source monitoring that are challenging given our dynamic neural inheritance. We manage these challenges culturally, collectively, and individually in part by setting up stabilizing and enduring external systems and inter-actions to buttress and support our naturally constructive memories (Donald 1991; Laland & Rendell 2013). But we also train up our more basic inherited cognitive systems, knitting them together to be better able to latch on to and exploit this ubiquitous social and worldly scaffolding, to be tuned to attend in the right ways to memory processes or to the phenomenological and metacogni-tive cues that help us work out the sources of our images, feelings, and thoughts. This enculturation of human memory is develop-mentally slow and uneven, even where it delivers more or less stable outcomes, though we won't know how diverse the processes and results are until a more thorough cross-cultural cognitive psychology of memory really looks beyond the WEIRD (Western, educated, industrialised, rich, democratic) participants on which much psychology has to date been based (Henrich, Heine, & Nor-enzayan 2010).

A cognitive archaeology of memory, then, can probe some of the ways that memory capacities might have been harnessed and shaped in particular historical circumstances. Were there relevant changes in the constraints for identifying and linking past events more precisely and in attributing experience to the right sources? There may be spaces between the basic memory capacities of the earliest anatomically modern humans and the richer, ambitious, and heterogeneous ways in which we later sought to tap and track our past.

To put this program into practice, we need to identify some of the relevant functions of memory across the periods in question. What did the inhabitants of Çatalhöyük need to remember, and how did those needs differ from the primary functions in play earlier, before such new settlements? This requires, first, a diachronic focus, examining Neolithic lifeways with their new scale and complexity to pick out key changes, and second, some indication of possible archaeological sig-natures of variation in these scaffolded, cul-turally mediated forms of remembering, identifying at least some kinds of revealing material trace. While the research programs are tentative, we can build suggestions from both archaeology and cognitive theory.

BACKGROUND CONDITIONS

Hypotheses about cognitive change in the Neolithic need to be modest. Any such 'change' is likely to have been gradual, uneven, incomplete, variably implemented, multiply caused, and multiply instantiated – less a single rupture or decisive transition than an array of entangled and partial shifts. In considering interrelated non-cognitive back-ground conditions for cognitive change, we can treat newer features of Neolithic lifeways as coexisting with older practices and com-mitments rather than decisively replacing them. Wengrow and Graeber (2015) posit extensive periods in which economic and political arrangements that may look incom-patible to us alternate or operate together in the same social groups, across more 'egalitarian' and more 'hierarchical' social ecologies, in deliberate collective exploration of a range of possibilities. In a body of work that I deploy later, Woodburn (1980, 1982, 2005) insists that his distinction between 'delayed-return' and 'immediate-return' societies does not describe a one-way historical transition: instead, adaptable and flexible immediate-return systems continued to operate alongside delayed-return systems. Any cognitive change in the Neolithic, long after significant changes in the human brain, was responsive to and entangled in an array of environmental, economic, and technological developments, which were themselves unevenly distributed: and so such cognitive change – as in later periods – is not likely to show up as a once-and-for-all revolution.

Such caveats in place, we can state an over-dramatic hypothesis about memory in the Neolithic and then build an argument around it. The idea is, in the language of this volume's overall target claims, that perhaps a more integrated personal self emerged during or around the occupation of Çatalhöyük *in the form of* richer narrative personal memories of specific past events, partly *because of* new demands on tracking events and on social commitments over time, and *supported by* new social and material memory norms, practices, and technologies. As well as motivating and explaining this hypothesis, I want to ask if it is the right *kind* of hypothesis for the form of enquiry in which the authors of this volume are engaged, even if it turns out not to be plausible in detail. I start by describing existing archaeological suggestions about the relevant changes in a little more detail, before tracking back to examine key background conditions by comparing the distinct (if overlapping) lifeways of previous hunter-gatherer groups and the people of Çatalhöyük.

Although ideas about memory were not explicitly included in this project's scope, related claims have been advanced for both to the Neolithic in general and Çatalhöyük in particular. Drawing on niche construction theory, Watkins (2004, 2006, 2012, 2013, 2016) suggests that new forms of shared cultural memory are visible in the novel architectural and monumental building and ritual projects of early Neolithic South-West Asia. The symbolic imagery of this period, Watkins argues, reveals a novel reliance on external symbol systems that predated writing but still dramatically expanded and transformed human memory and cognition, as our 'evolved capacity for the "extended mind" was taken a huge step further' (Watkins 2012, 32; compare Donald 2001, 301–20; Renfrew 2007, 95–105). While his primary focus is on the strengthening and perpetuation of shared and social memory, Watkins sees episodic and autobiographical memory as one key medium (2012, 34; for recent psychological work connecting individual and collective memory, see Hirst, Yamashiro, & Coman 2018). To suggest how 'memory was formed, modified, shared, reframed and shared again' in the early Neolithic, Watkins refers to Ian Hodder's work on history houses and burial practices at Çatalhöyük, to which we can now again briefly turn.

Hodder is probing the notion of the house as a new kind of 'site for social memory', such that his unit of analysis is the small cohesive household group rather than the isolated individual, and the labels 'personal' or 'autobiographical' memory may look out of place. But the form of remembering at issue is specific, directed at particular objects, people, or past experiences. So whatever the agent or agents of memory, the component functions that Hodder claims to be newly visible at Çatalhöyük are just those that came to distinguish later capacities for remembering the personal past. Hodder distinguishes those social memories that were 'general and site-wide … embedded in practices and routines' from those which 'linked a specific past to a specific present', in which particular events, people, and places were precisely recalled (Hodder 2006, 143; Hodder & Pels 2010, 183). Key evidence for 'specific memory' of ancestors, events, and histories lies in a number of burial disturbances in which 'there are clear indications that the precise locations and nature of earlier burials were remembered years or even decades later': the heads of particular individuals who had been treated differently at burial are specifically sought, removed, and curated, demonstrating memory also of very particular locations (Hodder & Cessford 2004, 35; Hodder 2006, 144–7). Some accuracy in the locations of heads, sculptures, and installations remembered over decades is demonstrated: 'there were clear memories within house clusters of the exact location and significance of the burials beneath the platform floors' (Whitehouse & Hodder 2010, 137). Hodder builds a case on the basis of such practices for a special category of 'history houses', which concentrate unique symbolism, are differentiated one from another, and transmit specific regulatory codes (compare Hodder 2016a).

Puzzles might be identified about how this stress on a new specificity in some memory practices relates to the reverse suggestion made by Hodder in collaboration with Whitehouse that an 'increasingly routinized religious life' emerged at Çatalhöyük with stronger doctrinal authority, repetitive activities, and reliance on semantic rather than episodic memory (Whitehouse & Hodder 2010). Postponing that enquiry to another occasion, here I run with the primary line of postulated development, that of increasing specificity, which is a corrective to interpretations of Çatalhöyük lifeways as entirely levelled and routinized, as in Steven Mithen's assessment that for the inhabitants of Çatalhöyük, 'every aspect of their lives had become ritualized, any independence of thought and behaviour crushed out of them by an oppressive ideology manifest in the bulls, breasts, skulls and vultures' (Mithen 2003, 95). Hodder's search for specificity of memory pushes us to look harder at the nature of episodic memory, and at what kinds of specificity may have been available and required in distinctive settings.

Hodder plausibly argues that any forms of 'active memory construction' visible at Çatalhöyük are likely to have first emerged earlier and elsewhere, perhaps in the early Natufian period, and alongside a raft of related shifts in social, economic, and ritual practices. One significant point is that gradually 'people became entangled in longer-term, delayed return systems' (Hodder 2016b, 42): elsewhere Hodder makes this connection more firmly, arguing that 'the construction of longer-term memories, both specific and general, would have been the basis for the social, ritual, and economic practices involved in delayed-return societies' (Hodder & Cessford 2004, 36; compare Hodder 2007 on the 'emergence of greater temporal depth', and Hodder 2012, 84–85 on Woodburn). I can build on the general approach to memory sketched earlier to explore further these suggestions about shifts in Neolithic memory.

First we want to look at the possible demands on memory of the periods prior to the Neolithic. Sophisticated forms of human memory, in terms of the effective tracking of events, long predate the Neolithic. Across the later Pleistocene, even as hunting and foraging lifeways became more complex, our hunter-gatherer ancestors could deploy flexible *embodied* memory and a capacity for increasingly high-fidelity transmission of skills through *apprenticeship learning* (Sterelny 2012); memory for generic, repeated, or typical events; and some abilities to deploy both environmental features and artefacts, both portable and fixed, for mnemonic purposes, especially perhaps in the recall of important factual or semantic information, and perhaps as curated by specialists (Kelly 2015).

But at the same time, hunter-gatherer lifeways may not have imposed heavy extra demands on tracking the precise sources of event knowledge. In our worlds, such demands are met partly by social and technological scaffolding and partly by richer forms of autobiographical memory involving distinctive metacognitive and phenomenological features. Perhaps the hunter-gatherers did not need, or need so often or so much, the kind of rich and specific narrative memories of unique personal experiences that we often simply think of as 'memory'. Among smaller groups of hunters and foragers, at least, many or most experiences were shared, and many actions were joint actions. Information tended to be mutually available and easily shared. Trust was built and maintained over histories of interaction involving strong social emotions. Events and sequences were relatively predictable and rhythmic. The choices and decisions made in many contexts brought fairly immediate returns. Much practically and socially significant information and

know-how could be partly left in places, to be accessed again when needed as those with a relevant history came by again (Basso 1996; Ingold 2005; Sterelny 2012, 2013, 2014; Kelly 2015).

For these reasons, then, perhaps these hunting and foraging ancestors had less of a need to track the precise sources of information in the past and to be able sharply to distinguish information arising from one's own experiences from information derived from others', first-hand from second-hand experience, what we call memory from what we call testimony. There were, we might say, less pressing demands for specific forms of 'epistemic vigilance' (Mercier & Sperber 2017) in such small and fairly egalitarian societies. A view of this kind has recently been developed and defended in a provocative paper by the biologist and philosopher Eva Jablonka. For Jablonka, at a period before more modern forms of autobiographical memory emerged, 'an individual's memory of her own specific role in a group event was less distinct than it is for individuals in modern societies. In such settings, not only was recollection spurred on by others, other individuals contributed to the recall of the event that the individual had experienced' (Jablonka 2017, 844; and compare Mahr & Csibra 2018). Jablonka's case is built around points about the highly constructive nature of our basic biological memory capacities like those I sketched earlier. In these earlier periods, there was less of a need to be able to compensate for, scaffold around, or reduce any uncertainty resulting from the constructive and social nature of remembering. Sufficient compensation or scaffolding was provided by more or less stable small-world social and ecological supports, so monitoring or epistemic vigilance did not have to be individual or internalised.

In the mutualist cooperation characteristic of the earlier foraging societies of anatomically modern humans, resources were typically shared on the spot. As Sterelny notes, 'this form of cooperation does not pose problems about discount rates, the certainty of future interaction, or tracking individuals and their generosity over time . . . [or] on mechanisms for tracking and policing' (Sterelny 2014, 44). My modest extra suggestion is that this form of cooperation therefore also placed significantly different demands on memory. Woodburn hinted at a similar point in describing immediate-return systems as 'strongly oriented to the present': without strong commitments to specific other people 'deriving from the past', or obligations incurred in the present, 'which would require careful planning for future reciprocation', Woodburn saw people in immediate-return systems as characterised by 'a lack of concern about the past or the future' (Woodburn 1980, 106).

Recalling the general notes of caution I chimed earlier, a couple of disclaimers are required here. First, my account here does not rule out that *some* specific, rich episodic memories may have played significant roles in these earlier social worlds, especially those deriving from rare, high-arousal ritual activities or unusual natural events (Whitehouse 2004; Whallon 2011). The basic sensory, emotional, and self-referential components of autobiographical memory capacities were in place and would be deployed in response to intense stimuli. This is still some distance from the regular monitoring of the sources of

particular items of information involved in the forms of autobiographical remembering with which we are familiar. Second, this picture is not the ascription of 'a classically primitive type of social intelligence' to early hunters and foragers: Wengrow and Graeber are right to caution against depictions of early *Homo sapiens* 'as effectively (or perhaps stereotypically) childlike, living the only lives they were able to imagine' (Wengrow & Graeber 2015, 602). Though I have drawn on contemporary developmental psychology to characterise the malleability of enculturated autobiographical memory, the point is not that there was a linear shift or a process of maturation from forms of remembering typical of 'the childhood of man' to a single sophisticated modern capacity. Rather, just as there were and are a range of overlapping or hybrid socioeconomic systems, so there were and are many possible ways of tuning the diverse and interacting cognitive and affective components of our various human ways of being in time, as we adapt more or less effectively to dynamic environments and social demands.

If there is something to this point that the various features of memory did not always need to be knitted together in quite the same way, we could expect relatively minor shifts across some initial social and economic transitions, from more straightforward collaborative mutualist interaction to more reciprocation-based cooperation with greater division of labour and some increased planning horizons (Sterelny 2014). But what more substantial new conditions and new cognitive demands might then have introduced pressures to track the past, and the sources of information about the past, more precisely?

A HYPOTHESIS ABOUT NEOLITHIC MEMORY

Of the big-picture changes in demographics and lifeways in the Neolithic, and at Çatalhöyük in particular, which might have altered demands on personal memory, the most significant is likely to have been the expansion in group size in such larger settlements. As Sterelny and Watkins put it (2015, 677),

The less the group lives together and acts together as a single entity, the less information about others is available for free, as a side-effect of shared mutual activity; the more information is filtered through others' minds and voices, and the more information must be deliberately sought. Fractionation into family groups living and working together, or into differing economic roles, tends to create private information. Information about one's group and its members becomes less of an automatic, common pool resource.

In the new larger and more complex groups, social worlds 'were less intimate, less informationally transparent, and the expectation of repeated interaction was less secure' (Sterelny 2014, 50). With the population at Çatalhöyük perhaps ranging between 3,500 and 8,000 (Hodder 2007, 1–6), richly shared histories are no longer a default scenario, but become rarer, each person and household embedded in a world of virtual strangers (Coward 2016), as well as among greater numbers of ancestors, some of whom may have been buried under the current household. Group cohesion and commitment was less automatically maintained. Settlement also brings different relations to place, perhaps requiring new means to localise or materialise certain memory content, such as the informational use of monuments (Kelly 2015).

As archaeologists have argued, existing forms of memory – embodied and skill memory, and some forms of event memory – were supplemented and perhaps partly transformed by new and often larger-scale forms of social and material memory, with new affordances for the kind of hybrid mind that could effectively deploy new symbol systems and architectural or environmental markers (Watkins 2004, 2016). Other symbolic media, from centres of congregation or ritual activity in some settlements to smaller artifacts and ornaments could act as external anchors for individual and social identity. Although it is not clear what abstracted or recombinable symbols might have been in operation at Çatalhöyük (compare, for example, Bennison-Chapman's Chapter 5 in this volume), it is at least possible that expanded and more widely distributed access to some forms of information may have been enabled by new portable media such as small geometric objects or 'tokens', symptoms of transitioning towards Donald's 'theoretic culture' and a key phase in the history of distributed cognition, allowing new forms of 'mind invasion' as well as mind expansion (Donald 1991; Slaby 2016). But even when factual information comes to be shareable and socially negotiable with external symbol systems, such changes in human memory mostly relate either to processing capacities (working memory), or to fairly *general* semantic information.

To begin to identify pressures towards additional changes in personal or episodic memory, we can first note simple requirements of more delayed-return systems involving farming and domestication of plants and animals. Agricultural production comes to depend on earlier clearing of forests and land.

Particular commitments and developments in working the land have to be tracked over periods of months, seasons, and years. As I understand the Çatalhöyük evidence, there's no clear sign of private property or of the restricted ownership of resources, so memory is not yet so systematically objectified or concentrated in unshared resources (Ingold 2005). But movements towards a delayed-return system intrinsically encourage some temporal forms of abstraction with more temporally extended resource management and planning across longer investment horizons.

Both practical and social commitments in larger group settlements, then, perhaps require more effective capacities for tracking such commitments over longer time periods, and in particular for keeping track of the past source of the commitments. Plans often bring agreements, promises, and contracts in their wake, operating over longer timescales than in a shared world of shorter-term action-consequence pairings. The maintenance, fulfilment, and enforcement of more diverse and longer-term social commitments requires stronger, more secure memory for the source of current beliefs and feelings. But this is difficult when memory processes are naturally constructive, and when it's not easy to tease apart the sources of specific items of information. Remembering specific past events as part of richer narrative sequences comes to play a larger communicative and persuasive function, with memory's role as making a claim on the past (and on present activities and future plans constrained by that past) coming to the fore. Greater epistemic vigilance about the past is required, with memory to provide more or less mutually acceptable reasons for action on the basis of professed past experience. So, gradually, some people developed, or more regularly and firmly deployed, more individualised or internalised practices and mechanisms of memory control and memory checking, enabling firmer attribution of beliefs to their own past experience. Perhaps they attend differently to memory processes. Perhaps they deploy autonoetic consciousness and the range of phenomenological signs of recollective experience more effectively to track distinctions between self and other and between memory and imagination. Remembering is still fallible, imperfect, selective, and partial. But now perhaps people come to share both stronger capacities to track past events more precisely, and regulatory ideals about the normative importance of so doing. Such normative developments, by which we keep ourselves and each other in line over time, are related to new practices of responsibility-attribution and new forms of enforcing norms and punishing violations in increasingly competitive societies (perhaps after rather than at Çatalhöyük): they do not operate in the moral and political realm alone, but also have a directly cognitive element as people internalise a sense that they should be able to avoid confusing distinct past events.

One natural strategy for thus tracking decisions, plans, and resources over longer timescales is to expand the forms of externalisation in widespread use. It could thus be argued that my suggestion that a richer and more reliable autobiographical memory might have developed is redundant. As Kim Sterelny points out to me, one way delayed return economies work is to decouple tracking economic history from autobiographical memory. In the end, that is one thing money will do: it finesses the problem of remembering credits and debts. I have indeed been focussing here more on the 'internal' wing of shifting cognitive ecologies than on the development of the symbolic or technological solutions and forms of material engagement that have received more attention in archaeology to date (Donald 1991; Renfrew & Scarre 1998; DeMarrais et al. 2004; Sutton 2008; Malafouris 2013). But to point to the vital and increasing role of artifacts and 'exograms' in helping to stabilise and anchor is not to rule out parallel and integrated changes in the memory capacities and processes into which these external resources are taken up. Such developments are always hybrid and interactive, with new technologies affording and shaping new ways of using them, or on occasion actively leading changing memory practices as new norms for the right ways to manage the past emerge.

This compressed and speculative narrative stands in for a more realistic tale of the kind of gradual, uneven changes that would require long multichannel enculturation processes, with local variation but slowly increasing grip in larger societies. In developing her similar account, Jablonka emphasises the social nature of memory sharing in earlier social systems as imposing more strain on individual memory capacities:

Whereas in small, intimate societies collective memory aligned individual and social experiences, increased group cohesion, and allowed the social control of collectively-constructed individual false memory through correction by knowledgeable group members, such memory-control may often have failed as societies grew in size and migration among them increased.

(Jablonka 2017, 849)

Whereas in smaller groups the fusion or confusion of individual experiences would matter less, a more specialised form of autobiographical memory was required to control the reliability of communication about past events: in particular, 'humans had to remember not only who did what to whom, but also who *said* what to whom, and had to be able to distinguish between reported-imagined and first-hand experiences, something that is still a big problem today' (2017, 845). Likewise, as developmental psychologist Katherine Nelson argues, still in childhood now we must learn to resist this kind of fusion, confusion, or overwriting of memories, learning through enculturation a range of tricks to keep parts of the past separate and distinct and to enforce a clear distinction between one's own experience and that of other people (Nelson 2007, 228–9).

In both Jablonka's and my version of such a hypothesis about changes in memory in (pre-) historical timeframes, the idea is not that a single environmental transition drives or selects for a novel cognitive capacity. Rather, these are subtler processes of sociocognitive tuning that, we suggest, may have emerged more recently in our history than the basic memory mechanisms onto which they latch. A cognitive archaeology of memory precision seeks to identify a range of interacting and entangled factors driving a new individualising of memory, whereby people gradually and imperfectly came to learn how better to track specific past events and experiences, and to find more secure ways to stabilise constructive and social memory systems.

I have suggested that richer and more precise personal memories of specific past events may, in or around the Neolithic, have been *demanded by* new demands on tracking events and on social commitments over time, and *supported by* new social and material memory norms, technologies, and practices, and by new forms of enculturation that permitted distinct ways of deploying our basic memory capacities. The hypothesis can be challenged on developmental, psychological, ethnographic, and historical grounds. We need to specify which memory and responsibility-attributing practices might reveal evidence about different ways the components of episodic memory can be knitted together. If we reject the hypothesis, however, we owe alternative accounts of the evolution or historical development and the nature of rich and precise narrative autobiographical memory, and of any changing demands on remembering the past in and around the Neolithic. My hope is that it is at least the right *kind* of claim about cognitive change in the Neolithic, exhibiting the right kind of (potential) fit between the ultimate explanatory targets (self, consciousness, creativity, or cognition), their specific instantiation (here, personal memory), an array of interacting causal/ historical factors, and available forms of evidence. In refining or rejecting this hypothesis, we will want to develop better alternative ways to link theory and data, and cognition and history.

ACKNOWLEDGEMENTS

Earlier versions of these ideas were tried out in talks at Cambridge, Adelaide, and Wollongong. Many thanks to the organisers of these events, especially to Ian Hodder, Scott Haddow, and the Çatalhöyük team with their impressive energy for and commitment to robust discussions with cognitive philosophers in the middle of their final season on site. My thanks for questions and comments to John Barrett, Sven Bernecker, Anna Fagan, Ian Hodder, Dan Hutto, Chris McCarroll, Kirk Michaelian, Talia Morag, Jon Opie, Erik Rietveld, Sarah Robins, Trevor Watkins, and Mike Wheeler. Conversations with Eva Jablonka and Kim Sterelny helped me immensely, though my deployment of their ideas diverges from their intentions. I am also very grateful to Hodder, Jablonka, and Sterelny for comments on a penultimate version. For other assistance I thank Graeme Friedman and Christine Harris-Smyth.

REFERENCES

Addis, D. R. 2018. Are episodic memories special? On the sameness of remembered and imagined event simulation. *Journal of the Royal Society of New Zealand*, 1–25.

Allen, T. A. & Fortin, N. J. 2013. The evolution of episodic memory. *PNAS, 110*, 10379–86.

Ambrose, S. H. 2010. Coevolution of composite-tool technology, constructive memory, and language: implications for the evolution of modern human behavior. *Current Anthropology, 51*, S133–S147.

Basso, K. H. 1996. *Wisdom Sits in Places: landscape and language among the Western Apache*. Albuquerque: University of New Mexico Press.

Boyer, P. 2009a. Evolutionary economics of mental time travel? *Trends in Cognitive Sciences, 12 (6)*, 219–23.

Boyer, P. 2009b. What are memories for? Functions of recall in cognition and culture. In P. Boyer (ed.), *Memory in Mind and Culture* (pp. 3–28). Cambridge, UK: Cambridge University Press.

Brown, S. D. & Reavey, P. 2015. *Vital Memories and Affect: living with a difficult past*. London: Routledge.

Campbell, S. 2004. Models of mind and memory activities. In P. DesAutels & M. U. Walker (eds.), *Moral Psychology: feminist ethics and social theory*. Lanham, MD: Rowman & Littlefield.

Clark, A. 2003. *Natural-Born Cyborgs*. Oxford, UK: Oxford University Press.

Conway, M. A. 2005. Memory and the self. *Journal of Memory and Language, 53 (4)*, 594–628.

Conway, M. A. & Pleydell-Pearce, C. 2000. The construction of autobiographical memories in the self-memory system. *Psychological Review, 107 (2)*, 261–88.

Coolidge, F. L. & Wynn, T. 2005. Working memory, its executive functions, and the emergence of modern thinking. *Cambridge Archaeological Journal, 15*, 5–26.

Coolidge, F. L. & Wynn, T. 2008. The role of episodic memory and autonoetic thought in Upper Paleolithic life. *PaleoAnthropology*, 212–17.

Coward, F. 2016. Scaling up: material culture as scaffold for the social brain. *Quaternary International, 405*, 78–90.

De Brigard, F. 2014. Is memory for remembering? Recollection as a form of episodic hypothetical thinking. *Synthese. 191*, 155–85.

DeMarrais, E., Gosden, C., & Renfrew, C. (eds.). 2004. *Rethinking Materiality: the engagement of mind with the material world*. Cambridge, UK: McDonald Institute for Archaeological Research.

Donald, M. 1991. *Origins of the Modern Mind: three stages in the evolution of culture and cognition*. Cambridge, MA: Harvard University Press.

Donald, M. 2001. *A Mind So Rare*. New York: W. W. Norton.

Fivush, R. 2011. The development of autobiographical memory. *Annual Review of Psychology, 62*, 559–82.

Fowler, C. 2004. *The Archaeology of Personhood: an anthropological approach*. London: Routledge.

Harris, C. B., Rasmussen, A., & Berntsen, D. 2014. The functions of autobiographical memory: an integrative approach. *Memory, 22 (5)*, 559–81.

Heersmink, R. 2015. Dimensions of integration in embedded and extended cognitive systems. *Phenomenology and the Cognitive Sciences, 14 (3)*, 577–98.

Henrich, J., Heine, S. J., & Norenzayan, A. 2010. The weirdest people in the world? *Behavioral and Brain Sciences 33 (2)*, 61–135.

Hirst, W., Yamashiro, J. K., & Coman, A. 2018. Collective memory from a psychological perspective. *Trends in Cognitive Sciences, 22 (5)*, 438–51.

Hodder, I. 2006. *Çatalhöyük: the leopard's tale*. London: Thames & Hudson.

Hodder, I. 2007. Çatalhöyük in the context of the Middle Eastern Neolithic. *Annual Review of Anthropology, 36*, 105–20.

Hodder, I. 2011. An archaeology of the self: the prehistory of personhood. In J. W. van Huyssteen & E. P. Wiebe (eds.), *In Search of Self* (pp. 50–69). Grand Rapids, MI: Eerdmans.

Hodder, I. 2012. *Entangled: an archaeology of the relationships between humans and things*. Oxford, UK: Wiley-Blackwell.

Hodder, I. 2014. Çatalhöyük: the leopard changes its spots: a summary of recent work. *Anatolian Studies, 64*, 1–22.

Hodder, I. 2016a. More on history houses at Çatalhöyük: a response to Carleton et al. *Journal of Archaeological Science, 67*, 1–6.

Hodder, I. 2016b. *Studies in Human-Thing Entanglement*. Online publication, www.ian-hodder.com/books/studies-human-thing-entanglement.

Hodder, I. 2017a. Assembling science at Çatalhöyük: interdisciplinarity in theory and practice. In I. Hodder & A. Marciniak (eds.), *Assembling Çatalhöyük* (pp. 7–12). London: Routledge.

Hodder, I. 2017b. Consciousness and creativity at the dawn of settled life: the test-case of Çatalhöyük. Project description for Çatalhöyük workshop.

Hodder, I. & Cessford, C. 2004. Daily practice and social memory at Çatalhöyük. *American Antiquity, 69 (1)*, 17–40.

Hodder, I. & Pels, P. 2010. History houses: a new interpretation of architectural elaboration at Çatalhöyük. In I. Hodder (ed.), *Religion in the Emergence of Civilization: Çatalhöyük as a case study* (pp. 163–86). Cambridge, UK: Cambridge University Press.

Hoerl, C. & McCormack, T. 2017. Animal minds in time. In K. Andrews & J. Beck (eds.), *The*

Routledge Handbook of Philosophy of Animal Minds (pp. 56–64). London: Routledge.

Hutchins, E. 2010. Cognitive ecology. *Topics in Cognitive Science, 2 (4)*, 705–15.

Ingold, T. 2005. Time, memory and property. In T. Widlok & W. G. Tadesse (eds.), *Property and Equality, volume 1: ritualization, sharing, egalitarianism* (pp. 165–74). Oxford, UK: Berghahn Books.

Jablonka, E. 2017. Collective narratives, false memories, and the origins of autobiographical memory. *Biology and Philosophy, 32 (6)*, 839–53.

Kelly, L. 2015. *Knowledge and Power in Prehistoric Societies: orality, memory and the transmission of culture.* Cambridge, UK: Cambridge University Press.

Laland, K. N. & Rendell, L. 2013. Cultural memory. *Current Biology, 23 (17)*, R736–R740.

Leichtman, M. D., Wang, Q., & Pillemer, D. 2003. Cultural variations in interdependence and autobiographical memory: lessons from Korea, China, India, and the United States. In R. Fivush & C. A. Haden (eds.), *Autobiographical Memory and the Construction of a Narrative Self: developmental and cultural perspectives* (pp. 73–97). Hillsdale, NJ: Erlbaum.

Mahr, J. B. & Csibra, G. 2018. Why do we remember? The communicative function of episodic memory. *Behavioral and Brain Sciences, 41.*

Malafouris, L. 2013. *How Things Shape the Mind: a theory of material engagement.* Cambridge, MA: MIT Press.

Mercier, H. & Sperber, D. 2017. *The Enigma of Reason.* Cambridge, MA: Harvard University Press.

Michaelian, K. 2016. *Mental Time Travel: episodic memory and our knowledge of the personal past.* Cambridge, MA: MIT Press.

Miller, P. J., Potts, R., Fung, H., Hoogstra, L., & Mintz, J. 1990. Narrative practices and the social construction of self in childhood. *American Ethnologist, 17 (2)*, 292–311.

Miller, P. J., Chen, E. C. H., & Olivarez, M. 2014. Narrative making and remaking in the early years: prelude to the personal narrative. *New Directions for Child and Adolescent Development, 145*, 15–27.

Mithen, S. 2003. *After the Ice: a global human history 20,000–5,000 BC.* Cambridge, MA: Harvard University Press.

Nairne, J. S. & Pandeirada, J. N. 2008. Adaptive memory: remembering with a stone-age brain. *Current Directions in Psychological Science, 17 (4)*, 239–43.

Nelson, K. 2007. Development of extended memory. *Journal of Physiology – Paris, 101*, 223–29.

Nelson, K. & Fivush, R. 2004. The emergence of autobiographical memory: a social cultural developmental theory. *Psychological Review, 111 (2)*, 486–511.

Palombo, D. J., Sheldon, S., & Levine, B. 2018. Individual differences in autobiographical memory. *Trends in Cognitive Sciences, 22 (7)*, 583–97.

Pasupathi, M. & Wainryb, C. 2018. Remembering good and bad times together: functions of collaborative remembering. In M. L. Meade, C. B. Harris, P. van Bergen, J. Sutton, & A. J. Barnier (eds.), *Collaborative Remembering: theories, research, and applications* (pp. 261–79). Oxford, UK: Oxford University Press.

Poole, R. 2008. Memory, history and the claims of the past. *Memory Studies, 1 (2)*, 149–66.

Redshaw, J. & Suddendorf, T. 2018. Misconceptions about adaptive function. Commentary on Mahr & Csibra (2018). *Behavioral and Brain Sciences, 41.*

Reese, E. 2014. Taking the long way: longitudinal approaches to autobiographical memory development. In P. J. Bauer & R. Fivush (eds.), *The Wiley Handbook on the Development of Children's Memory* (pp. 972–95). Oxford, UK: Wiley-Blackwell.

Renfrew, C. 2007. *Prehistory.* New York: Random House.

Renfrew, C. & Scarre, C. (eds.). 1998. *Cognition and Material Culture: the archaeology of symbolic storage.* Cambridge, UK: McDonald Institute for Archaeological Research.

Rubin, D. C. 2005. A basic systems approach to autobiographical memory. *Current Directions in Psychological Science, 14 (2)*, 79–83.

Rubin, D. C. 2006. The basic-systems model of episodic memory. *Perspectives on Psychological Science, 1 (4)*, 277–311.

Salmon, K. & Reese, E. 2016. The benefits of reminiscing with young children. *Current Directions in Psychological Science, 25 (4)*, 233–38.

Schacter, D. L., Addis, D. R., & Buckner, R. L. 2007. Remembering the past to imagine the future: the prospective brain. *Nature Reviews Neuroscience. 8*, 657–61.

Slaby, J. 2016. Mind invasion: situated affectivity and the corporate life hack. *Frontiers in Psychology, 7*, 266.

Sterelny, K. 2010. Minds: extended or scaffolded? *Phenomenology and the Cognitive Sciences, 9 (4)*, 465–81.

Sterelny, K. 2012. *The Evolved Apprentice*. Cambridge, MA: MIT Press.

Sterelny, K. 2013. Life in interesting times: cooperation and collective action in the Holocene. In K. Sterelny, R. Joyce, B. Calcott, & B. Fraser (eds.), *Cooperation and Its Evolution* (pp. 89–108). Cambridge, MA: MIT Press.

Sterelny, K. 2014. Cooperation, culture and conflict. *British Journal for the Philosophy of Science 67 (1)*, 31–58.

Sterelny, K. 2015. Optimizing engines? Rational choice in the Neolithic. *Philosophy of Science, 82 (3)*, 402–23.

Sterelny, K. 2017. Artifacts, symbols, thoughts. *Biological Theory, 12 (4)*, 236–47.

Sterelny, K. & Hiscock, P. 2017. The perils and promises of cognitive archaeology. *Biological Theory, 12 (4)*, 189–94.

Sterelny, K. & Watkins, T. 2015. Neolithization in Southwest Asia in a context of niche construction theory. *Cambridge Archaeological Journal, 25 (3)*, 673–705.

Strathern, M. 1988. *The Gender of the Gift: problems with women and problems with society in Melanesia*. Berkeley: University of California Press.

Suddendorf, T., Addis, D. R., & Corballis, M. C. 2009. Mental time travel and the shaping of the human mind. *Philosophical Transactions of the Royal Society B: Biological Sciences, 364 (1521)*, 1317–24.

Sutton, J. 2002. Cognitive conceptions of language and the development of autobiographical memory. *Language & Communication, 22 (3)*, 375–90.

Sutton, J. 2008. Material agency, skills, and history: distributed cognition and the archaeology of memory. In C. Knappett & L. Malafouris (eds.), *Material Agency: towards a non-anthropocentric approach* (pp. 37–55). Berlin: Springer.

Sutton, J. 2009. 'The feel of the world': exograms, habits, and the confusion of types of memory. In A. Kania (ed.), *Memento: philosophers on film* (pp. 65–86). London: Routledge.

Sutton, J. 2010. Exograms and interdisciplinarity: history, the extended mind, and the civilizing process. In R. Menary (ed.), *The Extended Mind* (pp. 189–225). Cambridge, MA: MIT Press.

Sutton, J. 2015. Scaffolding memory: themes, taxonomies, puzzles. In L. M. Bietti & C. B. Stone (eds.), *Contextualizing Human Memory* (pp. 187–205). London: Routledge.

Sutton, J. 2018. Shared remembering and distributed affect: varieties of psychological interdependence. In K. Michaelian, D, Debus, and D. Perrin (eds.), *New Directions in the Philosophy of Memory* (pp. 181–99). London: Routledge.

Sutton, J., Harris, C. B., Keil, P. G., & Barnier, A. J. 2010. The psychology of memory, extended cognition, and socially distributed remembering. *Phenomenology and the Cognitive Sciences 9 (4)*, 521–60.

Sutton, J. & Keene, N. 2017. Cognitive history and material culture. In D. Gaimster, T. Hamling, & C. Richardson (eds.), *The Routledge Handbook of Material Culture in Early Modern Europe* (pp. 44–56). London: Routledge.

Tattersall, I. 2008. *The World from Beginnings to 4000 BCE*. Oxford, UK: Oxford University Press.

Tribble, E. 2011. *Cognition in the Globe: attention and memory in Shakespeare's theatre*. London: Palgrave.

Tribble, E. & Keene, N. 2011. *Cognitive Ecologies and the History of Remembering: religion, education and memory in early modern England*. London: Palgrave.

Tulving, E. 2002. Episodic memory: from mind to brain. *Annual Review of Psychology, 53 (1)*, 1–25.

Wang, Q. 2013. *The Autobiographical Self in Time and Culture*. Oxford: Oxford University Press.

Wang, Q. 2018. Culture in collaborative remembering. In M. L. Meade, C. B. Harris, P. van Bergen, J. Sutton, & A. J. Barnier (eds.), *Collaborative Remembering: theories, research, and applications* (pp. 297–314). Oxford, UK: Oxford University Press.

Watkins, T. 2004. Architecture and 'theatres of memory' in the Neolithic of southwest Asia. In E. DeMarrais, C. Gosden, & C. Renfrew (eds.), *Rethinking materiality: the engagement of mind with the material world* (pp. 97–106). Cambridge, UK: Macdonald Institute for Archaeological Research.

Watkins, T. 2006. Architecture and the symbolic construction of new worlds. In E. B. Banning & M. Chazan (eds.), *Domesticating Space* (pp. 15–24). Berlin: Ex Oriente.

Watkins, T. 2012. Household, community and social landscape: maintaining social memory in the early Neolithic of Southwest Asia. In M. Furholt, M. Hinz, & D. Mischka (eds.), *'As Time Goes By': monuments, landscapes and the temporal perspective* (pp. 23–44). Bonn: Rudolf Habelt.

Watkins, T. 2013. Neolithisation needs evolution, as evolution needs Neolithisation. *Neo-Lithics, 2,* 5–10.

Watkins, T. 2016. The cultural dimension of cognition. *Quaternary International, 405,* 91–97.

Wengrow, D. & Graeber, D. 2015. Farewell to the 'childhood of man': ritual, seasonality, and the origins of inequality. *Journal of the Royal Anthropological Institute, 21,* 597–619.

Whallon, R. 2011. An introduction to information and its role in hunter-gatherer bands. In R. Whallon, W. A. Lovis, & R. K. Hitchcock (eds.), *Information and Its Role in Hunter-Gatherer Bands* (pp. 1–27). Los Angeles, CA: Cotsen Institute of Archaeology Press.

Whitehouse, H. 2004. *Modes of Religiosity: a cognitive theory of religious transmission.* Walnut Creek, CA: AltaMira Press.

Whitehouse, H. & Hodder, I. 2010. Modes of religiosity at Çatalhöyük. In I. Hodder (ed.), *Religion in the Emergence of Civilization: Çatalhöyük as a case study* (pp. 122–48). Cambridge, UK: Cambridge University Press.

Woodburn, J. 1980. Hunters and gatherers today and reconstruction of the past. In E. Gellner (ed.), *Soviet and Western Anthropology* (pp. 95–117). London: Duckworth.

Woodburn, J. 1982. Egalitarian societies. *Man, 17,* 431–51.

Woodburn, J. 2005. Egalitarian societies revisited. In T. Widlok & W. G. Tadesse (eds.), *Property and Equality, volume 1: ritualization, sharing, egalitarianism* (pp. 18–31). Oxford, UK: Berghahn Books.

ADORNING THE SELF

Milena Vasić

THIS CHAPTER EXPLORES THE PHENOMENON of personal adornment at Çatalhöyük with the aim of getting one step closer to what it meant to be a person in the Neolithic. When discussing self, the Western notion of self as autonomous and egocentric is usually taken as a starting point; however, using the term "dividual," Strathern demonstrated that other concepts of self exist (Strathern 1988). According to Strathern, the Melanesian self is defined and redefined according to the relationships with particular places, objects, and people (Strathern 1988:13). While the dividual, composed of multiple divisible aspects of socially embedded self, is sociocentric and determined by social structures, the Western concept defines an individual as a highly egocentric and indivisible independent social actor. However, as Sutton notes in Chapter 10 of this volume, many authors now agree that all persons are to some degree both dividuals and individuals (Englund and Leach 2000:229; Hess 2006; Mageo 1995:283; Smith 2012; Sökefeld 1999), and as Sökefeld notes, both egocentrism and sociocentrism are integral aspects of every self (Sökefeld 1999:430).

"The self is ultimately an embodied self, and the symbolic capacity of material bodies can thus be 'employed' by this self so embodied as one way to act on the world" (Reischer and Koo 2004:307). Social theory recognizes the body as a sociocultural and historical phenomenon that serves both as a symbol and an active agent (Bourdieu 1977; Douglas 1970; Goffman 1959; Mauss 1973). The body has an active role in the social world, and it is a fundamental aspect of the acting self (Csordas 1990, 1994; Turner 1994). "The surface of the body, as the common frontier of society, the social self, and the psycho-biological individual becomes the symbolic stage upon which the drama of socialization is enacted, and bodily adornment in all its culturally multifarious forms, from body painting to clothing and from feather head-dresses to cosmetics, becomes the language through which it is expressed" (Turner 1980:112). The body, and consequently its adornment, is not just a reflection and expression of dominant cultural values, but also an arena for construction, negotiation, and performance of these values and consequently, the identities, with the power of mediating our relationship to the world around us.

Although personal adornment is an essential feature of humanity, bodily decoration[1] is a cultural phenomenon (Reischer and Koo 2004:297). That is, body adornment is not uniform across the time and space, but rather, components of this practice are heavily dependent on the sociocultural and historical context.

The Middle Eastern Neolithic is a period marked by some of the greatest transitions in human history (e.g., emergence of permanent settlements, technological advances and production intensification, farming and domestification, proliferation of rituals and symbolism), and an increase in both social complexity and the entanglement of humans and things, leading to both an augmented self of exclusive property and a stronger sense of both individual and dividual selves (Hodder 2011, 2012). As Hodder notes, with the emergence of ownership, it is likely that people started not just separating their belongings from other people's belongings, but also themselves from others (Hodder 2011). Similarly, in his study of the domestic material environment, Noble argues that in the process of the accumulation of objects, people accumulate being (Noble 2004). Things we own affect the ways in which we perceive ourselves and distinguish ourselves from others, and at the same time, sometimes, we display our personal possessions to others so that they can see who we are (Mittal 2006). The formation of one's self is heavily dependent on personal possessions, and whether an object is part of the self or not depends on the emotional attitude of a person toward this object (Chaudhary 2008:10). Self and possessions are therefore mutually constitutive; self is externalized into objects, and at the same time, the very same objects are incorporated into our self-image (Hegel 1977; Miller 1987).

Personal adornment is a powerful social medium that conveys messages and displays our self to others. At the same time, it is fundamental in, and plays a crucial role in, the formation and negotiation of our self. Personal adornment is neither passive nor static; rather, it is a fluid and potent agent that is an integral part of the formulation of identities, self, and consequently, personhood. The construction and transformation of external display and adornment that is performed through the context of its use and through the contact with others is therefore essential for understanding self-perception, as well as the perception of others. Therefore, personal adornment can be seen as part of the extended self (Belk 1988; Fowler 2004; Gell 1998; Mittal 2006).

Looking at the bodily decoration brings us one step closer to revealing the sense of self and identities of people who lived in prehistory. With its exceptional dataset, Çatalhöyük represents an outstanding source of information for exploring the notions of self in the Neolithic. Çatalhöyük offers a large and diverse material assemblage with different types of items related to bodily adornment, a variety of excavated deposits from over 1,000 years of the existence of the settlement, as well as a large number of burials.

Given the preceding, notions of self and personhood are not universal, and we cannot assume that the simplified scheme of a shift from partible to integrated self can be applied to Çatalhöyük society. The aim of this chapter is to explore personal adornment and determine what forms of self existed at Çatalhöyük, and whether the notion of self changed throughout the existence of this Neolithic settlement.[2]

PERSONAL ADORNMENT AT ÇATALHÖYÜK

Personal adornment significantly varies from culture to culture and can include a diverse assemblage and processes ranging from body modifications to dress and ornaments. The ways in which people adorned themselves at Çatalhöyük are sometimes hinted on wall paintings and figurines. These schematic depictions are quite rare; in contrast to the relatively large assemblage of personal adornment on-site, depiction of clothing and adornment does not seem to have been as important as the portrayal of the human body. Depictions of bodily adornment on figurines and wall paintings include body painting, hairstyles, facial hair, some sort of headgear, beads and/or bangles, and dress (e.g., Mellaart 1962:Plates VIIIb, IXa–c, XVIII; 1963:Plates XXIa–c, XXIIc–d, XXIII). The evidence of what the actual garments looked like is quite limited; however, textile fragments that were preserved in a small number of burials indicate that Çatalhöyük inhabitants used finely woven linen (Fuller et al. in prep.), and it is likely that they used other material as well, such as hide and fur.

Although they do not necessarily mirror the daily social relations (Hodder 1982:200), burials provide the direct association of artifacts and bodies and are therefore the source of the most substantiated evidence for what constituted personal adornment at Çatalhöyük. Burials demonstrate that bodily decoration at Çatalhöyük consisted of a variety of ornaments. Bodies were painted with red, blue, and green pigments and adorned with beads, bangles, rings, collars, potential hair and/or clothing pins, and various fasteners. Self-decoration at Çatalhöyük could have involved objects outside the spectrum of items that are usually considered ornamental, and some objects that are traditionally interpreted as tools could have also been used for bodily ornamentation. Nevertheless, burials have not produced thus far any evidence for tools, such as bone points or obsidian blades, being used for adorning the body.

Burial assemblage not only represents the main evidence for what constituted adornment at Çatalhöyük, but also provides information about how the bodies (of the dead) were decorated. Hands were adorned with multiple rings worn on different fingers, wrists with bracelets and possibly wrist guards, and upper arms with bangles and beads. The adornment on upper arms is also depicted on a figurine from building EVI 10 (Mellaart 1963:Pl. XXIc and Fig. 25). Both arms of this figurine are incised with multiple lines that, given the evidence from burials, represent either bangles or beads.

Artifacts originally interpreted as belt hooks and eyes (Mellaart 1964:Fig. 43) were found, individually or in sets, associated with different parts of the body (e.g., leg, shoulder, and potentially upper chest), which suggests that these artifacts were used to fasten garments in different ways. Their nonstrict association with a specific part of the body could also indicate different types of clothing. Similarly, objects made of boar tusk that Mellaart interpreted as collars (Mellaart 1964:Fig. 45) were found on the chest, but according to the burial of one individual, they were also worn on shoulders.

Beads represent the largest part of the assemblage related to bodily decoration, and over 48,000 beads, made from more than 100 different local and nonlocal materials were found in both burial and nonburial Neolithic contexts. Over 80 percent of beads were made from different rocks and minerals; however, beads were also made from shell, clay, animal bone, copper, wood, and there are even several examples of perforated human teeth. According to the evidence from burials, beads were used to adorn bodies in different ways, and bead strings were most commonly found around the neck, arms, and ankles.

Red ochre, cinnabar, azurite, and malachite were identified as red, blue, and green pigments that were used to paint the bodies of the dead. Body painting is also indicated on a few figurines; however, it is striking that only red pigment was used for these depictions. Incidentally, red ochre is the most common pigment, and it is also found in other contexts (e.g., wall paintings), while the occurrence of blue and green pigments seems to have been restricted to burial contexts. Some burial features contain more than one pigment, which demonstrates that bodies were sometimes treated with multiple colors.

Mellaart noted that several burials with red ochre treatment contained mirrors (e.g., Mellaart 1967:Fig. XII), and the co-occurrence of pigments and mirrors has further been confirmed in the recent excavations. Little can be said of the use of mirrors and their relation to personal adornment. Although other applications such as divination are plausible, it is also feasible that they were used as mirrors in the modern sense, that is, for looking at oneself (Hodder 2011:63, see also Vedder 2005). Their rarity and association with pigments and burials suggest that they might have been used in certain ritualized events.

Stamp seals represent another type of artifacts that could have been related to bodily adornment, although they are almost never found in burials. As no clay sealings have been found thus far, and given that they do not contain any sort of residue that would provide information about what kind of material they had been used on, their function at Çatalhöyük still remains a mystery (Türkcan 2013). Nevertheless, it is plausible that they were used for producing patterns on clothes and/or bodies. In addition, one stamp seal had a perforated handle, which could potentially mean that some of these objects might have also been worn, in which case, they definitely formed part of personal adornment. Their depictions include a range of motifs, some of which occur on other media (i.e., wall paintings and figurines); however, the motifs almost never repeat on stamp seals themselves. Given their rare occurrence on-site, and the individuality and uniqueness of depictions, it has been suggested that stamp seals were some sort of identity or property markers (Hodder 2006; Mellaart 1962; Skeates 2007).

Items of bodily ornamentation similar to the artifacts discussed earlier[3] occur across the Neolithic Middle East. For example, bangles were found at Kösk Höyük, Cafer Höyük, and Akarçay Tepe (Cauvin et al. 2011; Özbaşaran and Duru 2011; Öztan 2012), while similar examples of belt hooks and eyes have been noted at Aşıklı Höyük (Özbaşaran 2012). Body treatment with pigments, especially red ochre, is a recurring trait in prehistory, and therefore, it is far from confined to the Neolithic Anatolia. Beads of similar types have been found in the settlements contemporary or partially contemporary with Çatalhöyük, the most notable example being *Körtik Tepe* with its enormous bead assemblage (Özkaya and Coçkun 2011). Bodily ornamentation clearly involved manufacture of similar objects across the region, and it is possible that members of different communities adorned themselves in similar ways. Further investigation needs to be conducted in order to establish similarities and/or differences of practices encompassing adornment; however, it is evident that personal adornment formed a significant part of the Neolithic lifeways.

ADORNING THE DEAD

Items of bodily ornamentation are by far more common in burials than other objects are, and it is clear that body treatment played a significant role in mortuary practices. Similarly, the importance of adornment is also documented in the desire to depict various aspects of bodily decoration on figurines, no matter how rare they are. This goes well with the elaboration of head witnessed on a number of figurines, and together, they point to the importance of depicting features that might be indicative of identities (Nakamura and Meskell 2009).

While personal adornment is the most common form of "burial goods" at Çatalhöyük, only 22 percent of the studied individuals were found with any items related to bodily ornamentation. According to the analyzed burial assemblage consisting of 440 primary and secondary interred individuals,[4] the use of items described earlier was not confined in any way in the mortuary practices.

Pigment traces found directly on the bones imply that males were treated with pigments more commonly than females, while females were more often buried with lumps of pigments and pigment applicators. Although adults seem to have been associated with pigments more often than subadults, infants were treated with pigments far more than any other age group.

Some ornaments consisted of hundreds of beads, others included a single bead. Bead ornaments frequently comprised single strands of beads; however, the evidence also suggests that multiple strands of beads existed as well. Bead strings (i.e., necklaces, bracelets, and anklets) including various types, colors, sizes, and raw materials were found in burials of individuals belonging to different age and sex categories. Correspondingly, no restrictions in terms of colors and types have been noted, and similar beads were used to adorn the bodies of both males and females, adults and subadults. At the same time, the use of specific bead types or bead colors was not limited to particular types of ornaments such as bracelets or necklaces. Beads seem to have been combined freely; that is, some strings are quite simple and include one type, material, and color; others are diverse with multiple shapes, colors, and materials.[5]

Despite the large quantity of beads found in burials, only 52 individuals were found directly associated with beads. The direct associations of beads show that females were more frequently buried with beads than males. However, if both direct and indirect

Bead associations

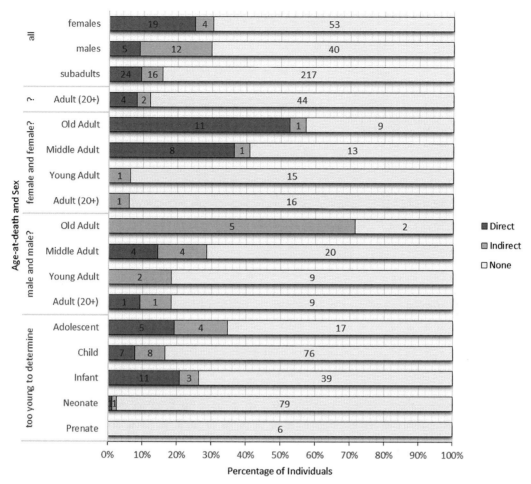

FIGURE 11.1 Age and sex categories with direct and indirect bead associations.

associations (items that were found directly on the body and items recovered from the fill, respectively) are taken into consideration, beads occur with the same percentage of males (29.8%) and females (30.3%). Consequently, given the relatively equal occurrence of beads with both sexes, it cannot be argued that there was a significant difference between males and females.[6]

Both direct and indirect associations show that the adults were more commonly buried with beads than the subadults, and it seems

that the placement of beads in burials correlates with age progression (Figure 11.1). The older the individuals were, the more likely they were to be buried with beads. Some discrepancies do exist (e.g., Young Adult category is almost never found with beads); however, this might be a consequence of a relatively arbitrary age categories that are based on our preconceptualized notion of biological age, rather than the social implications of what exactly it meant to be of certain age at Çatalhöyük. For example, if some of

Bead associations

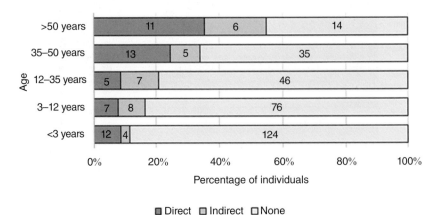

FIGURE 11.2 Alternative age categories with direct and indirect bead associations.

the categories are merged, occurrence of beads directly correlates with age progression (Figure 11.2).

Other objects related to bodily adornment, such as fasteners, bangles, and collars are generally not very common, and given their rare occurrence in burials, it is not possible to establish whether there were any restrictions in their use. "Belt hooks and/or eyes" have so far been discovered directly associated with two adult males and a child, while bangles were found adorning the upper arms of two adult females only. Rings have been found thus far only with one adult male and two (possibly three) subadults. However, given the normal distribution of their diameters from both burial and nonburial contexts, it is evident that individuals of different age groups, and likely both sexes, wore finger rings. Despite the small sample, it is clear that collars were used to adorn bodies of both males and females, while no collars have been found associated with children thus far.

The fact that collars were found on the chest of two females, and on a shoulder of a male, could potentially hint at males and females using these objects to adorn themselves differently.[7]

Given the preceding, sex does not seem to have been a major factor in self-decoration, and males and females were found associated with the same types of artifacts. Therefore, it can be argued that at least in some respects, men and women were not perceived differently within the society, and this is supported by other lines of evidence as well (e.g., figurines, diet, osteperiostitis, and trauma, see Agarwal et al. 2015; Hillson et al. 2013; Nakamura and Meskell 2009; Pearson 2013).

On the other hand, age does seem to have been a significant factor for status and social relations, and the correlation of objects and age progression has also been observed with other artifacts that occur in burials as well (Nakamura and Meskell 2013). Correspondingly, a focus on depicting age and maturity on figurines has also been noted (Nakamura and Meskell 2009), while depictions of subadults are completely absent. Age as an important social element is also demonstrated in the different diet between younger and older adults (Pearson and Meskell 2015).

Some ornaments in burials must have been gifts (especially the ones found in burials of subadults); however, others are likely to have been personal belongings of the dead. Given that subadults do get adorned with pigments, beads, and other items, the lack of clear-cut differences of adornment between subadults and adults is likely to be indicative of donations, and placement of similar ornaments that could have been worn by adults only might have symbolized the adult age that these infants and children never reached.

Objects sometimes display evidence of use and repair, which points to their use prior to interment. Regardless of whether the buried individuals were the original owners of these objects or not, their placement in burials attests to the importance of these items to their owners. On the other hand, some individuals were adorned with items that seem to have been completely new, and these objects might have been donations to the dead. Objects in burials are reflective of the presence of the living who put them there (Parker Pearson 1999). Therefore, these objects are not just gifts, but also represent commemoration of these people's participation in these events. Participants left part of themselves there, thus leaving a permanent mark of their involvement, as well as their relationship with the deceased.

The enduring relationship of people and their adornment is also evident in primary disturbed burials. Similar to the other prehistoric settlements in the Middle East (see Bonogofsky 2005; Kuijt 2008; Meskell 2008; Rollefson 1983; Simmons et al. 1990; Talalay 2004; Verhoeven 2002), bodily

FIGURE 11.3 Nassarius beads with the carefully placed long bones in a burial. (Photograph by Jason Quinlan)

dismemberment and circulation of body parts played an important part in Çatalhöyük society, and this is evident on the wall paintings, figurines, placements of body parts in the deposits related to building foundation and abandonment, as well as in their burial practices (Meskell 2008; Nakamura and Meskell 2009). Despite the circulation of body parts and the disturbance of burial features, there is evidence that suggests buried individuals kept their ornaments. For example, primary disturbed burial feature in B.77 contained the remains of at least two adults and a child. Over 80 *Nassarius* beads were found associated with the long bones of the two adults that were carefully placed together in the pit (Figure 11.3). This placement demonstrates the importance of commemoration, remembrance, and ancestry and indicates the special connection of these beads with the buried individuals.

CONTEXTUAL AND SPATIAL DISTRIBUTION

Although personal adornment played an important role in mortuary practices, the use of bodily ornamentation was far from confined to the sphere of the dead. The frequent occurrence of beads on floors, in middens, and the infill of buildings and their features such as bins, ovens, and hearths suggests that their use was also associated with other ritualized and daily life activities. In contrast, other items of personal adornment are not frequent, and outside of burials, they occur fragmented in middens and other tertiary deposits. Due to the very small number of collars, bangles, and elaborate fasteners, it is clear that they were not frequently made, and consequently, it can be argued that they were not used by many people living in the settlement. However, judging by the extensive use-wear on some of these items (e.g., 15067.f1, Russell 2007:177), they must have been used for a long time. These objects could have been used for as long as possible (at least the ones that were not placed in burials), and once they had been broken beyond repair, they were discarded. Therefore, similar items were used for adorning both the living and the dead.

As the same types of objects occur with both males and females in burials, there is no reason to infer that they were not similarly adorned in life. Perhaps certain elements of body adornment were only used on special occasions, but some must have been used in the everyday life as well. Objects such as collars and belt hooks and eyes must have formed an important part of the external display, and wearing them could not have gone unnoticed. They could have had different functions, such as marking certain sodalities or roles the people wearing them played in the society, and the use of these objects might have defined and reinforced the role and status of individuals wearing them.

While the contextual distribution is relatively straightforward, the spatial distribution of personal adornment shows no apparent patterning. Occurrence of adornment cannot be correlated to the size of buildings, their location, or type (i.e., history, elaborate, and houses with multiple burials, see Hodder 2014a:3). Quite small buildings can contain some of the most elaborate ornaments. Given the large quantities of beads, one would expect traces of bead manufacture across the settlement. However, evidence of in situ manufacture has been noted in only two buildings and few external spaces. Strikingly, no beads were recovered from burials in these two buildings (B.18 and B.75).[8]

Items of bodily ornamentation do not cluster anywhere, and similar objects occur in different parts of the settlement. For example, a necklace consisting of interlocking bone beads and few *Nassarius* shells was found directly associated with an adult female buried in the North Area. Mellaart found a group of the same type of bone beads in the 1960s in the South Area. Similarly, two large stone pendants that very much look alike were placed in the platforms below wall paintings in roughly contemporary buildings B.80 and B.77 that are located in two different areas of the settlement, while this kind of pendant has not been found elsewhere. Beads, fasteners, collars, and bangles were retrieved from burials in both North and South Areas. Given that the same types of ornaments were found in burials across the settlement, there is no reason to assume that there was any sort of differentiation of personal adornment among the individuals buried in contemporary buildings in the two excavated areas.

Neighboring buildings rarely contain similar artifacts. One of the notable exceptions represents two adults that were buried with collars on their chest in two adjacent buildings (EVII 12 and B.50). Another example comes from two roughly contemporary buildings B.1 and B.131 in the North Area. Two burial features in these buildings contained a child and an adolescent (B.1 and B.131, respectively) that were adorned with hundreds of very small disc beads. These two burials have the largest number of beads so far found at Çatalhöyük. The excavators noted strings of beads going across the body of the child buried in building B.1 (Cessford 2007). Similarly, in 2017, a very elaborate burial in B.131 was excavated. This burial contained a mirror, pigments, and over 3,000 beads, the large majority of which were very similar to the ones found in B.1. These beads were found around the neck, but also in multiple strands on the arm, wrists (hands?), and feet. Given the multiple rows, their direction, and position in the burial, it is possible that these beads were also used to wrap the body of this adolescent. Alternatively, they could have been attached on some sort of cloth. It is striking that these two individuals were buried in two adjacent buildings, and that they both had such a large number of beads that clearly were not just necklaces, bracelets, and anklets. Nevertheless, these examples are quite rare, and adjacent buildings generally contain completely different items of personal adornment.

Even individuals buried in the same building have different items associated with them, if they have any. Out of 61 individuals buried in the aforementioned building B.1, only 10 individuals were found associated with items related to bodily decoration. A similar pattern is observed in the neighboring building, B.131. Not every individual interred in this building was adorned with beads. Peculiarly, two individuals that were buried under the same platform in this building, were buried in a "mirror" position, and excavators noted the similar positioning and grave goods (a wooden bowl and beads) of these two individuals (Tung 2016:23). However, they were associated with different beads. One of them (young adult female) was found with a single stone bead between mandible and right hand, and the other one (possibly female middle adult) had a necklace and bracelets on the right arm consisting of a number of bone and stone beads of different types.

Spatial distribution of adornment reflects complex relationships that were not based on a physical proximity of buildings. This fits well with the general pattern of social geography on the site, which demonstrates that social organization functioned through a mosaic of networks crisscrossing the settlement (Hodder 2014b).

TEMPORALITY OF ADORNMENT

Material remains at Çatalhöyük reveal a stable society with a long tradition that involved certain conventions that endured for over 1,000 years. This stability is evident in personal adornment, but also architecture, burials, as well as other aspects of material culture.

The main temporal trends of personal adornment are continuity and slow gradual change, which corresponds to the dominant trends on site (Hodder 2014c). Items of bodily adornment were utilized from early on, and

Bead types

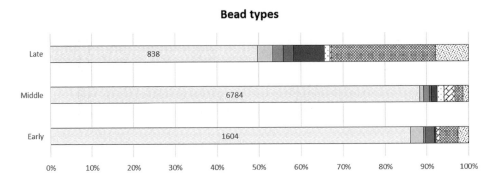

FIGURE 11.4 Bead types through time.

throughout the entire history of the settlement, in both burial and nonburial context. The practice of bodily decoration has gradually developed throughout the centuries of the settlement's occupation. Body painting seems to have been the most intense in the Early Period; however, its variety expands with the introduction of green and blue pigments in the Middle Period. Similarly, collars and belt hooks and eyes, although already present in the early levels, become more frequent in the Middle Period. The Middle Period exhibits a particular focus on the human hands witnessed on both relatively frequent handprints on walls and the number of bone rings recovered from this period. Personal adornment further develops with the introduction of stamp seals and mirrors in the middle levels, both of which are much more common in the Late Period (Türkcan 2013). Either the use of the stamp seals was intensified, or perhaps their use was extended to a larger number of people in the Late Period.

Similarly, depiction of adornment on figurines gradually expands from schematic representations of hair and/or hat to more elaborate depictions of facial hair, bead strings, bangles, garments, and body painting in the Middle and Late Periods (Vasić et al. 2014:213). Correspondingly, portrayal of humans on wall paintings evolves from schematic representations of the Early Period to details of facial hair, garments, and some sort of headgear in the Late Period.

Beads were used from the earliest levels onward, and the bead assemblage progressively expands, with new raw materials and types being added (Bains et al. 2013). The diversification of beads reaches its peak in the Late Period, when the quantity of disc beads, though they still represent the vast majority, drops to below 70 percent of the assemblage (Figure 11.4). Although already present in the early levels, blue beads are more common in the Late Period (Figure 11.5). In this period, beads also get bigger, and bead strings in burials become more diverse with a greater variety of colors, types, sizes, and raw materials than seen in the earlier levels (Figure 11.6). This diversity is also observed in the Late Period burials, some of which also contain unique types that had not been seen elsewhere. Particularity of the burials from

Bead colors

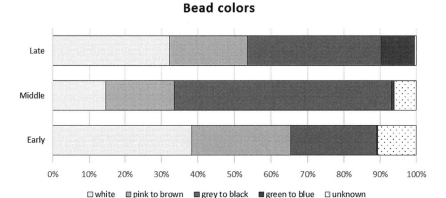

FIGURE 11.5 Bead colors across periods.

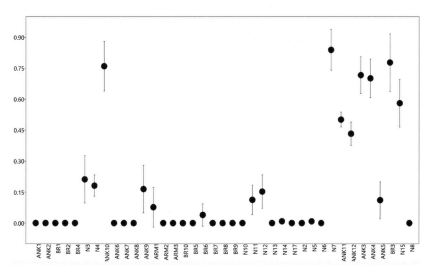

FIGURE 11.6 Diversity of individual bead strings in burials across the time.

this period is also witnessed in a changing frequency of individuals buried with beads. While adults were more commonly buried with beads in the early levels, the burial assemblage of the Late Period suggests that subadults have more bead associations than adults.

Burials of the Middle Period have a tendency toward certain level of standardization of adornment. This is the period when belt hooks and eyes seem the most common, as witnessed in their numbers in burials. Bead strings in these levels usually include only one type of bead, and there are noted repetitions of similar strings in different burials (e.g., ornaments consisting entirely of *Nassarius* beads, found in several burials). This is very much in contrast with the individuality and increased diversity of the Late Period's bead strings discussed earlier.

Although beads are more commonly found in burials than in the other types of deposits, their use in mortuary practices seems to reduce over time, and the presence of beads

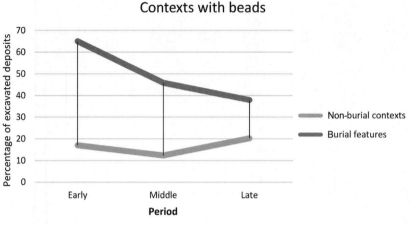

FIGURE 11.7 Contexts with beads.

in burials is at its lowest in the Late Period (Figure 11.7). Perhaps the decrease in the occurrence of beads in burials and the augmentation of their diversity when they do occur can be correlated to the increase in the number of secondary burials (see Chapter 12, this volume).

On the other hand, there is a slight increase in the occurrence of beads in nonburial context, and given an especially high quantity of complete beads that was noted in the Late Period middens, it could be argued that there was a shift in the roles beads, and consequently adornment, played at Çatalhöyük. The amplified occurrence of beads in nonburial contexts of the Late Period could be reflective of an increased importance self-decoration gained in daily life and other non-burial ritualized activities.

HISTORY HOUSES: CONTINUITY OF PRACTICES AND DISCONTINUITY OF ADORNMENT

One of the main characteristics of Çatalhöyük settlement is repetition of practices throughout the centuries of its existence. Sequences of houses that were built in the same spot and with a similar layout were defined as history houses (Hodder 2014a:3; Hodder and Pels 2010). Repetitive activities are not only seen in architecture and the internal arrangements (e.g., division of the living space into main and side room, or clean and dirty areas), but also across different media. For example, leopard reliefs were found decorating the walls of both EVII 44 and its subsequent EVI 44, while walls of both EVIII 8 and EVII 8 had depictions of vultures and human figures (Mellaart 1964:70). Similarly, placement of certain objects in the same location and repeated foundation burials of neonates were noted in the sequence of buildings B.65–B.56–B.44 belonging to the Late Period (Regan 2015).

While the repetition of practices is so clear in many aspects of material culture, it is remarkable that continuity is not very apparent in the adornment in the burials. For example, in the case of the aforementioned sequence from the Late Period, out of 31 interments in these three buildings, only

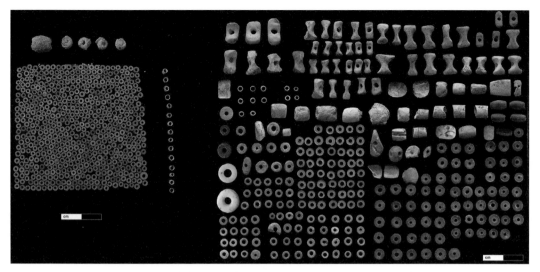

FIGURE 11.8 Some of the beads found with an adolescent in B.131 (left) and the child in B.129 (right). (Photographs by Ekin Ünal)

one individual was found directly associated with beads. A child buried in B.44 was adorned with three anklets. Although seven other burial features contained beads, the nature of their deposition was probably tertiary.

Continuity of adornment that does exist in few history houses, however, is not a coincidence. For example, Mellaart found belt hook and eye in both EVIB 20 and the subsequent EVIA 20 (Mellaart 1964:Fig. 43). Another example of continuity in burials was noted in two buildings in the North Area: B.131, and a building that was built on top of it, B.129. As previously mentioned, the body of an adolescent buried in B.131 was adorned with pigments and over three thousand beads, and this individual was also accompanied by a mirror. In addition to this adolescent, remains of a few more incomplete individuals were recovered from the same burial feature. In the building above it, B.129, in exactly the same location (under the north eastern platform), a child was buried

together with the remains of a few more individuals. Similar to the burial in the previous building, a relatively large number of beads, pigments, and two mirrors were recovered from this feature. Strikingly, beads found associated with this child were more colorful and of a wider range of types than the beads found with an adolescent in B.131 (Figure 11.8).

Continuity of adornment in history houses was not a prerogative, and the adornment of people who used and/or were buried in these buildings cannot be differentiated from the adornment of individuals buried in other buildings across the settlement. If the same group of people built, rebuilt, used these houses, and buried their dead in them, and if they used any distinguishing ornaments that would display association with their sodality (see Mills 2014), it is not apparent in burials. Quite the opposite, adornment of people buried in history houses does not implicate the desire or the necessity of displaying items characteristic for their sodalities in mortuary practices. This is quite clear in the diversity of burial goods of people buried in a single building, as well as different items of adornment found in the successive buildings.

Items of bodily ornamentation contributed to the creation and negotiation of identities at Çatalhöyük, and at the same time, they were a materialization of social organization and different relationships. It is possible that the adornment in burials is indicative of connections of the buried individuals with other groups in the settlement. Following Strathern, who argued that identities are created and recreated by multiple encounters with other people (Strathern 1988), the adornment in burials, and the diverse bead strings especially, can be interpreted as the material remains of different relationships. It is likely that beads were moved around frequently, and the assemblage we find in burials are material remains of social networking. The adornment in history houses demonstrates complex relationships, and its diversity could be a reflection of changing circumstances and affiliations over time.

SELF AT ÇATALHÖYÜK

As many authors have noted, personal possessions affect the ways in which we perceive ourselves and are essential in distinguishing ourselves from others. The intricate relationship of people at Çatalhöyük and their adornment is documented in burials, placement of beads in the deposits related to foundation and abandonment of houses, and also in their desire to repair broken objects. Broken ornaments, such as beads and collars, were sometimes repaired by adding a new perforation, thus extending their use life, while some objects were even recycled and made into something else. Russell notes a broken ring that was turned into a pendant (Russell 2005:352). Similarly, a fragment of a bangle was perforated, and perhaps used as a pendant. The most extreme example of alteration of objects represent human teeth that were perforated, presumably with the intention of being worn as pendants. This takes the circulation and reappropriation of body parts and objects to a whole new level; despite their rarity, perforated human teeth demonstrate that the notions of self and otherness were quite complex at Çatalhöyük.

Objects are not just an extension of self, they also bear the presence of others (Noble 2004:239). Self at Çatalhöyük was deeply embedded in the houses, and people at Çatalhöyük lived together with their dead (Hodder 2011). Given the small and confined areas of their houses, and a very dense layout of the settlement, individuals must have had a close contact with each other on a daily basis, as well as a close connection with their dead. Personal adornment is an intensely social practice that is performed through the context of its use and through the contact with others. Items of bodily ornamentation were consumed and displayed, as well as circulated in the events that brought people together, and perhaps even their manufacture itself carried multiple meanings.

Adornment as the physical remains of the embodied human self demonstrate that self at Çatalhöyük was both sociocentric and egocentric. The contextual and temporal distributions of items related to bodily ornamentation demonstrate that personal adornment formed an integral and essential part of different aspects of life and death at Çatalhöyük, and adornment must have played a funda-mental role in constituting and expressing both individuality and affiliations. Different combinations and ways in which objects might have been worn could have been an expression of individuality, and certain items must have been used to display and reinforce the roles people performed in the society.

At the same time, some objects might have been used to propagate social networks as well as their association with specific group(s). Beads, which are by far the most common type of adornment, are the embodiment of different relationships. Strings of beads are "composite artifacts through which chains of relations can be traced" (Fowler 2004:40). Each individual bead is an entity on its own, but through associations with other beads, as well as individuals, it gains new meanings and values. Although these values might have been partially based on the materiality of objects (e.g., rare or high-quality materials), they also must have consisted of specific sym-bolic, ritual, or other values, symbolic mean-ings and personal memories, as well as their connection to the individuals related to the manufacture or use of these objects.

Bead strings must have been continually altered, by adding new beads, removing the old ones, or perhaps even just changing their order. This is supported by the various levels of use-wear, as well as different expertise in their manufacture evident on some strings. The fluidity of beads could explain diversity in the assemblage, and lack of patterning in their spatial distribution. Beads might have been used to establish and reinforce relations among individuals and groups in the settle-ment, as well as connections to other groups outside the settlement. While we cannot be

certain of how these networks functioned, and how the bead strings were created, people of Çatalhöyük could have been donat-ing their beads to the deceased in order to make a statement, or reinforce their connec-tion to the deceased, or to the house in which the burial occurred. This is also supported by the fact that two buildings with evidence of bead making did not have any beads in the burials. Although interments in these two houses belonged to three neonates and one Young Adult (the age categories that are almost never adorned with bead strings), beads made in these buildings must have been used and potentially placed in burials elsewhere.

The prospect of bead ornaments in burials being a newly formed object should not be excluded, and neither should the possibility of more than one individual being involved in the creation of these strings. It is possible that a group of people came together, donated their beads, and formed a new string for the deceased. Use of beads was a highly social process, and personal adornment emphasizes a great level of sociality and networking at Çatalhöyük.

From the earliest levels onward, the deceased were adorned with similar items. Despite a certain extent of standardized prac-tices and tendencies in the material selection, burials demonstrate individuality and a variety of choices. Bodily decoration reflects the per-sonal choices as much as it reflects the rela-tionships between the individuals in charge of the burials and their dead. In contrast to the repetitive practices witnessed in so many aspects of life and death at Çatalhöyük, per-sonal adornment was possibly one of the most potent mediums for expression of individuality and a way to contradict the strict continuity of practices.

Transformations of self must have been related to major socioeconomic changes (Hodder 2011). Personal adornment must have played an important role in the new socioeconomic circumstances that came with and/or were of changes in settlements, such as the cattle domestication, intensified sheep herding, intensification of the use of stamp seals, mobility, decreased population density, and dispersal of the settlement (Hodder 2014c). The increased diversity of adornment witnessed in the Late Phase is indicative of a changing social expression and a growing complexity. The changes observed in this period could reflect not only an increased desire for individuality, but also more affiliations with different groups, or given the increased mobility witnessed on the skeletal remains (Sadvari et al. 2013), more connections with people from other settlements as well. Expansion of their networks could have brought more materials and ideas for new ways of presenting themselves to the members of their and other communities. Through relations within and outside the site, and between living and dead, personal adornment was able to mediate complex notions of personhood and identity. Bodily manipulation as the core of sociality would have been one of the main tools in the changing dynamics of social relations.

Given the continuity of adornment practices, it cannot be argued that there was a shift from partible to integrated self. On the contrary, it can be asserted that there was a strong notion of both integrated and partible selves throughout the occupation of the settlement. Fluidity of beads, discontinuity of adornment observed in most history houses, and the occurrence of similar items in various parts of the settlement demonstrate a great level of sociality and sociocentric decoration. On the other hand, individuality and elements of personal preferences are witnessed in the variability in the body treatment of the dead. Although an increase in diversity has been noted in the Late phase, variety and individual choices are indeed seen throughout the entire existence of the settlement. The self at Çatalhöyük must have been highly dynamic and changing according to the social context.

ACKNOWLEDGMENTS

I am grateful to Ian Hodder for the opportunity to participate in this volume. This paper is based on my PhD dissertation, and I would like to thank my supervisors Susan Pollock and Reinhard Bernbeck. I am also grateful to Carolyn Nakamura for her comments on the paper.

REFERENCES

Agarwal, S. C., P. Beauschesne, B. Glencross, C. S. Larsen, L. Meskell, C. Nakamura, J. A. Pearson and J. W. Sadvari 2015 Roles for Sexes. In *Assembling Çatalhöyük* edited by I. Hodder and A. Marciniak, pp. 87–96. Leeds: Maney Publishing.

Bains, R., M. Vasić, D. E. Bar-Yosef Mayer, R. Russell, K. I. Wright and C. Doherty 2013 A Technological Approach to the Study of Personal Ornamentation and Social Expression at Çatalhöyük. In *Substantive Technologies at Çatalhöyük: Reports from the 2000–2008 Seasons*, edited by I. Hodder. Monumenta Archaeologica, vol. 9. Los Angeles, CA: The Cotsen Institute of Archaeology Press.

Belk, R. W. 1988 Possessions and the Extended Self. *Journal of Consumer Research* 15(2):139–168.

Bonogofsky, M. 2005 A Bioarchaeological Study of Plastered Skulls from Anatolia: New Discoveries and Interpretations. *International Journal of Osteoarchaeology* 15(2):124–135.

Bourdieu, P. 1977 *Outline of a Theory of Practice*. Cambridge, UK: Cambridge University Press.

Cauvin, J., O. Aurenche, M.-C. Cauvin and N. Balkan-Atlı 2011 The Pre-Pottery Site of Cafer Höyük. In *The Neolithic in Turkey: The Euphrates Basin*, edited by M. Özdoğan, N. Başgelen and P. Kuniholm, pp. 1–40. Istanbul: Archaeology and Art Publications.

Cessford, C. 2007 Neolithic Excavations in the North Area, East Mound, Çatalhöyük 1995–98. In *Excavating Çatalhöyük: South, North and KOPAL Area Reports from the 1995–99 Seasons*, edited by I. Hodder. Cambridge, UK: McDonald Institute for Archaeological Research/British Institute of Archaeology at Ankara Monograph.

Chaudhary, N. 2008 Persistent Patterns in Cultural Negotiations of the Self: Using Dialogical Self Theory to Understand Self-Other Dynamics within Culture. *International Journal for Dialogical Science* 3(1):9–30.

Csordas, T. J. 1990 Embodiment as a Paradigm for Anthropology. *Ethos* 18:5–47.

Csordas, T. J. 1994 *Embodiment and Experience: The Existential Ground of Culture and Self*. Cambridge, UK: Cambridge University Press.

Douglas, M. 1970 *Natural Symbols: Explorations in Cosmology*. London: Barrie & Rockliff.

Englund, H. and J. Leach 2000 Ethnography and the Meta-Narratives of Modernity. *Current Anthropology* 41:225–248.

Fowler, C. 2004 *The Archaeology of Personhood*. London: Routledge.

Fuller, D. Q., S. D. Haddow, R. Hadad, K. Killackey, A. Bogaard, M. Charles, D. Filipović, L. Gonzalez Carretero and C. Knüsel in prep. The Earliest Evidence for Textile Trade: A Linen Shrouded Infant Burial from 7th Millennium BC at Çatalhöyük, Turkey.

Gell, A. 1998 *Art and Agency. An Anthropological Theory*. Oxford, UK: Clarendon Press.

Goffman, E. 1959 *The Presentation of Self in Everyday Life*. Garden City, NY: Doubleday.

Hegel, G. 1977 *The Phenomenology of Spirit*. Translated by A. V. Miller. Oxford, UK: Oxford University Press.

Hess, S. 2006 Strathern's Melanesian "Dividual" and the Christian "Individual": A Perspective from Vanua Lave, Vanuatu. *Oceania* 76:285–296.

Hillson, S., C. Larsen, B. Boz, M. A. Pilloud, J. W. Sadvari, S. C. Agarwal, B. Glencross, P. Beauchesne, J. A. Pearson, C. B. Ruff, E. M. Garofalo and L. D. Hager 2013 The Human Remains I: Interpreting Community Structure, Health and Diet in Neolithic Çatalhöyük. In *Humans and Landscapes*, edited by I. Hodder, pp. 339–396. Los Angeles, CA: Cotsen Institute of Archaeology Press.

Hodder, I. 1982 *Symbols in Action: Ethnoarchaeological Studies of Material Culture*. New Studies in Archaeology. Cambridge, UK: Cambridge University Press.

Hodder, I. 2006 *The Leopard's Tale: Revealing the Mysteries of Çatalhöyük*. London: Thames and Hudson.

Hodder, I. 2011 An Archaeology of the Self: The Prehistory of Personhood. In *In Search of Self: Interdisciplinary Perspectives on Personhood*, edited by J. W. W. van Huyssteen and E.P. Wiebe, pp. 50–69. Grand Rapids, MI: William B. Eerdmans Publishing Company.

Hodder, I. 2012 *Entangled: An Archaeology of the Relationships between Humans and Things*. Malden, MA: Wiley-Blackwell.

Hodder, I. 2014a Introduction and Summary of Summaries. In *Integrating Çatalhöyük. Themes from the 2000–2008 Seasons*, edited by I. Hodder, pp. 1–22. Los Angeles, CA: Cotsen Institute of Archaeology Press.

Hodder, I. 2014b Mosaics and Networks: The Social Geography of Çatalhöyük. In *Integrating Çatalhöyük. Themes from the 2000–2008 Seasons*, edited by I. Hodder. vol. 10. Los Angeles, CA: Cotsen Institute of Archaeology Press/British Institute of Archaeology at Ankara.

Hodder, I. 2014c Temporal Trends: The Shapes and Narratives of Cultural Change at Çatalhöyük. In *Integrating Çatalhöyük. Themes from the 2000–2008 Seasons*, edited by I. Hodder, pp. 169–184. Los Angeles, CA: Cotsen Institute of Archaeology Press/British Institute of Archaeology at Ankara.

Hodder, I. and P. Pels 2010 History Houses: A New Interpretation of Architectural Elaboration at Çatalhöyük. In *Religion in the Emergence of Civilization: Çatalhöyük as a Case Study*, edited by I. Hodder, pp. 163–186. Cambridge, UK: Cambridge University Press.

Kuijt, I. 2008 The Regeneration of Life: Neolithic Structures of Symbolic Remembering and Forgetting. *Current Anthropology* 49(2):171–197.

Mageo, J. M. 1995 The Reconfiguring Self. *American Anthropologist* 97(2):282–296.

Mauss, M. 1973 Techniques of the Body. *Economy and Society* 2(1):70–88.

Mellaart, J. 1962 Excavations at Çatal Hüyük: First Preliminary Report, 1961. *Anatolian Studies* 12:41–65, 103.

Mellaart, J. 1963 Excavations at Çatal Hüyük, 1962: Second Preliminary Report. *Anatolian Studies* 13:43–103.

Mellaart, J. 1964 Excavations at Çatal Hüyük, 1963, Third Preliminary Report. *Anatolian Studies* 14:39–119.

Mellaart, J. 1967 *Çatal Hüyük: A Neolithic Town in Anatolia*. London: Thames and Hudson.

Meskell, L. M. 2008 The Nature of the Beast: Curating Animals and Ancestors at Çatalhöyük. *World Archaeology* 40(3):373–389.

Miller, D. 1987 *Material Culture and Mass Consumption*. Oxford, UK: Blackwell.

Mills, B. J. 2014 Relational Networks and Religious Sodalities at Çatalhöyük. In *Religion at Work in a Neolithic Society: Vital Matters*, edited by I. Hodder, pp. 159–186. Cambridge, UK: Cambridge University Press.

Mittal, B. 2006 I, Me, and Mine – How Products Become Consumers' Extended Selves. *Journal of Consumer Behaviour* 5:550–562.

Nakamura, C. and L. M. Meskell 2009 Articulate Bodies: Forms and Figures at Çatalhöyük. *Journal of Archaeological Method and Theory* 16:205–230.

Nakamura, C. and L. M. Meskell 2013 The Çatalhöyük Burial Assemblage. In *Humans and Landscapes of Çatalhöyük. Reports from the 2000–2008*

Seasons, edited by I. Hodder, pp. 441–466. Los Angeles, CA: Cotsen Institute of Archaeology Press.

Noble, G. 2004 Accumulating Being. *International Journal of Cultural Studies* 7(2):233–256.

Özbaşaran, M. 2012 Aşıklı. In *The Neolithic in Turkey. New Excavations and New Research: Central Turkey*, edited by M. Özdoğan, N. Başgelen and P. Kuniholm, pp. 135–158. Istanbul: Archaeology and Art Publications.

Özbaşaran, M. and G. Duru 2011 Akarçay Tepe: A PPNB and PN Settlement in Middle Euphrates-Urfa. In *The Neolithic in Turkey*, edited by M. Özdoğan, N. Başgelen and P. Kuniholm, pp. 165–202. vol. 2, Istanbul.

Özkaya, V. and A. Coçkun 2011 Kortik Tepe. In *The Neolithic in Turkey 1. New Excavations and New Research: The Tigris Basin*, edited by M. Özdogan, N. Baçgelen and P. E. Kuniholm, pp. 89–127. Istanbul: Archaeology & Art Publications.

Öztan, A. 2012 Köşk Höyük: A Neolithic Settlement in Niğde-Bor Plateau. In *The Neolithic in Turkey: Central Turkey*, edited by M. Özdoğan, N. Başgelen and P. Kuniholm, pp. 31–70. Istanbul: Archaeology and Art Publications.

Parker Pearson, M. 1999 *The Archaeology of Death and Burial*. Stroud, UK: Sutton Publishing Limited.

Pearson, J. 2013 Human and Animal Diet as Evidenced by Stable Carbon and Nitrogen Isotope Analysis. In *Humans and Landscapes of Çatalhöyük. Reports from the 2000–2008 Seasons*, edited by I. Hodder, pp. 271–298. Los Angeles, CA: Cotsen Institute of Archaeology Press.

Pearson, J. and L. Meskell 2015 Isotopes and Images: Flashing out Bodies at Çatalhöyük. *Journal of Archaeological Method and Theory* 22(2):461–482.

Regan, R. 2015 The Sequence of Buildings 75, 65, 56, 69, 44 and 10 and External Spaces 119, 129, 130, 144, 299, 314, 319, 329, 333, 339, 367, 371 and 427. In *Çatalhöyük Excavations: The 2000–2008 Seasons*, edited by I. Hodder. Los Angeles, CA: Cotsen Institute of Archaeology Press/British Institute of Archaeology at Ankara.

E. Reischer and K. S. Koo, 2004 The Body Beautiful: Symbolism and Agency in the Social World. *Annual Review of Anthropology* 33:297–317.

Rollefson, G. O. 1983 Ritual and Ceremony at Neolithic Ain Ghazal (Jordan) *Paléorient* 9 (2):29–38.

Russell, N. 2005 Çatalhöyük Worked Bone. In *Changing Materialities at Çatalhöyük: Reports from the 1995–99 Seasons*, edited by I. Hodder, pp. 339–368. Cambridge, UK: McDonald Institute for Archaeological Research/ British Institute at Ankara.

Russell, N. 2007 Çatalhöyük Worked Bone 2007. In *Çatalhöyük 2007 Archive Report*, edited by I. Hodder, pp. 170–179.

Sadvari, J., M. Charles, C. Ruff, T. Carter and M. Vasić 2013 The People and Their Landscape: Changing Mobility Patterns at Neolithic Çatalhöyük. Paper presented at the Society for American Archaeology Symposium, Honolulu, Hawaii.

Simmons, A., A. Boulton, C. Butler, Z. Kafafi and G. Rollefson 1990 A Plastered Human Skull from Neolithic 'Ain Ghazal, Jordan. *Journal of Field Archaeology* 17(1):107–110.

Skeates, R. 2007 Neolithic Stamps: Cultural Patterns, Processes and Potencies. *Cambridge Archaeological Journal* 17:183–198.

Smith, K. 2012 From dividual and individual selves to porous subjects. *The Australian Journal of Anthropology* 23:50–64.

Sökefeld, M. 1999 Debating Self, Identity, and Culture in Anthropology. *Current Anthropology* 40 (4):417–447.

Strathern, M. 1988 *The Gender of the Gift*. Berkeley: University of California Press.

Talalay, L. E. 2004 Heady Business: Skulls, Heads, and Decapitation in Neolithic Anatolia and Greece. *Journal of Mediterranean Archaeology* 17 (2):139–163.

Tung, B. 2016 Excavations in the North Area. *Çatalhöyük 2016 Archive Report*:17–50.

Türkcan, A. U. 2013 Çatalhöyük Stamp Seals from 2000 to 2008. In *Substantive Technologies at Çatalhöyük: Reports from the 2000–2008 Seasons*, edited by I. Hodder, pp. 235–246. Los Angeles, CA: Cotsen Institute of Archaeology Press.

Turner, T. 1980 The Social Skin. In *Not Work Alone*, edited by J. Cherfas and R. Lewin, pp. 112–140. London: Temple Smith.

Turner, T. 1994 Bodies and Anti-bodies: Flesh and Fetish in Contemporary Social Theory. In *Embodiment and Experience: The Existential Ground of Culture and Self*, edited by T. J. Csordas, pp. 27–47. Cambridge, UK: Cambridge University Press.

Vasić, M. 2018 Personal Adornment in the Neolithic Middle East: A Case Study of Çatalhöyük. PhD Thesis, Institut für Vorderasiatische Archäologie, Freie Universität Berlin.

Vasić, M., R. Bains and N. Russell 2014 Dress: A Preliminary Study of Bodily Ornamentation at Çatalhöyük. In *Integrating Çatalhöyük: Themes from the 2000–2008 Seasons*, edited by I. Hodder, pp. 197–220. Los Angeles, CA: Cotsen Institute of Archaeology, Los Angeles.

Vedder, J. F. 2005 The Obsidian Mirrors of Çatalhöyük. In *Changing Materialities at Çatalhöyük: Reports from the 1995–99 Seasons*, edited by I. Hodder, pp. 597–619. Cambridge, UK: British Institute at Ankara/ McDonald Institute for Archaeological Research.

Verhoeven, M. 2002 Ritual and Ideology in the Pre-Pottery Neolithic B of the Levant and Southeast Anatolia. *Cambridge Archaeological Journal* 12(2):233–258.

FROM PARTS TO A WHOLE?
EXPLORING CHANGES IN FUNERARY
PRACTICES AT ÇATALHÖYÜK

Scott D. Haddow, Eline M. J. Schotsmans, Marco Milella,
Marin A. Pilloud, Belinda Tibbetts, and Christopher J. Knüsel

DEATH IS A UNIVERSAL AND PROFOUNDLY emotive human experience with social and economic implications that extend to communities as a whole. As such, the act of disposing of the dead is typically laden with deep meaning and significance. Archaeological investigations of funerary practices are thus important sources of information on the social contexts and worldviews of ancient societies. Changes in funerary practices are often thought to reflect organisational or cosmological transformations within a society (Carr 1995; Robb 2013). The focus of this volume is the role of cognition and consciousness in the accelerated sociocultural developments of the Neolithic Period in the Near East. In the introduction to this volume, Hodder identifies three commonly cited cognitive changes that can be measured against various archaeological datasets from Çatalhöyük. The funerary remains at Çatalhöyük are an obvious source of data for validating Hodder's third measure of change: a shift from a fluid and fragmented conception of the body and of selfhood to a greater awareness of an integrated, bounded personal self.

The notion of a highly distributed and partible self as a useful counterpoint to Western conceptions of an integrated and holistic self began to take hold in archaeological circles via ethnographies of personhood in India and Melanesia produced by McKim Marriott (1976) and Marilyn Strathern (1988), respectively (Fowler 2004). In each of these societies, personhood is seen as constructed and renegotiated through the actions and substances of others. It is through these interactions and exchanges that social relations are created and maintained. Marriott (1976) coined the term *dividual* to describe the composite character of selfhood in these societies. Many scholars have argued that the focus on cranial retrieval and other secondary burial practices observed during the Near Eastern Neolithic demonstrates a similar sense of partible personhood and a preoccupation with collectivity and sharing (e.g. Goring-Morris and Belfer-Cohen 2014; Hodder 2011; Kuijt 2000, 2001, 2008; Van Huyssteen 2014). Despite the criticisms of the dividual-individual scheme voiced in this volume by Sutton and Vasic in Chapters 10 and 11, we take it as a useful starting point, although we will point to difficulties in our conclusion.

In order to identify evidence in the funerary practices at Çatalhöyük for the emergence of higher-level forms of consciousness during the Neolithic and, more specifically, a shift to a more integrated and less partible conception of the self, it is important to first understand the nature of these practices, how they vary and whether this variation has a directional, i.e. temporal, trajectory.

FUNERARY PRACTICES AT ÇATALHÖYÜK

One of the most striking aspects of Neolithic Çatalhöyük is the seeming cultural conservatism apparent throughout its 1,100-year occupation (Bayliss et al. 2015). Seen on a macroscale, a considerable preoccupation with conformity, continuity and repetition is apparent in many aspects of life at the site (Hodder 2006; Hodder and Cessford 2004). A prime example of this tendency can be seen in the architectural layout of its buildings, which tend to conform to a similar layout: there is a large central room with smaller rooms typically located to the west or north of the central room. Ovens and hearths are almost always located along the southern wall, with the ladder entrance in the southeast corner. The central rooms are divided between 'clean' platform areas in the north and 'dirty' floors in the southern half of the building near the ovens and hearths. Wall paintings tend to occur in the same locations, usually along the north and east walls (Czeszewska 2014), while platforms, animal installations and walls are continuously replastered and repainted during the lifecycle of a building. After the abandonment and demolition of buildings, new structures are often rebuilt on the same footprint as the previous one, sometimes over several construction sequences (Farid 2014; Matthews 2005; Russell et al. 2014). A similar preoccupation with continuity and repetition is also evident in the funerary practices observed on-site.

During much of the occupation at Çatalhöyük, the overwhelming majority of burials occurred within houses, typically underneath the northern and eastern platforms of the central room, although perinate, neonate and infant burials are found in more variable locations within the house (Andrews et al. 2005; Boz and Hager 2013; Tibbetts 2017). Most intramural burials took place during the occupation phase of the house, although a smaller number of burials have been found that correspond with construction and abandonment phases. Perinates, neonates and infants also account for a large proportion of burials that occurred during the construction phase of houses, but are rarely found in abandonment contexts (Boz and Hager 2013).

Fully articulated skeletons, along with disarticulated and partially articulated skeletal elements, were commonly observed under house platforms and floors during the excavation projects of both Mellaart and Hodder (Haddow et al. 2016). However, the interpretation of this commingling has evolved since Mellaart's day. Mellaart interpreted the presence of disarticulated and commingled remains as evidence for secondary burial practices involving the exposure and excarnation of bodies prior to intramural burial: 'These burial habits ... strongly suggest that secondary interment was practised involving the reburial of parts of the skeletons after complete or partial decomposition of the flesh' (Mellaart 1962:51–52). Given the extreme flexion of some of the articulated skeletons, Mellaart also believed that these too represented secondary burials: 'Evidently care was taken to preserve the skeleton intact in anatomical position ...' (Mellaart 1967:204).

In contrast to Mellaart's view, the dominant narrative of the Hodder excavations has been that the majority of burials are primary rather than secondary in nature (Andrews et al. 2005; Andrews & Bello 2006). In this reading, the observed commingling of skeletal remains is interpreted as mainly the result of sequential disturbances to earlier primary interments by later ones (Boz & Hager 2014). Until recently, commingling of skeletal remains has been interpreted as largely the result of successive primary interments under house platforms: '... the majority of depositions are primary single interments. Burials containing multiple individuals interred in a single event rarely occur. Multiple event interments where primary burials are subsequently disturbed by new interments are common and result in the many primary disturbed skeletons at Çatalhöyük' (Boz & Hager 2013:415).

These interments are now defined as collective burials, as defined by Duday (2008) and applied by Crevecoeur et al. (2015). Knüsel and Robb (2016:657) define collective burial as 'human remains deposited successively over time rather than in a single episode, often inferred from variations in completeness and articulation among the remains'. As we shall see, however, recent observations, in combination with newly excavated material from the earliest and latest occupation levels, suggest that the funerary practices at Çatalhöyük were far more complex and variable than previously assumed.

Deposition Categories

A total of 816 individuals from stratified Neolithic contexts have been recovered during the Hodder-era excavations at Çatalhöyük. In order to assist the interpretation of the funerary practices, these have been assigned to one of six deposition categories that reflect the variable contexts from which skeletal remains have been recovered (Table 12.1). Primary burials, defined as the direct inhumation of an articulated corpse, are split between three depositional categories: (1) primary undisturbed: articulated skeletons found in their original interment location that have not been disturbed by later Neolithic activity; (2) primary disturbed: the in situ remains of articulated skeletons found in their original location that have been disturbed by subsequent Neolithic activity; and (3) primary disturbed loose: disarticulated or partially articulated skeletal elements found in grave fills that derive from disturbed primary burials. Individuals from the primary disturbed loose category are excluded from the total in order to avoid the potential for counting individuals twice. Secondary burials are defined as a partial or complete skeleton, typically in a disarticulated or partially disarticulated state, which has been intentionally moved by Neolithic people from a previous location to a subsequent interment location. The tertiary deposition category is reserved for isolated, disarticulated or partially articulated skeletal elements found outside typical burial contexts. Such non-interment contexts include middens and other external spaces, as well as house construction and abandonment layers. Last, human remains in the unknown

TABLE 12.1 Description of burial deposition categories employed by the Çatalhöyük Research Project

1. **Primary undisturbed**	An undisturbed, articulated skeleton, complete or nearly complete, found in its original place of interment
2. **Primary disturbed**	The in situ skeletal remains of a primary articulated skeleton found in its original burial location but subsequently disturbed/truncated by Neolithic people
3. **Primary disturbed loose**	Loose, scattered, disarticulated skeletal elements found in grave fills and deriving from a disturbed primary burial
4. **Secondary**	Partial or complete skeleton moved by Neolithic people from a previous location and deposited in a final interment context
5. **Tertiary**	Isolated, disarticulated or partially articulated skeletal elements found in non-interment contexts (e.g. room fill, midden)
6. **Unknown**	Unable to determine original deposition of bones

deposition category are typically recovered from heavily eroded surface layers or have been displaced by animal burrowing, such that their original deposition cannot be determined with certainty; in addition, highly commingled remains whose deposition cannot be clearly determined (e.g. secondary versus primary disturbed loose) are also assigned to the unknown deposition category. Figure 12.1 presents the number of stratified individuals by deposition

category. In this chart, individuals from unknown deposition contexts ($n = 75$) are excluded. As such, the total number of individuals is reduced from 816 to 741.

While primary burials dominate the skeletal assemblage ($n = 471, 64\%$), it is the rarer occurrence of secondary burials ($n = 96, 13\%$) at Çatalhöyük that are often the most intriguing. One of the most obvious examples of the secondary manipulation of body parts at Çatalhöyük can be seen in the practice of cranial retrieval, curation and redeposition. The discovery in 2004 of a plastered cranium and mandible clutched in the upper limbs of an articulated older adult female is the most conspicuous example of this practice (Boz & Hager 2013; Sadarangani 2014); while no further plastered crania have been found, there are numerous other cases of undecorated, disarticulated crania – often in association with disarticulated infra-cranial remains – found with primary burials and in other contexts.

Cranial Retrieval and Other Secondary Treatments

The occurrence of disarticulated crania in a variety of archaeological contexts, a commonly reported feature of Neolithic Near Eastern funerary practices (e.g. Bocquentin et al. 2016; Croucher 2006), raises the question of provenance. There are a number of instances of 'headless' primary burials at Çatalhöyük, the crania and mandibles having presumably been removed and retained before eventually being reburied. In most cases it appears that the cranium, mandible and in some cases cervical vertebrae were removed after a period of initial interment when the body had either partially or

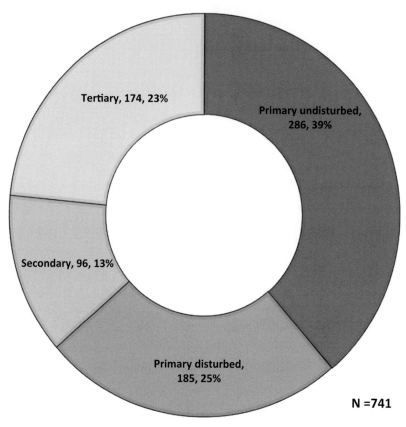

Tertiary, 174, 23%

Primary undisturbed, 286, 39%

Secondary, 96, 13%

Primary disturbed, 185, 25%

N =741

FIGURE 12.1 Distribution of individuals by burial context at Neolithic Çatalhöyük (individuals from primary disturbed loose and unknown depositions are excluded).

completely skeletonised (Andrews et al. 2005; Haddow et al. 2017). In other cases, however, it is not always clear if a skeleton had been intentionally targeted for retrieval, as earlier burials are sometimes disturbed by later interments, leading to the disarticulation or loss of skeletal elements (Haddow and Knüsel 2017). As such, the total number of primary burials in which we can say with some degree of confidence that the cranium and mandible were removed intentionally is 15 (Pilloud et al. 2016). This includes 12 adults (7 males and 5 females), 2 adolescents and 1 child. While disarticulated crania and mandibles are often found with loose and partially articulated infra-cranial bones at Çatalhöyük, at

least 52 isolated crania and/or mandibles have been recovered from secondary and tertiary contexts (Table 12.2), a figure that substantially exceeds the number of excavated 'headless' primary skeletons. Furthermore, the majority of these secondary remains are found in association with primary subfloor burials, rather than as separate deposits. A similar phenomenon has been observed at the Chalcolithic site of Souskiou-Laona in Cyprus (Lorentz 2010).

Of the 14 secondarily deposited crania/ mandibles, 5 are adults (1 young adult, 1 old adult and 3 adults who cannot be assigned to a specific adult category), and 9 are subadults (3 adolescents, 3 children, 2 infants and 1

TABLE 12.2 The distribution of elements of the cephalic extremity found in various contexts at Neolithic Çatalhöyük

	Males	Females	Unknown	Total
'Headless' individuals	7	5	3	**15**
Secondary crania/mandibles	2	5	7	**14**
Tertiary crania/mandibles	3	2	33	**38**

neonate). Of the 38 tertiary crania/mandibles, 27 are adults (1 old adult and 26 who cannot be assigned to a more specific adult category), and 11 are subadults (1 adolescent, 3 children, 3 infants and 4 neonates).

BODIES OF EVIDENCE: RECENT INSIGHTS AND NEW INTERPRETATIONS

The starting point for a re-evaluation of funerary practices at Çatalhöyük can be traced to a number of recent archaeological findings, including the excavation of a series of burials uncovered from buildings and spaces in the North Area of the site. In light of these findings, a number of patterns have emerged that provide fresh insights into many earlier observations that did not fit previous interpretative models. Furthermore, the addition of burial data from the earliest and latest levels of the site reveals that patterns of funerary behaviour were much less consistent throughout the occupation of the site than previously believed.

Case Study 1: Building 129

Between 2012 and 2015, several primary and primary disturbed subfloor burials located in the eastern platform area of Building 129 were found in association with loose crania and large amounts of disarticulated and partially

articulated infra-cranial remains (Haddow & Knüsel 2017; Knüsel et al. 2012). The variable treatment of human remains observed in Building 129 offers a microcosmic view of the range of variation in funerary practices encountered elsewhere at Çatalhöyük.

As noted earlier, loose crania and other disarticulated skeletal elements are often found in association with primary burials, but in some cases it is not always clear whether these derive from previously disturbed primary burials or were intentionally introduced into the grave from some other location. In this instance, however, it is clear that the supernumerary crania and other disarticulated remains did not derive from earlier burials in the same location but came from elsewhere.

Structure from Motion 3D modelling techniques enabled the identification of a retrieval pit located above the primary burial of an adult male in order to remove the cranium and mandible (Berggren et al. 2015; Haddow and Knüsel 2017). This type of retrieval pit has long been hypothesised to have been the means of obtaining crania at many Near Eastern Neolithic sites, but this is one of the few times, and the first at Çatalhöyük, that it has been confirmed archaeologically (see Goring-Morris and Horwitz 2007 for another case) due to difficulties in identifying smaller secondary pits stratigraphically. After the cranium and mandible were removed, partially and completely articulated remains of at least three individuals (including cranial and infra-cranial remains) were then placed in the pit before it was filled.

Case Study 2: Building 52

Beginning in 2013, two distinct skeletal assemblages were uncovered within adjacent platforms in Building 52 in the North Area of the site (Haddow et al. 2014, 2016, 2017; Knüsel et al. 2013). The two assemblages exhibit various degrees of commingling and represent the outcome of divergent funerary practices: one characterised by long-term, successive inhumations and the other by a single interment episode consisting of multiple individuals – a rare occurrence at the site. Each of these skeletal assemblages can be linked to the occupational history – or life course – of Building 52.

By analysing the manner in which the two sets of commingled remains from the northeast and northwest platforms were deposited, each assemblage reflects distinctive funerary behaviours that correspond to particular ways of entangling individuals (or parts of individuals) within Building 52 at different stages in its life course.

NORTHEAST PLATFORM

The skeletal remains of at least five individuals (three adults and two subadults), representing at least three separate burial events, were recovered from the northeast platform. These three interments occur at distinct phases in the use-life of the northeast platform. Compared with the northwest platform, which is lower in height, each primary interment in the northeast platform is separated by subsequent elevations and replasterings of the platform surface. There is also evidence that skeletal elements from the earliest burial were removed and later redeposited with the final interment.

NORTHWEST PLATFORM

The northwest platform contained the primary undisturbed remains of a middle adult male and at least six subadults in various states of articulation. Disarticulated subadult bones were also found scattered in the uppermost levels of the grave fill.

With the exception of a partial subadult skeleton deriving from an earlier burial in the same platform, it appears that all of these individuals were interred in a single burial event. Given their incomplete and partially articulated state, it appears that several of the subadults had been dead for some time before being buried with the adult. Where and for how long these remains were deposited or kept before being interred here is unknown, but in this sense, the subadults can be considered as secondary depositions, or even as grave inclusions.

Stratigraphically, this burial appears to be one of the last acts in the occupation of Building 52 before it was abandoned and intentionally burnt down. As such, it seems that the death of this adult male may have anticipated the abandonment and destruction of this building.

Case Study 3: Space 602

Another recent discovery has helped to bolster the new interpretative model and provides further food for thought. Unlike the majority of burials that occur during the occupation phase of houses, a series of intriguing inhumations was uncovered in 2015 within the infill of abandoned Building 132 (external Space 602) (Haddow et al. 2015). Two adult females, one adult male and an infant were recovered from separate grave cuts. Except for one grave (F.7634) located centrally within Space 602, their placement within the infill of Building 132 anticipated the layout of the north and eastern platforms of subsequent Building 77, which was constructed within the footprint of earlier Building 132. As such, these burials are among the very few found at Çatalhöyük that occurred in what would have been at the time an external space. Although the burials maintained a semblance of anatomical articulation, the bones themselves were very fragmentary and evinced multiple dry fractures. Additionally, many skeletal elements were out of place or missing entirely. In Feature 7632 (a young adult male, Sk. 21636) (Figure 12.2), for example, the left forearm of this individual was detached at the elbow and found tucked under the right upper limb (i.e. beneath the humerus) before the body was placed in the grave. In addition, the cranium was crushed flat, the base of the sacrum was rotated inferiorly and many of the thoracic vertebrae were no longer in articulation. The skeleton was very tightly flexed, and traces of phytoliths on the bones indicate that the body had been tightly bound (Haddow et al. 2015).

Each of the adults was buried with an unusually large and diverse number of grave

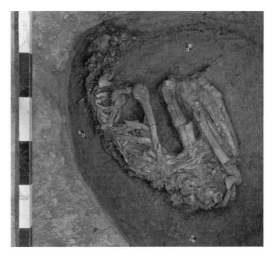

FIGURE 12.2 Burial F.7632, Sk (21636) in Space 602.

goods, including – variously – beads, obsidian and chipped stone blades, projectiles and scrapers, as well as a number of worked animal bone tools and pigment, some of which appears to have been applied directly to the bone. At this time, Building 132 was no longer occupied – only the shell of the house remained – and its successor, Building 77, had not yet been built.

Preservation of Organic Materials in Burnt Houses

While Mellaart uncovered a great deal of organic material, including textile, cord and wood from burnt houses at Çatalhöyük, it was not until 2009 that the Hodder-led team encountered and fully excavated such buildings. Since then, five burnt houses have been excavated, and each of these contained subplatform burials with exceptional preservation of organic material, including wooden bowls, animal hide, cord, textile, reed matting, basketry and in some cases carbonised human soft tissue. With the exception of phytolith impressions from reed baskets and matting, such findings are rare in unburnt contexts and furnish a glimpse of what were likely customary burial accompaniments at Çatalhöyük. The use of such materials suggest that great care was taken to tightly wrap and package the body, and this may have been done in order to retain the anatomical integrity of the body while it was kept above ground.

PUTTING TOGETHER THE PIECES: DELAYED BURIAL?

These recent observations have prompted a reexamination of previously excavated primary burials for similar anomalies. On closer inspection many primary skeletons do indeed show signs of an extended interval between death and final interment. Some skeletons are extremely hyperflexed, which suggests the removal or reduction of flesh prior to burial; such positions would likely be difficult to achieve if the body were fully fleshed. In addition, persistent joints such as the lumbar vertebrae, the knee, ankle and the sacro-iliac joint, as well as the humero-ulnar joint (as described in burial F.7632 earlier), are often disarticulated. Some bones are often out of place or missing entirely (e.g. basicranium, small bones of hands and feet). There are also differences in preservation between burials located in the same building and at times within the same platform. Last, the presence of packing and wrapping materials is associated with many of these tightly flexed inhumations.

Such observations suggest a number of potential behaviours, in particular the practice of delayed burial, in which the bodies of at least some members of the Neolithic population were kept above ground as part of a multistage funerary ritual that culminated in an intramural interment only after an extended interval above ground, possibly seasonal in nature, perhaps much longer. During this interval, soft tissue mass appears to have been reduced or removed without substantially compromising the anatomical integrity of the skeleton. If delayed burial was practiced at Neolithic Çatalhöyük, a number of questions arise: first, with regard to the manner in which bodies were presumably processed, and second, if there are spatio-temporal patterns underlying these and other secondary funerary practices. A number of potential means of removing or reducing soft tissue mass are currently being investigated, including the removal of flesh using tools or via exposure of the corpse to raptor scavenging, as well as rudimentary forms of natural mummification. The answers to these questions, especially regarding temporal changes, have important implications for our understanding of cognitive change and self-conception in the Neolithic.

Exposure and Excarnation (Anthropogenic versus Animal)

Manual excarnation, or the removal of flesh from a corpse using tools of some kind, has been observed in Neolithic contexts (see, for example, Erdal 2015; Robb et al. 2015) and may have been used at Çatalhöyük as a first stage in preparing a corpse for an extended period above ground. Verification of manual excarnation is typically made via the identification of linear markings on the diaphyseal surface of bones, either with the naked eye or microscopically (Fernández-Jalvo and Andrews 2016).

Exposure of the corpse as part of a delayed burial regimen has been proposed as the dominant funerary practice at Abu Hureyra in Syria (Moore and Molleson 2000). In Anatolia, clear cutmarks associated with flesh removal have been observed on a small percentage of human bones at PPNA Körtik Tepe (3.6% of 281 individuals) (Erdal 2015); if such practices occurred at Çatalhöyük they should also be observable. However, while cutmarks associated with bodily disarticulation (typically found in the vicinity of articular or peri-articular bone surfaces, i.e. joints) have been detected in a small number of cases (four individuals [2%] from primary disturbed contexts, one individual [0.6%] from a tertiary context), particularly pertaining to the separation of the head from the neck, there is an apparent lack of cutmarks associated with flesh removal. The overall frequency of cutmarks in the Çatalhöyük faunal assemblage is also low and has been attributed to the use of extremely sharp obsidian tools that lessens the need for deep cuts that would potentially leave marks on bone (Russell et al. 2013:241–242).

One of the more intriguing finds of Mellaart's excavations was a series of wall paintings depicting vultures attacking what look like headless bodies – these figures have been interpreted as depicting the process of excarnation prior to burial. During the current excavations, however, the idea of vulture excarnation playing a role in the funerary practices at Çatalhöyük was largely abandoned, as the predominant narrative surrounding funerary practices had moved away from the idea of delayed or secondary burial practices to a simplified model of death followed by immediate burial.

However, based on recent forensic taphonomic studies of raptor scavenging (Domínguez-Solera and Domínguez-Rodrigo 2011; Spradley et al. 2012), Pilloud et al. (2016) revisited the 'vulture hypothesis'. Raptorial birds are capable of stripping flesh from a corpse while leaving the body fully articulated, and they may do so while leaving very few, if any, marks on bones. While vulture excarnation cannot be established definitively in the absence of observable taphonomic evidence, there are a handful of unusual burials at Çatalhöyük in which such an interpretation may be justified. For example, Sk. 13609 from Building 49, was found missing both upper and lower limb elements, as well as the pectoral girdle (i.e. scapulae and claviculae). The axial skeleton, however, from the cranium to the sacrum, as well as the ribs and pelvic girdle remained in perfect articulation, and no cutmarks were observed on any of the bones (Pilloud et al. 2016). As such, the skeletal part representation of this individual could be compatible with more recent observations of raptor scavenging.

Mummification

Another means of preparing and preserving a corpse for an extended period above ground is by desiccation or mummification. Such techniques need not be as sophisticated as those practiced by the Ancient Egyptians, however. At the Bronze Age site at Cladh Hallan in the Western Isles of Scotland, for example, radiocarbon dating of the skeletal remains of two individuals revealed their remains to be several hundred years older than the building in which they were interred (Parker Pearson et al. 2005). One skeleton was revealed to be a composite of three different individuals, and histological analyses of the bones showed that the decomposition process had been artificially arrested soon after death via some form of mummification (Parker Pearson et al. 2005). A subsequent study has shown that rudimentary mummification practices were likely widespread in the British Bronze Age (Booth et al. 2015). The Cladh Hallan 'mummies', apparently kept in circulation for well over a hundred years, represent an extreme case of delayed burial but could explain the condition and appearance of some Çatalhöyük skeletons that show signs of an extended interval between death and burial, for example, the burials from Space 602 described earlier.

Possible methods for desiccating a corpse at Çatalhöyük may have included air-drying, smoking and other desiccating surface treatments such as the application of salts or ochre to the skin; or more advanced techniques such as the removal of internal organs to help reduce putrefaction. Combinations of these postmortem treatments are cross-cultural in nature and are documented *inter alia* for ancient Egypt (Aufderheide 2003; Papageorgopoulou et al. 2015), modern-day Papua New Guinea (Beckett et al. 2011; Beckett and Nelson 2015) and medieval Europe (e.g. Knüsel et al. 2010; Weiss-Krejci 2005).

Analytical Techniques

In the absence of preserved soft tissue, or cutmarks and other surface modifications of bone, microscopic analyses of bone using confocal and backscattered electron imaging are commonly used to characterise taphonomic changes associated with the burial of fleshed and unfleshed bodies (Bell 2012). For example, endogenous gut bacteria released during the early stages of decomposition are responsible for a particular pattern of bone microstructure alteration (Booth 2016; Jans et al. 2004; White and Booth 2014). As such, reduced levels of bacterial degradation of bone may indicate an intentional intervention by Neolithic peoples to reduce or halt the decomposition process, either through the removal (i.e. excarnation) or reduction (i.e. desiccation) of soft tissue body mass. Other histotaphonomic indicators that have the potential to identify particular types of body treatment, as well as burial environments, include collagen preservation (birefringence), microfissures, the inclusion of foreign materials in bone pores and staining (Hollund et al. 2012). These analyses are currently underway.

Spatio-Temporal Trends

There are substantial differences in the proportion of burial deposition categories between the three main excavation areas on the Neolithic East Mound at Çatalhöyük: North, South and TP/TPC/GDN. While the proportion of individuals from primary burials is nearly identical between the North and South Areas (68% and 66%, respectively), primary burials in the TP/TPC/GDN Areas make up only 37 per cent of the total number. Individuals from secondary contexts account for 13 per cent of the proportion of burials in the North Area and 3 per cent of the proportion in the South Area. In the TP/TPC/GDN Areas, however, secondary burials account for 43 per cent of the total number

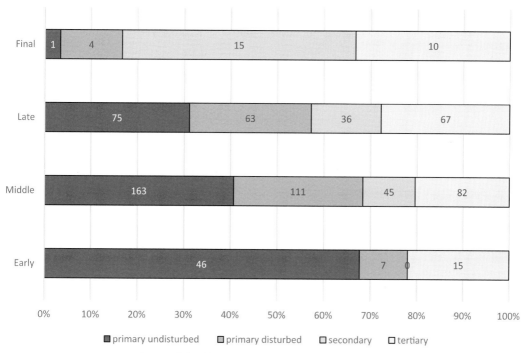

FIGURE 12.3 Temporal distribution of burial deposition categories through major occupation phases at Çatalhöyük.

of individuals. As we shall see, much – but not all – of the variation between excavation areas is due primarily to the occupation phases under excavation in each of these areas. For example, the South Area has the deepest stratigraphy, with material from the Early, Middle and Late occupation phases; the North Area contains only material from the Middle and Late phases, while the TP/TPC/GDN Areas have focused entirely on the Late and Final phases. The spatial locations of skeletal remains in secondary contexts vary substantially across the site. In fact, two North Area buildings, B.131 and B.129, account for 40 per cent of the total number of individuals found in secondary contexts. Building 131 contained the remains of 24 individuals (including 17 crania) in association with three separate primary burials, while

Building 129 contained the remains of 13 individuals (including 9 crania) in association with three separate primary burials. Building 129 was built on the footprint of the earlier Building 131 after it was abandoned and intentionally burnt. These two buildings are linked in other ways, including the very rare occurrence of obsidian mirrors in burials from both buildings.

Plotting changes in the proportion of burial deposition categories over time at Çatalhöyük (Figure 12.3) reveals that primary burials (undisturbed and disturbed) dominate the first three occupation phases at the site. Within the primary burial category, however, the proportion of undisturbed primary burials decreases substantially through time as disturbances of primary burials increase. These disturbances are usually the result of earlier burials being truncated by subsequent burials in the same house platform. As the proportion of primary burials decreases over time, the proportion of secondary deposits of human remains begins to rise. From the Early occupation phase, where no secondary burials have been found, the proportion increases steadily over time, eventually overtaking primary burials as the most common type of burial context in the Final occupation phase. In this phase, subfloor burials during the occupation of houses no longer took place. Instead, it appears that rooms or spaces were created within abandoned buildings for the accumulation of disturbed primary and secondary skeletal material (see, for example, discussion of Spaces 248 and 327 in Marciniak et al. 2015; Marciniak and Czerniak 2007). Last, the proportion of human remains found in tertiary contexts (i.e. middens, construction/abandonment infills) shows a slight increase over time, although it remains relatively stable in comparison to the primary and secondary deposition categories.

The increase in the proportion of individuals found in secondary contexts accords with trends observed across multiple data sets suggesting an increase in the mobility of the Çatalhöyük population over time as part of an ever-widening use of the landscape and its resources (e.g. Charles et al. 2014; Larsen et al. 2015; Pearson et al. 2007). Seen from this perspective, these secondary remains may represent individuals who died some distance from site and were not immediately returned for burial. As such, this temporal trend may be better characterised as a practical rather than cosmological shift in behaviour. As resource-acquisition regimes, availability and access tend to fluctuate seasonally, the trend is also more

consistent with prescheduled burial rites rather than a set liminal period. However, increased mobility does not sufficiently explain the rapid decrease in the proportion of primary burials between the Late and Final occupation phases. It is likely that there are multiple behaviours and intentions in operation here.

Another temporal trend worthy of note is the seeming increase in the degree of skeletal flexion over time. Primary burials from the earliest levels are more loosely flexed than burials from later levels, which might suggest that interments during the early occupation of Çatalhöyük occurred shortly after death while the body was still fully fleshed. In later levels, however, skeletons are usually found in less natural positions, with the upper and lower limbs typically more tightly flexed. Additional work is required in order to confirm these observations, however.

DISCUSSION

Given the excess of loose crania, mandibles and other disarticulated skeletal elements found in association with primary burial deposits and in other contexts, it seems likely that some segments of the population were never accorded a primary burial. Rather, their bodies, or in rarer cases parts of their bodies (primarily crania and sometimes mandibles), were retained for a time before eventually being deposited in a variety of contexts. Whether this practice occurred as part of a sharing/redistribution scheme for the purposes of social cohesion or stress alleviation, as many scholars have argued (see, for example, Whitehouse and Lanham 2004), is debatable. In fact, the presence of partial skeletons or disarticulated bones in secondary contexts at Çatalhöyük does not necessarily imply that bodies were 'partible' or that body parts were redistributed. The ratio of detached crania to 'headless' skeletons, for example, suggests that the redistribution of skeletal elements was a relatively rare occurrence. Thus, it may be time to de-emphasise 'skull retrieval and recirculation' at Çatalhöyük and replace it with an interpretative model in which bodies themselves appear to have circulated. In some cases, the loose or partially articulated skeletal elements found accompanying primary burials may actually represent what was left of an articulated corpse (originally held together by textile, hides, matting and cord) that was kept above ground for some time before gradually fragmenting and eventually being buried. In Medieval European contexts the cranium (and sometimes long bones) often served as a funerary synecdoche: the part that represents the whole, the head defining the place of burial (Binski 1996:55). Thus, many of the disarticulated bones found in secondary and perhaps tertiary contexts may represent the final deposition of a fragmented and skeletally incomplete individual, not the redistributed parts of a *dividual*. The important point here – and noted by other researchers (e.g. Croucher 2010; Goring-Morris and Belfer-Cohen 2014) – is that a one-size-fits-all model likely oversimplifies a situation in which multiple actions and intentions were at play.

Prescheduled/Seasonal Rites versus Prescribed Liminal Period?

One interpretation, offered originally by Mellaart (1964:92–94), is that intramural burials took place only at certain times of the year, when disruptions caused by opening holes in the platforms did not completely disrupt daily activities, perhaps during the spring or summer months. This possibility has also been raised by researchers on the current project (e.g. Fairbairn et al. 2005; Matthews 2005), but it has never been properly investigated until recently. If inhumations were scheduled on a seasonal basis, the variations in the degree of flexion and skeletal articulation observed among burials would reflect the amount of time between an individual's death and the burial rite itself. Alternatively, there may have been a prescribed liminal period between death and interment. Many social groups employ a very short liminal period, for example in Jewish and Islamic funeral traditions, while other cultures exercise a much longer interval, even decades (Metcalf 1981:576). If a prescribed liminal period was employed at Çatalhöyük, a standard level of flexion/articulation across all burials would be expected, but the observed variation argues against this interpretation. However, it could be that the liminal period was longer for some individuals than it was for others. The challenge is then to decode the selection criteria employed by the Neolithic inhabitants of Çatalhöyük. Obvious possibilities include age and sex groupings, membership in sodalities or in other social groups, or the social circumstances in which death occurred.

A delay in burial for some individuals might also reflect more practical considerations. Some inhabitants of Çatalhöyük likely spent a good part of the year away from the site as part of a seasonal cycle of resource management/acquisition, e.g. hunting, harvesting timber, sheep/goat pastoralism, obsidian and groundstone procurement, etc. (Asouti 2013; Charles et al. 2014; Fairbairn et al. 2005). Thus, some secondary burials may represent individuals who died away from site and were eventually returned for burial after the body had partially/fully decomposed. Variation in the degree of flexion and skeletal articulation might then reflect the amount of time before a body could be returned to Çatalhöyük for burial. Perhaps communal burial rites were scheduled at times during the year when the bulk of the population were most likely to be on site (Matthews 2005).

Other considerations include pragmatic issues of public hygiene associated with living in proximity to decomposing corpses such as escaping gases and insect infestation. The burial of a fully fleshed corpse under the floor of a house would also create structural instabilities caused by soil subsidence as soft tissue body mass is lost during decomposition.

Regional Comparisons

It is during the Final occupation phase at Çatalhöyük that the burial practices begin to resemble certain Late PPNB and Early Pottery Neolithic sites in the Levant and Mesopotamia, in which there appear to be very few burials within the settlement (e.g. Banning 1998; Bienert et al. 2004; Goring-Morris 2005; Rollefson 2001). Some researchers have interpreted this apparent selection for particular individuals as representing a form of early social differentiation (Rollefson 2002). Furthermore, Rollefson (2002) observes a similar increase in the proportion of secondary burial during the PPNC levels at 'Ain Ghazal. There are also similarities between

Late/Final phase Çatalhöyük and Late Neolithic Tell Sabi Abyad in Syria, where burials were found in abandoned rather than occupied houses (Akkermans 2008). Last, the burnt structure at LPPNB Bouqras in northern Iraq has been interpreted as a charnel structure for the storage and processing of bodies before final interment (Merrett and Meiklejohn 2007). This structure, as well as the 'collective burials' found at Late PPNB Ba'ja in Jordan (Gebel et al. 2006), appears somewhat similar to the 'burial chambers' (Spaces 248 and 327) in abandoned houses in the Final occupation phases at Çatalhöyük (Marciniak et al. 2015; Marciniak and Czerniak 2007).

CONCLUSIONS: EQUIFINALITY AND INTENTION

Returning to the question of whether or not there is evidence for a greater awareness of an integrated personal self, the funerary data do not appear to support the original argument as currently formulated: that an emerging sense of bounded identity and personal autonomy should be tied with a corresponding decrease in secondary burial (the fading of the so-called dividual). In fact, the increase in the proportion of human remains found in secondary and tertiary contexts observed at Çatalhöyük is exactly the opposite of what one would expect, as bodies actually become more fragmented over time, until 'whole bodies' (e.g. undisturbed primary burials) nearly disappear from the site. This trend continues in the early Chalcolithic settlement established on the West Mound at Çatalhöyük, where human remains in any context within the settlement are almost completely absent (Anvari et al. 2017; Biehl 2012).

If the original argument is turned on its head, however, the increase in human remains found in secondary/tertiary contexts (and the corresponding reduction in primary burials) during the Late and Final occupation phases at Çatalhöyük could be interpreted instead as representing a shift from an earlier egalitarian/collective mentality towards one in which certain people are singled out for secondary/delayed treatments as part of an emerging focus on particularly significant individuals – perhaps as part of a trend towards increased social differentiation/complexity. As we have seen, there are fewer primary burials on the Neolithic Çatalhöyük East Mound over time. And during the subsequent Chalcolithic occupation of the West Mound, burials within the settlement itself are almost entirely absent. Perhaps, then, primary burials at Çatalhöyük East represent a standard/collective mode of burial, while the secondary remains and delayed primary burials represent special treatments reserved for 'special individuals' – or 'special groups'. As secondary treatments increase through time, this could be interpreted as an increased focus on particular individuals/groups, although increased mobility and off-site deaths cannot be excluded here. If this was the case, however, it suggests that effort was expended to bring remains back to the site for burial, which suggests a strong sense of connection to the site and perhaps a special status associated with being interred there.

Furthermore, the reduced number of primary burials over time may represent a reduced emphasis on collectivism and social memory tied to houses, which is demonstrated in other Çatalhöyük data sets, for example the reduction in large-scale feasting activities; houses become more autonomous both spatially and in terms of production; symbolic systems previously linked with the house such as wall paintings and animal installations start to become portable with the emergence of stamp seals and eventually painted pottery on the Chalcolithic West Mound (Hodder 2014; Hodder and Doherty 2014; Marciniak et al. 2015; Marciniak and Czerniak 2007). Perhaps bodies (and increasingly only particular bodies) become more portable as well and less tied to houses.

In shifting from a macroscale view to a more fine-grained analysis of the funerary practices at Çatalhöyük, subtle patterns likely reflecting a much wider range of intentional behaviours than previously conceived begin to emerge. Furthermore, the addition of data from the earliest and latest levels of the site reveals unequivocal evidence of temporal changes in burial practices. It is clear that the increasing occurrence of disturbed, secondary and commingled remains at the site masks a variety of pathways that bodies, whole or fragmented, seem to have taken before their final deposition under house floors, external spaces or other contexts. For some individuals, however, the journey appears to have lasted longer than that of others. Decoding the motivations behind these practices and distinguishing between the equifinal behaviours that culminate in the archaeological record requires careful attention to the stratigraphic links between burial sequences and grave fills, as well as meticulous osteological and taphonomic analyses. In order to adequately address higher-level questions of sociocultural behaviour and cognitive change, it is crucial that these fundamental archaeological issues are sufficiently resolved.

While the rapid sociocultural changes observed during the Neolithic period have been described by some researchers as a part of a 'cognitive revolution' (e.g. Mithen 2004; Watkins 2010), archaeological data from the Upper Palaeolithic – including clearly intentional burial practices – have led other researchers to draw analogous conclusions for preceding periods (D'Errico and Vanhaeren 2016; Formicola 2007; Klein 2000; Mellars and Stringer 1989; Zilhão 2007; Zilhão et al. 2010). Similarly, sophisticated and highly flexible forms of sociopolitical organisation also appear to have existed well before the adoption of agriculture and animal husbandry (see Bar-Yosef 2002; Trinkaus and Buzhilova 2018; Vanhaeran and D'Errico 2005; Wengrow and Graeber 2015). With over a thousand years of Neolithic occupation and nearly 30 years of archaeological excavations conducted there, Çatalhöyük would appear to be an ideal source of data for detailed investigations of long-term sociocultural change. However, for wide-ranging and profound inquiries such as the emergence of consciousness and the nature of the mind, 1,000 years may not provide the time-depth required to properly address questions of this nature, and especially because Çatalhöyük occurs towards the end of the Neolithic period rather than at the beginning. As such, it will be necessary to take an even longer view, incorporating data from other sites and time periods.

REFERENCES

Akkermans Peter M. M. G. 2008. Burying the dead in Late Neolithic Syria. In *Proceedings of the 5th International Congress on the Archaeology of the Ancient Near East*, edited by J. M. Cordoba, M. Molist, C. Perez, I. Rubio, and S. Martinez. Madrid: Universidad Autónoma of Madrid, pp. 621–645.

Andrews, Peter and Silvia Bello. 2006. Pattern in human burial practice. In *The Social Archaeology of Funerary Remains*, edited by Christopher Knüsel and Rebecca Gowland. Oxford, UK: Oxbow, pp. 14–29.

Andrews, Peter, Theya Molleson and Başak Boz. 2005. The human burials at Çatalhöyük. In *Inhabiting Çatalhöyük: Reports from the 1995–99 Seasons*, edited by Ian Hodder. McDonald Institute for Archaeological Research and British Institute of Archaeology at Ankara, Cambridge, pp. 261–278.

Anvari, Jana, Jacob Brady, Ingmar Franz, Goce Naumov, David Orton, Sonja Ostaptchouk, Elizabeth Stroud, Patrick T. Willett, Eva Rosenstock and Peter F. Biehl. 2017. Continuous change: Venturing into the early Chalcolithic at Çatalhöyük. In *The Archaeology of Anatolia Volume II: Recent Discoveries (2015–2016)*, edited by Sharon R. Steadman and Gregory McMahon. Lady Stephenson Library, Newcastle upon Tyne (UK): Cambridge Scholars Publishing, pp. 6–39.

Asouti, Eleni. 2013. Woodland vegetation, firewood management and woodcrafts at Neolithic Çatalhöyük. In *Humans and Landscapes of Çatalhöyük: Reports from the 2000–2008 Seasons*, edited by Ian Hodder. Los Angeles, CA: British Institute at Ankara and Cotsen Institute of Archaeology Press, pp. 129–162.

Aufderheide, Arthur. 2003. *The Scientific Study of Mummies*. Cambridge, UK: Cambridge University Press.

Banning, Edward B. 1998. The Neolithic Period: Triumphs of architecture, agriculture and art. *Near Eastern Archaeology* 61(4):188–237.

Bar-Yosef, Ofer. 2002. The Upper Palaeolithic revolution. *Annual Review of Anthropology* 31:363–393.

Bayliss, Alex, Fiona Brock, Shahina Farid, Ian Hodder, John Southon and R. Ervin Taylor. 2015. Getting to the bottom of it all: A Bayesian approach to dating the start of Çatalhöyük. *Journal of World Prehistory* 28:1–26.

Beckett, Ronald G., Ulla Lohmann and Josh Bernstein. 2011. A field report on the mummification practices of the Anga of Koke Village, Central Highlands, Papua New Guinea. *Yearbook of Mummy Studies*, 1:11–17.

Beckett, Ronald G. and Andrew J. Nelson. 2015. Mummy restoration project among the Anga of Papua New Guinea. *The Anatomical Record* 298:1013–1025.

Bell, Lynne S. (ed.) 2012. *Forensic Microscopy for Skeletal Tissues*. New York: Springer.

Berggren, Åsa, Nicoló Dell'Unto, Maurizio Forte, Scott Haddow, Ian Hodder, Justine Issavi, Nicola Lercari, Camilla Mazzucato, Alison Mickel and James S. Taylor. 2015. Revisiting reflexive archaeology at Çatalhöyük: Integrating digital and 3D technologies at the trowel's edge. *Antiquity* 89:433–448.

Biehl, Peter. 2012. The transition of the megasite Çatalhöyük in the Late Neolithic and Early Chalcolithic. In *Proceedings of the 7th International Congress on the Archaeology of the Ancient Near East. Volume I: Mega-Cities and Mega-Sites. The Archaeology of Consumption and Disposal, Landscape, Transport and Communication*, edited by R. Matthews & J. Curtis. Wiesbaden: Harrassowitz, pp. 17–34.

Bienert, Hans-Dieter, Michelle Bonogofsky, Hans G. K. Gebel, Ian Kuijt and Gary O. Rollefson. 2004. Where are the dead? In *Central Settlements in Neolithic Jordan*, edited by H.-D. Bienert, H. G. K. Gebel, and R. Neef. Studies in Early Near Eastern Production, Subsistence and Environment 5. Berlin: Ex-oriente, pp. 157–176.

Binski, Paul. 1996. *Medieval Death: Ritual and Representation*. London: The British Museum Press.

Bocquentin, Fanny, Ergul Kodas and Anabel Ortiz. 2016. Headless but still eloquent! Acephalous skeletons as witnesses of Pre-Pottery Neolithic North-South Levant connections and disconnections. *Paléorient* 42(2):35–55.

Booth, Thomas, J. 2016. An investigation into the relationship between funerary treatment and bacterial bioerosion in European archaeological human bone. *Archaeometry* 58 (3):484–499.

Booth, Thomas J., Andrew T. Chamberlain and Mike Parker Pearson. 2015. Mummification in Bronze Age Britain. *Antiquity* 89(347):1155–1173.

Boz, Başak and Lori D. Hager. 2013. Living above the dead: Intramural burial practices at Çatalhöyük. In *Humans and Landscapes of Çatalhöyük: Reports from the 2000–2008 Seasons*, edited by Ian Hodder. Los Angeles, CA: British Institute at Ankara and Cotsen Institute of Archaeology Press, pp. 413–440.

Boz, Başak and Lori D. Hager. 2014. Making sense of social behaviour from disturbed and commingled skeletons: A case study from Çatalhöyük, Turkey. In *Commingled and Disarticulated Human Remains: Working toward Improved Theory, Method and Data*, edited by Anna J. Osterholtz, Katherine M. Baustian, and Debra L. Martin. New York: Springer, pp. 17–33.

Carr, Christopher. 1995. Mortuary practices: Their social, philosophical-religious, circumstantial and physical determinants. *Journal of Archaeological Method and Theory* 2(2):105–200.

Chapman, John. 2010. 'Deviant' burials in the Neolithic and Chalcolithic of Central and South Eastern Europe. In *Body Parts and Bodies Whole: Changing Relations and Meanings*, edited by Katharina Rebay-Salisbury, Marie-Louise S. Sorensen, and Juliet Hughes. Oxford, UK: Oxbow, pp. 30–45.

Charles, Michael, Christopher Doherty, Eleni Asouti, Amy Bogaard, Elizabeth Henton, Clark Spencer Larsen, Christopher B. Ruff, Philippa Ryan, Joshua W. Sadvari and Kathryn C. Twiss. 2014. Landscape and taskscape at Çatalhöyük: An integrated perspective. In *Integrating Çatalhöyük: Themes from the 2000–2008 Seasons*, edited by Ian Hodder. Los Angeles, CA: British Institute at Ankara and Cotsen Institute of Archaeology Press, pp. 71–90.

Crevecoeur, Isabelle, Aurore Schmitt and Ilse Schoep. 2015. An archaeothanatological approach to the study of Minoan funerary practices: Case-studies from the Early and Middle Minoan cemetery at Sissi, Crete. *Journal of Field Archaeology* 40:283–299.

Croucher, Karina. 2006. Getting ahead: Exploring meanings of skulls in the Neolithic Near East. In

Skull Collection, Modification and Decoration, edited by Michelle Bonogofsky. Oxford, UK: Archaeopress pp. 29–44.

Croucher, Karina. 2010. Bodies in pieces in the Neolithic Near East. In *Body Parts and Bodies Whole: Changing Relations and Meanings*, edited by Katharina Rebay-Salisbury, Marie-Louise S. Sorensen, and Juliet Hughes. Oxford, UK: Oxbow, pp. 6–19.

Czeszewska, Agata. 2014. Wall paintings at Çatalhöyük. In *Integrating Çatalhöyük: Themes from the 2000–2008 seasons*, edited by I. Hodder. Los Angeles, CA: Cotsen Institute of Archaeology, pp. 185–196.

D'Errico, Francesco and Marian Vanhaeren. 2016. Upper Palaeolithic mortuary practices: Reflection of ethnic affiliation, social complexity, and cultural turnover. In *Death Rituals, Social Order and the Archaeology of Immortality in the Ancient World 'Death Shall Have No Dominion'* edited by C. Renfrew, M. J. Boyd, and I. Morley. Cambridge, UK: Cambridge University Press, pp. 45–64.

Domínguez-Solera, Santiago and Manuel Domínguez-Rodrigo. 2011. A taphonomic study of a carcass consumed by griffon vultures (*Gyps fulvus*) and its relevance for the interpretation of bone surface modifications. *Archaeological and Anthropological Sciences* 3(4):385–392.

Duday Henri. 2008. Archaeological proof of an abrupt mortality crisis; simultaneous deposit of cadavers, simultaneous deaths? In *Palaeomicrobiology: Past Human Infections*, edited by Didier Raoult and Michel Drancourt. Berlin: Springer, pp. 49–54.

Erdal, Yilmaz S. 2015. Bone or flesh: Defleshing and post-depositional treatments at Körtik Tepe (Southeastern Anatolia, PPNA Period). *European Journal of Archaeology* 18(1):4–32.

Fairbairn, Andrew, Eleni Asouti, Nerissa Russell and John G. Swogger. 2005. Seasonality. In *Çatalhöyük Perspectives: Themes from the 1995–99 Seasons*, edited by Ian Hodder. Cambridge, UK: McDonald Institute for Archaeological Research and British Institute of Archaeology at Ankara, pp. 93–108.

Farid, Shahina. 2014. Timelines: Phasing Neolithic Çatalhöyük. In *Çatalhöyük Excavations: The 2000–2008 Seasons*, edited by Ian Hodder. Los Angeles, CA: British Institute at Ankara and Cotsen Institute of Archaeology Press, pp. 91–129.

Fernández-Jalvo, Yolanda and Peter Andrews. 2016. *Atlas of Taphonomic Identifications*. Dordrecht: Springer.

Formicola, Vincenzo. 2007. From the Sunghir children to the Romito dwarf: Aspects of the Upper Palaeolithic funerary landscape. *Current Anthropology* 48(3):446–453.

Fowler, Christopher. 2004. *The Archaeology of Personhood: An Anthropological Approach*. London: Routledge.

Gebel, Hans-Georg K., B. D. Hermansen and M. Kinzel. 2006. Ba'ja 2005: A two-storied building and collective burials. Results of the 6th season of excavation. *Neo-Lithics* 1(6):12–19.

Goring-Morris, Nigel. 2005. Life, death and the emergence of differential status in the Near Eastern Neolithic: Evidence from Kfar HaHoresh, Lower Galilee, Israel. In *Archaeological Perspectives on the Transmission and Transformation of Culture in the Eastern Mediterranean*, edited by Joanne Clark. Oxford, UK: CBRL and Oxbow, pp. 89–105.

Goring-Morris, A. Nigel and Anna Belfer-Cohen. 2014. Different strokes for different folks: Near Eastern Neolithic mortuary practices in perspective. In *Religion at Work in a Neolithic Society: Vital Matters*, edited by Ian Hodder. Cambridge, UK: Cambridge University Press, pp. 35–57.

Goring-Morris, A. N. and L. K. Horwitz. 2007. Funerals and feasts during the Pre-Pottery Neolithic B of the Near East. *Antiquity* 81:902–919.

Haddow, Scott and Christopher J. Knüsel. 2017. Skull retrieval and secondary burial practices in the Neolithic Near East: Recent insights from Çatalhöyük, Turkey. *Bioarchaeology International* 1:52–71.

Haddow, Scott, Christopher J. Knüsel and Marco Milella. 2014. Human remains. In *Çatalhöyük 2014 Archive Report*, pp. 80–92. www.catalhoyuk.com/sites/default/files/media/pdf/Archive_Report_2014.pdf.

Haddow, Scott, Christopher J. Knüsel, Belinda Tibbetts, Marco Milella and Barbara Betz. 2015. Human remains. In *Çatalhöyük 2015 Archive Report*, pp. 85–101. www.catalhoyuk.com/sites/default/files/media/pdf/Archive_Report_2015.pdf.

Haddow, Scott, Marco Milella, Belinda Tibbetts, Eline Schotsmans and Christopher J. Knüsel. 2017. Human remains. In *Çatalhöyük 2017 Archive Report*, pp. 103–141. www.catalhoyuk.com/sites/default/files/media/pdf/Archive_Report_2017.pdf.

Haddow, Scott D., Joshua W. Sadvari, Christopher J. Knüsel and Remi Hadad. 2016. A tale of two platforms: Commingled remains and the life-course of houses at Neolithic Çatalhöyük. In *Theoretical Approaches to Analysis and Interpretation of Commingled Human Remains*, edited by Anna J. Osterholtz. New York: Springer, pp. 5–29.

Hodder, Ian. 2006. *The Leopard's Tale: Revealing the Mysteries of Çatalhöyük*. London: Thames and Hudson.

Hodder, Ian. 2011. An archaeology of the self: The prehistory of personhood. In *In Search of Self*, edited by J. W. van Huyssteen and E. P. Wiebe. Grand Rapids, MI: Eerdmans, pp. 50–69.

Hodder, Ian. 2014. Çatalhöyük: The leopard changes its spots: A summary of recent work. *Anatolian Studies* 64:1–22.

Hodder, Ian and Craig Cessford. 2004. Daily practice and social memory at Çatalhöyük. *American Antiquity* 69(1):17–40.

Hodder, Ian and Christopher Doherty. 2014. Temporal trends: The shapes and narratives of cultural change at Çatalhöyük. In *Integrating Çatalhöyük: Themes from the 2000–2008 Seasons*, edited by Ian Hodder. Los Angeles, CA: British Institute at Ankara and Cotsen Institute of Archaeology, pp. 169–183.

Hollund, H. I., M. M. E. Jans, M. J. Collins, H. Kars, I. Joosten and S. M. Kars. 2012. What happened here? Bone histology as a tool in decoding the postmortem histories of archaeological bone from Castricum, The Netherlands. *International Journal of Osteoarchaeology*, 22(5):537–548.

Jans, M. M. E., C. M. Nielsen-Marsh, C. I. Smith, M. J. Collins and H. Kars. 2004. Characterisation of microbial attack on archaeological bone. *Journal of Archaeological Science* 31:87–95.

Klein, Richard G. 2000. Archaeology and the evolution of human behavior. *Evolutionary Anthropology* 9:17–36.

Knüsel, Christopher J., Catherine M. Batt, Gordon Cook, Janet Montgomery, Gundula Müldner, Alan R. Ogden, Carol Palmer, Ben Stern, John Todd and Andrew S. Wilson. 2010. The identity of the St. Bees Lady, Cumbria: An osteo-biographical approach. *Medieval Archaeology* 54:275–317.

Knüsel, Christopher J., Scott D. Haddow, Joshua Sadvari and Barbara Betz. 2013. Çatalhöyük Human Remains Team Archive Report 2013. Çatalhöyük 2013 Archive Report, pp. 111–133. www.catalhoyuk.com/sites/default/files/media/pdf/Archive_Report_2013.pdf.

Knüsel, Christopher J., Scott D. Haddow, Joshua Sadvari and Jennifer Byrnes. 2012. Çatalhöyük Human Remains Team Archive Report 2012. Çatalhöyük 2012 Archive Report, pp. 132–154. www.catalhoyuk.com/sites/default/files/media/pdf/Archive_Report_2012.pdf.

Knüsel, Christopher J. and John E. Robb. 2016. Funerary taphonomy: An overview of goals and methods. *Journal of Archaeological Science: Reports*, Special Issue on Funerary Taphonomy, edited by Christopher J. Knüsel and John E. Robb. 10:655–673.

Kuijt, Ian. 2000. Keeping the peace: Ritual, skull caching, and community integration in the Levantine Neolithic. In *Life in Neolithic Farming Communities: Social Organization, Identity, and Differentiation*, edited by Ian Kuijt. New York: Kluwer Academic/Plenum Publishers, pp. 137–164.

Kuijt, Ian. 2001. Place, death and the transmission of social memory in early agricultural communities of the Near Eastern Pre-Pottery Neolithic. *Archaeological Papers of the American Anthropological Association* 10:80–99.

Kuijt, Ian. 2008. The regeneration of life: Neolithic structures of symbolic remembering and forgetting. *Current Anthropology* 49(2):171–197.

Larsen, Clark Spencer, Simon W. Hillson, Başak Boz, Marin A. Pilloud, Joshua W. Sadvari, Sabrina C. Agarwal, Bonnie Glencross, Patrick Beauchesne, Jessica Pearson, Christopher B. Ruff, Evan M. Garofalo, Lori D. Hager, Scott D. Haddow and Christopher J. Knüsel. 2015. Bioarchaeology of Neolithic Çatalhöyük: Lives and lifestyles of an early farming society in transition. *Journal of World Prehistory* 28:27–68.

Lorentz, Kirsi O. 2010. Parts to a whole: Manipulations of the body in prehistoric Eastern Mediterranean. In *Body Parts and Bodies Whole: Changing Relations and Meanings*, edited by Katharina Rebay-Salisbury, Marie Louise Stig Sørensen, and Jessica Hughes. Oxford, UK: Oxbow Books, pp. 20–29.

Marciniak, Arkadiusz, Marek Z. Barański, Alex Bayliss, Lech Czerniak, Tomasz Goslar, John Southon and R. E. Taylor. 2015. Fragmenting times: Interpreting a Bayesian chronology for the Late Neolithic occupation of Çatalhöyük East, Turkey. *Antiquity* 89:154–176.

Marciniak, Arkadiusz and Lech Czerniak. 2007. Social transformations in the Late Neolithic and the Early Chalcolithic periods in Central Anatolia. *Anatolian Studies* 57:115–130.

Marriott, McKim. 1976. Hindu transactions: Diversity without dualism. In *Transaction and Meaning: Directions in the Anthropology of Exchange and Symbolic Behaviour*, edited by B. Kapferer. Philadelphia, PA: Institute for the Study of Human Issues, pp. 109–137.

Matthews, Wendy. 2005. Life-cycles and life-courses of buildings. In *Çatalhöyük Perspectives: Themes from the 1995–99 Seasons*, edited by Ian Hodder. Cambridge, UK: McDonald Institute for Archaeological Research and British Institute of Archaeology at Ankara, pp. 125–149.

Mellaart, James 1964. Excavations at Çatal Hüyük, 1963, third preliminary report. *Anatolian Studies* 14:39–119.

Mellaart, James. 1962. Excavations at Çatal Hüyük, first preliminary report, 1961. *Anatolian Studies* 12:41–65.

Mellaart, James. 1967. *Catal Huyuk: A Neolithic Town in Anatolia*. London: Thames & Hudson.

Mellars, Paul and Christopher Stringer 1989. *The Human Revolution: Behavioural and Biological Perspectives on the Origins of Modern Humans*. Edinburgh: Edinburgh University Press.

Merrett, Deborah C. and Christopher Meiklejohn. 2007. Is House 12 at Bouqras a charnel house? In *Faces from the Past. Skeletal Biology of Human*

Populations from the Eastern Mediterranean. (British Archaeological Reports International Series 1603) edited by M. Faerman, L. Kolska Horwitz, T. Kahana and U. Zilberman. Oxford: Archaeopress, pp. 127–139.

Metcalf, P. 1981. Meaning and materialism. The ritual economy of death. *Man* (New Series) 16(4):563–578.

Mithen, Steven J. 2004. Human evolution and the cognitive basis of science. In *The Cognitive Basis of Science*, edited by P. Carruthers, S. Stich, and M. Siegal. Cambridge, UK: Cambridge University Press, pp. 23–40.

Moore, Andrew M. T. & Theya I. Molleson. 2000. Disposal of the dead. In *Village on the Euphrates: From Foraging to Farming at Abu Hureyra*, edited by A. M. T. Moore, G. C. Hillman & A. J. Legge. Oxford, UK: Oxford University Press, pp. 277–299.

Papageorgopoulou, Christina, Natallia Shved, Johann Wanek and Frank J. Rühli. 2015. Modeling Ancient Egyptian mummification on fresh human tissue: Macroscopic and histological aspects. *The Anatomical Record* 298:974–987.

Parker Pearson, Michael, Andrew Chamberlain, Oliver Craig, Peter Marshall, Jacqui Mulville, Helen Smith, Carolyn Chenery, Matthew Collins, Gordon Cook, Geoffrey Craig, Jane Evans, Jen Hiller, Janet Montgomery, Jean-Luc Schwenninger, Gillian Taylor and Timothy Wess. 2005. Evidence for mummification in Bronze Age Britain. *Antiquity* 79(305):529–546.

Pearson, Jessica, Hijlke Buitenhuis, Robert Hedges, Louise Martin, Nerissa Russell and Katheryn Twiss. 2007. New light on early caprine herding strategies from isotope analysis: A case study from Neolithic Anatolia. *Journal of Archaeological Science* 34:2170–2179.

Pilloud, Marin, Scott D. Haddow, Christopher J. Knüsel and Clark Spencer Larsen. 2016. A bioarchaeological and forensic re-assessment of vulture defleshing and mortuary practices at Neolithic Çatalhöyük. *Journal of Archaeological Science: Reports* 10:735–743. DOI:10.1016/j. jasrep.2016.05.029.

Robb, John E. 2013. Creating death/an archaeology of dying. In *The Oxford Handbook of the Archaeology* of Death and Burial, edited by Liv Nilsson Stutz and Sarah Tarlow. Oxford, UK: Oxford University Press, pp. 441–457.

Robb, John E., Ernestine Elster, Eugenia Isetti, Christopher J. Knüsel, Mary Anne Tafuri and Antonella Traverso. 2015. Cleaning the dead: Neolithic ritual processing of human bone at Scaloria Cave, Italy. Antiquity 89(343):39–54.

Rollefson, Gary O. 2001. The Neolithic period. In The Archaeology of Jordan, edited by B. McDonald, R. Adams and P. Bienkowski. Sheffield: Sheffield Academic Press, pp. 67–105.

Rollefson, Gary O. 2002. Ritual and social structure and Neolithic 'Ain Ghazal. In Life in Neolithic Farming Communities: Social Organization, Identity, and Differentiation, edited by Ian Kuijt. New York: Kluwer Academic. pp. 165–190.

Russell, Nerissa, Katheryn C. Twiss, David C. Orton and G. Arzu Demirergi. 2013. More on the Çatalhöyük mammal remains. In Humans and Landscapes of Çatalhöyük: Reports from the 2000–2008 Seasons, edited by Ian Hodder. Los Angeles, CA: British Institute at Ankara and Cotsen Institute of Archaeology Press, pp. 213–253.

Russell, Nerissa, Katherine I. Wright, Tristan Carter, Sheena Ketchum, Philippa Ryan, Nurcan Yalman, Roddy Reagan, Mirjana Stevanović and Marina Milić. 2014. Bringing down the house: House closing deposits at Çatalhöyük. In Integrating Çatalhöyük: Themes from the 2000–2008 Seasons, edited by Ian Hodder. Los Angeles, CA: Cotsen Institute of Archaeology, pp. 109–121.

Sadarangani, Freya. 2014. The sequence of Buildings 53 and 42 and external spaces 259, 260 and 261. In Çatalhöyük Excavations: The 2000–2008 Seasons, edited by Ian Hodder. Los Angeles, CA: British Institute at Ankara and Cotsen Institute of Archaeology Press, pp. 191–219.

Spradley, M. Katherine, Michelle D. Hamilton and Alberto Giordano. 2012. Spatial patterning of vulture scavenged human remains. Forensic Science International 219:57–63.

Strathern, Marilyn 1988. The Gender of the Gift: Problems with Women and Problems with Society in Melanesia. Berkeley: University of California Press.

Tibbetts, Belinda. 2017. Perinatal death and cultural buffering in a Neolithic community. In Children, Death and Burial: Archaeological Discourses, edited by E. Murphy and M. Le Roy. Oxford, UK: Oxbow Books, pp. 35–42.

Trinkaus, Erik and Alexandra Buzhilova. 2018. Diversity and differential disposal of the dead at Sunghir. Antiquity 92(361):7–21.

Vanhaeren, Marian and Francesco d'Errico. 2005. Grave goods from the Saint-Germain-la-Rivière burial: Evidence for social inequality in the Upper Palaeolithic. Journal of Anthropological Archaeology 24:117–134.

Van Huyssteen, Wentzel. 2014. The historical self: Memory and religion at Çatalhöyük. In Religion at Work in a Neolithic Society: Vital Matters, edited by I. Hodder. Cambridge, UK: Cambridge University Press, pp. 109–133.

Verhoeven, Marc. 2002. Ritual and ideology in the Pre-Pottery Neolithic B of the Levant and Southeast Anatolia. Cambridge Archaeology Journal 12 (2):233–258.

Watkins, Trevor. 2010. Changing people, changing environments: How hunter-gatherers became communities that changed the world. In Landscapes in Transition, edited by B. Finlayson and G. Warren. Oxford, UK: Oxbow Books, pp. 106–114.

Weiss-Krejci, Estella. 2005. Excarnation, evisceration, and exhumation in medieval and postmedieval Europe. In Interacting with the Dead. Perspectives on Mortuary Archaeology for the New Millennium, edited by Gordon Rakita, Jane Buikstra, Lane Beck, and Sloan Williams. Gainesville: University Press of Florida, pp. 155–172.

Wengrow, David and David Graeber. 2015. Farewell to the 'childhood of man': Ritual, seasonality, and the origins of inequality. Journal of the Royal Anthropological Institute (N.S.) 21:597–619.

White, Lorraine and Thomas J. Booth. 2014. The origin of bacteria responsible for bioerosion to the internal bone microstructure: Results from experimentally-deposited pig carcasses. Forensic Science International, 239:92–102.

Whitehouse, Harvey and Jonathan A. Lanman, 2014. The ties that bind us. *Current Anthropology* 55 (6):674–695.

Zilhão, João. 2007. The emergence of ornaments and art: An archaeological perspective on the origins of behavioural 'modernity'. *Journal of Archaeological Research* 15:1–54.

Zilhão, João, Diego E. Angelucci, Ernestina Badal-García, Francesco d'Errico, Floréal Daniel, Laure Dayet, Katerina Douka, Thomas F. G. Higham, María José Martínez-Sánchez, Ricardo Montes-Bernárdez, Sonia Murcia-Mascarós, Carmen Pérez-Sirvent, Clodoaldo Roldán-García, Marian Vanhaeren, Valentín Villaverde, Rachel Wood and Josefina Zapata. 2010. Symbolic use of marine shells and mineral pigments by Iberian Neandertals. *Proceedings of the National Academy of Sciences* 107(3):1023–1028.

NEW BODIES: FROM HOUSES TO HUMANS AT ÇATALHÖYÜK

Anna Fagan

THE SUBJECT OF THIS CHAPTER CONSISTS OF a relational and ontological approach to the fundamental social changes that occurred at Çatalhöyük from 6,500 BCE and the revolutions in notions of selfhood and autonomy that followed. Previous explorations of personhood in the literature on the Neolithic in Southwest Asia, however, have relied heavily on post-Enlightenment Western conceptual dichotomies, most principally nature/culture. This opposition rematerialises as other dualisms, such as between the assumed converse conditions of humanity and animality, wild and domestic, hunter-gatherer and agriculturalist and so on, whereby controlling and taming the 'wild', people in turn are envisaged to have tamed and controlled both society and themselves. These notions essentially reiterate a common and archaic canon of thought. It is one concerned with the evolution of hominids to humans or, synonymously, with the transition from hunting to industry and the subordination of nature by human reason (Engels 1934, 34, 308, 178; Fried 1967; Glacken 1967; Service 1962). This convention, espoused in the middle of the last

century by Braidwood (1957, 22) and Childe (1942, 55), essentially questions the humanity of pre-agricultural peoples, considered to be more *homo sapiens* than 'person'. Through the revolution of subsistence, architecture, symbolism or sedentism, Neolithic peoples are portrayed as conquering some sort of intellectual and historical hurdle. These considerations find their most explicit expression in recent cognitivist approaches, which contend that the cultural transformations of the period were effected by a fundamental overhaul of the limits of the human mind (Mithen 1996). Living in larger social groups and engaging materially with monumental architecture is claimed to have engendered 'symbolic storage' and the accumulation of cognitive capital (Watkins 2004, 2005, 2006, 2008, 2010a, 2010b, 2012, 2014, 2016). This enabled humans to process greater and more complex volumes of information and externalise, represent and culturally construct the world around them in ways that were previously biologically inaccessible to our Palaeolithic forebears. As a consequence, Neolithic peoples are portrayed as culturally and intellectually similar to modern humans in fundamental ways that our hunting and gathering ancestors were not. By extension, one could apply the proposition to extant small-scale indigenous human groups, resulting in the same neo-evolutionary assumptions of biological inferiority prevalent in early twentieth-century anthropology.

Shamanistic or neuropsychological approaches have also been offered, where authors such as Lewis-Williams and Pearce (2005) have reasoned that hallucinatory experience might have been part of the stimuli responsible for the enigmatic imagery at Çatalhöyük and other notable Neolithic sites. While the authors are more than justified in arguing that humans may have deliberately altered their consciousness in prehistory, the problem lies in the entrenched anthropocentrism and the separation of imagery and shamanic practice from the social and corporeal contexts of its production. Even if only applied to art made *during* trance, the process and product of design should be understood as more complex in origin and function than mechanistic and faithful hallucinatory facsimiles (see Ingold 2013, 2015; Robinson 2013, 60). A similar problem emerges from broader understandings of the Çatalhöyük zoomorphic art as directly symbolic or representational: design is reduced to an objectification, rather than understood as an intrinsic ontological property.

Alternatives to these approaches, however, can be found in ethnographic case studies and recent theoretical innovations in anthropology that have reformulated understandings about human relationships with the environment. These new theoretical concepts have had the effect of rendering entrenched Western dichotomies and notions of universalism and relativism inadequate at interpreting the complexity and difference of other societies knowledge and experiences (Århem 1996; Descola 1994; Hill 2013; Latour 1993, 2004; Pedersen 2001; Stolze Lima 1999; Viveiros de Castro 1992, 1998, 2005; Willerslev 2007). As a result, this has generated more nuanced perspectives on personhood, agency, materiality and human–animal relations instigating a radical shift from epistemological to ontological questions and concerns in the field of archaeology (Alberti and Bray 2009; Borić 2013; Conneller 2004; Croucher 2012; Fowler 2004; Hamilakis 2013; Harris and Robb 2012; Knappett and Malafouris 2008; Pollard 2013; Weismantel 2013a, b, 2015). This chapter also takes an ontological and relational approach to better understand the shift in conceptions of selfhood in the upper levels at Çatalhöyük. By moving beyond the cognitivist explanations and the reductive and constraining parameters of the nature-culture paradigm, it becomes apparent that the greater focus on autonomy in the upper levels is not a strictly cognitive phenomenon but an ontological one, resulting from a reversal in the direction of vitality and a shift in the relational matrix: from what it means to be similar, to what it means to be *different*.

A deep concern with bodily difference is best articulated at the Pre-Pottery Neolithic site of Göbekli Tepe, in south-east Anatolia. The site is characterised by massive T-shaped pillars and statuary portraying a vast array of wild and often ferocious and predatory animals. Indeed, Göbekli Tepe and Çatalhöyük have often been compared due to their shared symbolic vocabulary and preoccupation with the animal world. However, while there are some iconographic similarities, I propose that these two sites occupy homologous albeit *distinct* cosmological landscapes. As I have explored elsewhere (Fagan 2017a), the enigmatic imagery, architecture and osteoarchaeological data at Göbekli Tepe hints that the human groups that built and utilised the site subscribed to an 'ontology of predation'. This cosmology, as outlined by Århem (2016) is deeply related to a hunting way of life wherein people entertain a close, intersubjective relationship with the principal predators and game animals on which their lives and livelihoods depend (see Viveiros de Castro 1998). Indeed, existence in such communities is defined not just through hunting to produce sustenance – but also by becoming sustenance for others. Thus, life is generated through exchanges of reciprocal predation: between humans and animals and the living and the dead. United in the common bond of becoming food for one another, all beings are 'active participants in an intricately interdependent system of resurrection' (Walens 1981, 6, 100; see also: Fausto 2007; Viverios de Castro 1998).

This ontology of predation seems to abound at sites throughout the early Pre-Pottery Neolithic in Upper Mesopotamia. It manifests in the keen interest in the animal point of view – the wearing of animal skins in rituals to gain their perspective, powers and knowledge, along with the visual articulation existential concerns such as human–animal hybridity and transformation (for a thorough discussion of the iconographic data, see Fagan 2016). Indeed, mutual practices of interspecific predation and consumption appear to be the key ontological principles driving social

engagements at Göbekli Tepe, where skeletonized and schematic human depictions appear to be preyed upon by animate and voracious predators – who occasionally clutch dislocated human heads in paws or talons. Similarly, totem-pole-like sculptures of animals holding human heads in succession seem to underline the metaphysical relations that exist between all beings: each animal a predator to some or prey to others. Such scenes, in conjunction with the potential evidence of intensive feasting found at the site (Dietrich et al. 2012), the remains of human bone with post-mortem ritual treatments uncovered in the enclosures' fill (Gresky et al. 2017), along with the high number of necrophageous corvids in the avifauna, evince a co-productive relationship: of animals feeding on or becoming humans and vice versa. Amongst other things, the Göbekli enclosures seem to have functioned as conduit points, wherein the spirits of powerful predators devoured the deceased, potentially aiding in human metamorphosis and the cycles of regeneration (Fagan 2017a).

Consequently, at Göbekli Tepe and potentially other hunting communities in the Early Pre-Pottery Neolithic, the relationship between the human living and the deceased was one of ontological discontinuity (see Viveiros de Castro 1998, 485). The living and the dead were not only socially estranged, but also metaphysically *different categories of being*. At Çatalhöyük, however, the cosmological makeup of the settlement must be understood in its particular historical and ecological context. While wild animal species certainly did not lose their significance at the site, the divide between humans and animals no longer constituted the sole ontological axis. Rather, in this densely packed permanent settlement, it was the similarities and differences between *human* persons that were integral to the construction of cosmology and identity (Strathern 1999, 252–3; see also Empson 2007; Humphrey 1996; Pedersen 2001). Eschatological concern was no longer founded on the post-mortem metamorphosis of humans into powerful wild animals, but instead, with the transformation of the dead into a collective body of *ancestors*. At Göbekli, there was conceivably no social or metaphysical continuity between the living and the dead, while at Çatalhöyük the cosmological world was *predicated* on continued relatedness between the living and the deceased. Århem (2016, 299) has recently made the same argument, comparing Southeast Asian animism with the particular form of animism known from primarily hunting human groups from Amazonia and the circumpolar regions. 'Southeast Asian animism', he contends, '[should] be understood in this light: as an ontological development associated with the transition from a hunting mode of life to a more settled, agricultural way of life in which livestock keeping has progressively reduced the role of hunting and where the village-centred domestication paradigm and its attendant sacrificial ideology rather than the venatic ideology of shamanism constitute the organizing ontological template'.

Transporting this concept to prehistoric Southwest Asia, we can see that the earlier Pre-Pottery Neolithic notion of animals inhabiting a social world isomorphic with the human world is replaced, at Çatalhöyük, by a society of ancestors inhabiting communities modelled on those of the living. Humans are no longer concerned with extra-human transformation (where humans become animals and vice versa), but *inter*-human transformation (where humans become other *humans*).[1] Indeed, the increase in figurines and the phenomenon of headlessness throughout the figurine corpus at the site (Hamilton 1996, 220–1; Meskell 2007, 114; Nakamura and Meskell 2009, 209; Talalay 2004), along with the curation of human skulls, might imply, to quote Humphrey, the need to literally see '*through the eyes of other people*, people who [are] dead and [have] become spirits' (1996, 189 quoted in Pedersen 2001, 423). In a landscape populated with more and more people, and especially in the upper levels – different *bodies* – the ability to exchange and explore different points of view across both human *and* animal ontological axes, essentially crossing social and cosmological boundaries, may have been especially profitable (see Humphrey 1996; Pedersen et al. 2007).

ÇATALHÖYÜK

Çatalhöyük has been described as an 'aggressively egalitarian' community (Hodder 2014b, 2016, 73), deeply ensconced in cross-cutting social contracts, relations and obligations that produced a consciousness of interdependence and shared substance. However, throughout the life of the long-lived settlement, we can witness gradual increases in stress, workload, obligations and morbidity resulting from the dense and permanent population. As I have argued elsewhere (Fagan 2016, 168–9, 2017b), while the village was a place of safety and stability, it was also one of *stagnation*. The perpetuation of life and the security of the community depended upon an entropic current of agentive forces flowing from the environs beyond into the settlement. It was the unbounded wild and the animal agents that dwelled therein that held supreme power over human life and livelihood, as houses, gardens and cultivated fields constituted loci of *consumption*, rather than *production*, where vitality and fecundity were expended and depleted (Descola 2012, 27; Ingold 2000, 84; van Beek and Banga 1992, 65, 69).

It is this notion that might illuminate the motives behind practices such as the deposition and display of exclusively *wild* animal parts and installations, the production of wild animal figurines, methodical refleshing and replastering practices and the association of human interments with aurochsen horns. Such phenomena may have served to preserve and delimit vitality and prevent entropic losses. Unlike smaller-scale, nomadic human groups who can move to new locations, the permanent dwellers at Çatalhöyük may have been living with and acting upon the existential risk of exhausting vital force. It is, therefore, significant that intensifications in animal installations, ritual activity, burials and architectural refleshing and replastering, occurred in conjunction and consequently, likely in reaction to increases in stress and morbidity resulting from a burgeoning permanent population, up until in Level VI/ South N/O. This is bolstered by the fact that we find significant decreases and drop-offs in socioritual behaviour after this time with the resultant shifts to greater mobility witnessed from South P onwards (Hodder 2014b, 16; Larsen et al. 2013). Consequently, it may be that part of the proliferation in ritual and symbolic activity witnessed at Çatalhöyük

was a response, in a time of escalating stress, disease, increasingly demanding workload, burgeoning population, multiple social contracts and potential environmental deterioration, to the need for greater invigoration and injection of the vitality and procreative capacities of wild animals into a stagnating and metaphysically starving village.

This long-lived sustainability strategy changed dramatically, however, after approximately 6,500 BCE (the end of Levels South O and North G), where pressures and entropic losses appear to have become intolerable and consequently combatted through population dispersal and shifts towards greater mobility (Cessford 2005; Hodder 2014b). Houses were burned, building continuity was broken and installations of wild animals decreased. Large elaborate buildings emerged with greater independence and economic self-sufficiency. Traditional ways of plastering houses were abandoned in favour of greater individual expression. The new houses now had street-level access, had pebbled inlaid floors and demonstrate evidence that they were productive complexes with yards including external ovens, hearths and middens. The previously pronounced focus on building continuity also disappeared: houses were occupied for a single generation only, and the dwellings of subsequent generations shifted across the neighbourhood area (Marciniak et al. 2015). The strict strategies and attitudes towards building termination also changed significantly. Interiors were no longer infilled and, instead, abandoned houses were left unoccupied, demonstrating less concern with the maintenance of mnemonic potential, with the transplantation of material potency through replication and reincorporation and the expression of ancestral continuity through architecture. Indeed, towards the end of Çatalhöyük, the institution of spatially and temporally interdependent houses as a trope and emblem for the community appears to have lost potency and meaning. The house matrix was no longer the key channel through which vitality was garnered and identity and belonging, articulated.

NEW BODIES

Indeed, the iconography and vital wild animal parts that previously powered houses and the community were replaced in the upper levels by new material bodies: decorated pots, stamps and figurines. The shift in design from the surfaces of houses to the surfaces of ceramics, as Buchli has argued, is perhaps anticipated by the earlier shift in ceramic technology at the site – from rough wares to more sophisticated forms that can be left unattended (2014, 288; Hodder 2006; Last 1996; Russell et al. 2013). By acting as a 'delegate' for the cook (Latour 2005), Buchli argues that ceramics developed virtual agency and thus greater importance, substantiated by the subsequent investment in their elaboration and specialisation. However, I would argue that delegation does not involve, as Latour proposes, an act of substitution and obedience on behalf of the pot, but rather, the pot acquires importance and sovereignty from going *beyond* human capacities, rendering persons dependent through these new affordances (Hodder 2012; Khatchadourian 2016).

Thus, I propose that whereas previously, vitality and transformability were localised in the matrix of houses and the literal *body* of the community,[2] following population dispersal and greater economic self-sufficiency, these fundamental powers were appropriated by *individuals*: pots and people.

This is evinced by the shift in loci of *design* – from house walls to ceramic and human bodies. Design, at Çatalhöyük, does not as appear to have been semantic or representational in nature, but rather, materially *transformative* (Fortis 2010; Gow 1989, 20–3, 1999; Trimm n.d., 20). Indeed, understanding design in these terms – as applied to transform – may shed light on the almost exclusive association of wall paintings with burial platforms: a tool to potentially transform the deceased from decaying [spiritual limbo] to *dead*. Moreover, in the later levels, this notion elucidates the shift in wild animal imagery – from the walls to the surfaces of objects that alter or transmute substances – such as cooking pots, that render raw food edible, and stamps, that legitimise and impart their vitality onto others. Thus, as Buchli notes, the previous 'efficacy of structures as containers and curators of powerful substances and forces' was overtaken by portable media (2014, 299). This progression towards newly independent and autonomous bodies articulates a significant ontological shift, from a focus on the collective to the individual, and from similarity to difference.

THE COMMODIFICATION OF VITALITY

The translocation of vital imagery from the membrane of house walls to the surfaces of portable stamps suggests appropriation, commodification, monopolisation, mobilisation, individualisation and legitimisation of previously house-based and communally oriented power. The pre-South-P settlement was dependent upon an entropic current of agentive forces flowing from the wild via animal remains, reliefs and installations. Following the increases in stress and morbidity, the old procedures for importing and managing generative force were no longer efficient, effective or sustainable. The images of hands, leopards, bear and wild boar that previously adorned house walls were reconstituted in the more mobile and practical forms of stamp seals (Türkcan 2013). Indeed, concentrating house-based imagery through miniaturisation and reconstituting that power in a new, more manageable and operational medium enabled governance and control over vital powers and their legitimising capacities. Imagery and its associated vitality could be transferred to skin or cloth and even potentially stamped on bread (Bogaard et al. 2014; Hodder 2014a, 2014b, 16, 2014c). The legitimising power stamps accorded persons is further exemplified by the inclusion of such stamps in burials, along with beads and other means of bodily decoration and individuation.

Indeed, in the earlier levels at Çatalhöyük, the community can be understood as a body of shared substance. As Lagrou has observed for the Cashinahua, 'People who live together, sharing food, bodily fluids and other physical and psychic influences, are said to become of a kind. Since they have been exposed to the same influences, their bodies start to resemble each other. A person's body is understood to be the product of the active intervention of close relatives who literally sculpt and model the body of their kin' (Lagrou 1998, 3). Similarly, prior to south-P,

it appears that people found meaning through resemblance and similarity. However, following the move to greater mobility and economic self-sufficiency, we find bodies – human and ceramic – become steadily more differentiated. The pottery in the levels from South O onwards demonstrates a greater diversity of forms, is of higher quality (Doherty and Tarkan 2013), has more decoration and serves a greater array of functions – many of which appear to be special purpose (Yalman et al. 2013). Stone vessels and andesite trays also become more common in the TP Area and on the West Mound (Wright, 2013), revealing an increasing focus on exchange and display (Hodder 2014b, 15–16).

FROM SIMILARITY TO DIFFERENCE

Indeed, just as pots emerged as distinctive individuated bodies with autonomy, so too did humans begin to differentiate themselves from one another. Whereas previously, in South G to M at Çatalhöyük, stone beads were produced from only a limited range of raw materials or colours (Bains et al. 2013), by South P onwards, a greater *variety* of stone beads can be observed, crafted from a diverse array of materials sourced from further distances and involving greater technological skill (Hodder 2014b, 16). Relatedly, spoons and spatulas are also more common in the upper levels, used presumably for the application of pigments in body ornamentation, amongst other things (Hodder 2014b, 16). Furthermore, the presence and increase of adornment in graves, even in disturbed interments, demonstrates the inextricability of ornamentation in individual bodily identity and *integrity*. Indeed, jewellery in many Amazonian communities is used – not simply to beautify or exhibit status – but rather as *ensouled* equipment: tools with which to *humanise* (Lagrou 2009; Santos-Granero 2012, 198). To be physically separated from these items and/or other toolkits – such as in death – would potentially deprive one of an essential component of personhood. Thus, in this sense, the burial of ornaments and certain artefacts with the dead would serve to secure the permanency of death and, moreover, render the deceased recognisable to kin in the afterlife (Fagan 2016, 178). Indeed, the importance of jewellery in identity making is demonstrated by finds of whole pendants in burials, revealing evidence of extensive use after repair, and that they were kept long after losing their perforation (Hodder 2011, 62).

However the greatest expression of human bodily difference comes from the corpus of well-made and extremely corpulent figurines from the upper levels at the site. As Meskell et al. (2016) have pointed out, human figures with a focus on adiposity come almost exclusively from the later levels (after Levels North G and South P) and the most technologically impressive examples from very late in the South Area. What is particularly striking about the late figurines is their overt naturalism and attention to detail that clearly articulates a real morphology. For instance, figurine 20736 – an extremely large, mature, female representation recovered from a platform in the TPC area – demonstrates studied physiological knowledge of the body (Figure 13.1). The stone has been deeply undercut to display the extreme adiposity of the stomach flap, fat rolls and arms. However, in the earlier levels at least, evidence for obesity and

FIGURE 13.1 Corpulent, mature, female figurine from Building 150 in the TPC area at Çatalhöyük. (Photo: J. Quinlan)

comorbid diseases are lacking in the osteoarchaeological record. Indeed, the Çatalhöyük population appears to have been in good health, evidenced by their relatively normal growth, development and their access to a varied and nutritious diet (Larsen et al. 2015). Unfortunately, not many skeletons have been recovered from the TP and TPC levels.

Consequently, in order to speculate on how obesity might have manifested in some of the residents, I suggest the following hypothesis. Following the population decline that occurred within the community from South P onwards (Cessford 2005), there was likely less genetic diversity, resulting in the circulation of recessive genes that would produce obesity in genetically susceptible individuals. Indeed, the dearth of other archaeologically visible human groups in the region outside of Çatalhöyük during the Middle period suggests a low migrant population pool immigrated to the site (Baird 2002, 2005) resulting in even less genetic diversity in the considerably smaller community than was present in the Late period.

Furthermore, the development of obesity at the site may also have been a two-way arrow. If vitality and social esteem was predicated on adiposity, this, combined with little sufficient outbreeding would select for rare genetic defects such as *MC4R* mutations (considered the commonest monogenic cause of human obesity, see Farooqi and Rahilly 2008). Arguments that corpulence at Çatalhöyük arose simply because of lifestyle/dietary changes are problematic (Pearson and Meskell 2013). As demonstrated by failed overfeeding experiments of the constitutionally thin (Germain et al. 2014), simply exposing lean individuals to more food does not induce hyperphagia and fatness, but rather greater anorexigenic energy expenditure, waste and a general inability to store fat. The failure of overfeeding experiments to elicit morbid obesity (as opposed to moderate and transitory weight gain) in otherwise healthy individuals problematises the notion that simply excess energy intake and/or lifestyle behavioural patterns *alone* constituted the primary driver of disease; instead, the involvement of such factors are clearly secondary to the vulnerability to develop the pathology in the first place. Thus, rather than a disorder of energy balance, obesity is better configured as a polygenetic condition and neuroendocrine disorder.

Consequently, in a population that, at least in the earlier levels, rarely exhibited such bodily qualities, such *uniquely* fat bodies – in the context of newly independent households – might have been viewed as especially powerful through the manifestation of explicit difference. The ability to store and sequester vitality via adiposity would have been a potent trope and tool. Whereas earlier, it seems as though vitality was amassed in the house via the injection of the generative capacities of powerful wild animals, in the upper levels, it is *humans* – perhaps even particular families and/or lineages – who take ownership of vital power through fat accumulation. Indeed, throughout the earlier levels at Çatalhöyük, there's generally a deliberate denial or disregard for genetic relatedness. Children weren't raised by their genetic parents, and people who lived together or were buried together weren't necessarily family members. However, following the transformations in social relations and notions of identity coterminous with the emergence of the household as a self-productive unit, we have the first instances of archaeologically visible social differentiation. Moreover, household groupings may even, during this time, have been based on genetic similarity. So these figurines might not just evoke the status accorded to fatness and the social affluence that conveys, but also the newly sanctified power and significance of *genetic* relatedness – if obesity was a hereditary condition, particular to only a few families alone. Indeed, the association of the two corpulent female figurines with plastered platforms hints that these images might depict the deceased (perhaps powerful relatives or ancestors), revered for their ability to monopolise

FIGURE 13.2 Figurine 20736.x3 from the F.3855 platform in Building 150 from the TPC Area at Çatalhöyük. The figure has two diagonally connected perforations on its head, suggesting it was worn on the body.

generative power within their flesh. Indeed, two diagonally connected perforations on the head of 20736.x3 from the F.3855 platform in the TPC Area suggests that this figurine was worn on the body, perhaps associating its vitality and even its *hereditary* power with its wearer (Figure 13.2).

THE AUTONOMY OF SPIRITS

As I discussed in the introduction to this chapter, the preceding Pre-Pottery Neolithic

in south-east Anatolia, typified by sites such as Göbekli Tepe, seems to have been characterised by cosmological concerns such as interspecies metamorphosis and the animalisation of the human dead (Viveiros de Castro 1998, 485). Thus, in the hunting world of early PPN communities such as Göbekli, the living and the dead might be said to be metaphysically discontinuous (Viveiros de Castro 1988, 482–3). At Neolithic agrarian Çatalhöyük, however, the livings' connection to the deceased seems to have been predicated on continuing *relatedness* and the notion that ancestors – rather than animals – 'form a society mirroring that of the living' (see Århem 2016, 299). While there are occasional elements hinting at human-animal transformation at Çatalhöyük – for instance, the use of bird feathers for costume (Russell and McGowan 2003), the association of aurochsen horns with burial platforms, and the vulture wall paintings that might depict a real or mythological practice of excarnation – generally, images of metamorphosis and hybridisation are rare in the imagery and mortuary practices at the site. Indeed, the general death of animal bone and associated artefacts in grave fills suggests a concern in the early and middle levels with maintaining *human* ontological integrity.

It has previously been argued that during the later levels at Çatalhöyük, the dead became more distanced from daily life (Whitehouse et al. 2014, 149–50). Instead, I would propose that the later levels saw greater autonomy, agency and subjectivity of the deceased, who now, like the living, inhabited, and presided over their own households extricated from the dependencies of the collective. During the earlier levels, on the other hand, the material remains of the dead were integral to establishing and legitimising place-based relations, ancestral continuity and community collectivism. Due to the paucity of grave goods and undifferentiated interments, the collective of the dead, in the earlier levels at least, seems to have remained somewhat anonymous and *de*-personalised. However, following the move towards greater human autonomy throughout time, it appears that some of the dead followed suit, garnering independence and, as Århem has coined it, 'superhuman ancestrality' in the spirit world (2016, 299). Such notions reach their apogee with more complex funerary rites such as secondary burial and the appearance of tombs and potentially also cemeteries, which, as proposed by Århem, suggests that the society of ancestors now inhabited their own houses and villages respectively – modelled on the houses and villages of the living (2016, 299). The greater complexity of funerary rituals and the secondary interment of bones in communal, clan or family ossuaries may have served to transform the powerful and even harmful spirits of the deceased into benevolent and protective ancestors, reintegrating the dead into the community.

CONCLUSION

This chapter has explored concepts of *self* and *other* through the trope of bodily difference. In the early Pre-Pottery Neolithic, typified by the site of Göbekli Tepe in South-East Anatolia, people appear to have been preoccupied with the differences between human and animal bodies, trans-specific metamorphosis and the ontological-othering of the dead. At the long-lived, densely populated permanent agrarian settlement of Çatalhöyük, however, a new concern emerged: the similarities between the bodies of humans living (and dying) in the collective. Following the radical rupture in the community after ~6,500 BCE, the obsession with difference surfaced once more; however, this time, it was not *inter*- but *intra*-specific. It was the differences between persons – perhaps even households – that formed the productive spark.

A number of scholars have contended that human autonomy and independence in the Neolithic was a product of greater cognitive complexity (de Chardin 1955), instigated by dense and permanent sedentism and the symbolic storage capacities of material culture and the built environment (Mithen 2004; Watkins 2006). While I would agree that greater human independence is evident in the later levels at Çatalhöyük, I would argue that this was not the product of a cognitive revolution but rather, a *cultural* one, whereby autonomy was now sanctioned and legitimised through new material media. This does not imply that people's agency was previously precluded or, moreover, cerebrally absent. Rather, the particular social milieu of earlier Çatalhöyük was organised in such a way so as to deter and impede the accumulation of wealth, deviation, and stark differentials in status. The social shift witnessed in the upper levels was a product of localised, historically contingent and gradual transformations in relations, agents, identities, attitudes and practices. What fundamentally changed at the end of Çatalhöyük was not the awakening of a latent consciousness or the expansion of mental capacities, but rather the field of relationships within which identity came into being.

REFERENCES

Alberti, B. and Bray, T. L. 2009. "Animating Archaeology: Of Subjects, Objects, and Alternative Ontologies." *Cambridge Archaeology Journal* 12:337–43.

Århem, K. 1996. "The Cosmic Food Web: Human-Nature Relatedness in the Northwest Amazon." In *Nature and Society: Anthropological Perspectives*, edited by P. Descola and G. Pálsson, 185–204. London: Routledge.

Århem, K. 2016. "Southeast-Asian Animism. A Dialogue with Amerindian Perspectivism." In *Animism in Southeast Asia*, edited by K. Århem and G. Sprenger, 279–301. London: Routledge.

Baer, G. 1994. *Cosmología y shamanismo de los Matsiguenga*. Quito: Abya-Yala.

Bains, R., Vasić, M., Bar-Yosef Mayer, D. E., Russell, N., Wright, K. I., and Doherty, C. 2013. "A Technological Approach to the Study of Personal Ornamentation and Social Expression at Çatalhöyük." In *Substantive Technologies at Çatalhöyük: Reports from the 2000–2008 Seasons*, edited by I. Hodder, 331–64. Los Angeles: University of California Press.

Baird, D. 2002. "Early Holocene Settlement in Central Anatolia: Problems and Prospects as Seen from the Konya Plain." In *The Neolithic of Central Anatolia: Proceedings of the International CANeW Round Table, Istanbul, 23–24 November 2001*, edited by F. Gérard and L. Thissen, 139–59. Istanbul: Ege Yayınları.

Baird, D. 2005. "The History of Settlement and Social Landscapes in the Early Holocene in the Çatalhöyük Area." In *Çatalhöyük Perspectives: Themes from the 1995–99 Seasons*, edited by I. Hodder, 55–74. Cambridge, UK: McDonald Institute for Archaeological Research; London: British Institute of Archaeology at Ankara.

Becker, N., Dietrich, O., Götzelt, T., Köksal-Schmidt, Ç., Notroff, J., and Schmidt, K. 2012. "Materialien zur Deutung der zentralen Pfeilerpaare des Göbekli Tepe und weiterer Orte des obermesopotamischen Frühneolithikums." *Zeitschrift für Orient Archäologie* 5:14–43.

Bird-David, N. 1999. "'Animism' Revisited: Personhood, Environment and Relational Epistemology." *Current Anthropology* 40:67–91.

Bogaard, A., Ryan, P., Yalman, N., Asouti, E., Twiss, K. C., Mazzucato, C., and Farid, S. 2014: "Assessing Outdoor Activities and Their Social Implications at Çatalhöyük." In *Integrating Çatalhöyük: Themes from the 2000–2008 Seasons*, edited by I. Hodder, 123–48. Los Angeles: University of California Press.

Borić, D. 2013. "Theater of Predation: Beneath the Skin of Göbekli Tepe Images." In *Relational Archaeologies: Humans, Animals, Things*, edited by C. Watts, 42–64. New York: Routledge.

Boz, B. and Hager, L. D. 2013. "Intramural Burial Practices at Çatalhöyük, Central Anatolia, Turkey." In *Humans and Landscapes of Çatalhöyük: Reports from the 2000–2008 Seasons*. Los Angeles, CA: Cotsen Archaeology Institute.

Braidwood, R. J. 1957. *Prehistoric Men*. Chicago Natural History Museum Popular Series Anthropology, 37. Chicago: Chicago Natural History Museum.

Buchli, V. 2014. "Material Register, Surface, and Form at Çatalhöyük." In *Religion at Work in a Neolithic Society: Vital Matters*, edited by I. Hodder, 280–303. Cambridge, UK: Cambridge University Press.

Cessford, C. 2005 "Estimating the Neolithic population of Çatalhöyük." In *Inhabiting Çatalhöyük: Reports from the 1995–1999 Seasons*, edited by I. Hodder, 323–6. Cambridge, UK: McDonald Institute for Archaeological Research.

Childe, V. G. 1942. *What Happened in History*. Harmondsworth, UK: Penguin Books.

Conneller, C. 2004. "Becoming Deer. Corporeal Transformations at Star Carr." *Archaeological Dialogues* 11:37–56.

Croucher, K. 2012. *Death and Dying in the Neolithic Near East*. Oxford, UK: Oxford University Press.

de Chardin, P. T. 1955. *The Phenomenon of Man*. New York: Harper.

Descola, P. 1994. *In The Society of Nature: A Native Ecology of Amazonia*. Cambridge, UK: Cambridge University Press.

Descola, P. 2012. "Beyond Nature and Culture. The Traffic of Souls." *HAU: Journal of Ethnographic Theory* 2:473–500.

Dietrich, O., Heun, M., Notroff, J., Schmidt, K., and Zarnkow, M. 2012. "The Role of Cult and

Feasting in the Emergence of Neolithic Communities: New Evidence from Göbekli Tepe, South-Eastern Turkey." *Antiquity* 86: 674–95.

Doherty, C., and Tarkan-Özbudak, D. 2013. "Pottery Production at Çatalhöyük: A Petrographic Perspective." In *Substantive Technologies at Çatalhöyük: Reports from the 2000–2008 Seasons*, edited by I. Hodder, 181–92. Los Angeles, CA: Cotsen Institute of Archaeology.

Empson, R. 2007. "Separating and Containing People and Things in Mongolia." In *Thinking Through Things: Theorising Artefacts Ethnographically*, edited by A. Henare, M. Holbraad, and S. Wastell, 113–40. London: Routledge.

Engels, F. 1934. *Dialectics of Nature*. Translated by C. Dutton. Moscow: Progress.

Fagan, A. 2017a. "Hungry Architecture: Spaces of Consumption and Predation at Göbekli Tepe." *World Archaeology* 3:318–37.

Fagan, A. 2017b. "Consuming Life: Managing Vitality at Çatalhöyük." Paper presented at Çatalhöyük, Konya, 15 July 2017.

Fagan, A. 2016. *Relational Ontologies in the Pre-Pottery Neolithic Middle East*. PhD diss. The University of Melbourne.

Farooqi, I. S. and O'Rahilly, S. 2008. "Mutations in Ligands and Receptors of the Leptin-Melanocortin Pathway That Lead to Obesity." Nature Clinical Practice. *Endocrinology and Metabolism Journal* 4:569–77.

Fausto, C. 2007. "Feasting on People: Eating Animals and Humans in Amazonia." *Current Anthropology* 48: 497–530.

Fortis, P. 2010. The Birth of Design: A Kuna Theory of Body and Personhood. *Journal of the Royal Anthropological Institute* 16:480–95.

Fowler, C. 2004. *The Archaeology of Personhood*. London: Routledge.

Fried, M. 1967. *The Evolution of Political Society*. New York: Random House.

Germain, N., Galusca B., Caron-Dorval, D., Martin, J., Pujos-Guillot, E., and Boirie, Y. 2014. "Specific Appetite, Energetic and Metabolomics Responses to Fat Overfeeding in Resistant-to-Bodyweight-Gain Constitutional Thinness." *Nutrition and Diabetes* 4(7): e126.

Glacken, C. J. 1967. *Traces on the Rhodian Shore*. Berkeley: University of California Press.

Gow, P. 1989. "Visual Compulsion: Design and Image in Western Amazonia." *Revista Indigenista Latinoamericana* 2:19–32.

Gow, P. 1999. "Piro Designs as Meaningful Action in an Amazonian Lived World." *Journal of the Royal Anthropological Institute* 5:229–46.

Gresky, J., Haelm, J., and Clare, L. 2017. "Modified Human Crania from Göbekli Tepe Provide Evidence for a New Form of Neolithic Skull Cult." *Science Advances* 3 published online: 28 June 2017.

Hamilakis, Y. ed. 2013. *Archaeology and the Senses: Human Experience, Memory, and Affect*. Cambridge, UK: Cambridge University Press.

Hamilton, N. 1996. "Figurines, Clay Balls, Small Finds, and Burials." In *On the Surface: Çatalhöyük 1993–95*, edited by I. Hodder, 215–63. Cambridge, UK: McDonald Institute for Archaeological Research and British Institute of Archaeology at Ankara Monograph.

Harris, O. and Robb, J. 2012. "Multiple Ontologies and the Problem of the Body in History." *American Anthropologist* 114:668–79.

Hill, E. 2013. "Archaeology and Animal Persons. Towards a Prehistory of Human-Animal Relations." *Environment and Society: Advances in Research* 4:117–36.

Hodder, I. 2006. *The Leopard's Tale: Revealing the Mysteries of Çatalhöyük*. London: Thames and Hudson.

Hodder, I. 2011. "An Archaeology of the Self: The Prehistory of Personhood." In *Search of Self: Interdisciplinary Perspectives on Personhood*, edited by J. W. van Huyssteen and E. P. Wiebe, 50–69. Grand Rapids, MI: Eerdmans.

Hodder, I. 2012. *Entangled: An Archaeology of the Relationships between Humans and Things*. Chichester, UK: Wiley-Blackwell.

Hodder, I. 2016. *Studies in Human-Thing Entanglement*. Online-only publ. www.ian-hodder.com/.

Hodder, I. 2014a. *Çatalhöyük Excavations: The 2000–2008 Seasons. Volume 7*. Los Angeles, CA: Cotsen Institute of Archaeology at UCLA.

Hodder, I. 2014b. "Çatalhöyük: The Leopard Changes Its Spots. A Summary of Recent Work." *Anatolian Studies* 64:1–22.

Hodder, I., ed. 2014c. *Integrating Çatalhöyük: Themes from the 2000–2008 Seasons*. Los Angeles: University of California Press.

Humphrey, C. with Onon, U. 1996. *Shamans and Elders: Experience, Knowledge and Power among the Daur Mongols*. Oxford, UK: Clarendon Press.

Ingold, T., ed. 2000. *The Perception of the Environment: Essays on Livelihood, Dwelling, and Skill*. London: Routledge.

Ingold, T. 2013. *Making: Anthropology, Archaeology, Art and Architecture*. London: Routledge.

Ingold, T. 2015. *The Life of Lines*. New York: Routledge.

Khatchadourian, L. 2016. *Imperial Matter: Ancient Persia and the Archaeology of Empires*. Oakland: University of California Press.

Knappett, C. and Malafouris, L. eds. 2008. *Material Agency. Towards a Non-Anthropocentric Approach*. New York: Springer.

Lagrou, E. 1998. *Cashinahua Cosmovision: A Perspectival Approach to Identity and Alterity*. Ph. D diss., University of St Andrews.

Lagrou, E. 2009. "The Crystallized Memory of Artifacts: A Reflection on Agency and Alterity in Cashinahua Image-Making." In *The Occult Life of Things: Native Amazonian Theories of Materiality and Personhood*, edited by F. Santos-Granero, 192–213. Tucson: University of Arizona Press.

Larsen, C. S., Hillson, S., Boz, B., Pilloud, M. A., Sadvari, J. W. Agarwal, S., Glencross, B. A., Beauchesne, P., Pearson, J., Ruff, C. B., Garofalo, E., Hager, L. D., Haddow, S., and Knüsel, C. J. 2015. "Bioarchaeology of Neolithic Çatalhöyük: Lives and Lifestyles of an Early Farming Society in Transition." *Journal of World Prehistory* 28:27–68.

Larsen, C. S., Hillson, S. W., Ruff, C. B., Sadvari, J. W., and Garofalo, E. M. 2013. "The Human Remains II: Interpreting Lifestyle and Activity in Neolithic Çatalhöyük." In *Humans and Landscapes of Çatalhöyük: Reports from the 2000–2008 Seasons*, edited by I. Hodder, 397–412. Los Angeles, CA: Cotsen Institute of Archaeology.

Last, J. 1996. "Surface Pottery at Çatalhöyük." In *On the Surface. Çatalhöyük 1993–1995*, edited by I. Hodder, 115–71 Cambridge, UK: Cambridge University Press.

Latour, B. 1993. *We Have Never Been Modern*. Cambridge, MA: Harvard University Press.

Latour, B. 2004. *Politics of Nature: How to Bring the Sciences into Democracy*. Translated by Catherine Porter. Cambridge, MA: Harvard University Press.

Latour, B. 2005. *Reassembling the Social: An Introduction to Actor-Network-Theory*. Oxford, UK: Oxford University Press.

Lewis-Williams, D. and Pearce, D. 2005. *Inside the Neolithic Mind: Consciousness, Cosmos and the Realm of the Gods*. London: Thames and Hudson.

Marciniak, A, Asouti, E., Doherty, C., and Henton, E. 2015. "The Nature of Household in the Upper Levels at Çatalhöyük. Smaller, More Dispersed, and More Independent Acquisition, Production, and Consumption Unit." In *Assembling Çatalhöyük*, edited by I. Hodder and A. Marciniak, 151–65. London: Routledge.

Meskell, L. M. 2007. "Refiguring the Corpus at Çatalhöyük." In *Material Beginnings: A Global Prehistory of Figurative Representation*, edited by C. Renfrew and I. Morley, 137–69. Cambridge, UK: McDonald Institute for Archaeological Research.

Meskell, L., Nakamura, C., Der, L., Tsoraki, C., and Arntz, M. 2016. "Figurines." In *Çatalhöyük Archive Report 2016*.

Mithen, S. J. 1996. *The Prehistory of the Mind: The Cognitive Origins of Art, Religion and Science*. London: Thames and Hudson.

Mithen, S. J. 2004. "Neolithic Beginnings in Western Asia and Beyond." *British Academy Review* 7:45–9.

Nakamura, C. and Meskell, L. M. 2009. "Articulate Bodies: Forms and Figures at Çatalhöyük." *Journal of Archaeological Method and Theory* 16:205–30.

Notroff, J., Dietrich, O., and Schmidt, K. 2014. "Building Monuments – Creating Communities. Early Monumental Architecture at Pre-Pottery Neolithic Göbekli Tepe." In *Approaching Monumentality in the Archaeological Record*, edited by J. Osborne, 83–105. Albany: SUNY Press.

Notroff, J., Dietrich, O., and Schmidt, K. 2016. "Gathering of the Dead? The Early Neolithic Sanctuaries of Göbekli Tepe, Southeastern

Turkey." In *Death Shall Have No Dominion: The Archaeology of Mortality and Immortality – A Worldwide Perspective*, edited by C. Renfrew, M. Boyd, and I. Morley, 65–81. Cambridge, UK: Cambridge University Press.

Pearson, J. and Meskell, L. M. 2013. "Biographical Bodies: Flesh and Food at Çatalhöyük." In *Early Farmers*, edited by A. Whittle A and P. Bickle, 233–50. London: British Academy.

Pedersen, M. A. 2001. "Totemism, Animism and North Asian Indigenous Ontologies." *Journal of the Royal Anthropological Institute* 7:411–27.

Pedersen, M. A., Empson, R., and Humphrey, C. 2007. "Editorial Introduction: Inner Asian Perspectivisms." *Inner Asia* 9(2): 141–52.

Peters, J., Driesch, A., Von Den, A., and Helmer, D. 2005. "The Upper Euphrates: Tigris Basin, Cradle of Agropastoralism?" In *The First Steps of Animal Domestication*, edited by J. D. Vigne, J. Peters, and D. Helmer, 96–124. Oxford, UK: Oxbow Books.

Pollard, J. 2013. "From Ahu to Avebury: Monumentality, the Social, and Relational Ontologies." In *Archaeology after Interpretation: Returning Materials to Archaeological Theory*, edited by B. Alberti, A. M. Jones, and J. Pollard, 177–96. Walnut Creek, CA: Left Coast Press.

Robinson D. 2013. "Transmorphic Being, Corresponding Affect: Ontology and Rock Art in South-Central California." In *Archaeology after Interpretation: Returning Materials to Archaeological Theory*, edited by B. Alberti, A. M. Jones, and J. Pollard, 59–78. Walnut Creek, CA: Left Coast Press.

Russell, N. and McGowan, K. J. 2003. Dance of the cranes: Crane symbolism at Çatalhöyük and Beyond. *Antiquity* 77(297):445–55.

Russell, N., Twiss, K. C., Orton, D., and Demirergi, A. 2013. More on the Çatalhöyük Mammal Remains. In *Humans and Landscapes of Çatalhöyük: Reports from the 2000–2008 Seasons*, edited by I. Hodder, 213–58. (Çatalhöyük Research Project Series Volume 8). London: British Institute at Ankara.

Santos-Granero, F. 2012. "Beinghood and People-Making in Native Amazonia: A Constructional Approach with a Perspectival Coda," *HAU: Journal of Ethnographic Theory* 2:181–211.

Service, E. R. 1962. *Primitive Social Organization: An Evolutionary Perspective*. New York: Random House.

Stolze Lima, T. 1999. "The Two and Its Many: Reflections on Perspectivism in a Tupi Cosmology." *Ethnos* 64:107–31.

Strathern, M. 1999. *Property, Substance, and Effect: Anthropological Essays on Persons and Things*. London: Athlone.

Talalay, L. E. 2004. "Heady Business: Skulls, Heads, and Decapitation in Neolithic Anatolia and Greece," *Journal of Mediterranean Archaeology* 17:139–63.

Trimm, C. n.d. *Surfaces and Lines: Artefacts and Designs as Communicative Manifestations of Relationships in Amazonian Cosmologies* 1–33.

Türkcan, A. U. 2013. "Çatalhöyük Stamp Seals from 2000 to 2008." In *Substantive Technologies at Çatalhöyük: Reports from the 2000–2008 Seasons*, edited by I. Hodder, 235–46. Los Angeles: University of California Press.

van Beek, W. E. A. and Banga, P. M. 1992. "The Dogon and Their Trees." In *Bush Base: Forest Farm. Culture, Environment and Development*, edited by E. Croll and D. Parkin, 57–75. London: Routledge.

Viveiros de Castro, E. B. 1992. *From the Enemies Point of View: Humanity and Divinity in an Amazonian Society*. Chicago: University of Chicago Press.

Viveiros de Castro, E. B. 1998. "Cosmological Deixis and Amerindian Perspectivism." *The Journal of the Royal Anthropological Institute* 4:469–88.

Viveiros de Castro, E. B. 2005. "Perspectivism and Multinaturalism in Indigenous America." In *The Land Within: Indigenous Territory and the Perception of the Environment*, edited by A. Surralles and P. G. Hierro, 36–74. Copenhagen: International Work Group for Indigenous Affairs.

Walens, S. 1981. *Feasting with Cannibals: An Essay on Kwakiutl Cosmology*. Princeton, NJ: Princeton University Press.

Watkins, T. 2004. "Building Houses, Framing Concepts, Constructing Worlds." *Paléorient* 30: 5–23.

Watkins, T. 2005. "The Neolithic Revolution and the Emergence of Humanity: A Cognitive Approach to the First Comprehensive World-View." In *Archaeological Perspectives on the Transmission and Transformation of Culture in the Eastern Mediterranean*, edited by J. Clarke. Oxford, UK: Council for British Research in the Levant.

Watkins, T. 2006. "Architecture and the Symbolic Construction of New Worlds." In *Domesticating Space*, edited by E. B. Banning and M. Chazan, 15–24. Berlin: Ex Orient.

Watkins, T. 2008. "Supra-Regional Networks in the Neolithic of Southwest Asia." *Journal of World Prehistory* 21:139–71.

Watkins, T. 2010a. "New Light on Neolithic Revolution in South-West Asia," *Antiquity* 84:621–34.

Watkins, T. 2010b. "Changing People, Changing Environments: How Hunter-Gatherers Became Communities that Changed the World." In *Landscapes in Transition: Understanding Hunter-Gatherer and Farming Landscapes in the Early Holocene of Europe and the Levant*, edited by B. Finlayson and G. Warren, 106–15. London: Oxbow Books.

Watkins, T. 2012. "Household, Community and Social Landscape: Building and Maintaining Social Memory in the Early Neolithic of Southwest Asia." In *"As Time Goes By?" Monuments, Landscapes and the Temporal Perspective: Socio-Environmental Dynamics over the Last 12,000 Years*, edited by M. Furholt, M. Hinz, and D. Mischka, 23–44. Bonn, Kiel: Rudolf Habelt.

Watkins, T. 2014. *"Time and Place, Memory, and Identity in the Early Neolithic of Southwest Asia."* In *Space and Time in Mediterranean Prehistory*, edited by S. G. Souvatzi and A. Hadji, 84–100. New York: Routledge.

Watkins, T. 2016. "The Cultural Dimension of Cognition." *Quaternary International* 405: 1–7.

Watkins, T., Betts, A. V. G., Dobney, K., and Nesbitt, R. M. 1995. *Qermez Dere, Tel Afar Interim Report No. 3*. Edinburgh: Department of Archaeology, University of Edinburgh (Project Paper No. 14).

Weismantel, M. 2013a. "Inhuman Eyes: Looking at Chavin De Huantar." In *Relational Archaeologies: Humans, Animals, Things*, edited by C. Watts, 21–41. London: Routledge.

Weismantel, M. 2013b. "Coming to Our Senses at Chavin De Huantar." In *Making Senses of the Past: Toward a Sensory Archaeology*, edited by J. Day, 113–36. Carbondale: The Center for Archaeological Investigations, Southern Illinois University at Carbondale.

Weismantel, M. 2015. "Seeing Like an Archaeologist: Viveiros de Castro at Chavin de Huantar." *Journal of Social Archaeology* 0:1–21.

Whitehouse, H., Mazzucato, C., Hodder, I., and Atkinson, Q. D. 2014. "Modes of Religiosity and the Evolution of Social Complexity at Çatalhöyük." In *Religion at Work in a Neolithic Society: Vital Matters*, edited by I. Hodder, 134–58. Cambridge. UK: Cambridge University Press.

Willerslev, R. 2007. *Soul Hunters: Hunting, Animism, and Personhood among the Siberian Yukaghirs*. Berkeley: University of California Press.

Wright, K. I. 2013. "The Ground Stone Technologies of Çatalhöyük." In *Substantive Technologies at Çatalhöyük: Reports from the 2000–2008 Seasons*, edited by I. Hodder, pp. 365–416. Los Angeles, CA: Cotsen Institute of Archaeology Press.

Yalman, N., Tarkan, D., and Gültekin, H. 2013: "The Neolithic Pottery of Çatalhöyük: Recent Studies." In *Substantive Technologies at Çatalhöyük: Reports from the 2000–2008 Seasons*, edited by I. Hodder, 147–82. Los Angeles: University of California Press.

NOTES

CHAPTER 3. WHEN TIME BEGINS TO MATTER

1. Rituals are ambiguous: they integrate and segregate, stabilize and destabilize, equalize or confirm hierarchies, they transmit traditions and promote change (Benz and Gramsch 2006; Hayden 2014; Widlok 2013).

2. Special buildings existed that might be considered forerunners of later so-called communal buildings (e.g. Abbès 2014; Byrd 2005; Price and Bar-Yosef 2017:151; Stordeur and Ibáñez 2008), but their dimensions are hardly comparable to the megalithic buildings of Göbekli Tepe.

3. Human remains of both sites were analysed in 2007. Epigenetic traits on their teeth demonstrated more heterogeneous patterns than for PPNB sites (Alt et al. 2013, 2015).

4. Specialization on gazelle hunting seems possible (for a summary with further references, see Benz 2000:78–79; Lang et al. 2013).

5. The term PPNA should be avoided because these communities differ from contemporary cultures of the Levant.

6. For a general discussion of this behaviour, see Chapman 2000.

7. The conceptional difference between gift-exchange based on networking with *do ut des* principle and trade of commodities has to be emphasized here. The biography of objects and the balance of giving and taking are essential in exchange networks, whereas in trade ascribed values of objects gain in importance. "Gift exchange precipitates ... cultural remembering, ... commodity exchange generates ... cultural forgetting" (Connerton 2009:53).

8. Rollefson (2000:185) alluded to this problem in respect to increasing population and size at the late PPNB site of 'Ain Ghazal.

CHAPTER 7. THE MERONOMIC MODEL OF COGNITIVE CHANGE AND ITS APPLICATION TO NEOLITHIC ÇATALHÖYÜK

1. Pauketat advocates 'viewing the world as dynamic relationships mediated by bundles'.

2. Concept names are written in uppercase throughout.

3. Tversky, for example, recognizes 'two general forms of organization of knowledge, taxonomic, that is, subdivision into kinds, and partonomic, that is, subdivision into parts' (Tversky, 1989, p. 983).

4. Habel et al. (1995) draw attention to the difficulty of stabilizing the semantics of the parthood relation.

5. This article takes 'meaning', 'idea' and 'concept' to be synonymous and uses them interchangeably.

6. There is a philosophical dimension to this. If the accommodating concept in a meronomic construction is not COMBINATION (or some equivalent), the idea constructed is then more than simply the 'sum of the parts'. The construction conforms to requirements that philosophers generally consider to apply to concepts of wholes. Aristotle, for example, states that 'The whole is something over and above its parts, and not just the sum of them all' (Metaphysics, Book H, 1045: 8–10: Ross, 1924). In similar vein, John Stuart Mill writes 'it appears to me the Complex Idea, formed by the blending together of several simpler ones, should ... be said to *result*

from, or be *generated by*, the simple ideas, not to consist of them' (Mill, 1843/1965, p. 29).

7. At the consciousness and creativity conference, Colin Renfrew characterized his reaction to this aspect of the evidence as 'bemusement'.

CHAPTER 8. CONTAINERS AND CREATIVITY IN THE LATE NEOLITHIC UPPER MESOPOTAMIAN

1. This contribution forms part of the project *Containers of Change*, supported by the Alexander von Humboldt Stiftung and based at the Institut für Vorderasiatische Archäologie of the Freie Universität Berlin.

CHAPTER 11. ADORNING THE SELF

1. Although the terms *bodily adornment*, *decoration*, and *ornamentation* can carry a different connotation, they are used in this chapter interchangeably.
2. This chapter is based on research I conducted for my PhD dissertation (Vasić 2018).
3. Except mirrors.
4. The dataset is limited to burial features from the North and South Areas that were excavated between 1995 and 2013. Primary deposition here includes both disturbed and undisturbed skeletons (see Haddow et al., Chapter 12, Table 12.1).
5. It should be noted, however, that anklets display a higher diversity of colors and types than bracelets.
6. Due to high level of disturbance in Çatalhöyük burials, a large portion of material assemblage ends up in burial fills. Nevertheless, it is plausible that higher frequency of beads in the fills of burial features with males could be reflective of

somewhat different practices. Perhaps these beads never formed part of specific strings such as bracelets or necklaces, but rather, they could have been scattered on top of the buried individuals. If that is the case, a difference between treatment of males and females would be in females more commonly buried with bead strings, and beads being more frequently scattered on top of the males.

7. The small size of the sample and the level of disturbance in burials hinders the exploration of different emphasis that could have highlighted the importance of adorning specific body parts.
8. Given that B.18 was partially excavated in the 1960s, and building B.75 was heavily eroded, the information is incomplete. Nevertheless, based on the evidence that exists, individuals buried in these buildings were not accompanied by beads.

CHAPTER 13. NEW BODIES: FROM HOUSES TO HUMANS AT ÇATALHÖYÜK

1. For an exploration of these ontological concerns through the framework of Amazonian perspectivism as expounded by Viveiros de Castro, see Fagan (2016) and Pedersen (2001), who applies perspectivism to the North Asian region.
2. I argue (Fagan 2017b) that, "through the systematic sharing of goods, cooperative labour, the pooling and circulation of resources, collective feasting, festive and everyday rituals, and practices such as alloparenting, entangled cross-cutting social contracts and associations were created resulting in complete interdependence and shared substance such that *the collective itself* may be conceptualised as a body – an interweaved whole of beings, relations, and things (see Lagrou 1998, 3)."

INDEX

Abu Hureyra, 12, 259
adiposity. *See* obesity
African pygmies, 135
agency, 8, 22, 37, 40, 171, 211,
    274, 278, 282–83
agriculture, 8, 40, 72, 74, 77–78,
    82, 94, 112, 114, 127, 163,
    172, 222
    adoption of, 6, 23, 34, 266
    communities, 16, 107
    origins, 33, 36
    spread of, 15
    transition to, 31–32, 65, 95, 108,
    231
    worldview, 33
'Ain Ghazal, 12–13, 264
'Ain Mallaha, 71
Akarçay Tepe, 233
altered states of consciousness, 6
Amazonia, 276, 280
Anatolia, 5, 9, 12, 14–15, 18, 76,
    107–8, 114, 133, 170–71, 183,
    203, 234, 259, 274,
    282–83
ancestors, 15, 67, 81, 90–91, 96,
    169, 193, 205, 213, 219–20,
    222, 274, 276, 281–83
animals, 7, 34–35, 94, 111, 190,
    212, 276, 282
    art, 74, 77, 275
    bone cluster, 121
    bones, 282
    commodities, 108, 123–24

humans becoming or vice versa,
    276
    hunting, 275
    rituals, 275
    wild, 20, 203, 275, 277, 281
animism, 276
anthropomorphic, 111, 135
architecture, 7, 15, 33–35, 39, 65,
    72, 75, 78, 175, 273, 275, 278
    Ba'ja, 162
    Çatalhöyük, 133, 135–36, 145,
    239, 242
    Harappan, 135
    monumental, 71, 73, 80, 273
    residential, 12
art, 9, 20, 81, 191, 202–3, 274
    depictions of beads, 232
    figurative, 77, 191
    geometric, 191
    in the house, 9, 17
    mobiliary, 194, 203–4
    Palaeolithic, 6
    zoomorphic, 274
Aşıklı Höyük, 9, 14–15, 18, 191,
    203, 233
assimilation, 73, 80
auroch, 45, 277, 282
    skull, 13
Australia, 40, 135
    Aborigines, 33
Ayn Qasiyyah, 52
Azraq Basin, 50, 52, 242–44
Azraq Oasis, 52

Bademağacı, 191
Ba'ja, 79, 161–62, 264
basketry, 8, 117, 172, 182, 258
    pottery hybrids, 175–77
Basta, 12, 78–79
beads, 21–22, 211, 234, 240,
    244–46, 279
    circulation of, 205
    deposit of, 76, 244
    non-burial contexts, 242
    stone, 279
bear, 202, 279
Bechtel, William, 97–101
    architecture, 102–3
Beidha, 13
being-in-the-world, 24, 39
belt hooks, 21, 232–33, 236, 238,
    240–41
bodily ornamentation, 232, 234,
    238, 244
Boncuklu, 9, 14–15, 76, 107–8,
    114, 118, 127
bone, 13, 22, 48, 78, 211, 234, 237,
    254, 257–60, 275, 283
    beads, 21, 233, 238–39
    disarticulated, 23, 256,
    262–63
    hooks, 15
    marks on, 259
    pins, 21
    points, 44, 232
    pores, 260
    rings, 240

bone (cont.)
  spoons, 15
  tools, 22, 257
Bouqras. *See* Tell Bouqras
brain, 4–6, 23, 72, 90–92, 97–102,
    213–14, 218
brain architecture, 4, 101, *See also*
    processing architecture
brick, 22–23, 163, 165, 211
  making, 134
  mudbrick, 133–34, 136–45
  size, 17, 135, 145
Bronze Age, 17, 111, 260
bucrania, 14–15, 19
building, 74–78, 81, 119–22, 124,
    134, 136–40, 143–45,
    163–65, 171, 177–79, 181,
    238–39, 244–45, 251, 255,
    258–59, 277
  abandonment, 237, 251, 256,
    261–62
  Building 1, 239
  Building 10, 145
  Building 129, 243, 255, 261
  Building 131, 239, 243, 261
  Building 132, 257
  Building 150, *280, 282*
  Building 18, 238
  Building 3, 121
  Building 42, 121
  Building 44, 121, 145, 243
  Building 49, 195, 259
  Building 50, 239
  Building 52, 256
  Building 56, 145
  Building 63, 121
  Building 65–Building
    56–Building 44 sequence, 242
  Building 74, 133, 137–39,
    141–42, 145
  Building 75, 121, 238
  Building 77, 195, 237–38, 257
  Building 80, 194, 238
  Building 95, 134, 137–38,
    141–42, 145
  Building EVII 12, 239
  Building VI.A.50, 194
  Building VIB.65, 199
  ceremonial, 160

cult, 14, 77
  density of, 192
  elaborate, 192, 277
  fully excavated, 257
  life history, 39
  public, 9, 13–14
  size, 238
  techniques, 17, 136
built environment, 7, 31–33, 35,
    38–39, 49, 95, 143, 283
bull, 192, 219, *See also* auroch
bullae, 110–13, 116
Burdur-Lakes region, 9
burial goods. *See* grave goods
burial practices. *See* mortuary
    practices
burials
  beads, 232–39, 241–43, 245, 257
  ritual, 76, 178, 262, 264
  secondary, 21–22, 192–93, 242,
    250–53, 259–60, 262, 264,
    283
burning, 44–47, 51, 77, 114,
    164–65, 178, 256, 261, 264
  limestone, 7
  sediment, 48

cache, 37, 44, 47, 51–52, 116, 120
  clay objects, 122, 124
  mini-balls, 121, 126
Cafer Höyük, 233
Can Hasan, 15
Canadian Arctic, 40
  Inuit groups, 35
Cappadocia, 15, 18, 191, 203
Çatalhöyük Research Project, 17,
    19
cattle, 22, 204
  bones, 14
Cauvin, Jacques, 8, 22
Çayönü, 9, 14, 108
cemeteries, 9, 15, 283
Central Levant, 77
ceramics. *See* pottery
ceremonial centres, 9
chaîne opératoires, 175
Chalcolithic, 10, 12, 14, 183, 204,
    254, 265
childhood, 123, 221, 224

chipped stone, 22, 50, 257
circulation
  body parts, 192, 205, 237, 244
  Cladh Hallan "mummies",
    260
  goods and commodities, 114,
    127
  recessive genes, 280
  tokens, 127
Clark, Andy, 6, 92–93, 100–1
clay, 142, 176, 178, 182, 195, 203,
    233
  balls, 116
  fabrics, 178
  figurines. *See* figurines
  floors, 44
  Northern Mesopotamian, 172
  sealings, 233
  silos, 180
  unfired, 172
clay objects
  geometric, 94–96, 104, 107–28
cleaning, 204
  clean and dirty areas, 15, 192,
    242, 251
  floors, 44–46, 190
cognition, 17, 20, 23, 31, 33, 83,
    90, 94, 108, 153–54, 160,
    168–69, 171, 182, 210, 214,
    218, 225, 250
  collective, 82
  forms of, 95–96
  levels of, 95–96
  memory, 213
  scientific, 8
  social, 4, 212
  view of, 153
cognitive archaeology, 3–5, 23, 91,
    153–54, 171, 209–10,
    212–14, 217, 224
cognitive ecologies, 213–14, 224
cognitive niche construction, 92
cognitive revolution, 3, 5, 266, 283
cognitive science, 91, 93–94, 97,
    101, 103–4, 154, 166, 210,
    214, 216
commemoration, 80, 192, 237
commodification, 66, 80, 83, 278
  processes of, 66

complexity, 6–7, 17, 32, 38, 107, 143, 158, 194, 204, 216–17, 246, 265, 274
cognitive, 191, 283
counting, 124
ritual, 14, 283
social, 231
connectionism, 97–98
consciousness, 3, 6, 39, 65, 67, 90, 94, 133, 145, 153, 168, 209–10, 223, 225, 250, 266, 274, 276, 283
changes in, 38, 93
consciousness and creativity, 170, 173
creation of, 32
definitions of, 202
forms of, 95–96, 251
levels of, 5, 16, 18, 23, 93, 95–96, 104, 108–9, 113, 122, 128, 133, 211
social, 17
states of, 66
consumption, 163, 172, 193, 205, 275
by elites, 169
daily, 164
events, 49
loci of, 277
creativity, 3, 6, 16, 24, 31, 67, 82, 162, 168–71, 175, 182, 190–91, 203–5, 209–10, 225
conceptual, 153–54, 156, 160–65
creation of, 32
degrees of, 5, 194
forms of, 19, 173, 179
levels of, 16, 23, 65, 133, 211
rates of, 19–20, 38
role of, 174
cultivation, 8, 12, 33, 71, 74, 123
cuneiform, 111–12, 168

Dead Sea, 13
dead, the, 10, 22, 24, 47–49, 51, 75–76, 163–65, 178, 192–93, 201, 203, 205, 232–33, 237–38, 246, 250, 275–76, 280, 282–83

death, 21, 47–48, 80, 165, 244–45, 250, 256, 258, 260, 262–63, 265, 280
life after, 70
model of, 259
overcoming, 67
retrieval after, 78
decoration, 20, 22, 76, 118, 209, 246
applied on vessels, 181
bodily, 21, 231–34, 239–40, 245, 279
pottery, 279
self, 232, 236, 242
Department of Antiquities of Jordan, 42
dependencies, 65, 169, 176, 182–83, 282
Dhra', 13
disposal
contexts, 96, 120–21, 128
zones, 119
distributed cognition, 93–94, 97, 99–104, 212, 214–15, 222
distributed mind, 4, 6, 73, 168
distributed perspective, 91–93, 97, 102–4
distributed self, 20–22, 250
Djade al-Mughara, 191
domestication, 8
cattle, 133, 170, 246
plants/animals, 7, 12, 33, 222
Donald, Merlin, 6–7, 168, 171, 182, 222
dwelling, 16, 36, 39, 49
concept of, 32–36
domestic building, 14, 16, 74, 76, 161, 163–65, 277
in a landscape, 39
memory, 40
in the world, 36

economy, 16, 33, 81, 96, 172, 223
egalitarian
ecologies, 217
egalitarian community, 276
egalitarian society, 13, 220
egalitarian village, 82
Egypt, 135, 259–60

Ein Gev, 47, 52
Ein Qashish, 52
elaboration, 19, 111, 122, 169
ceramic, 278
figurines, 234
ritual, 15
embodied engagements, 99, 169, 171, 181
embodied interaction, 97, 99, 102–3, 215
embodied level of practice, 4
embodied memory, 209–10, 220, 222
embodied self, 230, 244
emotions, 76, 91, 213, 216, 220
Epipalaeolithic, 7, 12, 16, 21, 31–53, 74
Epipalaeolithic Foragers in Azraq Project, 42
Europe, 6, 33, 57, 263
evolution, 7, 169, 212
biological, 213
clay objects, 111
cognitive, 6–7
human, 171, 273
linear, 16, 65
social, 172
exchange, 7, 19, 38, 50–52, 79–80, 155, 168, 181, 193, 205, 276, 279, See also trade and exchange
long distance, 31
rates of, 20

farming. See agriculture
communities, 38, 65, 73
feasting, 49, 121, 265, 275
figurines, 21, 113–14, 116, 178, 209, 278
animals, 277
bodily adornment, of, 233–34, 240
bodily difference, 280–81
circulation of body parts, 237
difference by age, 236
difference by sex, 236
female, 203
human, 21, 74

figurines (cont.)
  treatment of, 211
  zoomorphic, 110–11
Fikirtepe, 15
flesh, 282
  decomposition, 252
  removal, 178, 193, 258–59
Fodor, Jerry, 99, 103, 153

gaming, 107, 122
  pieces, 96, 110, 113
  types of games, 122
GDN Area, 260–61
Göbekli Tepe, 9, 13, 74–76, 191,
  274–75, 282–83
Gordon Childe, 6, 273
grave goods, 79, 234, 239, 244,
  257
  paucity of, 283
Greece, 15
groundstone, 19, 21, 205, 264

habitus, 37
Hacılar, 191
Hacinebi Tepe, 116
Hallan Çemi, 13, 29, 88
Harifian, 43
Hayonim Cave, 71
headlessness, 193, 254, 259, 263,
  276
hearth, 12, 18, 39, 42, 47–48, 161,
  163, 190, 192, 203, 238, 251,
  277, See also oven
herding, 65, 77–78, 123, 246
histories, 192–93, 219
  containers, 179
  of interaction, 220
  life history, 32, 37, 40, 43, 48
  shared, 222
history house, 10, 218–19,
  242–44, 246
Hodder, Ian, 82, 93, 136, 163,
  209–11, 218–19, 231, 250,
  252, 257
Holocene, 66, 71, 73, 77, 170
home, 31, 33–34, 38–41, 48, 51
  home-making, 16, 32, 38–39,
  52
  house and home, 38

Homo sapiens, 4, 7, 212–13, 221,
  273
horns/horn cores, 10, 192, 277,
  282, See also bucrania
  burning, 47
house
  abandonment, 136, 244, 251–52,
  264, 278
  burning, 257, 277
  rebuilding, 18, 82
  storage, 13
household, 12, 78–79, 81, 107, 128,
  181, 205, 209, 218, 222,
  281–83
human mind, 3–5, 8, 16, 23, 92,
  153, 214, 273
human-animal, 274–75, 282
hunting, 12, 34, 74, 77–78, 123,
  263, 275–76, 282
  communal, 43, 49
  narrative scenes, 20, 203–4
  transition to industry, 273
  trophies, 209

identity, 21, 50, 70, 73, 77, 172,
  183, 204, 216, 222, 231,
  233–34, 244, 246, 264, 276,
  278, 281, 283
  adornment, 280
  bounded, 79, 82
  corporate, 66, 77
  group, 72, 80
  objectification of, 70, 80
  residential, 136
  social, 16, 39, 41, 65, 71, 81–82,
  179
India, 250
Indus Valley, 134–35
inequality, 80, See also social
  differentiation
infants, 234, 237, 251, 255
innovation, 6, 16, 31–32, 49, 69, 77,
  82–83, 94, 102, 133, 168–70,
  175, 180, 194, 203–5, 209
  conceptual, 153, 161–62, 164
  container, 169
  rates, 20, 38
  theoretical innovations in
  anthropology, 274

installations, 9, 19, 52, 76, 219, 251,
  265, 277, 279
Israel, 50, 111
IST Area, 19

Jablonka, Eva, 220, 224
Jarmo, 110
Jerf el Ahmar, 14, 76
Jericho, 13, 108
Jilat 6, 48, 52
Jomon, 33
Jordan, 12–13, 16, 36, 41, 50–51,
  111
Jordan Valley, 50

Keane, Webb, 155
Kebaran, 12, 43–50, 52
Kfar HaHoresh, 13
Kharaneh, 16, 31–36, 41–43, 47–53
Konya Plain, 14–15, 116, 170
Körtik Tepe, 74–77, 234, 259
Köşk Höyük, 191, 233

labour, 13, 99, 123, 136, 221
language, 100–1, 103, 154–55, 158,
  169, 213, 215, 218, 230
  of distributed cognition, 214
  modern, 155
  niche construction, 214
Lebanon, 50
leopard
  paintings, 193
  wall reliefs, 193, 242
Levant, 9, 12–14, 50, 66, 73, 80–81,
  170, 264
Lévi-Strauss, Claude, 6, 8, 68, 71
Lewis-Williams, David, 6

Malafouris, Lambros, 93, 171
measures, system of, 3, 18, 135
  Babylonian, 134
  Egyptian, 134
  Sumerian, 134
measuring devices, 3, 18, 24
mega-site, 12, 81
Melanesia, 250
Mellaart, James, 9–10, 136, 163,
  191, 194, 199, 232–33, 238,
  243, 252, 257, 259, 263

memories, 4, 21, 72, 75, 209, 217–20, 224, 245
  collective, 72–73, 75, 81
  construction of, 193, 201–2, 219
  episodic, 216, 221
  shared, 40
  social, 4, 219
memory, 15, 40, 69, 73, 76, 79, 81, 92, 209–10, 212–25
  as a social construct, 72
  capacities, 92
  distributed, 92, 214
  episodic, 212–13, 215, 219, 222, 225
  making, 16, 73, 193–94, 204–5
  personal, 22, 210, 212, 215–16, 222, 225
  social, 209, 218, 224, 265
mental architecture, 153
meronomic approach, 154–55
meronomic process, 20
Mesolithic, 33
Mesopotamia, 134, 181, 264
Mezraa Teleilat, 180
midden, 9, 14, 21, 39, 47, 144, 238, 242, 252, 262, 277
  clay objects, 107–8, 119–22, 124, 126
  deposits, 12, 48, 144
Middle East, 3, 5, 7–9, 11, 15–16, 18, 21, 24, 170, 191, 203, 231, 233, 237
mirrors, 233, 239–40, 243, 261
Mithen, Steven, 7, 19, 153, 219
mortality profiles, 43, 49
mortuary practices, 12, 38, 211, 218, 234, 237, 241, 244, 250–51, 259, 264–65, 282
mummification, 258–59
Mushabian, 43
myth, 8, 67, 70, 169

Natufian, 12–13, 32–33, 38–39, 41, 43, 52, 219
natural born cyborgs, 92, 214
Near East, 65, 107–14, 122–23, 127–28, 169–72, 176, 178–79,

182–83, 250, 253, 255, *See also* Southwest Asia
Neolithic
  package, 8, 37, 170, 172
  revolution, 170, 175
Neolithization, 33, 38
neonates, 123, 242, 245, 251, 255
networks, 32, 50, 70–71, 77, 80–81, 170, 192, 202, 205, 216, 239, 245–46
  communication, 76
  connectionist, 97–100, 103
  exchange, 49, 71, 77
  long distance exchange, 31, 49
  of sacred objects, 160
  of sites, 74
  social, 31–32, 36, 50, 52, 72, 81, 193, 245
  spatial, 76
neuroarchaeology, 90–91
  experiments, 90
neuroscience, 6, 90, 210, 215
Nevalı Çori, 14
Neve David, 52
niche construction, 33
niche construction theory, 218
North America
  Northwest Coast groups, 33
  West Coast groups, 33
North Area, *10*, 19, 118–19, 121, 239, 255, 261
Northern Levant, 13, 176
Northern Mesopotamia, 66, 73–74, 77, 116, 118, 128, 170, 175, 178, 183
  containers, 171–73, 176, 180, 183
  creativity, 169, 171
  symbols, 80–81
number system, 3–4, 134–35
  Babylonian, 135
  Harrapan, 135

obesity, 280–82
obsidian, 19, 259, 264
  blades, 232, 257
  cache, 190
  circulation, 205
  exchange, 15, 77, 193

mirrors, 261
  source, 127
ochre, 44
  body treatment, 233–34, 260
  floors, 52
  shells, 51
Ohalo II, 47–48, 51–52
ontology, 23–24
  field of, 157
  of predation, 275
oven, 39, 163–64, 178, 190, 203, 238, 251, 277
ownership, 223, 231, 281

paintings, 191–93, *See also* wall paintings
  cave, 6, 191
  geometric, 20
  narrative, 19
  skin, 191
Palaeolithic, 16, 21, 65, 83, 112, 266, 273
  bone implements, 191
  mind, 6, 168–69
Papua New Guinea, 135
Pauketat, Timothy, 155, 160
personhood, 21, 231–32, 246, 250, 273, 280, *See* identity, self
pigment, 116, 239, 243, 257
  body treatment, 232–34, 237, 240, 243, 279
Pınarbaşı, 14
population
  density, 14, 19, 23, 192, 246
  size, 81
pottery, 8, 19–20, 121, 127, 171–78, 203, 278–79
  containers, 180–83
  exchange, 193
  geometric designs, 193
  invention of, 133
  painted, 15, 204, 265
  sedentism, 7
Pottery Neolithic, 9, 12–13, 15, 170–71, 175–76, 179–80, 264
power, 8, 12, 15, 75, 162, 173, 204, 231, 277–79, 281–82
  hereditary, 282

power (cont.)
  of animals, 275
  of pottery, 172
  social, 204
practice
  communal, 13
  cultural, 31, 33, 170–71
  daily, 32, 34, 37, 39, 47, 77
  memory, 209, 212, 215, 219, 224
  religious, 12
  repeated, 37, 39, 75, 245, *See also*
    habitus
  ritual, 15, 123, 192, 219
  shamanic, 191
  shamanistic, 274
  social, 48, 205, 244
  theory, 37
Pre-Pottery Neolithic, 12, 73, 77,
    274–76, 282–83
  A (PPNA), 12–14, 108, 191,
    259
  B (PPNB), 12–14, 66, 79, 82,
    191, 264
  C (PPNC), 12, 264
processing architecture, 98, 102
production, 12, 18, 66, 71, 79–80,
    175, 190, 193, 203–4, 231,
    265, 274, 277
  agriculture, 222
  areas, 9
  choices, 136
  container, 175
  craft, 108
  domestic, 193, 205
  figurines, 277
  food, 112
  groundstone, 21
  history houses, 10
  industrial, 169
  lithic, 14, 41, 50, 77
  mass, 78
  paintings, 194, 204
  pottery, 20, 173, 175–76,
    178–79
  textiles, 8
property, 12, 181, 183, 211
  markers, 233
  private, 223
Pylyshyn, Zenon, 99, 103

raptor, 258–59
reflexivity, 69, 77, 81, 183
reliefs, 191
religion, 10, 183
  eschatological, 66, 70
remembering, 212, 214–16,
    219–21, 223, 225
  activities or practices, 213–14
  autobiographical, 210–11,
    215–16, 221
  episodic, 210
  forms of, 209–10, 217–18
Renfrew, Colin, 7–8, 18, 119,
    128
resources, 72, 75, 94, 170, 175, 204,
    214–15, 223–24, 262
  cognitive, 96
  computational of the human
    brain, 101
  counting of, 95, 112
  distribution of, 123
  narrative, 215
  non-biological, 92
  shared, 136, 221
  water, 52
  wild, 74
revolution, 8, 218, *See also* cognitive
    revolution, Neolithic
    revolution
  painted pottery, 172
  selfhood and autonomy, 273
ritual, 12–15, 69–70, 72–73, 75–77,
    81, 108, 123, 126–27, 135,
    192–93, 204, 218–19, 221–22,
    231, 233, 238, 242, 245,
    277
  animal skin, 275
  deposits, 178
  funerary, 258, 283
  house ritual, 10, 15, 18, 193
  post-mortem, 80, 275
  rites de passage, 69
  structures, 7, 13–14, 77

sacred v. profane, 69
sacred, the, 69, 193
Schmandt-Besserat, Denise, 7, 17,
    94, 108, 111–13, 117, 128
Scotland, 259

sedentism, 7–8, 11, 31, 39, 75, 80,
    113, 122, 168, 171, 273, 283,
    See also settled life
  adoption of, 23
  emergence of, 33
  incipient, 170
  processes of, 11
self, 93, 209–10, 215–16, 218, 221,
    225, 230–32, 244, 246, 250,
    264, 281, 283
  awareness of, 183, 212–13
  conception, 251, 258
  distinctions between self and
    other, 223
  expression, 169
  holistic, 250
  representation, 215
self-consciousness, 183
selfhood, 250, 273–74
self-image, 231
self-sufficiency, 193, 277–79
settled life, 23, 32, 183
settlement layout, 146
settlement pattern, 36
Sha'ar Hagolan, 12
shaman, 13
shamanism, 276
  trance, 191
sharing, 18, 21, 50, 66, 71, 78,
    192–93, 211, 250, 262, 279
  beads, 22
  food, 14, 193, 202, 279
  language, 155
  memory, 224
sheep, 111, 125, 127, 190, 193, 204,
    246, 263
Sheikh-e Abad, 108
shell, 19, 44, 51–52, 233, 238
  exchange, 49–50
Shir, 180
skin, 193, 260, 279
skull and skin, 90, 102
skulls, 219, 276
  circulation, 21, 263
  exhumation, 80
  plastered, 80–81
  skull cult, 79
social difference, 23, 79, *See also*
    social differentiation

social differentiation, 12–14, 16, 18, 65–66, 70, 75, 78, 80, 264–65, 281
social hierarchy, 33, 70
social organization, 10, 15, 31, 180, 213, 239, 244
sodalities, 18, 192–93, 202, 205, 238, 243, 263
South American tribes, 135
South Area, 10, 19, 118–19, 238, 261, 280
Southeast Asia, 276
Southern Levant, 12–13, 52, 77
Southern Mesopotamia, 111, 113
  written records, 124–25
Southwest Asia, 32–34, 36–40, 111, 218, 273, 276
specialization, 18, 75, 78, 204
speleothems, 19
stamp seals, 15, 17, 20, 114, 182, 203, 246, 265, 279
  adornment, 233, 240
  animal, 202
  geometric, 193–95, 200, 202
standardization, 118, 145, 211
  adornment, 241
  bricks, 17, 136
  clay objects, 116, 127
  process, 133, 140
  symbolism, 76, 80
status, 70, 73, 75, 80, 236, 238, 265, 280, 283
  cognitive, 102, 104
  figurines, 281
storage, 13–14, 38, 43, 49, 76–77, 79, 112, 125, 172, 179, 204, 264
  bins, 13
  information, 97, 107–8, 113, 121, 123, 126, 128
  pottery, 181
  rooms, 13, 182
  shared, 14
  structures, 13, 179

symbolic, 18, 94, 168, 171, 182, 191, 273, 283
Strathern, Marilyn, 230, 244, 250
Sumer, 113, 135
symbol, 5, 7, 98, 102, 230
  systems, 4–5, 96–97, 99–101, 103, 218, 222
Syria, 13, 50, 76, 111, 114, 169, 191, 259, 264

taxonomy, 156, 158, 209
teasing/baiting of animals. *See* hunting, narrative scenes
technology, 9, 93–94, 174–75, 177, 211–12, 218, 224–25
  administrative, 127
  changes in, 8
  container, 175
  containers, 169
  lithic, 50
  pottery, 6, 278
  production, 136
  storage, 180
Tell 'Abr, 14, 76
Tell Bouqras, 177, 191, 264
Tell el-Kerkh, 180
Tell Halula, 180, 191
Tell Hassuna, 180
Tell Qaramel, 13, 76
Tell Sabi Abyad, 114, 118, 128, 169, 172–73, *177*, 178–80, 182, 264
Tepecik-Çiftlik, 191
textile, 176, 232, 257, 263
Tikopia, 3
tokens, 7, 16–18, 23, 73, 94, 107–15, 125–28, 202, 222
toys, 109, 113, 123
TP Area, 114, 118, 121, 137, 195, 260–61, 279–80
TPC Area, 260–61, 280, 282
trade and exchange, 7–8, 12, 19, 38, 203, 211
Turkey, 3, 9, 13, 15, 111, 191

Ulucak Höyük, 191
'Umm Dabaghiyah, 191
Upper Mesopotamia. *See* Northern Mesopotamia
Uyyun al-Hammam, 52

value, 119, 125–26, 128, 139, 142–43
  commodification, 169
  indicators of, 124
  intrinsic, 107, 119
  notions of, 3, 179
  relative, 7
  symbolic, 125, 128
values, 4, 7, 245
  cultural, 230
vultures, 219, 242
  excarnation, 259

Wadi al-Hasa, 52
Wadi Mataha, 52
wall paintings, 9, 82, 193, 204–5, 232–33, 238, 251, 265, 278
  adornment, 233
  circulation of body parts, 237
  geometric, 190–91, 193–203
  humans, 240
  vultures, 193, 259, 282
wall reliefs, 9, 19, 82, 193, 242, 279
Watkins, Trevor, 7, 19, 95, 128, 218, 222
wealth, 75, 283
weights, 3, 7, *See also* measures
West Mound, 204, 264–65, 279
writing, 3, 7, 17, 101, 111, 113, 124, 218
  alphabetic, 168
  appearance of, 110–11, 171
  origins, 112

Yorghan Tepe, 111